LIMERI
INSTI

D1336849

Scientific Examination of Questioned Documents

Revised Edition

CRC SERIES IN FORENSIC AND POLICE SCIENCE

BARRY A. J. FISHER, Series Editor
L.A. County Sheriff's Department

TECHNIQUES OF CRIME SCENE INVESTIGATION
Fifth Edition
Barry A. J. Fisher

SCIENTIFIC EXAMINATION OF QUESTIONED DOCUMENTS
Revised Edition
Ordway Hilton

ADVANCES IN FINGERPRINT TECHNOLOGY
Henry C. Lee
R. E. Gaensslen

INSTRUMENTAL DATA FOR DRUG ANALYSIS
Second Edition, Volumes 1–4
Terry Mills, III
J. Conrad Roberson

INSTRUMENTAL DATA FOR DRUG ANALYSIS
Second Edition, Volume 5
Terry Mills, III
J. Conrad Roberson
H. Horton McCurdy
William H. Wall

Scientific Examination of Questioned Documents

Revised Edition

ORDWAY HILTON
Examiner of Questioned Documents
Landrum, South Carolina

CRC Press
Boca Raton   Ann Arbor   London   Tokyo

Library of Congress Cataloging-in-Publication Data

Hilton, Ordway.
    Scientific examination of questioned documents / Ordway Hilton.
        p.   cm.
    Originally published: Rev. ed. New York : Elsevier,
c1982. (Elsevier series in forensic and police science)
    Includes index.
    ISBN 0-8493-9510-0
    1. Writing–Identification. 2. Forgery. I. Title. II. Series:
Elsevier series in forensic and police science.
HV8074.H49 1993
363.2'565–dc20

for Library of Congress   93-8522
                                                                                                    CIP

To my wife
LILLIE ATKINSON HILTON
for helping to make this book possible

Contents

Preface

This book is a guide to all aspects of a questioned document for attorneys, investigators, document examiners, and others. It attempts to cover the broad spectrum of this work as practiced today—not only the scientific examination of questioned documents, but also the steps to be taken by the field investigator and trial attorney. Disputed document inquiries encompass extensive and varied technical examinations, unique phases of investigation, and specialized legal presentations. The coordinated efforts of the persons responsible for every step ensure a successful conclusion.

Today there is widespread use of the document examiner's services both in civil law practice and in criminal cases. His services, however, are not confined to potential court trials, but also deal with personnel problems, security work, and investigations in the business world, as well as assistance to troubled individuals.

Many techniques have been developed by which the physical facts contained within the document can be discovered, revealed, and demonstrated. The courts of most jurisdictions accept the assistance derived from these skills, a significant change from the practices of 75 or more years ago, when presentation of findings was curtailed whenever possible. Early cases consisted almost entirely of handwriting identification and the detection of forgery. Today these problems are still common, but examiners are confronted with typewriting and other mechanical impressions, erasures and alterations, photocopies, and many additional problems involving inks, writing instruments, and paper. In fact, if there is a question about any type of document, the document examiner is consulted for the solution.

The preface to the first edition (in 1956) noted that no comprehensive treatment of the questioned document had appeared for over 20 years. Within the succeeding five years two texts were published.[1] Now another 20 years has elapsed since an up-to-date treatise has appeared. During that period many new instruments and materials for preparing documents have been introduced, including porous tip and roller pens, single element and electronic typewriters, and dry-process copiers. Recognizing and identifying their work has presented challenges to the progressive document examiner. In response to these new problems there have been significant modifications in technique. At the same time, workers in the field have developed other new methods, such as thin-layer chromatography, infrared luminescence, and examination with dichroic filters, to answer older questions more completely and accurately. In a number of respects document examination today is more advanced than it was, or had to be, in the 1950s. The innovations in methods and the recognition of current problems have in some measure made all former texts obsolete. Consequently, a substantial revision of the previous edition was needed.

A comprehensive approach to any document problem in essential. Many times the question of a document's authenticity, or its fraudulent nature, is answered only by a careful consideration and correlation of all or a number of the various attributes that make up the document. In accomplishing such a study, however, it is necessary to know exactly what each of its elements may contribute to the composite picture. Therefore this presentation deals with individual parts of a document and single problems rather than directly with such broader topics as whether a document is authentic or forged.

One possible exception is a chapter, new to this edition, on the age of a document. It brings together many aspects of a question that, at least in civil cases, is so frequently raised. However, the discussion in another chapter of some particular element of the document may itself reflect on the question of age by showing that the document could not have been prepared on its date.

The discussion of examination methods has been deliberately curtailed. The governing principles and basic mode of attack are presented so that the reader who is confronted with a questioned document problem may gain a clearer idea of what can be done. Examination techniques have not been expanded so that this book might serve as a training manual, although with its present scope it can be used as a guide for a course of training under a qualified document examiner-instruc-

---

[1]Wilson R. Harrison, *Suspect Documents, Their Scientific Examination* (New York: Frederic A. Praeger, 1958). James V. P. Conway, *Evidential Documents* (Springfield, Ill.: Charles C Thomas, 1959).

tor. With many problems the footnotes cited expand on the methods.[2]

The work of the field investigator, the efforts of the attorney preparing for trial, and the techniques of presenting evidence in court form an important part of document examination. Since errors and oversights in any of these steps may be just as serious as failure to consider the physical evidence contained within the document itself, several chapters are devoted to this phase of the work. The technical questions are not isolated from the case as a whole, but must be fully coordinated with the initial investigation and the courtroom presentation.

[2]For other worthwhile papers not included, see the *Syllabus/Bibliography of Selected Books and Articles Related to Forensic Document Examination* (American Board of Forensic Document Examiners, 1979).

Acknowledgments

A number of research papers by fellow workers have been cited. No one document examiner can hope to keep abreast of all aspects of this work without the published writings of others, and these examiners have all made significant contributions to the general fund of knowledge condensed in this book.

The first five years in which the author practiced in New York City were in association with Elbridge W. Stein. In our many discussions of questioned document examination, there were references to drafts of the first edition of this book, in which Mr. Stein was greatly interested. Upon his retirement he left with the author a number of files dealing with some important and some unusual cases of his career, with the expressed permission to use any illustrations contained in them. A number of these photographs have been adapted as illustrations in this book, and each is specifically acknowledged.

A number of illustrations were originally published in the *Journal of Criminal Law, Criminology and Police Science,* of which the author was Police Science Editor for nearly 30 years. These appear with the permission of the journal. In addition, illustrations that appeared in articles in the *Journal of Forensic Sciences* and the *Journal of Police Science and Administration* are reprinted with permission.

The author appreciates the detailed, critical review of the manuscript by John J. Harris and Patricia R. Harris of Los Angeles and Roy A. Huber of Ottawa, Canada. Many of their comments and suggestions helped to clarify points in the final editing of the text.

Scientific Examination of Questioned Documents

Revised Edition

I

INTRODUCTION AND BASIC DEFINITIONS

1

Preliminary Considerations

This is an age of documents. We depend on them in many of our encounters with the complexities of modern life. They feature in our financial, legal, business, social, and personal affairs. Hardly a day goes by without some document playing a part in the life of every one of us. With their widespread use it is almost axiomatic that analytical methods should be developed to establish facts concerning documents—their source, authenticity, age, or original state. These are the techniques that are to be described in the ensuing chapters.

Documents and Questioned Documents

What is a document? It may be more complex than merely writing on a paper. In the broadest sense a document is any material containing marks, symbols, or signs that convey meaning or a message to someone. While the great majority of documents are written on paper either by typewriter or by hand with pencil or pen and ink, many other substances can be used for the same purpose. Wills written on wood have been offered for probate.[1] Signs painted on walls and windows make up a common class of documents; carved letters on tombstones and cornerstones all record history. These and many other combinations of materials and writing instruments form the vast store of documents with which man has recorded his acts and thoughts.

Among all these documents is a small group which, though numerous by count, actually constitutes but a minute part of the whole. This

---

[1]Clark Sellers, "Strange Wills," *Journal of Criminal Law and Criminology* 28 (1937): 106–117.

group is known as *questioned* or *disputed documents*—those suspected of being fraudulent or whose source is unknown or background
is disputed.

A questioned document, like other documents, may have been prepared with any of the numerous materials available. Sometimes the
very materials of which it is constructed bring discredit and suspicion
upon it. Many times, however, its elements are entirely in keeping
with its history and purpose, and yet there are those who contest its
authenticity.

Not all questioned documents are fraudulent. Not all are instruments
of crime. There may be a variety of reasons for questioning a document
other than to invalidate it or to establish the basis for a criminal action.
Many documents are examined closely only to identify their authors
or to establish their source. Of those suspected of being fraudulent,
probably at least half are exactly what they claim to be—perfectly
authentic documents. But the remainder, which involve fraud, forgery,
blackmail, or a host of other lesser crimes or offenses, are instruments
that may represent to the individual concerned sizable wealth, property
or personal possessions, or reputation and respectability. Thus, the
truth about these questioned documents assumes importance of large
magnitude to all whom they concern.

Examiner of Questioned Documents

The profession of examiners of questioned documents grew out of the
needs of the courts for assistance in interpreting evidence relating to
the preparation and subsequent treatment of documents.[2] It is actually
a pure forensic science in that it developed within the legal system
rather than being derived from other professions, such as medicine,
dentistry, or chemistry, to be applied to legal problems.

These individuals have specialized in the study and investigation of
documents to determine the facts about them, their preparation, and
their subsequent treatment. Not only must these examiners be able
to identify handwriting, typewriting, and printed matter, but they must
be able to distinguish forgery from genuineness, to analyze inks, papers,
and other substances that are combined into documents, to reveal
additions and substitutions in a document, and to restore or decipher
erased and obliterated writing. When records produced by complex
modern business machines are suspected of having been manipulated,
document examiners may be among the first to be consulted. Certainly

---

[2]A. S. Osborn, "A New Profession," *Journal of the American Judicature Society* 24 (1940). This
paper is reprinted by A. S. Osborn and A. D. Osborn in *Questioned Document Problems*, 2nd ed.
(Albany: Boyd, 1946), Chapter 31, pp. 358–367.

their experiences and training must be broad and varied if they are to cope successfully with all the problems brought to their attention.

The reader must recognize that a document examiner is trained not only to examine various elements of the document but also to consider the whole document. He is concerned with identification of the factors which make up the document and the detection of manipulation or falsification.

Many of his problems involve handwriting, and consequently he is often referred to as a handwriting identification expert.[3] In his study of handwriting, his aims are different from those of a graphologist or grapho-analyst.[4] The graphologist seeks to derive character and personality traits from an individual's handwriting, not unlike the psychologist who, by means of various testing techniques, endeavors to discover similar information. The graphologist deals only with handwriting and no other part of the document. The document examiner, on the contrary, examines handwriting to identify the writing or to detect evidence of forgery. He also investigates other aspects of the document, when appropriate, and those documents in which there is no handwriting or it is but a small part of the whole. It is the unusual person who can work in both fields and produce top-quality opinions involving identification questions and graphological findings.

The document examiner must be more than a technician; he must be a scientist, for the methods at his disposal are those of applied science. Each question with which he is confronted is an individual research problem, but, like all scientific investigations, each has as its ultimate goal the discovery of the facts. To reach this goal the examiner must be thorough, accurate, and entirely without bias. His task is not to prove by some devious means certain preconceived ideas of those who consult him, but to establish the facts that tell of the document's preparation and subsequent history through a study of its identifying details and the collation of its elements with those of known specimens.

The document examiner's work does not end with the discovery of the identifying details in a document. He must properly interpret them and through logical reasoning arrive at a correct conclusion regarding

---

[3]"Handwriting identification expert" or "handwriting expert" is the heading used in classified telephone directories, a ready source of names for locating local examiners, but unfortunately not necessarily a reliable listing. The *American Bar Association Journal* carries a classified list under "handwriting experts," which is an unscreened listing. Only *Martindale–Hubbell Law Directory* screens examiners before accepting a listing.

[4]Grapho-analyst is a designation given graphologists in North America who have completed a correspondence course in graphology, which designates the person as a Certified Grapho-Analyst (CGA). A more advanced course entitles the person to be a Master Grapho-Analyst (MGA). The classified telephone directory listing "handwriting analyst" covers all workers who profess to examine handwriting to reveal personality traits rather than identify handwriting.

the problem at hand. After arriving at an opinion, he must be prepared to demonstrate the basis and reasons for his opinion in a manner that a layman, be he judge, juror, or interested party, thoroughly understands. Thus, he becomes both a teacher and an advocate for the truth. The skilled examiner, by means of photographic enlargement, charts and sketches, and careful explanation of the factors involved, should be able to make his findings apparent to all who are willing to judge with an open mind.

Standards

The answer to certain questions can be found by a direct examination of the questioned document, but the more common problems require comparison of the disputed material with specimens from known sources. These known, authentic specimens, commonly referred to as *standards*,[5] must be carefully selected so as to be truly representative. They should, in fact, be a condensed and compact sample that contains a true cross section of the genuine or authentic material from the particular source. Unless the standards fulfill these conditions they cannot be considered adequate and accurate.

When it is necessary to make a collation with known specimens in order to solve the problem at hand, like things must be compared. This rule holds true whether the question is that of examination of inks, papers, handwriting, typewriting, or any other part of a document. For example, ink studies are most precise when the strokes compared are of similar density, and handwriting or typewriting examinations are more apt to lead to correct and certain findings if the known and disputed matter are documents of a similar class. In contrast, to mention but two questions that are raised rather often, little can be determined from a comparison of handwriting with handlettering or signatures with holographic documents.

Reference Collections

A somewhat special class of standards consists of the compiled material in the document examiner's reference collections. These are essential to his work. Here he gathers together and classifies source material such as typewriting specimens, inks, paper, pencils, pen points, and sample specimens from check writers. By constantly enlarging and bringing these reference collections up to date, the document examiner

---

[5]The term was first used by A. S. Osborn, *Questioned Documents*, 1st ed. (Rochester: Lawyer's Co-Operative, 1910), to describe known writing and typewriting specimens. Today some workers use the term examplars rather than standards.

has at his finger tips the necessary source material with which to answer many basic questions.

Instruments

Progress in document examination has resulted in no small measure from the development and special application of scientific instruments that are suited to this work. The camera and the magnifying lens are the two most useful tools. Both can reveal details, but the modern document camera both reveals and records, so that it becomes an indispensible instrument.

Various kinds of microscopes are needed to determine the facts, especially the steroscopic binocular microscope, which gives a three-dimensional enlargement, and the comparison microscope, which is specially constructed to facilitate side-by-side study of microscopic details. Modern versions have special lighting features and lens systems to facilitate a variety of examinations. Various measures and test plates have been devised for particular problems.[6] Control of illumination is important and is accomplished by the selection of the quality of light (that is, daylight, incandescent, or fluorescent light), and control of the direction and angle of illumination. Special lighting equipment, such as simple light boxes for transmitted light studies and the RCMP oblique light unit, which produces even-intensity, low-angle illumination for special photographic use,[7] are useful units. Not only is visible light from these special sources employed, but invisible radiation in the ultraviolet and infrared portions of the spectrum are also used by photographic techniques and by means of electronic units that convert the invisible infrared reactions into a visible image for immediate study. More recently, a narrow-band visible-light source coupled with special equipment has been used to produce luminescence in the infrared range.[8] The electrostatic reaction, which is used to produce modern photocopies, has also been adapted to read very weak writing impressions in an otherwise blank sheet of paper.[9] All these tools, together with chemical testing, especially by means of thin layer chro-

---

[6]Osborn, *Questioned Documents*, 2nd ed. (Albany: Boyd, 1929), devotes a chapter, "Special Instrument, Measures and Appliances," pp. 79–96, to test plates of his design. O. Hilton, "An Innovation in Typewriter Test Plate Design," *Medicine, Science and the Law* 14 (1974): 205–208, and Hilton, "A Test Plate for Proportional Spacing Typewriter Examination," *Journal of Criminal Law, Criminology and Police Science* 47 (1956): 257–259, has updated typewriter test plate designs to assist in modern problems.

[7]N. W. Duxbury and J. W. Warren, "Deciphering and Photo-Recording of Indented Writings," *Royal Canadian Mounted Police Seminar* No. 4 (Ottawa: Queen's Printer, 1956), pp. 27–35.

[8]John Costain and George W. Lewis, "A Practical Guide to Infrared Luminescence Applied to Questioned Document Problems" *Journal of Police Science and Administration* 1 (1973): 209–218.

[9]D. J. Foster and D. J. Morantz, "An Electrostatic Imaging Technique for the Detection of Indented Impressions in Documents" *Forensic Science International* 13 (1979): 51–54.

matography (TLC), have made possible a marked and steady progress in document investigation.

Scientific Examination of Documents

How is the document examiner's investigation different from that of the layman who may try to judge the facts by himself? When inspecting a document the layman is principally concerned with the obvious and gross features, but the document examiner's inquiry, as has already been indicated, is exhaustive in its detailed study. Not only is he equipped by special training to recognize and evaluate the pertinent attributes of a document, but he is never satisfied until he has discovered every detail that may have any bearing on the problem. Thus, the important aspects of his examination virtually begin at the point where the layman leaves off.

The document examiner's study is directed toward one end, the discovery of those elements of a document that become its identifying attributes or characteristics, or may reveal how it was prepared or in what way it may have been modified. Actually, all the elements of a document help to identify it, but the most individual or unusual have the greatest importance. Since any single characteristic, even the most individual ones, may be found in documents from another source, no single element can by itself be the sole basis of an identification. In fact, many identifying characteristics are part of a large group of documents prepared at different sources. While it is obvious that these group or class characteristics alone cannot identify a document, or the handwriting or typewriting on it, they must be considered and evaluated in every examination. The final identification, therefore, is based upon not one or two but the combination of all characteristics present in the document.

The examination of documents is a scientific procedure only if the examiner seeks out similar characteristics and at the same time remains constantly alert to any evidence of differences. Further, one must distinguish between actual differences and variables that are present in every individual's writing, as well as in the work of any typewriter or other office machine or device, every pen or other writing instrument, and in paper and inks from a single source. The true scientist looks for evidence that leads to the solution of the problem, and after reaching an apparent solution, makes sure that there is no neglected evidence that might invalidate or modify the findings. The document examiner also ascertains that differences that can disprove an identification have not been overlooked. Variations must be distinguished from basic differences in order to avoid an inaccurate conclusion. The examiner must be completely satisfied that the standards are representative of the person's handwriting so that unusual variations are not misinterpreted as distinguishing characteristics. Basic, true differences establish nonidentity, but variables cannot necessarily invalidate a conclusion of identity based upon a unique combination of similarities. In other words, the document examiner must be ever critical so that when a final conclusion is reached it is completely accurate.

Probability of Accidental Coincidence

Any identification by means of physical attributes involves the concept of the probability of accidental coincidence. In applying this theory to a document problem, it is necessary to establish a sufficient number of identifying attributes in common between the known and disputed specimens so that the chance of their having originated at two different sources is so unlikely that for all practical purposes it can be considered nonexistent. In most document problems it would be impossible, or at least extremely impractical, to measure mathematically the degree of probability of accidental coincidence.[10] Many identifying attributes of handwriting, for example, occur in gradually varying degrees with no sharp line of demarcation between the different steps. For instance, while writing skill may well differ among ten writers, each one cannot be put into a particular class that has its limits fixed in sharply defined terms. These basic conditions prevent arithmetic determination of a probability factor.[11]

---

[10]Two important trials involving testimony of document examiners have seen special testimony on the probability of accidental coincidence as a test of the accuracy of their identifications. The trial of Sylvia Ann Howland in Massachusetts is an excellent example of how this kind of testimony should be presented. Osborn *Questioned Documents*, 2nd ed., ably discusses pertinent aspects of this case in a footnote on p. 348 and again on p. 350.

On the other hand, People v. Risley, 214 N.Y. 75, 108 NE 200 (1915), was reversed upon appeal because of the improper handling of testimony by a mathematician as an expert on the theory of probability. In this case, as opposed to the Howland matter, no basic data upon which to establish the probability had been derived from the evidence in the case, nor did the mathematician show experience in the field of typewriting identification to validate his basic assumptions.

[11]The lack of a sharp line of demarcation in document examinations introduces a concept of mathematics not considered in calculating the probability factors in the Howland and Risley cases. In the calculations employed in these two cases, only a discrete probability function was considered. The present condition introduces the continuous probability function. The discrete case can be likened to a series of dots or points in an area—these can be counted; the continuous case can be likened to a line or curve, which can be considered to be made up of an infinite or countless set of minute points packed tightly together. In theory, both problems are handled alike, but in practice the calculations of the continuous case may become extremely complex. This second or continuous function would be encountered in document problems in measuring skill, freedom, fluency, shading, angularity, and the like—all important considerations in determining whether a signature is genuine or forged. Since these factors are essential to accurate identifications, arithmetic calculations of a measure of likelihood of accidental coincidence becomes impractical in questioned document examination.

A further complication in applying mathematical measures of probability to handwriting problems arises out of the interdependence of certain writing habits. One of the basic premises of the probability multiplication theorems is that each individual probability factor must be completely independent

(continued)

Despite our present inability to measure mathematically the improbability of chance duplication in a document problem, the document examiner depends on the principles of probability in reaching his conclusion. He must therefore evaluate through experience the relative certainty of his identification. Actually, the scientific examiner requires a much more positive identification than the bare minimum, by which it would be safe in a practical way to say that the disputed matter could not have originated at any source different from that determined from the available evidence. The requirements for an identification are that all identifying details of the disputed matter must occur in the same way in the known specimens unless there is a logical explanation for an obvious deviation. In other words, there must be no significant deviations or differences between the two.

Nonidentity of Source

To establish that the known and disputed material have different sources requires that there is at least one basic, significant difference between them—one fundamental identifying characteristic that does not occur in the same way in both sets of specimens. Such a determination presumes extended writing specimens including extensive broad-based standards that reveal a full picture of the known writer's habits and ability. Actually, in virtually all problems of nonidentity there is a number of differences, but a single one, if fundamental in nature and not due merely to chance, would be sufficient for the proof. It is a basic axiom of identification in document problems that a limited number of basic differences, even in the face of numerous strong similarities, are controlling and accurately establish nonidentity.

Natural Variation

In all document problems there is yet another important element that must be considered—the question of natural variation. No repeated act is always accomplished with identically the same results regardless of whether it is produced by a machine or human effort. An individual's handwriting is made up of a complexity of habitual patterns that are

---

footnote[11] (continued)
of every other. Applying the theory to the general handwriting problem, however, requires very careful analysis to be sure that each factor is actually independent. For example, if a writer's habit is to fail to close his a, one would also expect to find in his handwriting g's and o's with open tops. By the same token, the characteristics derived from writing systems may appear in different letters, and the system relationship destroys the independence. As an example, an r started like an n and the looped vertical staff of the d are both common to the Palmer system, but not to every other modern writing system. Actually, this interrelationship between factors involves consideration of the statistical concept of correlation and greatly complicates probability determinations.

A further discussion of this problem can be found in Hilton, "Relationship of Mathematical Probabilities to Handwriting," *Royal Canadian Mounted Police Seminar* No. 5 (Ottawa: Queen's Printer, 1958), pp. 121–130.

repeated within a typical range of variation around the model patterns; the individuality of typewriting is influenced to some extent by the variation in the depth of impression and "play" in the moving parts of the machine; paper has its tolerances of composition and physical dimensions. In the case of handwriting the proper consideration of natural variation is essential in order to distinguish between forged and genuine writing.[12] Regardless of the class of problem, variation is ever present and must be accurately evaluated. It is as much a basic part of the identification as each identifying characteristic itself.

The Opinion

All these factors are a part of the document examiner's opinion, which in its essence is a collection of observed physical facts evaluated in the light of basic rules of identification and experience. It is a summation of details woven together systematically into a whole so that one logical and obvious conclusion alone is possible. All the facts disclosed in the course of the examination are valueless unless they are properly compiled and evaluated—an act that can be accomplished only by one who through experience and study has come to know the importance and limitations of each. Thus the document examiner by his interpretation of the meaning and value of each identifying element is able to arrive at an opinion that describes the true basic conditions bearing on the disputed document.

The findings derived from the examination of a document are more than a mere opinion. In virtually every problem the conclusions are subject to a demonstration that can make the reasons for them apparent to all. In many cases, if presented properly, this demonstration becomes so clear that those who witness it feel that they themselves could have, and did, arrive at exactly the same conclusion without the assistance of the document examiner. He is no longer expressing a dogmatic and individual opinion. He is merely discussing what is obvious to all at hand, yet what prior to this demonstration and explanation would have been far from obvious to most persons present.

Basis of Effective Court Presentation

Trials of cases in courts of English-speaking countries generally require that the document examiner give testimony concerning his opinion. Effective presentation of this kind in the trial is a matter that requires

---

[12]Lucas reports a case in which the proof of forgery of three questioned signatures was based primarily on the lack of variation of these questioned signatures as compared with the variation present in 83 genuine specimens. See A. Lucas, *Forensic Chemistry and Scientific Criminal Investigation*, 3rd ed. (London: Edward Arnold, 1937), pp. 139–140.

coordinated effort between the document examiner and the trial attorney. The attorney must understand the theory of the technical proof and appreciate its details. The document examiner must know the legal restrictions on his testimony. Into this presentation the proficient trial attorney brings a background of legal training and courtroom experience, while the qualified document examiner supplies a technical knowledge supplemented by extensive experience in a small sphere of legal procedure. Complete coordination of these qualifications and the integration of them into the problem at hand requires thorough pretrial conferences between the document examiner and the attorney. These discussions are not only proper from an ethical point of view, since both parties are thus better able to aid justice by the most effective presentation of the facts, but also proper in a practical way, for smooth and orderly presented testimony saves time of the court and all present. Technical testimony can be a difficult subject for the court and jury to understand. Therefore, it must be simply and directly presented so that its basic elements and conclusions are entirely clear.

Indefinite Findings

Although it may have been inferred from this discussion that all conclusions resulting from the examination of a document are definite and positive, this is certainly not the case. Some questions, either because of their inherent nature or because of the material at hand or the opportunity available for study, can be answered only with reservations or qualifications. Certainly, these results are hardly satisfactory either to the document examiner or to the contestants, but it does not alter the fact that qualified opinions are encountered from time to time. In fact, some classes of problems do not permit definite solutions, except possibly in rare instances. The reader will find specific examples of these problems in subsequent chapters. The examiner who claims to employ methods that never lead to an indefinite or partial solution, regardless of the problem, is one whose opinions should be accepted with great caution, if not suspicion. There are cases in which, when the evidence is studied and properly evaluated, the conclusion cannot be rendered in positive terms but must be expressed with clear reservations.

Scope of Document Problems

Problems arising from documents include a wide field of investigations. Handwriting or typewriting identification and the detection of forgery are often believed to cover completely all of the questions which are undertaken; although they certainly are very common problems, they cannot be said to exhaust the scope of this work. Problems involving inks, paper, erasures and insertions, and mechanical impressions represent some of the other questions encountered.

All document problems actually fall into two basic groups: those that require known specimens from an individual source for their ultimate and complete solution, and those that are completed either by a study of the questioned document alone or by its comparison with reference collections. Since questions and materials involved are so varied, little can be said in general regarding either group of problems. Through a study of the subsequent chapters, the reader can come to appreciate the scope and limitation of each class of document problems.

2

Definitions of Terms

The examination of documents, like most technical subjects, has developed a specialized vocabulary. Many of the terms have been derived from related fields such as penmanship, the typewriting and printing trades, and paper and ink manufacturing; others have come into existence in order to describe concisely something unique to document examination, or to several disciplines of forensic science.

Today there is a need for both standardization and simplification of terms. Unlike most scientists, the document examiner is not primarily concerned with discussing his findings with highly trained associates but with presenting his conclusions clearly to the layman—to attorneys and other parties who submitted the problem to him or to judges and jurors during a trial. It is well, therefore, to keep to a very minimum the use of technical terms, and whenever one must be used, to explain its meaning fully. The need for standardization of terminology is also acute, but because of the lack of formal training programs and a comprehensive professional organization to accomplish this end, it is a much more difficult problem than in many other scientific fields.

In this chapter no attempt will be made to prepare an exhaustive list of definitions. The terms that appear are principally confined to those encountered in the course of this text. Certain terminology peculiar to some parts of the country will not be found. This selection, moreover, does not seek to establish criteria that should be universally accepted; rather these definitions are primarily intended to clarify the meaning of basic terms which appear in this book.

Throughout the text most terms when first encountered are explained in relation to the application under scrutiny. However, where a term is used again in a later section a reader might desire clarification of its meaning. This chapter is especially designed for such a ready reference.

Six general headings have been employed to facilitate reference to definitions. First "General Terms" are described, that is, those applicable to all phases of document examination. The next section, "Handwriting," deals with the special terminology related to handwriting, signatures, and handlettering problems. It is followed by a consideration of terms pertaining to typewriting identification. The section on "Altered and Damaged Documents" includes terms peculiar to the solution of questions involving erasures, alterations, and substitutions. "Other Identification Problems" include the particular terms encountered in the examination of inks, paper, pencils, pens, printed matter, and the like. Finally, terminology common to document photography is taken up.

General Terms

Certification. The recognition of a particular level of professional qualifications. A national organization, the American Board of Forensic Document Examiners, Inc., has set up a certification program for document examiners based upon a review and testing of their qualifications. This nationwide program, established in 1978, will ultimately provide a register of well-qualified document examiners.

Characteristic. Any property or mark that distinguishes and in document examination commonly refers to identifying details. There are two groups of characteristics, class and individual.

Class characteristic. Not all characteristics encountered in document examination are peculiar to a single person or thing, and one that is common to a group may be described as a class characteristic.

Collation. As used in this text, critical comparison or side by side examination.

Comparison. The act of setting two or more items side by side to weigh their identifying qualities. It implies not only a visual but also a mental act in which the elements of one item are related to the counterparts of the other.

Conclusion. A scientific conclusion results from relating observed facts by logical, commonsense reasoning in accordance with established rules or laws. The document examiner's conclusions are so derived. See *Opinion,* the usual legal term.

Disputed document. A term suggesting that there is an argument or controversy over the document, and strictly speaking this is its true meaning. In this text, as well as through prior usage, however, "dis-

puted document" and "questioned document" are employed interchangeably to signify a document that is under special scrutiny.

Document. In its fullest meaning, any material that contains marks,
symbols, or signs either visible, partially visible, or invisible that
may ultimately convey a meaning or message to someone. Pencil or
ink writing, typewriting, or printing on paper are the more usual
forms of documents.

Document examiner. One who studies scientifically the details and
elements of documents in order to identify their source or to discover
other facts concerning them. Document examiners are often referred
to as handwriting identification experts, but today the work has
outgrown this latter title and involves other problems than merely
the examination of handwriting.

Examination. The act of making a close and critical study of any material, and with questioned documents is the process necessary to
discover the facts about them. Various types of examinations are
undertaken, including microscopic, visual, photographic, chemical,
ultraviolet, and infrared examinations.

Exemplar. A term used by some document examiners and attorneys
to characterize known material, but the author in preparing this text
has used the older, better established, term, standards. (See
Standards.)

Expert witness. A legal term used to describe a witness who by reason
of his special technical training or experience is permitted to express
an opinion regarding the issue, or a certain aspect of the issue, which
is involved in a court action. His purpose is to interpret technical
information in his particular specialty in order to assist the court in
administering justice. The document examiner testifies in court as
an expert witness.

Fluorescence. See *Ultraviolet examination.*

Forensic science. The field of science that is used in the judicial process. A number of scientific disciplines commonly make up the more
active segments of forensic science. Some are derived from the physical, medical, and dental sciences, and the best-qualified workers
specialize in the court-oriented aspects of each discipline. Questioned document examination is a notable part of forensic science
in that it developed directly from the need of court experts to answer
problems regarding documents instead of growing out of established
fields of science.

Grapho-analysis. A form of graphology commonly practiced in the
United States. It has no relationship to handwriting identification.
(See *Graphology.*)

Graphology. The art of attempting to interpret the character or personality of an individual from his handwriting; also called grapho-

analysis. Such an undertaking is beyond the realm of the document examiner's work.

Handwriting identification expert. A common name for the document examiner. (See *Document examiner.*)

Holographic document. Any document completely written and signed by one person; also known as a holograph. In a number of jurisdictions a holographic will can be probated without anyone having witnessed its execution.

Individual characteristic. A characteristic that is highly personal or peculiar and is unlikely to occur in other instances. (Cf. *Class characteristic.*)

Infrared examination. The examination of documents employing invisible radiation beyond the red portion of the visible spectrum. Infrared radiation can be recorded on specially sensitized photographic emulsions or it can be converted by means of an electronic viewing device into visible light for an on-the-scene study of the evidence.

Infrared luminescence. A phenomenon encountered with some dyes used in inks and colored pencils that, when illuminated with a narrow band of light in the blue-green portion of the spectrum, give off a luminescence that can be detected in the far-red or near-infrared range. The technique is useful in distinguishing between certain inks and colored pencils, and in detecting or deciphering erasures.

Microscopic examination. Any study or examination made with the microscope in order to discover minute physical details.

Natural variation. Normal or usual deviations found between repeated specimens of any individual's handwriting or in the product of any typewriter or other record making machines.

Oblique light examination. An examination with the illumination so controlled that it grazes or strikes the surface of the document from one side at a very low angle; also referred to as a side light examination.

Opinion. In legal language, the document examiner's conclusion. Actually, in court he not only expresses an opinion but demonstrates the reasons for arriving at it. Throughout this book opinion and conclusion are used synonymously.

Qualification. The professional experience, education, and ability of a document examiner. Before he is permitted to testify as an expert witness, the court must rule that he is a qualified expert in his field.

Quality. A distinct or peculiar character. In this text, "quality" is used in describing handwriting to refer to any identifying factor that is related to the writing movement itself.

Questioned document. Any document about which some issue has been raised or that is under scrutiny. (See also *Disputed document.*)

Reference collection. Material compiled and organized by the document examiner to assist him in answering special questions. Reference collections of typewriting, check writer specimens, ink, pens, pencils, and papers are frequently maintained.

Sample. A selected, representative portion of the whole. In this text, the term follows closely the statistical usage.

Standard. A condensed and compact set of authentic specimens which, if adequate and proper, should contain a true cross section of the material from a known source. They are used by the document examiner as the basis for his identification or nonidentification of the questioned document, as for example the known handwriting which serves to establish who wrote the disputed letter.

Transmitted light examination. An examination in which the document is viewed with the source of illumination behind it and the light passing through the paper.

Ultraviolet examination. Ultraviolet radiation is invisible and occurs in the wavelengths just below the visible blue-violet end of the spectrum (rainbow). The invisible rays react on some substances so that visible light is emitted, a phenomenon known as ultraviolet fluorescence. Thus, ultraviolet examination may be made visually or photographically by recording either the reflected ultraviolet or visible radiation.

Handwriting

Assisted signature. See *Guided signature.*

Baseline. The ruled or imaginary line upon which the writing rests.

Copybook form. The design of letters that is fundamental to a writing system. This term is derived from the old methods of teaching handwriting from a copybook containing engraved script printed on each page for the student to imitate.

Cross mark (his mark). Historically, many who could not write signed with a cross mark or crude X. This authenticating mark is still used today by illiterates, and if properly witnessed, it can legally stand for a signature. In this book ballot marks are also referred to as cross marks because of the common practice of marking with an X.

Cursive writing. Writing in which the letters are for the most part joined together.

Disguised writing. A writer may deliberately try to alter his usual writing habits in hopes of hiding his identity. The results, regardless of their effectiveness, are termed disguised writing.

Forgery. Strictly speaking, a legal term that involves not only a non-genuine signature or document but also an intent on the part of its maker to defraud. Outside the courtroom, however, it is used synonymously with a fraudulent signature or spurious document. The document examiner confines the use of the term to any signature or holographic document written by someone other than the person himself.

Fraudulent signature. A forged signature. It involves the writing of a name as a signature by someone other than the person himself, without his permission, often with some degree of imitation.

Freehand imitation (forgery). A fraudulent signature that was executed purely by simulation rather than by tracing the outline of a genuine signature. The term "simulated forgery" has identical meaning.

Guided signature. A signature that is executed while the writer's hand or arm is steadied in any way; also classified as an assisted signature. Under the law of most jurisdictions such a signature authenticates a legal document provided it is shown that the writer requested the assistance. Guided signatures are most commonly written during a serious illness or on a deathbed.

Habit. Any repeated element or detail that may serve to individualize writing.

Handlettering. Any disconnected style of writing in which each letter is written separately; also called handprinting.

Imitated signature. Synonymous with *Freehand forgery.*

Left-handed writing. See *Wrong-handed writing.*

Line quality. A term characterizing the visible record in the written stroke of the basic movements and manner of holding the writing instrument. It is derived from a combination of factors including writing skill, speed, rhythm, freedom of movement, shading, and pen position.

Manuscript writing. A disconnected form of script or semiscript writing. This type of writing is taught young children in elementary schools as the first step in learning to write.

Model signature. A genuine signature that has been used to prepare an imitated or traced forgery.

Movement. An important element of handwriting. It embraces all the factors related to the motion of the writing instrument—skill, speed, freedom, hesitation, rhythm, emphasis, tremor, and the like. The manner in which the writing instrument is moved, that is, by finger, hand, or arm action, may influence each of these factors.

Natural writing. Any specimen of writing executed normally without an attempt to control or alter its identifying habits and its usual quality of execution. It is the typical writing of an individual. (Cf. *Disguised writing.*)

Patching. Retouching or going back over a defective portion of a writing stroke. Careful patching is a common defect in forgeries.

Pen emphasis. The act of intermittently forcing the pen against the paper surface with increased pressure. When the pen point has flexibility this emphasis produces shading, but with more rigid writing points such as ball point pens heavy pen emphasis can occur in writing without any evidence of shading.

Pen lift. An interruption in a stroke caused by removing the writing instrument (pen) from the paper.

Pen position. The relationship between the pen point and the paper. Specifically, the angle between the nibs of the pen and the line of writing and between the pen point and the paper surface are the elements of pen position. Both conditions may be reflected in the writing, but is not always revealed except when writing was prepared with a nib pen.

Pen pressure. The average force with which the pen contacts the paper, as estimated from an examination of the writing. Pen pressure, as opposed to pen emphasis, deals with the usual or average force involved in the writing rather than with the periodic increases.

Retouching. See *Patching.*

Retracing. Any stroke that goes back over another writing stroke. In natural handwriting there may be many instances in which the pen doubles back over the same course, but some retracing in fraudulent signatures represent a reworking of a letter form or stroke.

Rhythm. That element of the writing movement marked by regular or periodic recurrences. It may be classed as smooth, intermittent, or jerky in its quality.

Shading. A widening of the ink stroke due to added pressure on a flexible pen point or to the use of a stub pen.

Significant writing habit. Any characteristic of handwriting that is sufficiently uncommon and well fixed to serve as a fundamental point in the identification.

Skill. In any act there are relative degrees of ability or skill, and a specimen of handwriting usually contains evidence of the writer's proficiency.

Slant. The angle or inclination of the axis of letters relative to the baseline.

Speed of writing. Not everyone writes at the same rate, so that consideration of the speed of writing may be a significant identifying element. Writing speed cannot be measured precisely from the finished handwriting but can be interpreted in broad terms as slow, moderate, or rapid.

Splicing. A term used by document examiners to denote the slight overlapping of two strokes after an interruption in the writing. It may be a part of imitated, fraudulent signatures that are prepared one or two letters at a time.

Spurious signature. In this text, a fraudulent signature in which there was no apparent attempt at simulation or imitation. It is a common form of forgery encountered in investigations of fraudulent checks where the person passing the check depends on the surrounding circumstances rather than upon the quality of the signature for his success.

System (of writing). The combination of the basic design of letters and the writing movement as taught in school. Writing through use diverges from the system, but generally retains some influence of the basic training.

Traced forgery. Any fraudulent signature executed by actually following the outline of a genuine signature with a writing instrument. Such a signature may be produced with the aid of carbon paper by first tracing a carbon outline and then covering this with a suitable ink stroke, or the forgery may be traced from an outline made visible by light coming through the model signature and the fraudulent document.

Tremor. A writing weakness portrayed by irregular, shaky strokes.

Writing condition. Both the circumstances under which the writing was prepared and the factors influencing the writer's ability to write at the time of execution. Circumstances pertaining to preparation involve the writer's position (sitting, standing, abed, etc.), the paper support and backing, and the writing instrument; writing ability may be modified by the condition of the writer's health, nervous state, or degree of intoxication.

Wrong-handed writing. Any writing executed with the opposite hand from that normally used. Some workers refer to this writing as "with the awkward hand." It is one means of disguise. Thus, the writing of a right-handed person written with his left hand accounts for the common terminology for this class of disguise as "left-handed writing."

Typewriting

Alignment defect. Characters that write improperly in the following respects: a twisted letter, horizontal malalignment, vertical malalignment, or a character "off-its-feet." These defects can be corrected by special adjustments to the typebar and type block on a typebar machine.

Baseline alignment. The alignment of the base of characters horizontally along an imaginary line. The lower projections of letters are excluded in determining the baseline. Improper baseline alignment would involve those letters printing above or below the established baseline.

Carbon impression. Any typewriting placed on the paper by the action of the typefaces striking through carbon paper. Generally, carbon impressions are "carbon copies," but sometimes original typewriting is made directly through a carbon paper or carbon film ribbon.

Character. In connection with typewriting identification, letters, symbols, numerals, and points of punctuation.

Clogged (dirty) typeface. With use the typefaces become filled with lint, dirt, and ink, particularly in enclosed letters, such as o, e, p, and g. If this condition is allowed to progress without cleaning, there comes a time when the written impressions actually print with the clogged areas shaded or solid black.

Defect. Any abnormality or maladjustment in a typewriter that is reflected in its work and leads to its individualization or identification.

Electric typewriter. A typewriter equipped with an electric motor that assists in operating the typebars and the carriage movements, while the typebars or type element is activated by a series of mechanical linkages. In the electronic typewriter such mechanical parts have been eliminated.

Electronic typewriter. A typewriter in which most mechanical parts have been replaced by electronic controls. With all such machines, mechanical linkages between the keys and the typing action are replaced by electronic circuits controlled by microprocessors, and most other actions such as escapement, fine alignment, and ribbon action, are also controlled electronically.

Escapement. The spacing along the line of typewriting, that is, the basic letterspacing; also termed pitch.

Horizontal malalignment. An alignment defect in which the character prints to the right or left of its proper position.

Machine defect. Any defect in typewriting resulting from the malfunctioning of the machine rather than the typebar or type element.

Normally, these defects include improper escapement spacing (that is, each letter underspaces or overspaces a fraction of the basic unit) and defects in printing brought about by improper alignment of the typing unit and the roller. In other words, machine defects tend to affect all the characters on the machine rather than any particular character.

Malalignment. See *Alignment defect.*

Manual typewriter. A machine whose operation depends solely upon the mechanical action set in motion by striking a letter or character key. During the first 50 or more years in typewriter history, all machines were manually operated.

Off-its-feet. The condition of a typeface printing heavier on one side or corner than the remainder of its outline.

Permanent defect. Any identifying characteristic of a typewriter that cannot be corrected by simply cleaning the typeface or replacing the ribbon. Actually, this term is not absolutely accurate, since all defects in typewriters undergo modification and change with time.

Platen. The cylinder that serves as the backing for the paper and absorbs the blow from the typeface.

Proportional spacing typewriting. A modern form of typewriting resembling printing in that letters, numerals, and symbols do not occupy the same horizontal space as they do with the conventional typewriter. For example, the i occupies two units, the o three, and the m five.

Rebound. A defect in which a character prints a double impression with the lighter one slightly offset to the right or left.

Ribbon condition. Cloth or multiple-use typewriter ribbons gradually deteriorate with use, and the degree of deterioration is a measure of the ribbon condition.

Ribbon impression. Typewriting made directly through a cloth or carbon film ribbon is called a ribbon impression. Original typewriting is made in this way.

Single element typewriter. Typewriters using either a type ball or type wheel printing device. The IBM Selectric machine was the first modern typewriter of the group.

Transitory defect. An identifying typewriter characteristic that can be eliminated by cleaning the machine or replacing the ribbon. Clogged typefaces are the most common defects of this class.

Type ball. A device containing all the typefaces of some single element typewriters and which by rotation and tilting prints the type.

Type element. The type ball or type wheel of a single element typewriter.

Typeface. The printing surface of the type block or type element. On the typebar machine the type block is attached an arm, known as the typebar.

Typeface defect. Any peculiarity in typewriting resulting from actual damage to the typeface metal. It may be an actual break in the outline of the letter where the metal is chipped away, sometimes referred to as broken type, or a distorted outline of the letter because of bent or smashed typeface metal. The defect can be corrected only by replacing the type block or element.

Type wheel. In modern use, a series of characters mounted on flexible arms around a circular core. The wheel rotates to position each type, which is printed by a plunger striking against the back of the typeface forcing it against the ribbon and paper.

Twisted letter. Each character is designed to print at a certain fixed angle to the base line. Wear and damage to the type bars and the type block may cause some letters to become twisted so that they lean to the right or left of their correct slant.

Vertical malalignment. The result of a character printing above or below its proper position. See also *Baseline alignment.*

Word-processing unit. Any typewriter or other printing unit that is combined with a memory system and is thus capable of automatic typewriting or repetitive typewriting of certain matter. Material can be stored on disks, tapes, or memory chips.

Altered Documents

Altered document. A document that contains some change, either as an addition or a deletion.

"Blank" paper. A sheet of paper that contains no visible or readily visible writing. At times a "blank" paper may contain impressed or latent writing that can be made legible with proper treatment.

Charred document. A document that has become blackened and brittle through burning or through exposure to excessive heat.

Decipherment. The process of making out what is illegible or what has been effaced. In this book decipherment refers to the process of reading or interpreting the erased or obliterated material that is illegible without actually developing or restoring the original writing on the document itself. (Cf. *Restoration.*)

Efface. To rub out, to strike or scratch out, or to erase.

Erasure. The removal of writing, typewriting, or printing from a document. It may be accomplished by either of two means: a chemical eradication in which the writing is removed or bleached by chemical agents, e.g., liquid ink eradicator; or an abrasive erasure in which the writing is effaced by rubbing with a rubber eraser or scratching out with a knife.

Ink eradicator. A chemical solution capable of bleaching ink.

Insertion. The addition of writing and other material within a document such as between lines or paragraphs, or the addition of whole pages to a document.

Interlineation. The act of inserting writing or typewriting between two lines of writing.

Lift-off ribbon. A modern typewriting ribbon whose ink can be completely removed with a special adhesive tape to leave an apparent blank area; also sold as a correctable ribbon.

Obliteration. The blotting out or smearing over of writing to make the original invisible or undecipherable.

Restoration. Any process in which erased writing is developed or brought out again on the document itself. (Cf. *Decipherment.*)

Secret inks. A material used for writing that is not visible until treated by some developing process; also referred to as sympathetic ink.

Sequence of strokes. The order in which writing strokes are placed on the paper.

Smeared-over writing. An obliteration accomplished by covering the original writing with an opaque substance.

Sympathetic ink. See *Secret ink.*

Writing impression. The small writing indentation completely or virtually devoid of any pigment. It may be made on the sheet of tablet paper that was immediately below the one on which writing was done or remain after pencil or typewriting has been thoroughly erased.

Writing offset. The result of a paper coming in contact with fresh ink writing. It may be the mirror image of entire words or sentences, as are sometimes found on a blotter, or merely fragments of words or letters.

Other Identification Problems

Aniline inks. See *Synthetic dye inks.*

Ball point pen. A writing instrument having as its marking tip a small, freely rotating ball bearing that rolls the ink onto the paper. Many of these pens use a highly viscous, nonaqueous ink, but in recent years construction of some pens has been adapted to use water-based inks. See *Roller pen.*

Blue-black ink. The class of fluid ink that writes blue and darkens with age to a neutral gray or black. It contains a blue dye, but the permanent marking substances are almost-colorless iron tannates and gallates, which gradually darken after exposure to air.

Carbon ink. Inks of the carbon class, consisting of finely ground carbon particles suspended in water. Their manufacture dates from antiquity, and they are still used as drawing inks and very occasionally as writing inks.

Colored pencil. A pencil whose marking pigment is not black.

Copy pencil. A pencil whose marking substance consists of a mixture of graphite and an aniline dye. When the pencil stroke is moistened the dye develops into a strong purple or, in some cases, a blue color. The developed stroke is more difficult to erase than ordinary pencil writing. Some refer to this kind of writing instrument as an indelible pencil.

Dye inks. See *Synthetic dye inks.*

Engraved printing. Letterheads and other matter that are printed from a metal plate containing an etched design, for example. With this type of work the ink is slightly raised above the surface of the paper.

Felt tip pen. See *Porous tip pen.*

Fiber tip pen. See *Porous tip pen.*

Flexibility of pen point. A quality of the nib pen that varies with different pens and can be measured by the amount of pressure necessary to cause a spreading of the nibs or a given degree of shading.

Fountain pen. A modern nib pen containing a reservoir of ink in a specially designed chamber or cartridge. After complete filling, the pen may be used to write a number of pages without refilling.

Hard point pen. A modern writing instrument in which the point is a perforated plastic unit. It uses a water-based ink and produces a stroke similar to the porous tip pen, but is capable of making carbon copies like a ball point or roller pen.

Indelible pencil. See *Copy pencil.*

Ink. A colored fluid or viscous marking material used for writing or printing.

Iron tannate or iron-base ink. See *Blue-black ink.*

Latent fingerprints. Any deposits or traces from the finger tips that are completely invisible. With proper treatment they can be developed or made visible.

Lithographic or offset printing. Printing from a smooth surface plate that has been treated so that the printing areas are ink attracting and the nonprinting areas are ink repelling. Originally this process used a smooth stone surface, but today most offset printing is prepared from specially treated zinc or paper plates.

Look-through of paper. The appearance of paper when viewed by transmitted light, thus disclosing the texture or formation of the sheet.[1]

Nonaqueous ink. Ink in which the pigment or dye is carried in any vehicle other than water. Inks of this class are found in ball point pens, typewriter ribbons, and stamp pads, and are widely used in the printing industry.

Offset printing. See *Lithographic printing.*

Pen. Any writing instrument used to apply inks to the paper.

Pen nib. One of two divisions or points that form the writing portion of a dip pen or fountain pen.

Pencil. A writing instrument in which the marking portion consists of a compressed stick of graphite or colored marking substance usually mixed with clays and waxes.

Pencil grade. A qualitative description of the hardness or softness of a pencil, that is, how dark a stroke it is capable of making.

Porous tip pen. A modern writing instrument in which the marking element or point consists of a porous material through which the ink can flow. These pens are commonly known as fiber tip or felt tip pens or may be referred to as soft tip pens.

Roller pen. A type of ball point pen that uses aqueous ink.

Surface texture of paper. The surface of any sheet of paper when viewed under magnification is not absolutely smooth and flat, but irregular and rough. Surface texture describes this property.

Synthetic dye inks. Any ink consisting simply of a dye dissolved in water together with the necessary preservatives. Various dyes are used in commercial ink manufacture today; the aniline dyes were the first of these, and some writers still refer to inks of this class as aniline inks.

Watermark. A translucent design impressed in certain papers during the course of their manufacture.

Photographs and Other Reproductions

No attempt will be made in this section to prepare an exhaustive list of photographic terms; rather, fundamental terms that are employed repeatedly, together with special terms of document photography, are defined according to their use in this text. There are many elementary

---

[1]*Dictionary of Paper* (New York: American Paper and Pulp Association, 1940), p. 217.

and basic photographic publications that will assist in clarifying the photographic discussions, two useful ones being *Photography*, Vol. 1, Naval Training Course, NAVPERS 10371, U.S. Government Printing Office, 1952, and C. E. Kenneth Mees, *Photography*, (New York: MacMillian Company, 1937).

Camera. Basically, a light-tight box designed to hold photographic film. It is equipped with a lens system by which the image is focused on the film and a shutter device by which the desired amount of light is admitted to expose the film.

Color film. Two classes of films are available for color photography today: color reversal films for color transparencies and color negative films from which color prints or slides (transparencies) can be made. Both are useful in certain document problems.

Color sensitivity of films. Modern black-and-white photographic films fall into three ranges of color sensitivity. "Color-blind" or blue-sensitive films record the blue portion of the spectrum in proper tones of gray, but all other colors are photographed as black. Orthochromatic films accurately record blue, yellow, and green, but photograph red and black alike. Finally, panchromatic films are fully color sensitive, photographing all colors of the visible spectrum in their proper tones of gray. To photograph documents correctly, films must be chosen in accordance with their sensitivity and the colors present.

Contact print. A photographic positive made by exposing the photographic paper while it is held tightly against the negative.

Contrast. The tonal difference between the darkest and lightest portions of a negative or print.

Cut-out exhibits. A photographic exhibit made up of words and letters cut from photographs of different documents and arranged side by side. Some writers refer to these exhibits as "juxtaposition photographs."

Display exhibit. A greatly enlarged photographic court exhibit that is made to such size that it must be placed upon an easel before the jury box. These exhibits may also be referred to as "bromide enlargements."

Emulsion. A coating on all photographic films and papers, consisting of light sensitive silver salts in a gelatin medium.

Film. For black-and-white photography consists of a transparent base (cellulose acetate or other material) that supports the light sensitive emulsion. Photographic plates in which the film base is replaced by a glass sheet have occasional use in document photography.

Filter. A colored glass or gelatin that is inserted in the lens system to modify the color characteristics of the light that strikes the film. There are two types of filters. A compensating filter only slightly weakens a particular color band within the spectrum and thus may improve certain color rendition. A contrast filter, on the other hand, transmits only one relatively narrow color band or wavelength of light and completely absorbs the balance, causing them to photograph as black. Contrast filters are employed in document work principally to eliminate interfering color marks or to intensify weak traces of a complementary color.

Grain size. The light sensitive silver halides that are impregnated in the emulsion exist as small crystals and upon development are converted to pure silver granules. Under the microscope these crystals are found to vary in size with different types of films and photographic papers; this characteristic is known as grain size.

Hand exhibit. A photographic court exhibit designed to be held and examined by the individual juror or a pair of jurors.

Infrared luminescence photography. Photography using infrared sensitive films and filters to record luminescence in the infrared light range. It is a useful tool in questioned document work.

Infrared photography (direct). Reactions in the infrared (invisible) portion of the spectrum recorded by the illumination of a document with a source rich in infrared radiation and by using infrared emulsions and filters.

Lens. One or more optical ground glasses that focus light rays in a manner similar to that of the pupil of the eye. The function of the camera lens is to focus an image of the object being photographed on the film surface.

Microphotograph. Copies of documents at a greatly reduced scale on small film sizes. They are used in certain commercial record systems. Throughout this text the term designates copies made on 35-mm and smaller film sizes. The line of demarcation has been chosen arbitrarily and may not necessarily agree exactly with views of other writers.

Negative. See *Photographic negative.*

Photocopy. A reproduction of a document made on paper by any office or commercial system.

Photograph. A reproduction made with a camera and light sensitive material. The process normally requires two steps: the preparation of a negative on film and the printing of the final positive from it.

Photographic negative. The transparency produced when black-and-white film is exposed in a camera and then developed. The term is derived from the appearance of the transparency, in which white areas of the original appear the darkest or most opaque, while the darkest portions of the original are almost clear. With color film the light–dark reversal is coupled with a change of colors to the complements of those in the original material.

Photographic positive. A print made by passing light through the negative generally onto photographic paper. In this print the tonal values are directly proportional to those of the original, that is, light areas of the original appear light, and dark areas dark.

Photomicrographs. A photograph made through a compound microscope and may be a greatly enlarged image of a small area. A similarly enlarged photograph may be prepared with only a lens of very short focal length and is accurately termed a photomacrograph. It is extremely difficult to distinguish between photographs made by the two processes, and both are often incorrectly referred to as a photomicrograph.

Photostat®. A commercial reproduction in which a negative copy, white writing on a black background, is made directly on photosensitive paper. The process employs a special camera equipped with a lens and inverting prism. The inverting prism causes the writing in the negative copy to run from left to right, i.e., in the same direction as in the original rather than backward. A photostatic positive, that is black writing on a white background, must be prepared by rephotostating the negative copy. The method is obsolete and has been replaced by various dry photocopying methods.

Print. See *Photographic positive.*

Projection prints. A print made by focusing light from the negative on the printing paper by means of a lens system. These positives are generally enlargements. Some workers refer to them as "bromides" because of the type of paper emulsion originally used.

Resolving power. The maximum number of distinguishable lines per millimeter that can be recorded by photographic material or by a lens. Not all photographic materials or lenses have the same characteristics in this respect.

Standard photograph. In this text, any document photograph that is not a microphotograph. For the most part, a standard photograph is made on film sizes of $2\frac{1}{4} \times 3\frac{1}{4}$ in. or larger. The negative image is only slightly reduced and more generally is of natural size or enlarged.

Ultraviolet photograph. Any photograph that records the document under ultraviolet illumination. With some of these the ultraviolet radiation strikes the film, but with others a filter is employed so that the only visual fluorescence caused by the ultraviolet is recorded.

Xerox®. A positive photocopy made directly on plain paper. Although Xerox is a trade name, its success, like Photostat's before it, has resulted in many people referring incorrectly to all present-day photocopies as xeroxes.

II

WHAT EXAMINATION
OF A DOCUMENT MAY REVEAL

Witnesses are frequently produced in court to describe in detail the preparation and history of a contested document when in fact the most accurate and complete story may be contained within the document itself. Every article used in its preparation has certain characteristics, and each step toward its completion and in its subsequent handling affects to some degree its ultimate condition and appearance. Of these factors, some may be so highly individual that they positively identify the source, while others may influence the physical appearance little, if at all. More generally, though, all play their role in its identification so that a rather accurate resumé of its history can be reconstructed from an extensive technical examination. Just how complete this resumé is, of course, depends upon the factors involved in each individual case, but in many instances it is more accurate than the memory of those persons present at the document's inception and of those who may have handled the document during its life. At times it can refute claims of parties interested in the document or help to substantiate these claims. The ensuing chapters describe in detail the extent of the information to be derived from these examinations.

Everyone knows that a document is the product of a combination of several materials, such as ink and paper, put together by means of certain common instruments like the pen, the pencil, or the typewriter. Almost everyone, however, fails to appreciate fully that each of these materials and instruments has its individual and class characteristics, which in combination help to personalize and identify the document's source and history. Furthermore, once a document is completed, any changes, either deliberate or accidental, may produce inconsistencies that are typical of and distinguish it as an altered document. It thus becomes necessary to discover and evaluate correctly each of these factors to reconstruct as much of the document's history as possible.

3

Instruments and Materials
Used to Prepare Documents

The Pen

Since ancient times the nib pen has been the principal writing tool. However, during the last 30 years it has been superceded in large measure by the ball point pen and to some extent by other special types of pens, especially the porous tip or fiber tip pen and the roller pen. For over a century, the pencil has been substituted for the pen in preparing certain documents, and during this century the typewriter has become an important instrument for document preparation. Despite all these competing writing instruments, the nib pen is still to be found, usually in the form of a fountain pen, but very occasionally as the steel dip pen, which even as late as the 1930s enjoyed widespread use. A number of special types of pens, including drawing, lettering, quill, and stylographic pens[1] have been or are still available. Each class has its peculiarities by which its work can be recognized and may at times assume special importance in the investigation of a disputed document (Figure 3.1).

Ball Point Pen

The ball point pen was introduced to the American market in 1945, at the close of World War II.[2] Its popularity grew rapidly despite early

---

[1]The stylographic pen consists of a small cylindrical tube fitted with a plunger at the tip. When the pen is pressed on the paper the plunger is raised slightly, causing the ink to flow. A pen of this design writes a stroke of uniform width regardless of the direction of its movement and, because of its design, is an easy writing pen especially adapted to disconnected lettering. Its peculiarity of design and writing quality distinguishes its work. Few of these pens are available today, although the principle is used in the pen portion of some lettering guide sets.

[2]The ball point pen was actually first sold in Europe as early as 1935, but by 1939 sales totaled only about 25,000 pens (*Fortune,* July 1946, p. 144). Ladislo Biro began manufacture of these pens in

(continued)

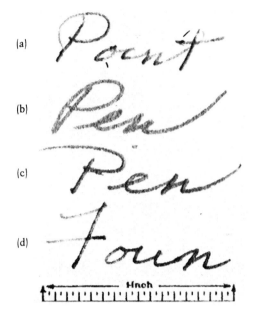

(a)

(b)

(c)

(d)

Figure 3.1. Enlarged segments of writing with the four common, contemporary pens show some of the writing qualities of each. (a) The ball point pen has a number of writing defects including "gooping," as shown by the indicated dark ink spot in the t crossing and the skipping in the lower portion of the o. (b) The flat even inking of the porous point pen is sometimes accompanied by hairline dragging of ink along the edge of the line (not illustrated). (c) The roller writer has a stroke very similar to the porous tip, but also leaves a writing groove like that of the ball pen, as suggested by the dark edge inside the turn of the P. (d) The dark flowback at the right end of the F and at the bottom of the vertical stroke is a typical action of the nib pen. Dark nib tracks, as suggested along the edge of this downstroke, are a further identifying mark.

faults. With it the nibs of the conventional pen were replaced by a small steel ball. The ball is held in place at the tip of the pen by a housing that allows it to rotate freely during the writing process, rolling the ink onto the paper, ink which is picked up on the ball as it revolves through the adjacent ink chamber. Ball point pen ink is a pastelike substance of high viscosity, which contrasts with the water-soluble fluid ink used by the nib pen.

The work of the ball point pen can be recognized and distinguished from other writing instruments both by its ink and the details of the

footnote² (continued)
Argentina in 1943 and sold them in limited numbers in South America (*Readers Digest*, December 1946, p. 60). A few found their way to the United States by 1945. It was his pen that lead to the introduction by Reynolds of the domestically made ball point pen in the fall of 1945, and the accompanying promotional program quickly jumped sales into the millions. Thomas Whitside, in *The New Yorker* (February 15, 1951), tells of the pen's early history and promotion.

stroke. In lighter strokes the rolling of the pastelike marking substance catches only on the edges of the higher fibers, and in the heavier strokes the pressure on the ball forms a groove or compression in the center of the stroke. Inks in use today set up or dry quickly on the paper. Furthermore, the ink supply, an integral part of the writing unit, is sufficient to write for weeks or months of use. When the ink is exhausted, many pens are designed so that the entire writing unit can be removed and discarded and a new unit with its ink supply inserted. Actually, this creates a new pen. Other characteristics of the ball point pen are derived from the size of the ball, which controls the width of the writing stroke and the quality of the stroke produced.

Ball point pens can be differentiated by ink characteristics, particularly color, by the ball size, and by the defects present in the writing stroke, which includes "gooping" of the ink, that is, small dotlike, dark deposits especially at turns in the writing, skipping or short gaps in the stroke, and striations within the stroke.[3] Very fine "burr striations" may occur at times in a distinctive enough pattern virtually to individualize the pen.[4] Nondestructive tests, including visual, microscopic, infrared, and ultraviolet examinations, may permit one to distinguish between the work of two pens. Studies of the ink strokes using dichroic filters[5] or infrared luminescence[6] are further means of distinguishing between similar but not identical inks. None of these tests alters or damages the document. Certain chemical tests discussed in the following section on inks can further extend the means of differentiating between ball point pens.

Porous Tip Pens

More recently the porous tip pens, that is, fiber or felt tip pens, have assumed some popularity. The writing point of this pen is porous and allows a supply of fluid ink to be spread on the paper. Broad tips pre-

---

[3]A more detailed treatment of the characteristics of the ball pen can be found in O. Hilton, "Characteristics of the Ball Point Pen and Its Influence on Handwriting Identification," *Journal of Criminal Law, Criminology and Police Science* 47 (1957): 606–613. A discussion of the early pens is found in Elbridge W. Stein and Ordway Hilton, "Questions Raised by Examiners of Signatures and Documents," and C. H. Lindsly and Robert Casey, "Behavior of Ball Point Pens and Ink as Seen by a Principal Manufacturer," *American Bar Association Journal* 34 (1948): 373–378. Also see Jacques Mathyer, "Ball Pens and Expert Appraisal of Written Documents," *Internnational Criminal Police Review* 43 (1950): 357–360, and Wilmer Souder, "Composition, Properties and Behavior of Ball Pens and Inks," *Journal of Criminal Law, Criminology and Police Science* 45 (1955): 743–747.

[4]David A. Black, "Identifying Ball Pens by the Burr Striations," *Journal of Criminal Law, Criminology and Police Science* 61 (1970): 280–282.

[5]See Royston J. Packard, "Selective Wavelength Examination Applied to Ink Differentiation Problems," *Journal of Forensic Sciences* 9 (1964): 100–106.

[6]Linton Godown, "New Nondestructive Document Testing Methods," *Journal of Criminal Law, Criminology and Police Science* 55 (1964): 281–284. Also see Ronald M. Dick, "A Comparative Analysis of Dichroic Filter Viewing, Reflective Infrared, and Infrared Luminescense Applied to Ink Differentiation Problems," *Journal of Forensic Science* 15 (1970): 557–563.

dominated in the early pens, but as the pen was more widely accepted a moderate width tip became more common. Fine and very fine tips have been developed, some of which have a hard perforated plastic tip. Flair produces both a fiber tip and a porous plastic tip, their Hardhead, with a moderate width tip. The hard tip pens produce a stroke very similar to the pure fiber tip pen except that under some conditions they can create a slight furrow or tough. With all, the ink tends toward intense colors, and the pens deliver a heavy, though quick-drying, stroke. While the writing strokes are rather distinctive and can be distinguished from those of ball point pens and generally from those of fountain pens, a particular pen rarely develops enough individuality to distinguish it from others containing similar ink. Pens of this class are factory filled, and many of them are of the throwaway type in which the whole writing instrument is discarded when the ink is exhausted. The exact color may vary slightly from one lot to another, as well as between manufacturers. In addition, stroke width is dependent upon the size of the tip. With use, pens may produce a distinctive imperfect stroke. These factors serve as a means of distinguishing between the writing of some pens.

Roller Pens

It was only a few years after the introduction of the ball point pen that the first attempt was made to produce a ball point pen that would use fluid ink, but it was not until the late 1960s that such a pen was perfected so that it wrote with sufficient reliability to assure general acceptance. These pens produce a stroke not unlike that of a porous tip pen except that the ball tends to emboss the paper. Differences in ink distinguish their work from that of the conventional ball pens. With use some stroke defects do appear, but a particular pen does not develop sufficient individuality to distinguish it from others of the same class.

Fountain or Nib Pens

Today the fountain pen is the most common nib-pointed pen. The writing characteristics vary. The width of the nib point (Figure 3.2) and its degree of flexibility are two factors in this variation. Occasionally, a steel-pointed dip pen may be encountered; with very old documents, there is a good chance that some were prepared with such a writing instrument. Normally, a particular nib pen cannot be individualized by its work; that is to say, it cannot usually be determined that a specific pen wrote the document. Still, not all of these pens produce

Figure 3.2. A photomicrograph made through the comparison microscope shows the difference in two ink strokes, indicating two different nib widths.

the same writing strokes,[7] which makes it possible to say in some situations that a certain pen was not used to execute a questioned document or that more than one pen was used to write a document.

Nib pens produce a stroke different from those of other types of pens. The nibs can make a distinctive darker double track within the stroke, but this double track is not as pronounced with modern, stiff-pointed fountain pens as it is with more flexible points.

The property of the fountain pen to write lengthy documents with comparable ink densities from page to page can distinguish it from the steel dip pen. The latter produces more intense writing each time it is filled, and gradually the intensity of the strokes diminishes. If the point of a fountain pen is flexible, definite shading can be a part of the writing, which is recognized by the gradual increase in the width of the stroke due to the pressure of the pen, particularly on downstrokes. Further, differentiation results from the nib width, which can best be determined by careful study of the upstrokes of the letters under magnification. These factors permit the examiner to distinguish between writings by different nib pens.

It is seldom possible to identify the work of a particular pen of this class, although a few cases are on record in which some unusual defect permitted such an identification.[8] Even so, evidence developed from the examination of nib and other classes of pens may be of unique value. To be able to say that a document was prepared with a certain type of pen means very little as a general rule, but if the testimony of

---

[7]The reader desiring to delve more deeply into the question of the identification of nib pens should refer to A. S. Osborn, *Questioned Documents*, 2nd ed. (Albany: Boyd, 1929), Chapter 11, "Writing Instruments," pp. 151–161.

[8]When a pen is found that is sufficiently defective to suggest that an identification of its work might be possible, there should be in existence a quantity of writing done by it. The pen itself may still be available. If either the pen or sample writing or both are located, they should be made available for study and comparison.

a witness with a fraudulent document can be refuted by physical evidence derived from such examination, the pen stroke assumes greater importance as evidence.

Historic facts about pens and the alleged age of documents have a way of becoming embarrassingly inconsistent for the uninformed forger. Forgeries prepared with steel pens or fountain pens, dated years before the invention of these instruments, leave little argument over their authenticity. The same could be true of ball point pen writing. In these cases other elements no doubt indicate fraud, but none can be more conclusive than the information derived from the pen study alone.

Among the most significant pen examinations are instances in which it is possible to demonstrate with clarity that added portions, especially of a modifying nature, have been inserted with a pen different from that originally used in the preparation of the document. Fortunately, ignorance or lack of care on the part of those attempting to perpetrate fraud may lead to these errors. On the other hand, the use of two or more pens to make periodic entries in documents, such as a record or account book, may provide evidence of authenticity (Figure 3.3). Certainly, any suspected documents that appear to have been written with more than one pen should be investigated and the evidence weighed in the light of the usual or normal mode of preparing such a document, as well as in the light of testimony of those responsible for its preparation.

Examination of the work of pens does not always lead to conclusive solutions, but information so obtained adds to the total picture. In many instances, this evidence, combined with additional facts derived from a study of other elements of the document, has led to definite proof of either genuineness or forgery.

Figure 3.3. Changes in the pens and inks used for four different entries are perfectly consistent with the differences in the dates of writing.

Writing Inks

The history of ink dates back to ancient times. Among the earliest materials used was carbon, which produces a very permanent ink. Today it is still employed in certain drawing inks, often referred to as India inks. During the Middle Ages iron-gall ink was developed, which ultimately was improved to become the modern blue-black ink. Until the ball point pen became the popular and most common writing instrument, this class of ink was widely used. Various natural dyes were also adopted for colored inks, but gradually with the development of aniline and other synthetic dyes were replaced by these materials. The changeover came in the late 1800s and the early 1900s.[9] Synthetic dyes form the coloring matter in almost all present-day inks.[10] During the 1930s dyes were developed that required the use of strong alkaline solution instead of the mild acid ink, and these newer inks enjoyed limited commercial popularity.[11] With all of the inks discussed to this point, water was the chief solvent.

With the introduction of the ball point pen in the mid-1940s, a different type of ink was needed. It is a thick pastelike material using organic chemical solvents rather than water.[12] In this respect it resembles inks used for typewriter ribbons and for printing, but of course it must have its own special properties. Thus today inks are available that use water and organic solvents as their base.

In the last 20 years fluid water-based inks have found expanded use, first in the porous tip or fiber tip pen and more recently in the roller writer, that is, the type of ball point pen that uses fluid ink. The fiber tip pen marked a modification of the felt marking pen, which had had some specialized use and employed a non-water-based ink. One can see that the variety of pens that have been developed requires a corresponding variety of inks, even though fluid inks are used in several different classes of pens. As a result, the document examiner has developed the ability to distinguish between the different classes of ink as well as the different types of pens. Some of these determinations may be made with a high degree of certainty.

Document examiners are called upon not only to differentiate be-

---

[9]An early history of writing inks has been compiled by David N. Carvalho, *Forty Centuries of Ink* (New York: Banks Law Publ. Co., 1904). An extremely useful tabulation of historic events in the development of inks and pens is found in Julius Grant, *Books and Documents* (New York: Chemical Publ. Co., 1937), pp. 41–44.

[10]C. A. Mitchell and T. C. Hepworth in *Inks, Their Composition and Manufacture*, 4th ed. (London: Griffin, 1937), thoroughly investigated all classes of modern inks that were in use at the date of publication. A briefer and less technical discussion of present-day inks can be found in A. Lucas, *Forensic Chemistry and Scientific Criminal Investigation*, 4th ed., (London: Arnold, 1946), pp. 79–88.

[11]At this time the Parker Pen Company introduced their "51" and "Superchrome" ink, which is a highly alkaline dye rather than a slightly acid solution found in the more common dye inks.

[12]See Wilson R. Harrison, *Suspect Documents, Their Scientific Examination* (New York: Praeger, 1958), p. 217.

tween inks, but also to identify the source of particular ink. Very similar, but different, inks can be distinguished by proper tests, but a positive identification of the source of an ink is unlikely. The best that can be stated is that the questioned ink is the same kind as that found at the suspected source and could have originated there.

Differentiation between inks can be accomplished by both visual, nondestructive tests and by chemical tests, which generally involve alteration of some parts of the document. Nondestructive tests are almost universally employed as the first step in any ink study. They start with an examination of the ink for color and the appearance of the stroke on the paper using hand magnifiers or the binocular microscope under various types of illumination. Relative color qualities may be altered with a change of illumination from daylight to fluorescent or tungsten light. Ultraviolet, infrared, infrared luminescence, and dichroic examinations are additional nondestructive tests that may assist in distinguishing between similar inks.

A microscopic spot test—the reaction of a minute drop of chemical reagent on a portion of the ink stroke viewed under the microscope—helps to determine that the document was written with a particular class of fluid ink, e.g., iron base, synthetic dye, or carbon ink.[13] These tests when properly performed make only a microscopic change in the document. Although not employed as much today as formerly, they are of particular value in demonstrating that two different inks were employed on a single document, but unfortunately, they do not necessarily distinguish between brands of the same class of ink.

Since the 1950s the most common chemical ink testing is chromatography,[14] especially thin-layer chromatography (TLC).[15] The

---

[13]Chemical spot tests for differentiation between inks are reported by several writers. Modern tests are included in Lucas, *Forensic Chemistry and Scientific Criminal Investigation*, pp. 88–92, while A. J. Quirke in *Forged, Anonymous and Suspect.Documents* (London: Routledge, 1930), discusses similar tests (pp. 177–179). Further tests, especially by French workers, and a survey of microchemical testing methods are set forth by H. T. F. Rhodes, *Forensic Chemistry* (New York, Chemical Publ. Co., 1940), pp. 94–104. Mitchell and Hepworth, *Inks, Their Composition and Manufacture* deal at length with these tests.

[14]Chromatographic analysis was suggested or hinted at by Mitchell and Hepworth, *Inks, Their Composition and Manufacture*, 3rd ed., 1924, p. 158, but was not developed for tests on questioned documents until rather recently. A number of workers have contributed applications of the technique to testing and differentiating between inks, especially synthetic dye inks. Indications are that particular brands of ink can in some instances be distinguished. See, for example, Wilmer Souder and W. Harold Smith, "Comparison of Writing Inks by Paper Chromatography," *Identification News* (November 1951): 4; A. W. Somerford, "Comparison of Writing Inks by Paper Chromatography," *Journal of Criminal Law, Criminology and Police Science* 43 (1952): 530–539; Charlotte Brown and Paul R. Kirk, "Horizontal Paper Chromatography in the Identification of Ball Point Pen Inks," *Journal of Criminal Law, Criminology and Police Science* 45 (1954): 334–339.

[15]A. H. Witte, "The Examination and Identification of Inks," *Methods of Forensic Science*, Vol. 2, edited by Frank Lundquist (New York: Interscience, 1963), pp. 56–61; D. A. Crown, R. L. Brunnelle, and A. A. Cantu, "The Parameters of Ballpen Ink Examination," *Journal of Forensic Sciences* 21 (1976): 917–922.

method requires cutting or scraping a very small sample of ink from the paper, a step that may require a court order or an agreement among all parties to the dispute. With adequate reference files, the source and an estimation of the age of the writing may be derived. By these tests two inks can be compared to establish whether they are the same. TLC represents the most sensitive test available today.

The most recent development in ink manufacturing is the addition of traces of rare-earth elements to the ink. The tagging material is changed periodically and the detection of a particular element can be used to determine from the manufacturer when the questioned ink was produced. Again a small sample of the ink must be cut from the document.

Chemical tests are an important part of the identification of inks. Chemical composition has been determined by a combination of tests and demonstrated in legal proceedings in order to show that the document could not have been executed on the alleged date. Some of the more famous cases occurred in the latter part of the 19th and the early years of the 20th century.[16] It was during that period that ink manufacturers introduced synthetic dyes in writing inks. Today chemical tests for composition may be less spectacular since manufacturing has become more standardized, but thin-layer chromatography can disclose very minute differences in the composition of two inks with unusual clarity.

The combination of the various tests can reveal important information, especially when there is suspicion of a fraudulent entry in a handwritten document. With comprehensive reference material, it is sometimes possible to make an accurate judgment about the brands of inks that appear on a document and possibly whether the inks are consistent with the alleged date of the document.

In general it may be said that ink examinations offer more opportunities to disclose fraud than clearly to substantiate genuineness. The inconsistencies between various parts of the document can at times, although not always of course, lead to the former conclusions, but consistent results do not conclusively establish that the document was necessarily prepared at one time. Nevertheless, there may be important instances when these tests do permit definite interpretations.

---

[16]Among these cases was the trial before Chancellor McGill of New Jersey of the Gordon will dispute in 1891. In this case the interlineation in an alleged draft of a will was written with a red aniline dye ink that had not been discovered until some years after the date of the draft. See William Hagan, *Disputed Handwriting* (New York: Banks, 1894), pp. 209, 253–282 (reprinted by AMS Press, New York, 1974). C. A. Mitchell in *The Expert Witness* (New York: Appleton, 1923), p. 115, refers to the trial of Alexander Humphrey in Edinburgh, 1839, in which a document alleged to have been written in 1639 was shown to have been written with "modern ink."

Pencils

Historically speaking, pencils are a modern instrument. According to histories, graphite, the "lead" of today's pencils, was first discovered in England in 1564.[17] From a limited use in the 16th century, the pencil has grown in popularity, until today it is found in every home, office, and school. Obviously, because of its widespread use numerous questions arise regarding its identification.

Let us first examine the general properties of pencils. Like pens, pencils can be grouped into classes based on their physical properties. The graphite forming the marking substance is in the course of manufacture mixed with clay and waxes and baked. The amount of graphite and clay and the period of baking are factors that determine the hardness of the lead.[18] Pencils designed for drawing work may be extremely hard, i.e., capable of writing only a light stroke even with heavy writing pressure. At the other extreme are the soft drawing pencils, which make relatively dark lines with only slight pressure. Somewhat midway between these two extremes are the several grades of common writing pencils. Thus pencils can in a general way be classified by their relative grade or hardness.

In addition to the hardness of the lead, there are various qualities of lead that result in a large measure from the quality of ingredients used in the manufacture. Inexpensive pencils are made with less-refined graphite and clay, while the top grade uses fine materials and is manufactured under excellent quality controls. Microscopic study of pencil strokes helps to differentiate between the cheaper and more expensive writing leads.

When a specimen of pencil writing is examined, it may be very difficult to establish the particular hardness of the pencil used, although broad groupings such as soft, medium, or hard may be recognized. The differences between two adjacent grades prepared by the same manufacturer are slight. Two writers using the same grade of pencil may produce slightly different effects because of individual habits of pressure and emphasis. Furthermore, a change of writing background from a hard table top to a softer writing pad modifies the density of the stroke produced, and this is also influenced by relative sharpness of the point. With extended documents, softer points in wood encased pencils may wear down appreciably during the writing of several pages, whereas a harder lead holds its point much longer.

---

[17]Carvalho, *Forty Centuries of Ink*, p. 262. The entire chapter (pp. 261–271) relates the history and development of the pencil.

[18]Early pencils were a pressed mixture of clay and graphite. The "lead" of these pencils was not baked and consequently was very soft, giving only a broad stroke. Modern pencils, in which the clay and graphite mixture is baked to give added hardness, came into use about 1810 [W. E. Woodward, *The Way Our People Live* (New York: Dutton, 1944), p. 120 footnote].

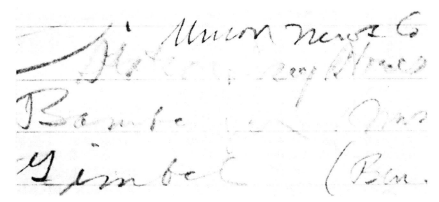

Figure 3.4. The four pencil-written entries show the probability of three different pencils. The first entry was made with a sharp, soft point, a softer grade than any of the others. The more intense writing with a lack of embossing established this conclusion. The second line was written with a relatively dull point, while the last two lines show a sharper point. The second pencil could have been partially sharpened to write these last lines or a different but similar pencil could have been used.

On the other hand, the question does arise of whether all the writing on a page was prepared at one time or with a single pencil. Differentiation between pencils, especially when the writing is done by one person, may be more readily achieved than attempting to establish the actual grade. A sharp change in the width of the stroke, in its clarity, in embossing, or in intensity may be evidence of two separate writings. Study of the pencil stroke may indicate writing of a single document on more than one kind of writing background or writing with more than one pencil (Figure 3.4). These conditions are more consistent with preparation of the parts on separate occasions than with continuous writing at one time. Complete uniformity strongly suggests continuous writing, but is not absolute proof of the latter. If the writing was prepared with a mechanical pencil on several different occasions but with the same writing background throughout, there may be little evidence of the interruptions.

It can seldom be established that a particular pencil was used to write a document.[19] Identifications of this nature must be based upon microscopic flaws in the writing stroke, resulting from impurities in the graphite, and involves extensive microscopic examination combined with controlled lighting and photography. Usually, a pencil does

---

[19]Rex v. Wood is a famous English case in which expert testimony regarding copying pencils played a part. See C. A. Mitchell, *The Scientific Detective and the Expert Witness* (New York: Appleton, 1931), pp. 164–165. A complete discussion of the investigation of copy pencils can be found in C. A. Mitchell, *Documents and Their Scientific Examination* (London: Griffin, 1935), pp. 118–137.

not have sufficient individuality to permit a definite conclusion of this nature.

A copy pencil, often referred to as an indelible pencil, forms a special subclass. In its manufacture, an aniline dye is combined with the graphite. The dye has little color until moistened; then the stroke assumes a pronounced blue or purple color and cannot be readily erased with an ordinary rubber pencil eraser. Identification and segregation of these pencils parallel very closely the pattern in the case of black leads except that the dye allows some additional group classification and there is less variation in the hardness of the leads.[20]

Colored pencils, especially red and blue, have widespread use, and their work may become questioned. Within each color group there are a variety of tints. Some pencils are water soluble, some are not. A drop of water will resolve this question. Some contain high-quality leads producing smooth strokes, while poorer grades write a flawed stroke. All these factors, plus the basic lead width, distinguish different pencils.[21] Besides visual and microscopic examinations, ultraviolet, infrared, and infrared luminescence examinations can be used to distinguish between the work of different pencils (Figure 3.5). Identifying a particular make by these factors is a risky undertaking. Materials change from time to time with all manufacturers. There are brands produced by certain manufacturers who sell to a group of wholesalers, each of whom brands the same pencil with his own trade name. Uniformity of all identifying factors suggests that one pencil of a particular color was used throughout a document, but it does not establish this with a high degree of probability.

Pencil examinations are basically restricted to visual study, but these examinations can be supplemented with the use of the binocular microscope and hand magnifiers. It is important to consider the degree of embossing, the condition of the point, and intensity of the strokes. Spotlight illumination at different, especially low, angles can reveal a secondary color sheen. Except with colored pencils, infrared and ultraviolet examinations are not of particular assistance. Since black pencils all contain a basic carbon ingredient, they react in a similar manner under infrared study. With colored pencils, some absorb infrared radiation, others do not. An ultraviolet study helps to differentiate between some dyestuffs. Infrared luminescence also can separate some similarly colored strokes. Chemical tests for dyes and impurities

---

[20]A recent study, Stephen Cain, A. A. Cantu, Richard Brunnelle, and Al Luter, "A Scientific Study of Pencil Lead Components," *Journal of Forensic Science* 23 (1978): 662–671, shows that American-made pencil lead can be distinguished by chemical test. However, to date the writers have been unable to develop a procedure for testing small samples of pencil lead taken from paper.

[21]A more detailed discussion of colored pencils can be found in Ordway Hilton, "Identification and Differentiation between Colored Pencils," *Forensic Science* 6 1975: 221–228.

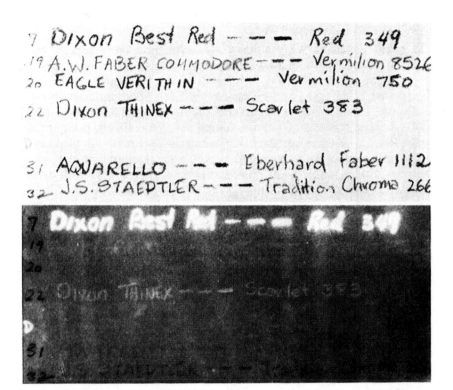

Figure 3.5. The upper sections show six red pencils of similar tints. The lower section shows their reaction in an infrared luminescence test. Note the different intensity in the bright luminescence of pencils 7 and 22 and the dark recording of pencil 32. The others are virtually or completely invisible. If these writings were the work of unknown pencils, the test would permit differentiation of 7, 22, and 32 from each other and from the other writings.

are seldom employed in the United States because there are frequently court restrictions on altering the condition of the document. Mitchell and other English and European authorities have suggested chemical spot testing of strokes as a means of differentiation, and chromatography would be of value with some colored pencil problems.

Evidence derived from the examination of pencil strokes may not necessarily form a definite solution to the problem at hand. Instead, this information combined with other physical document evidence may assist in reconstructing the circumstances surrounding the preparation of a questioned document. If fraud has actually been attempted, however, inconsistencies in the pencil strokes may assist in revealing it.

Crayons and Marking Pencils

The heavy greasy or waxy colored markings from both crayons and marking pencils are similar to and distinctive of these instruments alone. Although neither was developed for the preparation of formal documents, both can be encountered in problems involving anonymous letters or as identifying marks on documents and packages. The marks of these instruments differ from colored pencils and from the similar broad strokes of marking pens. Variations in the shade of color may permit differentiation between products of several manufacturers. Neither instrument tends to develop peculiarities from which an individual identification could be made, but the fact that a suspect in an anonymous letter or other investigation has in his possession a crayon or marking pencil matching in color the questioned writing is the type of lead that suggests further investigation. The alert investigator would undoubtedly take steps to obtain specimen writings with a similar instrument or to have the suspect's writing compared with the questioned material. It must be recognized that writing with this class of instrument, as well as with chalk on a blackboard, can be identified with proper writing standards.

The Typewriter

One of the paradoxes of document examination is the typewriter. To most laymen the machine represents a perfect disguise for the anonymous letter writer or the best means to keep secret the document's source. The truth is, however, that the typewriter actually supplies more evidence pointing to the origin of writing than any other class of writing instrument. Ultimately, when specimens are available from all possible machines, the particular one used can be identified. For the present, however, we shall direct .our attention to what can be determined from examination of the document alone.

At this point some readers will undoubtedly ask, How is this possible when all typewriting looks alike? Fortunately, all typewriting does not look alike. From the beginning of the typewriter's development in the 1870s, each manufacturer in this country designed his typefaces according to his own ideas of legibility and beauty. This method of production continued in this country well into the 1950s, when several domestic companies began the manufacture of some or all of their machines abroad and modified their manufacturing procedures to conform with European practices. As the typewriter developed in Europe, some companies followed the American pattern of type manufacturing, but the majority purchased their type from specialty manufacturers. This practice led to not every make of machine having distinctive, individualized type.[22] Thus a great number of working typewriters today and many that were used in the past have type designs peculiar to the particular make, although a number do not.

Type design as well as mechanical features of the typewriter have not been constant.[23] Periodically throughout the world there have been modifications in type design and, especially since the early 1950s, introductions of a number of new fonts. Design changes have also occurred with the product of typeface manufacturers.[24] Thus, because of individuality and changes, it is possible many times, although not in every instance, to ascertain and to demonstrate the make of machine and in some cases its date of manufacture, within a period of relatively few years, by simply studying the work of the typewriter itself. Several methods have been devised that permit typewriting examiners to enter into reference collections and to locate the information necessary to establish the make and model of the typewriter used.[25] This work is not complete, however, so that with a number of the more modern fonts and designs within them, no ready search scheme is currently available.

Letterspacing on the great majority of domestic machines has traditionally been 1/12 in. (elite spacing) and 1/10 in. (pica spacing). In Europe corresponding type sizes have been used on machines with various metric spacing. For example, elite size type has not only used the metric equivalent of 1/12 in. 2.12 mm, but also 2.00, 2.20, 2.23, 2.25, and 2.30 mm, while pica spacing includes 2.50 and 2.60 mm in addition to 2.54 mm, the metric equivalent of 1/10 in. Thus some different makes of European-made machines with identical type design can be differentiated by letterspacing, and certain letterspacings have been used by only a small group of manufacturers.

For many years the information derived from a study of this nature would enable the examiner to advise the field investigator exactly what kind of a machine to look for. Even today with the influx of machines

---

[22]The complexities of identifying the make of a European typewriter are ably discussed by Jean Gayet, "The Identification of Makes of Typewriter by the Script," *International Criminal Police Review* 27 (1949): 10–20 and 28 (1949): 16–26. In contrast to this, the typeface design is the controlling factor in determining the make of American typewriter. See Ordway Hilton, "Identification of the Make of Typewriter," *International Criminal Police Review* (1951): 287–293.

[23]A. S. Osborn, *Questioned Documents*, 2nd ed., p. 584. Osborn's earliest work on typewriting identification appeared in *The Albany Law Journal* 63 (1901).

[24]The changes in pica typeface designs during the 20th century have been documented by Josef Haas, *Atlas der Schreibmaschinenschrift, Pica.* 1972. This text documents changes by companies who manufacture their own type as well as all the manufacturers who produce typefaces exclusively.

[25]Among the available schematic search methods are Ordway Hilton, "A Systematic Method for Identifying the Make and Age Model of a Typewriter from Its Work," *Journal of Criminal Law and Criminology* 41 (1951): 661–672, for United States standard pica and elite fonts; David A. Crown, "The Differentiation of Pica Monotone Typewriting," *Journal of Police Science and Administration* 4 (1976): 134–178, for domestic and foreign fonts.

made abroad, it is still possible to eliminate certain makes of machines and thus to narrow the search of the particular typewriter in question. In smaller communities it may be that upon rare occasions only one machine might be found with the particular design of type and letter-spacing of the questioned material, but this naturally represents an exceptional case.

The first typewriter manufactured for commercial use was a manual, typebar machine on which a single type block was connected to a particular key on the typewriter by means of a series of mechanical linkages. In the course of early development of the typewriter, other classes of machines were developed, but until the 1960s the typebar machine dominated the market. During the 1920s, the first electric machines were made, but until about 1950 relatively few of these typewriters could be found in use in the business world. Today some kind of electric typewriter is found in most commercial establishments, and electric portable machines are also in use. Virtually all information on typewriting identification published prior to 1960 dealt exclusively with manual and electric typebar machines.

Proportional Spacing Typewriters

As implied in the opening paragraphs of this section, the first typewriters printed all letters in the same space of $\frac{1}{10}$ in. This practice continued with the addition of other unit spacing, such as $\frac{1}{12}$ in. for elite, until 1939, when IBM produced the first proportional spacing typewriter,[26] marketed as the Executive typewriter. This machine produced typewriting that resembled printing, with some letters occuping different units of spacing, ranging from two to five units (Figure 3.6). IBM machines had three units of spacing: $\frac{1}{32}$, $\frac{1}{36}$, and for a time $\frac{1}{45}$ in. The Executive typewriter had extensive sales in the 1950s, but after 1960 sales declined and the typebar models were ultimately discontinued. Two companies in the United States, Remington and Olivetti (Underwood), produced competing machines for a time, and subsequently two European manufacturers, Olympia and Hermes, entered the field for a few years (Figure 3.7). The combination of unit spacing and type design distinguishes the different makes and models, and the introduction of each new type font established a new potential dating criterion.

---

[26]Ordway Hilton, "Problems in the Identification of Proportional Spacing Typewriting," *Journal of Forensic Science* 3 (1958): 263–287.

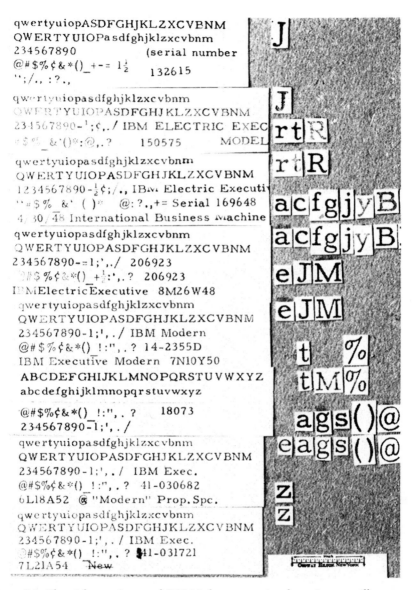

Figure 3.6. The eight specimens of IBM Modern proportional spacing type illustrate early design changes made in the popular font. The font was introduced in 1942. Two major changes were made, but some letters were changed earlier than others. See the reference cited in footnote 26 for more detail on this and other IBM proportional spacing fonts. *(Reprinted from the Journal of Forensic Sciences.)*

```
qwertyuiopasdfghjklzxcvbnm
QWERTYUIOPASDFGHJKLZXCVBNM
1234567890-=½;',./ RemStatesman
!@#$%¢&*()_+¼:",.? ES2251688
Remington Statesman 1N17Y58
Monticello 661 1/32 unit

qwertyuiopasdfghjklzxcvbnm
QWERTYUIOPASDFGHJKLZXCVBNM
1234567890-=½th;'],./HermesElectric-Var
!@#$%¢&*()_+¼°:"[,.? 4137009
HermesElectric-Varia 6L26J72

qwertyuiopasdfghjklzxcvbnm
QWERTYUIOPASDFGHJKLZXCVBNM
1234567890-=½];¢,./OlivettiGraphika
!"#$%_&'()*+¼[:@,.? 180268
OlivettiGraphika-Cassandrafont5Nl9Y58

qwertyuiopasdfghjklzxcvbnm
QWERTYUIOPASDFGHJKLZXCVBNM
1234567890-=½;',./OlympiaModel50M
!@#$%¢&*()_+¼:",.? 27-386513
OlympiaModel 50M typestyleJewel68

qwertyuiopasdfghjklzxcvbnm
QWERTYUIOPASDFGHJKLZXCVBNM
1234567890-=½];',./ Olivetti Editor 5
!@#$%¢&*()_+¼[:",.? E-3 13-604CC03
4/24/72 Mfs.Tn. New Demo Windsor
```

Figure 3.7. Examples of typewriting from machines of the four companies besides IBM who manufactured proportional spacing typewriters. The third specimen, Olivetti Graphika, was the only manually operated proportional spacing machine. It was available in this country and Europe in 1958.

Single Element Typewriters

IBM introduced the Selectric typewriter in 1961. This machine has changed the concept of typewriting identification. The Selectric is a typing unit consisting of two distinct parts, the machine and the type ball or element, which contains all letters and characters. The element is interchangeable from one machine to another and replaces the type-bars of the traditional typewriter. Depressing a type key causes the ball to rotate and tilt in order to position the proper character and then to strike the paper.[27] This single element type ball machine has become

---

[27]Ordway Hilton, "Identification of the Work from an IBM Selectric Typewriter," *Journal of Forensic Sciences* 7 (1962): 286–302.

the dominant typewriter in the progressive business office. Its widespread adoption has since 1974 lead to other companies producing similar machines. An important characteristic of the type ball machine is the ability to change the element so that two or more styles can be used on a single document without removing the paper from the machine.[28] All IBM Selectric type styles differ from similar fonts used on typebar machines and from single element type styles of other manufacturers.

IBM's exclusive manufacturing of the type ball machine ended in 1974–1975 when Caracters SA (CSA) of Switzerland made plated type balls available to other machine manufacturers. Adler (Germany), Royal (United States), Facit (Sweden), Hermes (Switzerland), Olympia (Germany), and Silver Reed (Japan) all use these type balls and except for some fonts, particularly pica and elite, all apparently use CSA's standard production of type styles. Adler and Royal have some modification in their pica and elite styles. Remington also entered the field in 1975. It is reported that Remington is manufacturing type balls in its Holland factory under license by CSA and uses distinctive type styles very similar but not identical to IBM's. Remington's machine is built under a patent exchange with IBM, and the type balls are interchangeable with the IBM elements. The other companies use different type ball design, although Adler and Royal elements (cores) can be interchanged, as can the Hermes and Olympia elements since both are made in the Hermes plant.

In 1975 Olivetti introduced a very different type ball office machine with its own design of type and a typing element of cast metal. The company manufactures a portable type ball machine, again with very distinctive type designs produced in Olivetti's own plants. The element is of unplated plastic. Beginning in 1978, these machines were manufactured by SCM in the United States, and the same machines now are marketed by both comapnies.

In 1978 Brother (in Japan) introduced a single element type ball machine. It uses an unplated plastic element with a unique type design.

Thus, to summarize present manufacturing, in addition to the type designs of IBM, CSA supplies a number of manufacturers with usually identical type styles. Remington manufactures its own elements with a unique type design, as does Olivetti, and both Olivetti and SCM market identical portable machines, with the same elements. Brother also has distinctive type styles. Since all type ball machines use $1/10$ in. (2.54 mm) for pica fonts and $1/12$ in. (2.12 mm) for elite fonts, an unknown specimen of typewriting may not be related to a particular make

---

[28]Ordway Hilton, "Identification of Work from a Selectric II Typewriter," *Journal of Forensic Sciences* 18 (1973): 246–253.

of machine. However, the designation of a limited number of machines is possible on the basis of letter design.

Word Processing Systems and Electronic Typewriters

Word processing systems are relatively new in the business world, having first become available in the early 1970s. The documents prepared by any of these systems have a direct relationship to typewriting identification, and in the coming years the document examiner will be concerned more and more with this class of documents.

A word processing system reduced to its fundamentals is the combination of a typewriter and an information storage, editing, and search system involving either magnetic cards, tapes, disks, or solid-state memories. As the systems have developed, more sophisticated editing and storage systems have been developed, and the need for faster operating automatic typewriters has been recognized. The features of the competing systems are not necessarily the concern of the document examiner except in the way that any particular feature might affect the identification problem. His concern is the finished document produced by this method, the automatically typed text, when it is involved in a questioned document problem.

In the early 1970s most of the systems used the Selectric typewriter or, in one or two cases, a typebar typewriter for the input and output unit. With the development of the Xerox 800 word processor and the Diablo printer as an output unit, the type wheel typewriter entered the field. The type wheel, often referred to as the daisy wheel, is a hub surrounded by a series of spokes or arms each of which contains a single typeface at the end. After a letter is rotated to align the typeface to print, the printing is accomplished by a plunger striking the back of the typeface forcing it against the ribbon and paper. With it the speed of automatic typewriting was ·increased from between 150 and 180 words per minute with Selectric typewriters to 350 words per minute with the type wheel printers. The type wheel has brought about a new series of typefaces, most being very similar in style to those available for typebar or type ball machines but differing in subtle details.

There are a number of systems that do not type the input copy, using instead a video display and an electronic keyboard for the draft copy, which is edited from the display and placed in the storage. Only the final edited copy is printed by the output unit, appearing as a typewritten copy.

Other recent developments involve the IBM jet ink printer. This is a nonimpact system in which there are no typefaces. Instead the letter image is formed by electrostatic deflection of ink droplets. For the document examiner, the work of these newly introduced printing units constitutes another challenge, an identification problem that is still being studied. Letter designs parallel other IBM type designs. The ink droplet formation allows initial recognition of the printing process.

The Mag Card IBM word processor is a highly developed type ball machine that uses magnetic cards as the storage medium. It was the first single element typewriter to produce a type ball capable of handling proportional spacing typewriting.

When Xerox introduced its model 800 it introduced an advanced concept in typewriting. Mechanical linkages between the keyboard and the type wheel had been replaced by an electronic system in the typewriter or input–output unit. This machine was the first electronic typewriter, but of course the Xerox 800 is in addition a complete word processing system. The system is capable of preparing copy in pica, elite, and proportional spacing fonts, or any combination of them, since the type wheels are interchangeable.

The first machines to be sold as electronic memory typewriters came on the market in 1978. Many of their features were the result of the developments in word processing systems, but they are compact units only slightly larger than the electric typewriters that have been part of standard office equipment for years. Actually they bridge a gap in their functions, and their cost falls between that of the Selectric and other type ball machines and the word processor.

IBM released its machine before others. It is a type ball machine, an advance over the Selectric typewriter. One model can handle pica, elite, and proportional spacing fonts, the other only pica and elite. The mechanical connections that operate the Selectric type ball are replaced by an electronic system. One model has a small-capacity memory chip, and there are a number of automatic features not found on electric typewriters.

Within a few months QYX, a division of Exxon Enterprises, Inc., released its electronic typewriter. It is a type wheel machine with a minimum of mechanical parts. The type wheel is interchangeable, giving capability for pica, elite, or proportional spacing typewriting. The basic machine, designated as Level 1, has a number of automatic features and includes a one-line memory chip with additional capability of storing phrases and formats. The QYX typewriter is available in five levels, each of which has additional features, such as larger memories and more editing and search facilities than the lower levels. The machine can be easily upgraded to a higher level by inserting the necessary electronics within a few hours at the owner's office. The use of type wheel printing makes possible higher-speed automatic typewriting in the higher levels of the machines so that all models above the basic typewriter are actually capable of some word-processing procedures.

Two additional electronic typewriters with memory systems have been developed. Olivetti uses the type wheel printer and a display unit for initial copy, which is either stored when edited or immediately automatically printed. Several models with different features are available.

Royal has also produced an electronic version of its type ball machine. This machine also incorporates text editing and storage facilities and of course automatic printing among many special operations.

Each of these four electronic machines uses a distinctive series of typefont, although with IBM and Royal it is not known at this time whether their designs differ in any details from the design of type found on their type-ball electric typewriters. However, with only a few companies capable of producing metal-plated typing units, others entering the field may well turn to the same suppliers, and typeface duplication will occur in this field as it did in the case of other classes of typewriter (Figure 3.8).

There is no sure way at this time of determining that a document has been prepared on an electronic typewriter as opposed to a machine of any other class. If the typewriting was done directly, without using the editing and automatic typing facilities of the more advanced models, minor typing errors may well be corrected in the course of typing by the correcting lift-off key that is a part of these machines, as it is in most other single element typewriters today.

Throughout this discussion it has been pointed out what might be determined from a document about the make of typewriter used to prepare it. Trial attorneys may find this information of value when dealing with a perjurer. The detailed description of how a fraudulent document was prepared could be refuted by establishing that either the make of machine used is inconsistent with the testimony or the type design had not been introduced until after the date of the document (Figure 3.9). The fraudulent character of more than one important will or deed has been demonstrated conclusively in this manner.

Thorough examination of the entire document may reveal inconsistencies in typeface design. Depending on the class of typewriter used, this may, with typebar machines, be evidence that more than one typewriter was used. The condition is not always evidence of fraud, but when important or modifying portions have been prepared with a second machine, the presumption becomes extremely strong. Because of the individuality of each typewriter—a phase of this work that more logically is part of Chapter 11—even the use of a second typewriter of the same make and age-model can be detected provided that it has been used to write more than a few words.

Additions can also be detected even though the same machine was used throughout. When a document is removed from and replaced in

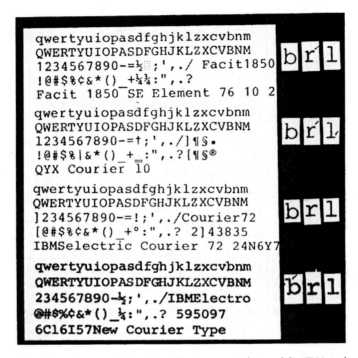

```
qwertyuiopasdfghjklzxcvbnm
QWERTYUIOPASDFGHJKLZXCVBNM
1234567890-=½   ;',./ Facit1850
!@#$%¢&*() +¼¾:",.?
Facit 1850 SE Element 76 10 2

qwertyuiopasdfghjklzxcvbnm
QWERTYUIOPASDFGHJKLZXCVBNM
1234567890-=†;',./]¶§•
!@#$%|&*() +_:",.?[¶§®
QYX Courier 10

qwertyuiopasdfghjklzxcvbnm
QWERTYUIOPASDFGHJKLZXCVBNM
]234567890-=!;',./Courier72
[@#$%¢&*() +°:",.? 2]43835
IBMSelectric Courier 72 24N6Y7

qwertyuiopasdfghjklzxcvbnm
QWERTYUIOPASDFGHJKLZXCVBNM
234567890-½;',./IBMElectro
@#$%¢&*()_¼:",.? 595097
6C16I57New Courier Type
```

Figure 3.8. Examples of specimens of Courier style type manufactured by IBM and Caracters S.A. (CSA), the two principal suppliers of the plated type ball for single element machines. The right-hand column shows distinguishing typefaces. Facit uses a CSA type ball, QYX a CSA type wheel. The Selectric is IBM's type ball version, and the fourth specimen shows the original IBM design, found on the IBM typebar machine. Only the typebar version has the long upper serif on the b and the h. CSA uses a shorter pump handle on the right-hand side of the r than does either IBM machine, and the CSA type wheel version of the l has a shorter lower right serif than the other styles.

Figure 3.9. An alleged 1918 letter was typewritten on a Remington machine. It was offered to substantiate a claim against an estate. The change in the M and w design was made in 1946, and the type design alone proved forgery.

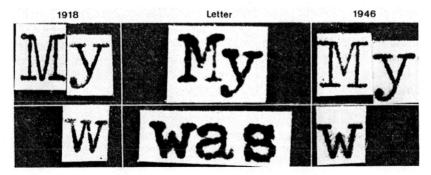

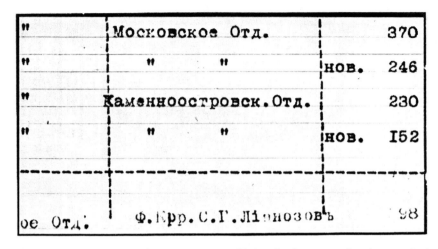

Figure 3.10. The last line of typewriting was added to the document after the paper had been removed from the machine and reinserted. Two factors establish this. The line of typewriting is not parallel to those above, and there is a sharp difference in the inking of the ribbon. In continuous typewriting, each line is parallel to all others. The document involved a dispute over stock in a White Russian company based in Paris.

the typewriter it contains evidence of this act. Despite the greatest care, it is very difficult to reinsert the paper in exactly the position it was originally. Continuous typewriting aligns in such a way that all lines are parallel (Figure 3.10) and spaces are in multiples of $\frac{1}{6}$ in.[29] with the letters forming vertical columns with those above and below (Figure 3.11). If a typewritten sheet is reinserted in the same machine, the added lines may well not be parallel, or the horizontal and vertical spacing may be slightly off. These facts can be determined by a detailed study combining both the microscope and special measuring devices. The findings can also be demonstrated photographically. If there is considerable lapse of time between the two writings and a fabric ribbon was used, the ribbon may show evidence of greater wear, or a new one may have been put in use, so that the inked impressions of the two parts are not consistent. In some instances, especially with a personal typewriter, the type may show accumulations of ink and dirt because of lack of periodic cleaning. Any one of these factors refutes the claim that the page was all typed at one time.

---

[29]This is the normal interlinear spacing for domestic machines. Preparation of several carbons will cause the line spacing to be slightly greater, while slight variation in the diameter of the platen can also modify this spacing and help to individualize the machine. Some American typewriters are designed with other units of line spacing, as are many European makes.

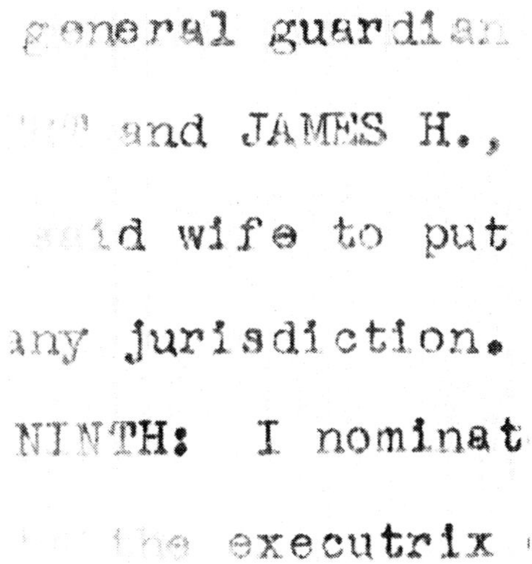

general guardia

and JAMES H.,

d wife to put

any jurisdiction.

NINTH: I nominat

he executrix

Figure 3.11. With continuous type-writing the letters print in vertical columns throughout the page. That the last two lines are not in the same vertical alignment as those above establishes that the typewriting had been interrupted by removing and reinserting the paper before writing paragraph "Ninth."

Computer Printouts

Problems involving the work of high-speed computer printers have not yet entered into many questioned document cases. However, the extensive and expanding use of computers presents potential problems involving the questioned document examiner.

At present there are several classes of high-speed printers.[30] They include the matrix, impact, and nonimpact printers. The latter two classes have distinctive subgroups, and it is possible to distinguish between the three basic groups and certain of their subgroups by critical study of the printouts.

The matrix-type printer is distinctive, forming letters and numerals as a pattern of dots by a series of printing rods. The design of characters and their defective elements permit the identification of a particular matrix printer.

The second class, impact printers, includes the single element type head, similar to the Selectric type ball, or wheeltype printer, the chain printer, and the drum printer. IBM and Univac use the type ball units, whereas Xerox and Diablo use a flywheel with typefaces attached to short plastic or metal arms. Again typeface design factors help to distinguish between different makes, although there is a vast selection of type units that can be used on each make of machine. With the

---

[30]Janis Winchester, "High Speed Computer Print Outs," presented at the 1976 Annual Meeting of the American Society of Questioned Document Examiners, San Francisco, and "Computer Print Quality Defects—Significance for the Document Examiner," presented at the 8th International Meeting in Forensic Sciences, Wichita, Kansas, 1978.

chain printer, the typefaces are attached in a long chain that revolves rapidly and are printed by impact on each individual type unit. The drum printer contains a series of 133 hammers that strike against the printer to print the appropriate letter. Because of high speed, drum rotation units of this type require special synchronization.

There are also nonimpact printers that use a phototransfer method to combine portions of letters in order to form a specific letter. A more recent development, an ink jet printer, produces copy by spraying the ink onto the paper through small holes to form a matrix or dot design.

Careful examination can distinguish between certain of these units and class of prints. Each class has its own particular characteristics of design and classes of defects that may develop. In this way an examiner may determine the kind of unit that prepared the copy, and he might ultimately identify a particular printer.

Carbon Copies

Occasionally, carbon copies are questioned (Figure 3.12). If these are clear, sharp impressions, most of the facts derived from the typeface design can be ascertained. Actually, certain writing defects may appear more clearly in the carbon copy than in the original. In some instances, however, because of worn carbon paper, the preparation of several copies, or excessive handling, little can be told from them (Figure 3.13). Insertion of material may show more clearly in the carbon copy than the original. Malalignment of the added lines is far more likely since

Figure 3.12. This executed copy of a will was submitted for examination to determine whether it was the original (ribbon) or an executed carbon copy. The halo effect around all letters except AMAR (top line) reveals that it was a carbon copy. The spelling of the surname, CALAMAR, had been corrected after the page was completed by erasing and typing these four letters directly on the carbon sheet. Note in the M the ribbed impressions from the ribbon threads. No original copy of the will could be found.

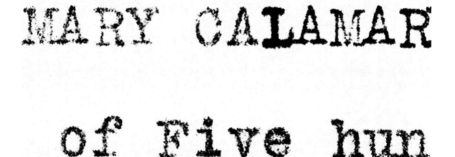

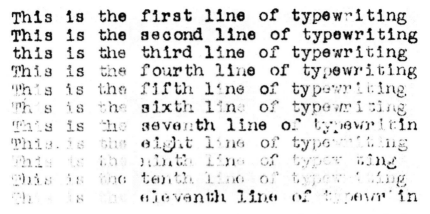

This is the first line of typewriting
This is the second line of typewriting
this is the third line of typewriting
This is the fourth line of typewriting
This is the fifth line of typewriting
This is the sixth line of typewriting
This is the seventh line of typewritin
This is the eight line of typewriting
This is the ninth line of typewriting
This is the tenth line of typewriting
This is the eleventh line of typewritin

Figure 3.13. These 11 specimens were made to demonstrate the deterioration of carbon paper with repeated use by fixing a piece of carbon paper so that each line was typed over exactly the same area. The line-by-line deterioration of "This is the" shows how the pigment is exhausted when the same letter strikes repeatedly in exactly the same position. The balance of each line is made up of different words typewritten over the same area. This leads to the splotchy outlines where part of the pigment has been depleted and part has not been disturbed. Note particularly the word "seventh."

once the original and carbon are reinserted further aligning of the hidden carbon copy must be made virtually by guesswork.

Proof that a carbon copy and an original were typewritten simultaneously may become an issue. Generally, the two copies can be superimposed exactly line by line using transmitted light. A full page of original and carbon typewriting, however, may not exactly superimpose vertically. The linespacing of the original is slightly wider due to the small increase in diameter of the original paper surface compared with the carbon copy. While the difference is very slight, it can be recognized in a full page of typewriting. With an old machine in poor mechanical condition, though, the difference can be greater, and there are times when the lines are not exactly parallel throughout. The two sheets may slip slightly as they are rolled around the platen because of the weak pressure between the platen and feed rollers. Under such circumstances, it becomes necessary to make a very detailed examination comparing all typewriting errors and peculiarities in order to show that the two were prepared together (Figure 3.14). On the other hand, this procedure can be followed when it is suspected that a "carbon copy" has been manufactured for variation in touch, spacing, indentations, and accidental variation in the type impressions may be found even when the copying has been carefully and accurately executed.

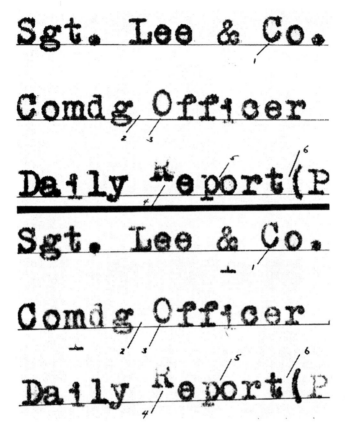

Figure 3.14. At the top is a portion of the original (ribbon) copy of a police report, and below, one of several carbon copies. The original and each carbon copy had been submitted as separate, detailed, antigambling, daily inspection reports. At the trial-board hearing it was necessary to show that the several daily reports had been typed at one time. Proof of that fact rested upon a combination of a great number of typing individualities and errors like the six illustrated. 1, 3, and 4 designate letters printing above the baseline because of improper operation of the shift key. 2 shows the omission of a period after the abbreviation "Comdg" and 6 the omission of a space before the parenthesis. 5 is an example of crowding due to irregular typing rhythm. The identical combination of chance variables would not be likely to occur in both documents if written at different times.

A further question occasionally arises with an original typewritten document: Was a carbon copy prepared with the original? Under some circumstances, the question can be answered. The solution involves a detailed microscopic study of all points where the typefaces penetrated the paper, making a slight break. It has been established that ink from the carbon paper can be drawn up through the break as the typeface withdraws from the hole. In contrast, when no carbon copy is made, the edge of the hole will show some clear edges of the paper, but the determination is not a simple one and requires a most careful, detailed study. Occasionally, offsets will be found on the back of the sheet from material printed on the backing of the carbon paper, but this determination is not positive proof because a similar condition can be found on the back of the first sheet, if comparable material was on the surface of the backing sheet that some typists use when typing only an original.

A further test involves the linespacing, which is slightly greater than standard spacing ($1/6$ in. for machines made in the United States), because of the increase in the diameter of the paper resulting from the additional sheets for the carbon copies.[31]

Comparison of the linespacing from a sheet of typewriting made on the machine without any carbon copies to the linespacing in question can give an estimation of the number of copies made.

Typewriter Ribbons

Two kinds of typewriter ribbons are in common use today. Fabric ribbons, which are found on some office machines and to a greater extent on portable typewriters, date back to the earliest machines manufactured. During the last 20 years or so, carbon-coated ribbons on either plastic film or occasionally paper tapes have been introduced and enjoy widespread use on office typewriters. Paper tape served as the basis of earlier ribbons of this class, but has been superceded by polyethylene film base. Cloth ribbons are designed to be used and reused, running forward and backward as they are wound on a pair of spools, and can be reused for an extended period of time. Carbon film ribbons in contrast are designed for only a single run or use and are then discarded. The kind of ribbon and its quality have a definite influence on identification problems.

Throughout the history of the typewriter, fabric ribbons have been gradually improved. The first ribbons were of cotton fabric, and this material still is used, but silk and now nylon fabric are used for the better grades. Originally, inking of the ribbons was done manually by the user, but by the turn of the century these ribbons were being factory

---

[31]Celso M. R. del Picchia, "The Mathematical Determination of the Number of Copies of a Type-written Document" *Forensic Science International* 15 (1980): 141–147.

inked. Modern ribbons give good service for extended periods of use, especially with the better grades. The cheaper grades of fabric ribbons have fewer, coarser threads per inch, while the best grades have higher thread count and threads of a finer quality. The latter produce the sharpest type impression among fabric ribbons. The carbon film ribbons give an excellent, sharp typeface impression. Their work has a uniform characteristic, since each impression is made through an unused area of the ribbon and no part is reused. Top-grade carbon film ribbons are capable of reproducing slight typeface defects clearly in the printed copy.

The cloth ribbons are impregnated with a high-viscosity ink. Black inks are a combination of finely ground carbon, various types of oils, and dyes or toners, which give the ink the proper black intensity. Since the ink has fluid quality, some ink is pressed onto the paper when the ribbon is struck by the typeface, and then the ink flows through the fabric to replenish the supply at the point of impact. Thus with fabric ribbons, fresh ribbons give very intense letter impressions, but as the ink is used up, gradually print gives weaker and weaker impressions (Figure 3.15). This characteristic is unique to this class of ribbons. The work of the ribbon can also be recognized, especially with moderate to weaker inked strokes, by the appearance of ribbed texture of the ribbon in the type impression.

Black carbon film ribbons have an ink coating of wax, impregnated with carbon particles and toners. When a letter is struck, a part of the ink adheres to the paper leaving a weak outline of the letter on the ribbon itself. Unlike in fabric ribbons, there is no flow of ink into the exhausted areas, which is the reason that these ribbons cannot be reused. Should they be reused, impressions from the second use would contain weak or broken areas in the letter forms where the original typing had removed most of the carbon coating. The work of these ribbons can be recognized by the very sharp, solid letter impressions.

Both classes of typewriter ribbons, fabric and carbon film, are available in a variety of colors. The carbon is replaced by color pigments and dyes, while the other ingredients are similar to those of the black ribbon.

A recent development is the IBM Tech III ribbon, which has been introduced for the Selectric II. This is a ribbon that uses a polyethylene base rather than fabric, but the ink and the base have been modified so that there is some ink recovery after a letter is printed, and the area of the ribbon can be reused much as with a fabric ribbon. Reuse of the Tech III ribbon is more limited than is the case for fabric ribbons. Typing impressions through these ribbons are sharper than impressions through top-quality fabric ribbons and are similar to typing with a

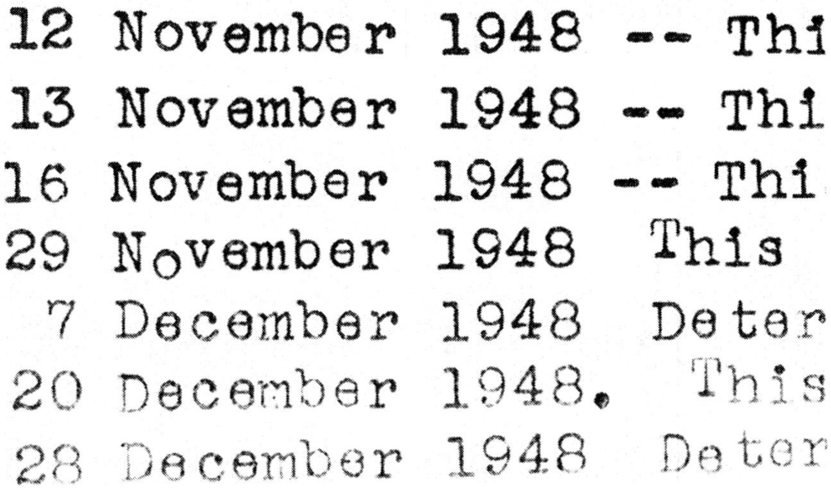

12 November 1948 -- Thi
13 November 1948 -- Thi
16 November 1948 -- Thi
29 November 1948   This
7 December 1948   De ter
20 December 1948.   This
28 December 1948   De ter

Figure 3.15. Dated specimens from the same ribbon shows its gradual deterioration. Both the darker color and the wider strokes in the earlier specimens are indicative of a fresh ribbon, while the very light impression and the thinner strokes of the December typewriting are typical of a ribbon with extensive use. The pattern of deterioration varies with different ribbons and the amount of daily use.

single-use carbon ribbon. At present the use of this ribbon is limited to the Selectric II typewriter.

A further innovation in film ribbon inkings was introduced a few years ago. This is the correcting or lift-off ribbon, designed originally for the IBM Correcting Selectric,[32] but rather widely used today on single element machines. When first written, the ink of these ribbons does not adhere strongly to the paper, so that with a second typing of the same letter through the lift-off ribbon, which has a highly tacky coating, the ink of the original typing can be removed. Only a blank impression remains. This class of inks gradually acts upon the paper and becomes more difficult to lift off several days after it was originally written. Tests on mail received indicates that the ink can be removed, not nearly as effectively, even after it has been on the paper for a period of days. Because of the ease of correcting typographical errors, the correcting typewriter and ribbon have become popular and other companies have introduced machines with similar correcting devices.

---

[32]M. A. Casey and D. J. Purtell, "IBM Correcting Selectric Typewriters: An Analysis of the Use of the Correcting Film Ribbon in Altering Typewritten Documents," *Journal of Forensic Science* 21 (1975): 208–211.

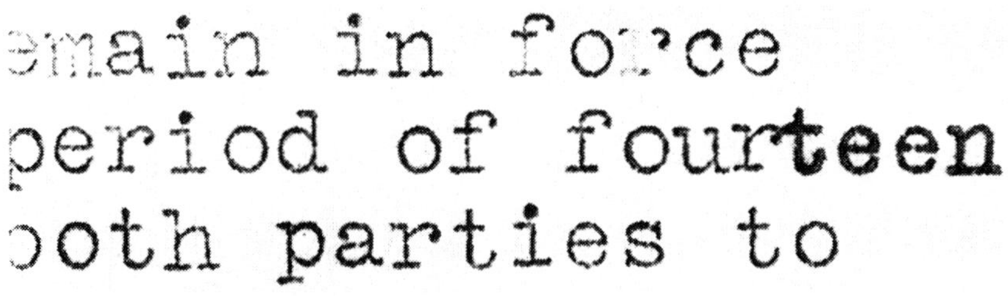
emain in force
period of fourteen
both parties to

Figure 3.16. The darker, heavier impression of the last four letters in "fourteen" (end of second line) clearly reveals an addition to the original text. Not only is the insertion made with a fresher ribbon than the original matter, but it was written with a different typewriter. Note the difference in the length of the cross-stroke of the t of "teen" and of "to" below. *(From the files of Elbridge W. Stein.)*

Examination of the typewritten impression can disclose the following useful information:

1. whether fabric or carbon film ribbon was used,
2. if a fabric ribbon, the thread count (that is, the number of threads per inch),
3. color of the ink, both the primary and the reflected secondary color,
4. intensity of the ink due either to the original inking or with fabric ribbon due to use, and
5. chemical reaction of the toner disclosed by chromatographic analysis or spot testing.[33]

This latter factor can assist in differentiating between the works of different ribbons.

When a document was not typewritten continuously, ribbon impressions may reveal a significant difference between the two parts. Dissimilarity in any of the identifying factors may be present either because more than one ribbon was used or the fabric ribbon was more nearly exhausted when the sections were added (Figure 3.16). These conditions are not found in a continuously written document.

With fabric ribbons a study of the type impressions may help to date a document (Figure 3.17). No chemical tests have been developed that permit an estimate of how long typewriting has been on the paper, but by comparison of the ink intensity in a series of dated typewritten papers covering the life of the ribbon or a major portion of it, the date of the questioned typewritten material can be estimated. A careful study of the degree of ribbon exhaustion, as shown in the typed impres-

[33]H. E. Cassidy, "Chemical Reactions from Typewriting," *Journal of Criminal Law and Criminology* 33 (1942): 188–192, particularly p. 191.

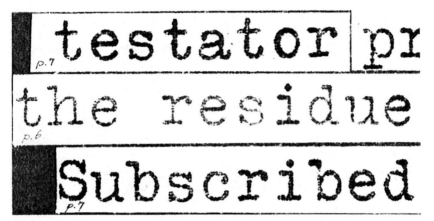

Figure 3.17. A difference in the ribbon condition on the pages of a typewritten will helped to establish that the substituted pages had been prepared at different times. The top and bottom lines are from page 7, the signature page. Words from page 6 are shown in the center. The heavier impression and wider strokes (page 7) indicate that the ribbon, although used, was not as worn as when page 6 was written. (See Figure 3.34 for other evidence in this case.)

sions and matching of the condition found in the disputed document, establishes a close approximation of the date or period of time in which the document was prepared. This test cannot be applied to a single-use carbon ribbon. With the single-use ribbons, it is possible to examine the ribbons themselves and to read what had been typed with the particular ribbon. These ribbons are generally long and the used portions accumulate in a discarded chamber. With some of the more modern machines, the used and unused ribbons are built into a cassettelike unit. The used ribbon with its type impressions forms a means of linking the document to a particular typewriter or to establish that it was prepared more recently than on its date. However, this technique can be used only when one has access to the machine shortly after the preparation of a questioned document. With bicolored fabric ribbons there have been cases on record in which black letter impressions could be deciphered on the red portion of the ribbon. Again a link was made between the suspected machine and a questioned document that contained both red and black typewriting.

Correction Liquid and Paper

A rapid and easy means of changing typewritten texts or correcting typing errors is to paint over the typewriting with a white opaquing liquid. When dry, the paper surface is clear and the corrected text can be typed over the original. That there has been an alteration can be easily recognized by critical visual inspection. Normally, the original text can be deciphered, if needed, by studying the back of the paper, but with most unclear areas the original text can be made visible by applying the thinner solution to the covering material and blotting with absorbent tissue. Liquid Paper®, introduced in 1951, was the first commercially available brand.

In 1960 correction paper became available. This specially coated paper is inserted in front of the typewriter ribbon and the letter or words to be removed are retyped. A white impression is made over the original letters covering it sufficiently that the correction appears without interference from the first typing. Again it is possible to deciper the original with study. The white-covered letter can be seen against the paper with properly controlled lighting. Unlike liquid coverup material, the correction tape must be used before the paper has been removed from the machine; otherwise reinsertion would require absolutely perfect realignment for the original material to be completely obliterated. Carbon copies can be corrected at the same time as the original, by inserting a second paper between the carbon paper and the second sheet.

When correcting typewriters were introduced, correction paper was produced in tape form to be used with standard ribbons in place of the lift-off tape.

Adding Machines, Calculators, and Cash Registers

The work of an adding machine is questioned only infrequently, despite its widespread use. Certain electronic calculators, which have been developed in recent years, are also provided with recording devices and are used in place of the old-fashioned adding machine. The construction of both classes of machines and particularly the process of printing differs greatly from typewriters, but there are certain similarities in the methods and principles of identification. In a measure the identification is modified by how the machine prints. Not all adding machines or recording calculators print in the same way.

Manufacturers of these instruments may use styles of numerals different from their competitors (Figure 3.18). Furthermore, in the case of adding machines, the older companies have modified the design of numerals or symbols from time to time (Figure 3.19). Manufacturers who specialize in producing typefaces for typewriters also supply typefaces for adding and calculating machines. Thus it is possible, particularly with present-day practices in manufacturing, for several companies to use the same typeface supplier and purchase identical type styles. Nevertheless, design is one means of establishing the probable

Figure 3.18. The design of numerals on several makes of adding machines differ. Shown are machines of the 1950–1960 period: (1) Underwood Sundstrand, (2) R. C. Allen, (3) Remington Rand, (4) Smith-Corona, and (5) Victor. Besides numeral styles, spacing between columns further assists in distinguishing some makes. The digits 1–6 in each specimen are actual printings from the tapes and illustrate the spacing found on the machine.

source of a tape. Since these machines generally print an individual column of numbers from a single segment of type, typewheel, or set of types, the distance between columns is a second means of distinguishing between makes of machines and at times with proper reference material to establish the manufacturer.

Many of these units print through a ribbon that is comparable to a typewriter ribbon, and here is a further method of distinguishing the work of several different machines. The degree of ribbon wear or exhaustion is also a means of determining whether two questioned adding machine tapes were prepared at the same or different times.

Among the smaller electronic calculators, some machines print record of their work by a nontypeface method, such as by infrared radiation on an infrared sensitive tape providing additional means of establishing the make of machine that prepared the record.

One can see that adding machines and electronic calculators are not all alike, and it may be possible from a study of the work of a machine to establish its probable source.

Cash registers also print records in a way similar to adding machines and calculators. Columns of type print through ribbon from separate

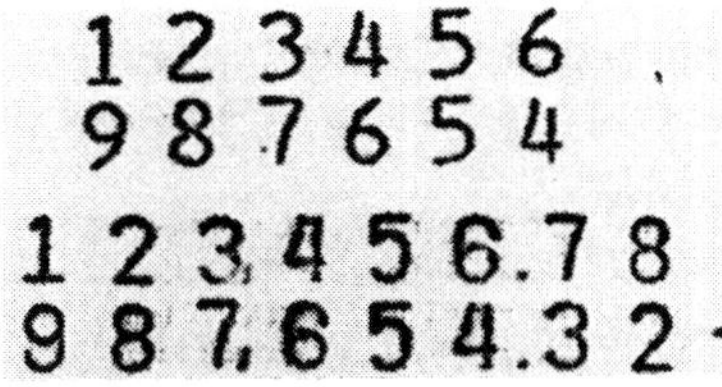

Figure 3.19. Numeral design of two different age-models of Victor machines. Note the design change in the 6 and 9.

wheels or segments. Today some sales slips are printouts from computer systems, while others are produced by the old-type cash registers.

Printed register receipts occasionally come into dispute.[34] They may be altered and offered as a receipt for merchandise that has been shoplifted. In this and other cases, it can be important to establish the source of a particular sales slip or register receipt. Although the principles of identification are similar to those of other machine record problems, it is often helpful for the examiner to inspect the cash register or printout system in question in order to appreciate fully its identifying characteristics. This procedure holds true for all business machines that produce documentary records. No examiner can be entirely familiar with every modern business machine or with all production models. However, the important fact is that security personnel and law enforcement officials and attorneys as well as businessmen should recognize that there are identification potentials in all mechanical records, which may have significant value in a particular problem or investigation.

Mechanical Recording Devices

In addition to the office machines discussed in the previous sections there are a wide variety of special-purpose devices using metering units that record time and date information or weights or measurements. Probably the most familiar of all these is the time clock, which has had a long and diversified use both for employee records and such other purposes as visitors' passes in security areas and parking lot fees.

The time clock is normally an automatic stamping unit that records the time shown on the clock and in some instances the date. Older units required manual manipulation of the printer to stamp the card or other document, but nowadays time clocks automatically stamp when a document is inserted into the machine. The design of the data so stamped, if questioned, may indicate certain makes of clocks and eliminate others. Furthermore, these units may develop certain individuality so that one can be distinguished from others of the same make and model.

Printing is normally made through a fabric-inked ribbon by metal typefaces. The typefaces can become worn, which assists in machine identification. The deterioration or wear of the ribbon can also help to distinguish among units where several of the same design are in use in one business. The amount of inking on the ribbon may be of further

---

[34]J. Warren, "Cash Register and Cash Adding Machine Identification," *Royal Canadian Mounted Police Seminar* No. 5 (Ottawa: Queen's Printer, 1958), pp. 89–99.

value in verifying the date of a time stamp in question simply by comparing with undisputed stamps and matching the ink intensity.

Businesses and consumers depend upon printed records from devices metering fluids, such as fuel oil or gasoline, and of weights. Some of these devices print through inked ribbons; with others the typefaces stamp directly against the paper surface, which is made up of a series of thin sheets and interleafed carbons.[35] With the latter system the striking pressure transfers ink from the carbon to the various copies. All these units have their particular characteristics of manufacture, including the size and design of the characters and the spacing between them. Individuality is developed through use, so that the document examiner may be able to establish which unit prepared the documents in question, besides being able to distinguish between different manufacturers' products and models of the same factory.

Generally, with problems of this nature, the document examiner needs to confer with service or production personnel of the manufacturer regarding characteristics of its product. The document examiner cannot be familiar with all specialized devices, but understands the principles of identification. He is able to derive pertinent information from individuals who know the mechanics of their products. On the other hand, the serviceman or production engineer may have little knowledge of what might identify or individualize a particular unit. Thus this teamwork may be essential in answering the basic problems at hand.

Check Writers

Check writers were designed originally as a device to prevent anyone from manipulating or raising the value of a check and have come to enjoy extensive use in the commercial world. They are such a standard part of business checks that criminals who specialize in passing worthless checks frequently employ check writers in conjunction with printed check forms to make their product appear "more genuine." While checks imprinted by a check writer are difficult, but not impossible, to raise they are also not necessarily a mark of authenticity.

A check writer prints the amount of the check while simultaneously perforating or embossing the surrounding area.[36] Some even emboss

---

[35]This latter type of printer can be found on fuel oil trucks. The device prints a record of the number of gallons of oil pumped. See Ordway Hilton, "Individualizing Oil Delivery Imprints," *Journal of Forensic Sciences* 21 (1975): 213–217.

[36]David J. Purtell, "The Identification of Checkwriters," *Journal of Criminal Law, Criminology and Police Science* 45 (1954): 229–235. James T. Miller, "Role of Check Protector Identification in Law Enforcement, Exemplar and Comparison Problems," *Police Science and Administration* 3 (1975): 259–266.

Figure 3.20. Design of printing type of various makes of check writers of the 1950–1960 period with the date of first use. (1) Todd, 1946; (2) F. & E. Excel, 1949; (3) Safeguard, 1942; (4) Paymaster, 1949; (5) Toledo, 1945; (6) Speedrite, 1949; (7) International, 1935; and (8) Defender, 1938. *(Specimens furnished by the Todd Co., Rochester, New York.)*

the area containing the payees name, as well as printing the amount. Writers have been marketed that simply print the amount without any embossing. The printed value is stamped in such a way as to leave no room for inserting additional figures, while the "shredding" or embossing makes other kinds of manipulation more difficult. Furthermore, the ink used cannot easily be removed. Nevertheless, checks prepared with check writers have been manipulated,[37] but critical visual examination followed by microscopic study under proper lighting should reveal such acts.

Like all mechanical devices for preparing documents, check writers have individuality. Each make is distinguished both in mechanical

---

[37]How a check prepared on a check writer was raised is told by John L. Harris "Eyeing the Evidence," *Southern California Alumni Review* 21 (May 1940). In this instance two impressions for $7.00 and $20.00 were cut and fitted together in a single check to create the amount of $720.00.

Figure 3.21. Specimen showing the periodic redesigning of the printing matrix of Todd check writers in 1946, 1939, 1934, 1928, and 1928 (top to bottom). *(Specimens furnished by the Todd Co., Rochester, New York.)*

design and in its printed work (Figure 3.20). A particular machine may have sufficient individuality to identify its work, a problem discussed in more detail in Chapter 12. Much of the effort for improving check writers has been to make their work less susceptible to "raising," which has led to periodic redesigning of the printing matrix and its figures (Figure 3.21). These changes can be documented in a reference collection of check writer specimens from which it is possible to form a judgment as to the make and approximate date of manufacture of the writer used.[38]

Closely related to the check writer is the facsimile signature, which is printed by a signature plate. This metal plate is generally incorporated into a more complex check writing machine, which also prints the amount of the check. It contains a facsimile signature generally surrounded by an individual background pattern. It prints through a ribbon similar to the ribbon used on some check writer imprints. A particular plate can be identified by signature and the background pattern. The plate itself, which can be removed from the check writing machine, must be kept under secure storage to prevent misuse.

Hand and Impression Stamps

As an office labor-saving device, the hand or impression stamp is convenient and useful; as a field of investigation for the document examiner, it is rather infrequent but diversified. Much of its diversity lies in the great variety of stamps in use: those of fixed letter design, those made up entirely of loose type, the facsimile signature stamp, those

---

[38]James T. Miller, "Role of Check Protection Identification in Law Enforcement, Exemplar and Comparison Problems," *Journal of Police Science and Administration* 3 (1975): 259–266.

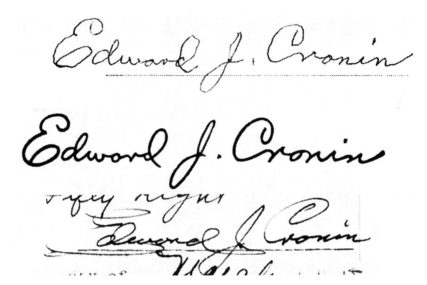

Figure 3.22. The upper signature was a forgery found on an alleged will of Edward J. Cronin, who had served as Secretary of State for the Commonwealth of Massachusetts. The center specimen was his facsimile signature printed on official election notices. It had served as a model for the forgery. Below is a genuine signature of Cronin's, which he used for personal business. The simplified form had been written by him to serve as a model for the facsimile and was never used for any other purpose. The printer had complained that the business signature was too ornate to reproduce well in printed form.

with rotating sections of the time–date stamp variety, the date stamps with movable strips of type, and any combination of these. The diversity is not limited to classifications based upon makeup. The actual material from which the stamp is constructed and its mode of manufacture add to the possible varieties. Rubber stamps are undoubtedly the most common, but metal hand stamps are also in use. Occasionally, linoleum, wood, plastic, and other materials are the basis for the printing surface. Some are machine made, others handmade. With machine-formed stamps there may be some handwork that influences the identification problem. Every aspect of the stamp's makeup may affect its work and its identification, and individuality of a particular stamp is in part derived from steps in its manufacture,[39] and in part from use.

A rubber facsimile signature stamp is a highly individualized impression stamp. Much of the manufacturing process requires handwork.

[39]Maureen A. Casey, "The Individuality of Rubber Stamps," *Forensic Science International* 12 (1978): 137–144. David J. Purtell, "Identification of Rubber Stamps," *Royal Canadian Mounted Police Seminar* No. 4 (Ottawa: Queen's Printer, 1956), pp. 124–136.

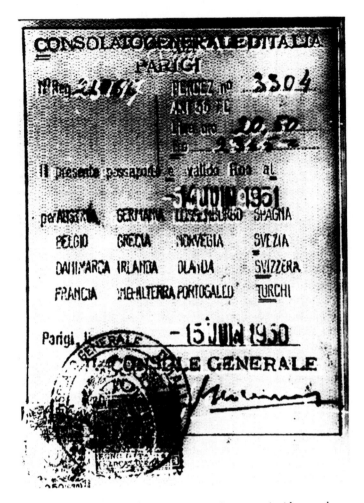

Figure 3.23. The failure of two "identical" stamp impressions to coincide exactly assisted in proof that they were forgeries. Both were found in a suspected passport. If genuine, they would have been made from the same rubber stamp. Actually, they were set with a small "commercial printing press" using loose rubber typefaces. The type had been torn down between printings and was reset. Only the underscored letters can be matched together at one time. *(Illustration used with the kind permission of Jean Gayet, formerly of the staff of the Lyon (France) police laboratory, and reprinted from his article "A Method of Superimposed Photography Applied to Criminalistics,"* Journal of Criminal Law, Criminology and Police Science *44 (1953): 338. The article describes in detail the photographic method employed to make the illustration.)*

The actual cutting of the signature outline is hand done. The signature itself is made from a single example of the writer's signature. The combination produces an individually designed stamp, and of course use could further individualize it. A typical problem presented to the document examiner with respect to these signatures is to determine whether the signature is handwritten or a stamp impression. Distinguishing qualities of the stamp impression are the unevenness of the line edges and the line thickness and the difficulties exhibited in the tapering of ending and beginning strokes. These qualities can distinguish the imprint from a duplicate or copy of the stamp. In addition, stamp pad ink has a different quality or appearance from writing inks when examined under magnification, which is an additional means of recognizing a hand stamp signature. Stray ink marks from dirt on the stamp or areas around the signature can also be encountered from time to time.

Another class of facsimile signature is the printed signature. The sharp difference in printing and writing ink is the usual means of recognizing these signatures. They are frequently affixed to printed material. The signatures can be made by preparing a metal printing cut using the old linecut process. At times these signatures differ in detail from the person's regular signature. Modifications may be made in order to provide for clearer printing or for personal reasons (Figure 3.22).

So much depends on the disputed stamp impression and the circumstances surrounding the investigation that it is difficult to generalize about what a technical examination might uncover. Many times the

Figure 3.24. The registered envelope contained a song written by an amateur song writer, Al L. Smith. He claimed that Irving Berlin had stolen the music for his chorus of "You're Just in Love," a hit tune from *Call Me Madam,* from Smith's song. Its chorus music was virtually the same as Berlin's. It became important to show whether the song was in the envelope when it was mailed. (See Figure 3.25 for comparison of portions of the envelope.)

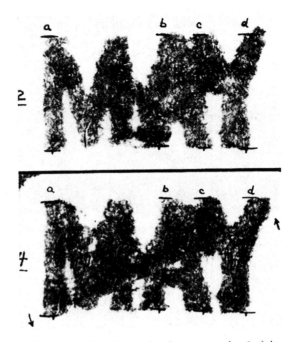

Figure 3.25. The word "MAY" at the top was found in the hand stamp number 2 of the envelope (Figure 3.24) and was printed entirely on the upper flap of the envelope. Below is the same word from hand stamp number 4, which, except for the left stroke of the M, falls partly on the upper flap and partly on the end flap. The arrows show the edges of the top flap.

Comparison of the two imprints from the same stamp reveal that measurements b, c, and d are shorter in number 4 than the corresponding distances in number 2. Measurements of a are the same in both impressions. In resealing the envelope after receipt the flap was pushed down slightly too far on the right side. Excessive handling of the envelope during litigation caused the seal of extra glue to be broken slightly, and it was found that some of the ink of the three strokes of number 4, which were shorter, actually extended under the edge of the flap.

In ruling that Irving Berlin had not stolen this song from Smith, Justice Frank of the Supreme Court of New York County stated, "The court was convinced by Hilton's testimony."

subject matter of the stamp points directly to its source, while on other occasions it merely forms an additional lead. A number of stamps are in themselves individual; some have sufficient peculiarities to identify their work; others are practically devoid of any but the most general characteristics. The questions may be raised of whether two impressions were made from a single stamp or if one is a forgery of the other (Figure 3.23). The ink offers little assistance except when the stamp has been used with more than one color, or when there is a question

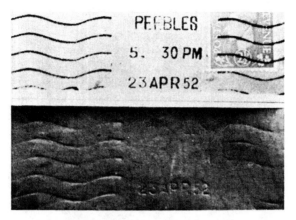

Figure 3.26. Definite proof that certain papers were mailed in a particular envelope may sometimes be found in a clearcut embossed impression of the cancellation on the contents. At the top is shown the corresponding portion of the envelope that contained the lower sheet.

of whether two or more impressions were all printed at once. While inconclusive findings are more often the rule than positive identification, stamp impressions should by no means be passed over without consideration. By their very nature, they are always a potential source of information in both the preliminary field investigation and in the ultimate proof of facts.

Before leaving the subject of stamp impressions we should consider briefly one specialized kind—postal cancellations. They are often completely neglected, even in anonymous letter problems where they may contain definite information about the source of the letter. Postal cancellations may assist in other investigations also, especially as a means of positively dating a document. Because of their importance in this respect, they have been forged in attempts to substantiate a previous fraud. Registration stamps may aid in showing whether an envelope has been tampered with after mailing (Figures 3.24 and 3.25). Complete investigation of a suspected document that has gone through the mail should include careful examination of the mailing envelope, the cancellation thereon, and possible impressions of the cancellation on the contents (Figure 3.26).

Mimeograph and Office Duplicating Methods

The needs of modern business have led to the development of the stencil duplicator and a number of other duplicating processes. By these methods a quantity of copies of typewritten material can be prepared at a lower cost and in a shorter time than by low-cost offset printing. The methods discussed in this section are those in which the duplicating procedure is carried out before any copies are made and does not include photocopying techniques. The stencil duplication or Mimeograph type is common. A rather similar method, Multilith, is also available.[40] A slightly slower, though none the less useful technique, is a gelatine and spirit duplicator or hexagraph. Each has its inherent advantages and disadvantages and raises specific identification problems.

Stencil duplication (Mimeograph) prints from a typewritten or handwritten paper stencil. The typewriter cuts into and almost perforates the stencil, so that the ink flows through it at these thinner points; any handwriting on the stencil is impressed with a stylus. All stencil copies are run off a drum-type machine, which inks the back of the stencil and rolls it across the paper to print the copy.

The Multilith process is a form of offset printing from a paper master. The typewriting is done on a heavy paper sheet with a specially inked multilith ribbon. Handwriting and sketches can be readily added to the master sheet either by pen with special ink or by special pencils and crayons. The copies are run by using the master on an offset printing press. The surface of the master is moistened. The typewriting ink repels the water but attracts the press ink, which in turn is repelled by the moist, unmarked parts of the master. The master, before it is printed, looks like any typewritten material, and the printed copy is similar to but distinguishable from material prepared on a stencil duplicator.

The master copy for a gelatin or spirit duplicator is typewritten on regular typewriting paper with a ribbon or carbon paper impregnated with duplicating ink. The master sheet may also be handwritten with the duplicating ink or a copy pencil. This original copy is placed in contact with a moist gelatin surface on the drum of a spirit duplicator. When printing the copy, a portion of the ink is transferred onto the final sheet. The amount of ink taken up by the printing surface is sufficient to make a limited number of copies. More copies can be printed with the spirit duplicating process than with the water–gelatin technique.

Problems arising from documents prepared by these methods generally involve the identification of typewriting or in rather rare instances, of handwriting. Once in a while a question peculiar to the type of duplicating process may be encountered. Little basic research

---

[40]The names Mimeograph and Multilith are trademarks, registered with the U.S. Patent Office.

has been carried out toward the identification of or differentiation among inks used in these processes. Consequently, the results of any ink study may be inconclusive. It may upon occasion become important to know whether two apparently identical sheets were actually printed from the same master. A detailed comparison of the typewriting and handwriting may permit a definite conclusion. With Mimeograph stencils that are rerun after being put aside for a time, this can sometimes be determined from a study of the finished product. The later run tends to lack the sharpness and clear quality of the initial set.

Address Stencils and Plates

The speed of addressing circulars, business letters, periodicals, and so on from a large repeated mailing list is greatly increased with the use of modern addressing plates or stencils. Two methods are available: One, known as Addressograph, uses an embossed metal plate; the other is a paper stencil method similar in principle to the Mimeograph.[41] Some of the methods have also been adapted to payroll and various account systems. Computer-controlled systems and automatic typing units have become competitive with these methods in recent years.

The embossed metal plates are made on special machines that impress a characteristic design of type into the plate. The plate prints

---

[41]Addressograph is a registered trademark. Equipment for preparing and printing the plates is manufactured by the Addressograph–Multigraph Corp. Charga-Plates (registered trademark), used by some department stores, employ a similarly embossed plate.

Paper addressing stencils and printing equipment are manufactured by the Elliott Addressing Machine Co.

Figure 3.27. The enlarged photograph shows the characteristic ribbon imprint between letters of an Addressograph plate impression. The entire information on the plate is printed simultaneously through a wide ribbon, causing the ribbon marks.

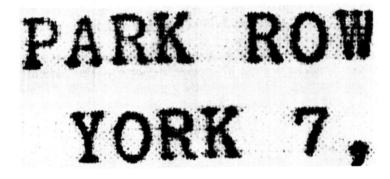

through a wide cloth ribbon. The finished copy resembles typewriting, but the design of the letters is distinctive. Furthermore, close examination of the finished product reveals ribbon traces over the entire area of the address rather than just within the outlines of the letters as in typewriting (Figure 3.27). Occasionally, there may be plate individuality, and the methods of identification follow the techniques and principles of typewriting identification.

Where the paper stencil method is used, the stencils are cut on a standard typewriter so that the type design is exactly like that of other typewriting. No ribbon is used. In printing, the plates are inked from behind, and the ink penetrates through the thin typewritten portions of the stencil. The finished product, the addressed envelope, has the same quality as a paper stencil duplicate (Mimeograph).

Printed Matter

The printed portions of a document are very likely to go unchallenged, and in general nothing is lost by this attitude. Printed documents can, however, contain physical facts of great importance.[42] Since type and presses are less accessible to the general public, their misuse is rather infrequent, yet in some instances, it is imperative that a part or the whole of a document must be printed if a fraudulent scheme has any chance of success. On the other hand, the printed portion of a genuine document that is under attack may contain significant evidence pointing toward its authenticity. If all factors of a document are to be analyzed, its printed portions must also be studied and interpreted correctly.

During the last few decades there have been significant changes in the production of printed matter. Whereas formerly most high-grade printing was produced by the letterpress technique, that is, using metal type, today offset printing has been adapted to longer press runs and a variety of printing problems. Its uses range from inexpensive, quick service printing of poor to average quality to top-quality work including books, magazines, and newspapers. Both methods, however, produce printed material that can be individual and distinctive.

The two printing methods represent distinctly different techniques. Letterpress utilizes raised type, while offset printing is produced from a smooth plate that has been treated so that the ink adheres to only the portions to be printed. In inking letterpress type the ink rollers make contact with only the raised portions of the typefaces, which in

---

[42]Jan Beck, "Printed Matter as Questioned Documents," *Journal of Forensic Science* 12 (1967): 82–101.

turn are pressed directly against the paper to deposit the ink outlines. In contrast, the offset plate has two different areas, the letter areas, which repel water, and the remainder of the plate, which absorbs water. In operation the plate is first moistened, and then the ink rollers pass over it. The moist areas do not accept the oil-base ink, but the other areas do. The inked plate transfers the ink to an intermediate blanket roller, which in turn prints on the paper.

With letterpress printing, the metal type is set either by hand for small jobs or, in most instances, by a machine such as the Linotype. This type must be arranged in units that make up the printed page. Depending on the type of presses used, these pages of type are further processed or transferred directly to the press for printing.

With offset printing, copy is prepared on paper to match the final printed page exactly. With the widespread use of offset printing, a number of special units have been developed to produce the copy. Typefaces may be of the traditional printing styles or, with certain classes of work, simply ordinary typewritten pages. In fact, hand-produced copy can be converted into an offset plate. The copy is photographed and, by a series of steps, transferred to a metal, plastic, or paper plate. Because of the variety of ways in which the copy can be prepared, study of the printing can assist in narrowing the possible sources of the suspected material, provided of course that ample reference material is at hand. The quality of the press work may also assist in eliminating some shops or suggesting others. Consultation may involve the combined work of the document examiner and a well-qualified printer.

Offset and letterpress printing can be distinguished through very careful examination. The slight embossing of letterpress work or the quality of letter imprint are elements to be considered. If the press work is not of the highest quality, the differences may be recognized more readily. Likewise, poor shop work in preparing assembled master copies for offset reproduction may reveal slight flaws in the finished printing. With both methods there are a great number of possible type designs, and some are very similar for the two processes.

Typeset material can be a fertile field for technical examination. Many different fonts are in use today, but not all shops can supply each.[43] Determination of a font used to print a suspected document may greatly assist in locating the plant at which the printing was done. At times information concerning such matters as the way the type was set, i.e., by typesetting machine or by hand, and the quality of the

---

[43]R. R. Karch, *How to Recognize Type Faces* (Bloomington: McKnight & McKnight, 1952), is a source book of American printing type designs and presents a systematic method of identification.

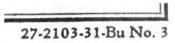

27-2103-31-Bu No. 3

Figure 3.28. Code numbers appearing on printed forms often give information about the source and date of printing. In this case the third group of digits, 31, indicates a 1931 printing.

typesetting or the presswork, can be derived from a study of the document itself, which may have some value in the investigation of the problem. Many standard forms prepared by letterpress or offset have printing codes that identify their source (Figure 3.28). Thus certain questions can be answered from the printed document alone, but far more can be told by comparison of it with known material, a problem discussed more fully in Chapter 12.

Engraved and Lithographed Forms

Questions regarding the origin or genuineness of engraved or lithographed material are encountered in document problems from time to time. While these documents resemble ordinary printed material, the methods of preparation are different.[44]

The finest-quality work is produced by engraving or etching a reusable steel or copper plate to print engraved letterheads, business cards, and similar material. In reusing, it is always possible that slight flaws may be found in the plate due to mishandling, but this is unusual. Otherwise it would be difficult to distinguish the work of different runs. Letterheads, currency, and stock and bond certificates are common documents prepared by engraving today.

This class of printing can be easily distinguished from lithographed forms, since the engraving produces raised ink while lithographs are smooth surface printing. The lithograph process is similar to offset printing in the final product. Birth, marriage, and baptismal certificates, some letterheads, and check blanks are among the common documents prepared by lithography. In the majority of problems, however, the most valuable information is derived from comparison of the disputed material with specimens from known sources or different printings, rather than from the disputed document alone.

---

[44]Forms of either class are printed from solid plates rather than from the assembled pieces of type used for ordinary (letterpress) printing. Engraved (intaglio) printing uses a plate with the design cut into the face; offset printing is produced from a smooth plate in which only the printing areas hold ink.

Paper Examination

Numerous kinds of paper made specifically for writing purposes are in common use today. These are produced in large quantities, thousands of sheets at a time, all of identical composition. Still, many papers differ sharply from one another, and products of the same mill made only a day or so apart may have properties by which they can be distinguished. Furthermore, some documents are written on paper that was manufactured for purposes other than writing, with physical properties unlike those of writing paper. Consequently, scientific study of the paper properties of a disputed document may disclose controlling evidence.

Knowledge of paper making and of the materials employed is essential to accurate identification of paper and for differentiating between closely related specimens. Laboratory study enables the paper specialist to determine from the finished sheet the materials that went into it and some details of its processing.

All papers are composed of closely matted fibers. In this country, these are principally rag and specially treated wood fibers. The former are used exclusively in the best grades of writing paper, while the latter are common to inexpensive stationery. However, many writing papers of good quality combine the two classes of fibers. Other paper fibers used in other parts of the work include straw, esperato grass, and hemp.

The wood used for writing papers is for the most part broken down into pulp by the sulphite process, in which the wood is cooked in a solution of bisulphite of lime to reduce it to a pliable fiber. Three other processes of wood treatment may be used. The wood may be ground mechanically into very small pieces, or cooked in either caustic soda (soda process) or a sodium sulphide solution (sulphate process).

Regardless of how the pulp has been prepared, it is made into paper by mixing it with a large quantity of water. To this stock a bleach may be added, and the stock is then beaten for several hours, during which loading materials and dyes can be introduced. More water is added until the beaten stock is made up of about 99% water. Then it starts its run through the paper machine. On the machine water rapidly drains off while the fibers are shaken on a large screen in order to mat them together to form a wet but continuous web. The web of paper is lifted from the screen and passed through rollers to remove more water and is finally dried, usually by heat. The extent of treatment at each step varies with different papers, and may be reflected in the finished sheet. Certain papers undergo special finishing such as calendering (i.e., passing them through heavy, heated rollers to smooth the surface) or coating with clay, alum, or starch to be more suitable for some particular use. One special coating encountered in typewriting papers facilitates easy erasing and can be distinguished by careful visual examination.

Figure 3.29. Three packs of 3 × 5 index cards are photographed to show the fine striations along the edges, which were left by nicks in the cutting knife when the cards were trimmed. Note the different pattern on each pack.

After these cards had been taken from a file and grouped by this method, it was possible from a study of the data on them to make an accurate estimate of when the file had been set up.

Laboratory investigation of a paper sample can involve visual, physical, microscopic, ultraviolet, and microchemical tests. All but the last can be made without altering the condition of the document; some microchemical tests, which are necessary for accurate determination of the composition of the paper, require that a small portion of the document be cut away and reduced to pulp. With this type of testing a skilled paper microscopist can report accurately on the fiber content, and when wood fibers are present, on how they were treated to form the pulp.

An objection to cutting off part of the document may be raised. If it is necessary only to differentiate between several pieces of paper, the destructive chemical tests may be omitted in favor of other kinds of examination. Thickness accurately measured with a micrometer can in itself be significant. Exact measurements of the length and width help to establish whether all sheets were cut at the same time. On the other hand, the edges of a stack of sheets, cut as a group, may show microscopic striations from nicks in the cutting blade, which will permit positive grouping of the sheets[45] (Figure 3.29). Surface texture and the "look through," i.e., the fiber pattern as seen by transmitted

---

[45]The problem of identifying the work of paper cutting knives is discussed by David J. Purtell, "The Identification Paper Cutting Knives and Paper Cutters," *Journal of Criminal Law. Criminology and Police Science* 44, (1953): 262–268.

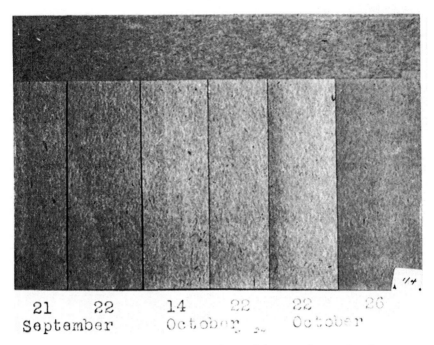

21   22   14   22   22   26
September   October   October

Figure 3.30. The six documents of known date and the seventh, questioned one across the top were photographed under ultraviolet radiation. All visual and physical characteristics of the documents were similar. However, the questioned and the October 26 paper showed a similar ultraviolet fluorescence, which differed from the others. This condition indicated that the date of the questioned sheet was proper.

light, depend on manufacturing techniques and are means of distinguishing between many papers. The color and quality of fluorescence under ultraviolet radiation may assist in segregating specimens, but investigation[46] and plant procedures indicate that these tests must be interpreted with caution (Figure 3.30).

In finer grades of writing paper, watermarks are an outstanding identifying characteristic, and have been carefully cataloged according to manufacturer.[47] The watermark gives not only a quick clue to the paper's source but also the date of its first use. Some marks contain specific dating information. Other papers, especially those for currency, contain secret threads—an irregular pattern of small colored threads

---

[46]O. Hilton, "Pitfalls in the Use of Ultraviolet Examination to Differentiate Between Writing Papers," *Journal of Criminal Law and Criminology* 40 (1949): 519–522.

[47]*Lockwood Directory of Paper Manufacturers*, a yearly publication. *The Paper Catalogue* (Oradel: Walden Mott).

—to protect against forgery and to identify them further. These paper properties should receive early and thorough consideration in order to individualize the specimen at hand.

Thus far we have considered paper characteristics that may occur in any problem. Frequently, however, physical facts are discovered that raise the question, For what use was this sheet originally intended? It may be that the size is unusual. Was the sheet previously used? Examination of a hand-trimmed edge could disclose evidence of this nature. The matching of perforations or torn edges on two pieces may establish that they were once one. Headings, rulings, or any printed material warrant careful scrutiny. Folds, especially those that do not properly fit into the present document, should be thoroughly studied. The relationship of these factors to the document at hand may control the ultimate opinion.

The technical examination of paper has become so complex that there are today highly trained paper specialists who devote their entire attention to the study of paper. While they are primarily interested in problems concerning paper manufacture, their constant research has made possible the improved techniques of examining the paper of disputed documents.[48]

Envelopes

In investigations of anonymous letters the mailing envelope consistently plays its most prominent role. Yet even in these cases there is a strong tendency to neglect it completely, considering it merely an insignificant container for the all-important letter. This situation is deplorable, for the envelope may well reveal equally significant facts regarding the identity of the writer or the source of the letter. Here, particularly in the early stages of the investigation, the postmark, the writing, the stamp, and all the details of the envelope itself should be very thoroughly examined.

It might be well to note at this point that the manner of addressing an envelope is often highly individual. Arrangement of the items on the envelope, abbreviations, spellings, punctuation, indentations, size of writing, particularly the relative size of address and return, the locations of the return address, the alignment of the writing, and the crowding or spreading of items must be given full consideration. Al-

---

[48]Research carried on at the Institute of Paper Chemistry, Appleton, Wisconsin, as well as in other paper laboratories, has laid the groundwork for many tests used in forensic studies. Graff's microscopic techniques for fiber analysis are among the more important contributions applicable to questioned document examination. Paper fiber identification is fully treated by John H. Graff, *Pulp and Paper Microscopy*, 2nd ed. (Appleton: Paper Institute, 1942).

though the writing of both the letter and envelope may contain elements of disguise, it is not infrequent that the writer places this carefully disguised writing on the envelope in his own habitual manner.

Of the elements that tell of source, history, and background of an envelope, those of the paper from which it is constructed are highly significant. Nothing that identifies paper should be overlooked. In addition, there are peculiar to an envelope such features as the manner in which the paper is cut and folded, a factor that assists in ascertaining the source of manufacture or sale, and the glue used for sealing, which varies with manufacturers. Some envelopes contain inconspicuous printing of the name or logo of the manufacturer. These are the elements by which its source may be established or the alleged similarity of the two envelopes evaluated.[49]

Since first introduced in 1839,[50] sealed envelopes containing important or confidential papers have been subjected to tampering. Examination of the edges of a flap may reveal small tears, creases, stains, loose paper fibers, or the presence of excess glue resulting from lifting and regluing a flap. Examination by transmitted light may show internal tears or irregular deposits of glue. Fluorescent and chemical tests can show the presence of two dissimilar glues when the flap has been resealed.[51] When there is writing or handstamps across the edge of a flap, the lack of perfect registry may be additional evidence of tampering. Opening and resealing an envelope without leaving some indication is a difficult task.

Sealing Tapes and Labels

Not every document or object is transmitted in an envelope. Some are wrapped or boxed, and the sealing is accomplished with paper or other types of tape. These tapes may be gummed with a water-soluble glue or may be of the pressure-sensitive type. Purtell and Casey have discussed the possibility of identifying the source of paper tapes and discussed their manufacturing characteristics.[52] In addition, binding tapes may have a plastic or cloth base. Information about the source of any of these tapes has its greatest potential in criminal investigations.

---

[49]M. P. Bertocchi, "Envelope Association Through Manufacturing Characteristics," *Journal of Forensic Sciences* 22 (1977): 827–834.

[50]W. E. Woodward (The Way Our People Live) footnote, p. 16.

[51]Chemical tests for common types of adhesives are reported by Lucas, *Forensic Chemistry and Scientific Criminal Investigation,* 4th ed., p. 338. J. A. Radley, *Photography in Crime Detection* (London: Chapman & Hall, 1948), pp. 71–72 and Illustration 41, discusses ultraviolet examination.

[52]D. J. Purtell and M. A. Casey, "Paper Tapes and Labels Encountered in Document Examination," *Journal of Forensic Sciences* 11 (1966): 496–506.

With cloth tapes the examiner also has the threads of the fabric to consider. If they are cut or torn, it may be possible to match the thread ends to the tape from which the piece was taken. In addition consideration must be given to the adhesive, and such a match may clearly identify its source.[53]

Purtell and Casey also indicated that the stocks for labels and identification stickers are manufactured in a similar manner. Many labels also contain printed portions that may be individual or typical of a particular source. Of course mailing stickers with return addresses on them are easily identified, but there are others that only provide space within a particular design for address and return address. Differences in design of print, paper stock, adhesives, or dimensions in combination may lead to a single supplier within a community.

Problems involving any of these materials are infrequent, but the document examiner and those interested in the source of a particular document may find that the characteristics of the tape or label used is one other factor in identifying where a document originated.

Postal Cards

The illustrated postal card displays a good deal of information about its source in a quite obvious manner, but it also may contain less obvious information concerning its date of first use. Such factors as card stock, color of inks, and the peculiarities of a particular printing help to establish these dates. Likewise, a government postal card can be dated by its stamp design, and the date of first sale could be of significance.[54] These documents do not commonly play a prominent part in legal disputes, but under the right circumstances they can be thoroughly studied with a promise of helpful conclusions.

Cardboard

Cardboard in any variety is rarely a part of an important document, but at times it is involved in criminal investigations. Should it become important to trace the material to its source or to learn of the previous or intended use, the characteristics by which paper is identified, particularly color, thickness, surface texture, and composition, must be studied. In reality cardboard is a special form of paper, and the poten-

---

[53]Katherine Keeler, "Comparison and Identification of Adhesive Tape Used in the Construction of a Bomb Mechanism," *Journal of Criminal Law and Criminology* 28 (1938): 904–908.

[54]Dating information is contained in *Stamps and Stories*, 7th ed. (Washington, D.C.: U. S. Postal Service, 1980).

tialities of technical investigations into its background parallel very closely those of paper problems.

Blotters

The widespread use of the ball point pen has virtually eliminated the need for blotters, and they are only rarely encountered today. Modern fluid ink writing produced by the porous point pen or the roller pen deposits only a limited amount of water-based ink on the paper. These writing instruments have not increased the demand for blotters. Of all writing instruments in use at this time, the fountain pen alone may deposit enough ink to warrant the need for a blotter.

Blotting of a fresh ink stroke removes a portion of the ink and leaves definite traces of the action in a weaker and characteristic stroke. No examination of the document or the pen stroke, however, tells anything about the particular blotter used. Any information of this sort must come from the offsets on the blotter itself. When it has had only slight use, it may be possible to decipher the various offsets through examination with a mirror or by reversal and intensification of a photographic negative, and thus to connect it definitely with the preparation of a particular document.

Carbon Paper

For the writer of detective fiction, the examination of impressions in carbon paper plays a startling role. True, under proper conditions these examinations have value, but generally not to the extent assigned by these writers. It can be observed that each time a carbon sheet is used, especially with a typewriter, an impressed offset is left in it. This impression can be read with the assistance of oblique lighting or from a carefully made photograph (Figure 3.31). Its decipherment may be of value in police investigations, and these techniques, coupled with comparison of the marking pigment, its color, and its intensity, may establish that a particular sheet of carbon paper was used in the preparation of a suspected document. Solving the problem depends primarily on the questioned carbon paper having seen little use.

If there is a suspicion that pages have been substituted in a document and the carbon copy is available for study, it may be possible to show that the carbon paper of the substituted page differs in color, condition, or chemical composition from that of the other pages. Visual, microscopic, and chemical tests, especially chromatography, can establish these facts. Modern carbon papers consist of pigments and dyes in a waxlike coating, and different dyes, pigments, and coating materials are found on sheets of the various manufacturers and on papers in-

Figure 3.31. The two pieces of carbon paper were found in an antigambling raid. The right-hand one had been used only once, and this photograph shows that it was used to make a carbon of a policy slip. The left-hand carbon had been reused a number of times, and it was impossible to make out any information of value.

tended for particular uses.[55] Each time the paper is used, a portion of the coating material is deposited on the document, a process that in time exhausts the carbon paper. These documents consequently contain evidence of the carbon paper used and of its general condition at

---

[55]A comprehensive analysis of the characteristics of carbon paper is to be found in R. R. Wissinger, "Carbon Paper and Other Duplicating Papers," in *Specialty Papers*, edited by R. H. Mosher (Brooklyn: Ramsen, 1950).

the time of use. The accumulated weight of these factors has been instrumental in disclosing many instances of substitutions.

Seals and Authenticating Devices

In earlier times wax seals often took the place of a person's signature, since writing was then an accomplishment of the scholar, and many a person in high position could not even sign his own name. Today in some parts of the world these seals are still extensively employed to supplement signatures in authenticating documents. In this country, however, they are falling into disuse except for occasional use as a protective seal for envelopes to discourage tampering with them while in transit.

No protective device, however, has yet been devised that someone has not tried to evade or forge by one means or another. The wax seal is no exception. Two methods have been employed to forge a seal. The first involves the preparation of a mold or cast of the embossed design contained in the genuine wax seal. To form the forged design, this cast is impressed on the heated wax in the same manner as the original metal die. These forged impressions tend to lack the sharpness of original seals and may contain other defects. The second technique actually transfers the genuine seal by lifting it from an authentic document and reaffixing it to the forgery by heating the underside of the wax slightly or by attaching the seal with a small amount of fresh wax. Transferring has been known to crack the seal, a defect the forger may attempt to remedy by skillful patching with additional wax. These manipulations accomplished with the addition of fresh wax often result in a seal composed of two different waxes, which may be disclosed by examination under ultraviolet light and the microscope.[56]

The embossed seal, such as that used by a notary, is far more common in this country. Corporate seals are another common form of these seals. The impression is fixed in the paper by pressing it between two metal plates, one a positive die with the design of the seal raised on its surface, the other a negative with the depressed design. Forgery of these seals is uncommon, for it would entail preparation of an imitation die, or formation of the outline by drawing with a sharp instrument, either of which could undoubtedly be detected by a detailed comparison with genuine specimens. An alternative technique is simply to prepare a weak impression of a similar seal and to depend on the carelessness of all parties concerned to fail to detect the defect. With weak impres-

---

[56]Analysis of sealing wax can also include the determination of the melting point, the amount of resins, and the amount and nature of the ash (Lucas, *Forensic Chemistry and Scientific Criminal Investigation*, 4th ed., p. 322).

sions the seal can best be read by side-light illumination or by applying a fluorescent paste to the raised surface by means of a small roller and examining under ultraviolet radiation.[57] Actually, it seems, few persons ever bother to try to make out the design of the seal, its presence being regarded sufficient to authenticate the document.

Adhesive Stamps

Stamps of all varieties, including both postal and revenue, may find their way into a document investigation. They serve primarily as a ready means of dating the document, although in rarer instances, matching of the perforations with stamps found at a particular source can establish the origin of the document. For the postal authorities, reuse of a previously canceled stamp forms a special document problem. The investigation of adhesive stamps is an extended study in itself,[58] and while most of the problems of the philatelists do not bear upon questioned document problems, consideration of these items in relation to specific documents may be in order.

Grouping and Binding Devices

Many devices are available for grouping and binding documents—paper clips, pins, staples of various designs, grommets, rubber bands, metal file binders, spindles, adhesives, spring clips, not to mention the cruder devices of turning or dog-earing the edges of the paper itself. The majority of these leave telltale traces of their use, while the remainder may in certain instances implant typical marks in the document, particularly if employed over an extended period of time.

Documents that have been bound together by pins, metal file binders, or spindles bear imprints typical of these devices and indicative of their size. Beyond this, however, little if anything can be determined about the individual instrument used. Careful study of the pinholes, however, may allow accurate reconstruction of the grouping of several sheets and determination of whether some pages have subsequently been inserted after the original assembly.

Paper clips and spring clasps generally leave very little trace of their use (Figure 3.32). If the documents are fastened by these devices for a long time, they may bear imprints corresponding to the outline of the

---

[57]This fluorescent technique was first suggested by J. Gayet, "A Method of Superimposed Photography Applied to Criminalistics," *Journal of Criminal Law, Criminology and Police Science* 44 (1953): 384–386.

[58]Publications of Scott Publ., New York, are considered standard works on postage stamps of the world, but many volumes deal with specialized studies on certain countries or issues.

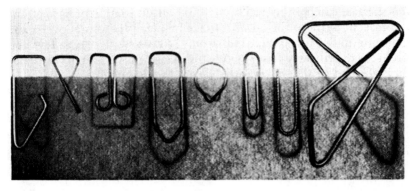

Figure 3.32. Eight different sizes and shapes of paper clips. The lower portion of the
exhibit, made with transmitted light, reveals both the shadow outline of the portion of
the clip behind the paper and the visible portion.

clips or a portion of the outline as a rust stain. It is more difficult to
establish that several sheets bearing these impressions were once a
single unit than if they had been pinned, but a pattern of clip imprints
in some sheets different from that in others suggests that certain pages
may have been substituted.

A positive identification of source is potentially present in the wire
staple used to bind papers, though to date there has been no reported
use of the technique. There are in common use today two kinds of
wire staplers. One drives a ready-cut staple through the paper and
mechanically fastens it with a single stroke. The other in a single
action cuts an unshaped staple from a roll of wire, shapes it, and pushes
it through the paper into a secured form (Figure 3.33). Identification
can be accomplished by application of comparative micrography techniques, which have been successfully employed to identify the microscopic striations of tool marks left on the object by impact or by the
action of the cutting edges.[59] Thus, two objects upon which the same
tool was used bear similar striations or marks. This technique can be
applied to the cut end of the second type of staple, or to the surface of
any staple upon which the driving portion of the stapler acts, in order
to effect an identification of a particular machine. Sample staples fastened by the suspected machine are required as standards. Comparisons
should be made by means of a comparison microscope with carefully
controlled light. Sufficient points of identification are not always pres-

---

[59]For methods used in these identifications see C. M. Wilson, "Comparison and Identification of
Wire in a Coal Mine Bombing Case," *Journal of Criminal Law and Criminology* 28 (1938): 904–908.

Figure 3.33. Seven different sizes and designs of paper staples found in New York City stationery stores in the 1950s. (1) Bates (0.31 in.); (2) Arrow (0.32 in.); (3) Tot (0.34 in.); (4) Commander (0.41 in.); (5) B-8 (0.44 in.); (6) Standard (0.50 in.); and (7) Scout (0.50 in.). The Bates forms the staple from wire; the others use precut staples.

ent in problems involving tool marks for positive conclusions, but if there are, the technique allows clearcut individualization.

Whenever it is suspected that pages have been substituted in a document bound with staples, a careful study of all staple holes in each sheet should be made (Figure 3.34). If a sheet does not contain the same number of holes as other pages, or if the position of the hole on a sheet does not match those of other sheets, then it is clear that at one time not all the pages were part of the present unit.

The assorted glues, pastes, and adhesive tapes with which papers are sometimes held together may often be distinguished by means of microscopic, chemical, ultraviolet, chromatographic, or spectrophotometric techniques.[60] In this way it may be possible to detect regluing with a second adhesive after the sheets had been separated for the purpose of inserting additional papers.

---

[60]B. B. Coldwell and M. Smith, "The Comparison and Identification of Adhesives on Questioned Documents," *Journal of Forensic Sciences* 11 (1966): 28–42.

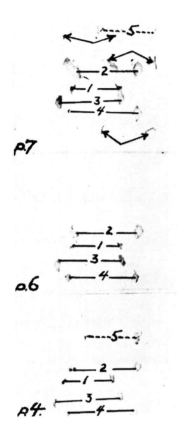

Figure 3.34. A study of the staple holes in the seven pages of a will and its legal back revealed that it had been opened and restapled a number of times. Page 7, the signature page, bore a date of August 1930. Substitution of pages 4 and 6 is clear. Page 6 had only four holes, which corresponded with those numbered 1–4 on page 7. Page 4 contained these four and one additional set. The legal back had the same pattern of holes as page 6 and a printer's code dating it in 1931. (See Figure 3.28.) Therefore the last substitution was made after execution. Probate was denied.

Conclusions

Basically, the examination of a questioned document is a detailed analysis of all its elements, prominent and minute. The final opinion is an evaluated summation of the findings of these separate studies. These unit analyses form important segments of the whole, but it is only occasionally that any one of them, standing alone, controls the final conclusion. Not only must several of these be considered in combination, but also other studies, to be treated in subsequent chapters, play important roles in framing the ultimate answers to the questions raised.

4

Alterations in Documents

On numerous occasions documents are altered during their preparation or after their completion with full knowledge of all parties concerned and without an attempt on the part of anyone to perpetrate fraud. However, there are other instances—more numerous than generally believed—in which an addition or other alteration is made with intent to cheat some party in an otherwise fair and legitimate transaction. When such an act has been committed, or is suspected, a document examiner may be consulted in the hopes that he can reveal evidence that will disclose the fraud. Since these calls for assistance are not infrequent, effective techniques have been devised through extensive research and experimentation not only to disclose evidence of the alterations or additions, but also to demonstrate what has been changed and what the original contents were.

Documents are changed in several ways, and each method requires a separate technique for detection and for the restoration or decipherment of the original material.[1] The most common procedures include the removal of portions by erasure, obscuring the writing by opaque marks, and the addition of material either by interlineation or by extending portions of the document. We have already seen examples of fraud, and the steps taken to detect them, when the alteration involves tampering with seals and embossed impressions. Now we shall consider the more common problems in which handwriting or typewriting

---

[1]Throughout this discussion the term *restoration* is used to denote those techniques in which the original material is actually brought out (restored) on the document itself. On the other hand, *decipherment* implies that the method involves simply reading the original material, although sometimes the decipherment can be demonstrated photographically.

has been removed from the document or expunged in some manner. Under these conditions the ultimate objective is always to restore the original writing so that it can be read in its entirety, but there are instances when only portions can be deciphered.

Erasures

It is common knowledge that writing, typewriting, or printing may be removed by either chemicals, abrasion, or scratching with a sharp instrument like a knife. Not all of these methods are successful in removing each class of marking medium, but all are encountered in a series of problems.

Virtually all erasures can be detected by a thorough examination. On a rare occasion, an extremely skillful bleaching of fluid ink writing with a chemical erasing fluid might remain undetected, but the combined effect of two factors should leave some evidence of the act itself. First, the chemicals react with the paper to form visible or latent stains, and if an attempt is then made to write over the erased area with a fountain pen, the fluid ink is very apt to spread out microscopically wherever the paper sizing has been affected by the liquid. A similar result may be observed when the writing was done with a soft tip or fiber tip pen. With ball point pen inks chemicals bleach the ink only with great difficulty, and except for the most persistent person trying to remove the ink, some stains will probably remain. Overwriting with a ball pen may not appear to be abnormal, but some evidence of erasing probably will remain. Examination with oblique lighting, the microscope, photography, and especially ultraviolet radiation or infrared luminescence should establish in most instances that there has been alteration. In contrast to this, even very skillful erasures by means of abrasion or scratching generally leave much more definite telltale traces consisting of disturbed paper fibers and portions of the original strokes that were not completely removed. These erasures are consequently more easily detected.

Although the first step is always to ascertain that an erasure has been made, in any investigation of this nature the step that is of greatest importance to those who stand to be defrauded by the alteration is the restoration or decipherment of the erased matter. By restoration is meant that the original writing is revealed on the document either temporarily or permanently, while decipherment includes any method, photographic or otherwise, that permits determination of what has been erased. Whether or not this is to be successfully accomplished depends both on the original writing medium and the manner in which it has been erased.

Note that the erasure most likely to pass undetected—the chemical erasure of an iron-base ink—is at the same time the most likely to be successfully restored (Figure 4.1). Several techniques can bring about a restoration, and the most effective is to fume the document with sulfocyanic acid fumes.[2] Since the original ink is only bleached by the eradicator, its iron constituent is left in the paper, and the sulfocyanic fumes combine chemically with the iron to cause the writing to reappear in a clear red color. An advantage of this method is that the restoration gradually fades out or can be rapidly removed by fuming with amonium hydroxide and the process repeated at a subsequent time. If this same type of ink is removed by an abrasion or scratching, there is again a chance for successful restoration unless the paper was badly gouged during the erasing process. Unfortunately, such damage is often encountered with this method of erasing, and the result then is at best a partial restoration. During the years when the nib fountain pen was the most common writing instrument, this class of ink was widely used, but today it is only rarely encountered. It is not used in modern porous or roller pens.

With other classes of fluid ink that do not contain iron salts, the restoration problem is much more difficult and generally less successful. In the case of synthetic dye inks found in porous tip or roller pens, bleaching removes not only the color but virtually all of the chemicals from the paper as well. Here again is an example of the fact that nonchemical erasures, while more easily detected, are less readily deciphered. With these inks, photographic techniques (Figure 4.2) or examination under ultraviolet radiation (Figure 4.3) and infrared luminescence are standard methods, although not every erasure can be successfully deciphered. (These methods can also be used effectively with iron-base inks.[3])

Carbon ink is very difficult to expunge completely. Chemicals do not bleach it, but an abrasive erasure or a skillfully used knife edge or razor removes the ink effectively. Decipherment of the original ink is usually extremely difficult. If it has been completely erased, the problem may be virtually impossible. However, whenever there are some traces of the original writing, these may be intensified photographically

---

[2]This method was developed by M. E. O'Neill and is described in detail in his article, "The Restoration of Obliterated Ink Writing," *Journal of Criminal Law and Criminology* 27 (1936): 574–577. A. Longhetti and P. L. Kirk, "Restoration and Decipherment of Erasures and Obliterated or Indented Writing," *Journal of Criminal Law and Criminology* 41 (1950): 518–519, suggest applying the liquid reagent as a fine mist by means of a nebulizer.

[3]The use of ultraviolet radiation to decipher erased writing is ably discussed by Elbridge W. Stein, "Ultraviolet Light and Forgery," *Scientific American* (October 1932): 204–206.

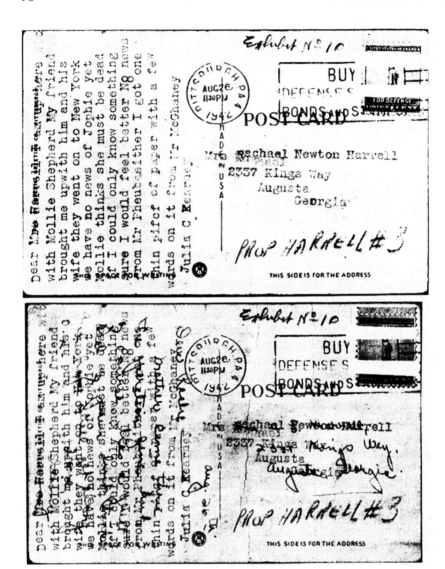

Figure 4.1. At the top is a postal card as offered in evidence in connection with a claim against an estate. After chemical fuming the card appeared as shown below. This evidence completely refuted the assertions of the claimant. The original writing on the document had been written with an iron-tannate ink.

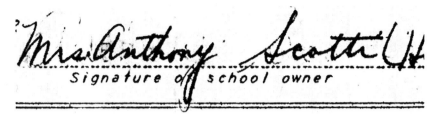

Figure 4.2. The original signature, Anthony Scotti, had been removed using an abrasive eraser. The best decipherment was achieved by photographing with carefully controlled lighting in order to intensify the fragments. Mr. Scotti's signature had been written with a blue dye ink.

Figure 4.3. Above is a portion of the endorsement area of a check. Loss of background indicates a chemical erasure.

The same area was photographed under ultraviolet radiation, which revealed a weak outline of a second endorsement and a passbook number below it.

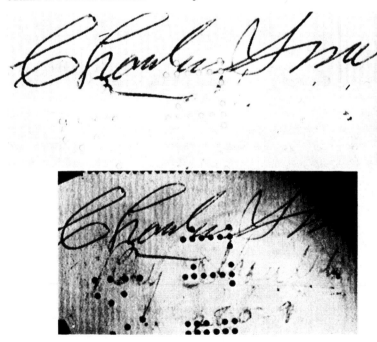

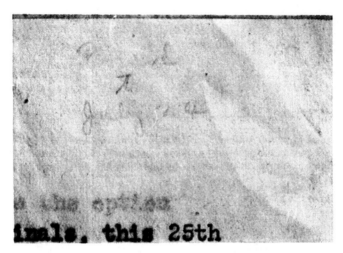

Figure 4.4. The partially erased date, July 24, was written with a red pencil. Photographic decipherment was accomplished by using a green filter to intensify the remaining weak strokes.

by using ordinary copying or infrared sensitive film to bring about at least a partial decipherment.

Ball point pen ink does not erase easily.[4] Commercial ink eradicators are only partially effective, but hard rubbing with an abrasive eraser can remove the ink and at the same time leaves clear evidence of the act. Extensive rubbing is necessary to effect a full erasure because the ink penetrates the paper and is not all on the surface. In addition the indentation of the ball track may remain. Photographic, ultraviolet, and infrared luminescence methods, while not foolproof, are the better ways of deciphering the original matter.

The decipherment of erased pencil writing, regardless of whether a black, indelible, or colored pencil was used, not only presents a difficult but also an arduous and lengthy task. The erasure can be made with a soft rubber eraser, which in the hands of a skillful person hardly disturbs the paper surface. Even so, except when the writing was ex-

---

[4]Erasable ball pen ink is a recent development. This writing can be rather easily erased, but not without some evidence of the act left on the document. The most extensive study of this problem is found in Peter Pfefferli and Jacques Mathyer, " 'Eraser Mate' Un Stylo à Bille à Encre Effaçable," *Revue International de Criminologie et de Police Technique* 4 (1979): 407–419. See also William J. Flynn, "Paper Mate's New Erasable Pen," *Journal of Police Science and Administration* 7 (1979): 346–349. Both studies indicate that the ink can be erased with a soft pencil eraser within a short time after writing (1 or 2 hours) and, depending upon the paper, may in some instances still be erasable 70–80 hours later (Flynn). Once permanently set, the ink is as difficult as other types of ball pen inks to erase.

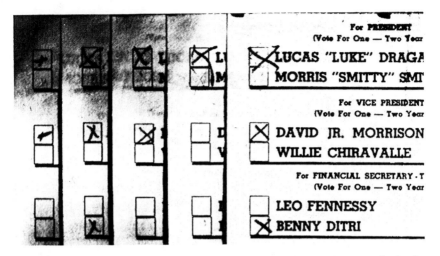

Figure 4.5. Five ballots in a union election were altered. The erased crossmarks for the second presidential candidate were revealed by combining oblique lighting with infrared sensitive film.

ecuted with a very light touch, slight indentations of the original strokes may remain after complete obliteration, and when incomplete, some carbon or pigment traces are to be found. Both the indentations and traces serve as the basis of decipherment. Visual and photographic examination under controlled light, involving both oblique illumination and low intensity diffused light, are effective methods of reading the erased matter[5] (Figure 4.4). At times reflected infrared photography is needed (Figure 4.5) and with colored pencils infrared luminescence. Specially compounded chemical solutions[6] may intensify the writing impressions (Figure 4.6). With indelible pencil writing some of the unerased dye can be made more visible by moistening with a fine spray of alcohol.[7] If during the erasing process the paper surface was badly roughed, the problem becomes more complicated because controlled, side-light illumination does not produce as clearcut results (Figure 4.7). Under favorable circumstances a complete decipherment can be

---

[5]Modern photographic methods of deciphering erased pencil writing, including a discussion of a newly developed technique of using a low intensity diffused light source, are discussed in the author's article, "Photographic Methods of Deciphering Erased Pencil Writing," *International Criminal Police Review*, No. 85 (February 1955): 47–50.

[6]One such solution, called Grapho-Detector, is commercially marketed by Faurot Protective System, Inc., Moorestown, New Jersey. A formula for a similar solution appears in H. T. F. Rhodes, *Forensic Chemistry* (New York: The Chemical Publ. Co., 1940), p. 135.

[7]For techniques used in this kind of restoration refer to Longhetti and Kirk, "Restoration and Decipherment of Erasures and Obliterated or Indented Writing," p. 519.

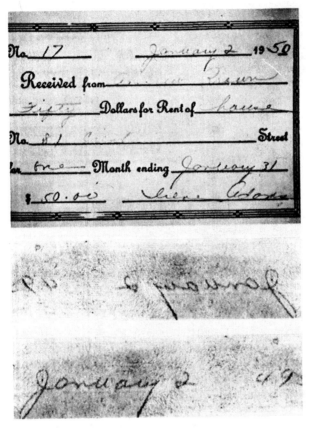

Figure 4.6. The year in the rent receipt, shown at the top, contained evidence of a pencil erasure. The back of the document was treated with a chemical staining solution, with the results shown in the center and reversed photographically below.

achieved, but there are many cases where only part of the original matter can be read (Figure 4.8).

Typewriting with a standard record ribbon is extremely difficult to expunge completely without seriously damaging the paper, but once removed it is equally hard to decipher.[8] Should traces of the original matter remain, they may be intensified photographically, with either infrared-sensitive or contrast emulsions, just as erased carbon ink or pencil writing is handled (Figure 4.9). Even though the pigment is all removed, on many occasions impressed outlines of the letters remain.

---

[8]Typewriting ribbon manufacturers have made an "erasable ribbon," one in which the ink is a synthetic dye without any carbon constituent and which can be bleached with fluid ink eradicator. The ribbon has not been widely used. Therefore the discussion in this section is based upon the use of the more common black record ribbon, which contains carbon as its principal marking substance.

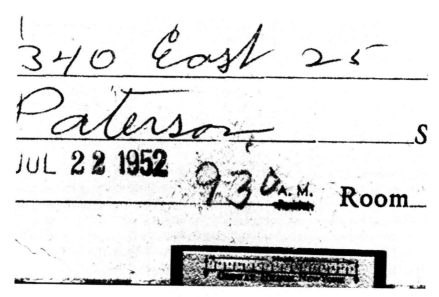

Figure 4.7. A portion of a hotel registration card shows the time of a morning registration. It was offered as an alibi that the defendant in a grand larceny case was several hundred miles away from the scene of the crime at the time. The very disturbed paper background can be seen in the oblique light photograph reproduced here. The only part of the original writing that could be deciphered is a groove through the printed A.M. of the time indicating that the original registration was P.M. not A.M. Following expert testimony and during the weekend recess of the court, a guilty plea of second degree larceny was arranged.

Figure 4.8. This daily report form was involved in a civil suit alleging that a paper winding machine was defective. Numerous reports contained entries, "Down for reels," showing the number of minutes lost per day due to the malfunctioning of the winder. Most were absolute fabrications, like this one, but in others only time losses had been increased. On this sheet, the indentations from the erased pencil writing were intensified by oblique light photography. "Trouble getting paper over" indicates a mill problem not related to the winder.

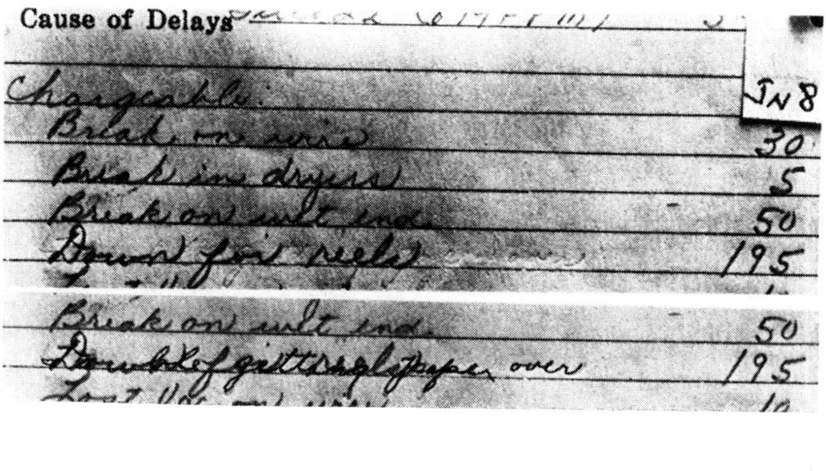

Figure 4.9. The partially erased typewriting of Anthony Scotti's name was intensified photographically using a high-contrast film.

This condition is especially common when a lift-off ribbon has been used with a correcting typewriter. Virtually all of the pigment is removed but the impression of the letter is intensified.[9] Side-light photographs, a plastic cast technique,[10] or application of the chemical solution used in pencil problems may lead to full or partial decipherment. Nevertheless, cases are encountered in which the erasure has been so thorough that none of the techniques gives satisfactory results.

Problems resulting from the removal of a stamp impression or printed matter, or from an erased carbon copy, are less frequent, and the best results are apt to lead only to a partial decipherment. The methods depend for the most part on photographic intensification of the partially erased material (Figure 4.10). Controlled lighting, and under some circumstances reflected infrared, infrared luminescence, or ultraviolet photography, may improve the results (Figure 4.11). The latter two techniques are most effective when the impression was bleached out with chemicals, the former when there are some fragments of the original impression. Often with these problems the paper

Figure 4.10. The erased carbon copy of a bill of sale originally bearing the name Herman Heft was deciphered using contrast photography.

---

[9]See M. A. Casey and D. J. Purtell, "IBM Correcting Selectric Typewriter: An Analysis of the Use of the Correctable Film Ribbon in Altering Typewritten Documents," *Journal of Forensic Sciences* 21 (1976): 208–212.

[10]A method of making a plastic cast or replica of writing and typewriting impressions was developed by Longhetti and Kirk, "Restoration and Decipherment of Erasures and Obliterated or Indented Writing," pp. 519–522.

Figure 4.11. Visual and microscopic examination of "JUN" disclosed evidence of an abrasive erasure in the area of the U and that the U was in pencil rather than black stamping ink. Note the microscopic ribs along the lighter side of the U, typical of marking across the paper fibers with a weak pencil stroke.

This infrared photograph revealed the fragment of the tip of an erased A (marked by arrow) of "JAN." *(From the files of Elbridge W. Stein).*

surface has been seriously damaged by abrasive erasing. Such cases as well as the usual problems require repeated experimentation with various methods to arrive at the most satisfactory solution, and some are never solved completely.

Despite excellent results on many erasure problems, there are cases in which the restoration or decipherment of erased writing may not be successful. So much depends on the individual case—the materials erased; the care and handling of the document prior to undertaking the restoration or decipherment; the time between the writing, erasing, and attempted restoration or decipherment; and other factors often individual to the particular problem. Each restoration or decipherment may involve a great deal of experimentation and time. While the previous paragraphs have indicated photographic and scientific techniques that may be helpful, much progress is usually made by visual study aided by magnifiers and sometimes reducing lenses under various controlled-lighting conditions, including oblique or subdued lighting, as well as moderate-intensity daylight illumination. Thus, when an erasure is first suspected, it is well to submit the document for examination immediately. This eliminates unnecessary handling, which may reduce the chances of success, and also allows sufficient time to investigate the problem thoroughly.

Associated Evidence

While associated evidence may not necessarily involve technical study, it does serve a very useful role in the decipherment and verification of decipherments of erased and altered documents. Associated evidence would be any other documents that relate closely to the altered document (Figure 4.12). One obvious example would be a carbon copy, which might not have been available to the individual who made the erasure or change in the original. Locating the carbon copy would reveal immediately what had been erased. Other types of evidence might involve accounting records in which one such record had been changed but other entries in the bookkeeping system had not. Thus, anyone familiar with the manner in which the books are kept would be able to locate the associated entries and reconstruct the original entry.

It is always possible that portions of the associated evidence have also been altered. For example, in an accounting record, the erasure and change of a particular entry may require that the totals at the end of a section or a page be changed as well. Although great care may have been taken with the critical entry, it is not uncommon for the changes in the subtotals or totals to have been made carelessly or with only partial erasing. The result is that the original totals can be deciphered more readily than the key erased figure. In such a way, the critical entry could be reconstructed. Many other examples could be pointed out, and often consultation with the examiner himself may bring to mind where to look for this type of evidence.

Cutting

A rare, though not unheard of, alteration of a document can be achieved by skillful cutting away of some portions and then inserting new material to fill the gap. Of course, it is necessary to devise some means of securing the inserted material in place. The document may be pasted to another sheet, or stamps or tape may be affixed to the back of the document. Check protector imprints have been altered by this means[11] (Figure 4.13). Careful inspection of the paper will reveal the alteration,

---

[11]John L. Harris, "Eyeing the Evidence," *Southern California Alumni Review* 21 (May 1940).

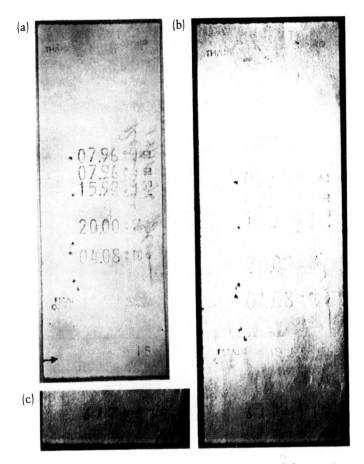

Figure 4.12. An altered register receipt from a K-Mart store was used as a defense against a charge of shoplifting. The accused claimed that she had purchased the merchandise, was returning it, but had started home to get the sales receipt when apprehended. The key identification number and the two letters "NO" at right angles [bottom of (b) and traced over in (c)], agreed with the internal record tape of the register and established that this purchase was made several weeks after the crime, on November 15. The decipherment of weak purple ink impressions was accomplished by ultraviolet photography.

but casual observers and even those who handle the document in business transactions, businessmen and bank employees, have been fooled by checks altered in this manner.

If the paper is thick, only the top layer need be cut out and the inserted material cut so that it fits accurately into the depression. Contest cards and parimutuel tickets are known to have been produced

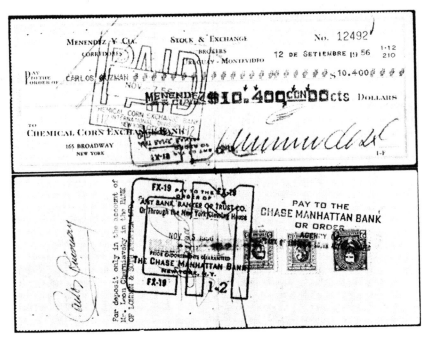

Figure 4.13. A ten-dollar check raised with a knife and a manipulated check writer was successfully negotiated through New York City banks. The South American company returned it to its New York bank claiming forgery. Technical study revealed two small sections cut from the check and patched with similar check paper. Arrows indicate the upper cut between "10" and "00" and following the two zeros. Apparently "*CON*" and "cts" had been removed. The stamps on the back hold the patches in place.

with key numbers modified in this way[12] (Figure 4.14). Detection of the alteration of course is possible, but what was there originally normally cannot be ascertained.

Interlineations and Additions

Fraud can be committed just as effectively by addition as by subtraction. The insertion of a modifying clause or sentence may completely change the meaning of a document in as thorough a manner as the erasure of a key portion. The skill with which these modifications are inserted varies from case to case, but as with erasures effective methods

---

[12]Maureen A. Casey, "Alteration of Pari-Mutual Tickets," *Journal of Criminal Law, Criminology and Police Science* 62 (1971): 282–285.

Figure 4.14. With a nonwinning $1000 card, the number was cut out, but only the surface layer of the card was removed. A card of another value with the winning $1000 number was manipulated in the same way, and the number was pasted into this card. Careful examination and photography showed the court the knife lines, which revealed the fraud.

have been developed by which many fraudulent interlineations or additions are revealed.

Obviously, the crude insert of some important clause between the lines or crowded along a margin immediately arouses suspicion, and rightfully so. However, many additions are carefully worked into the form of the document when very convenient space either within it or immediately above the signature was provided by careless preparation. When these insertions are skillfully done, they may pass unnoticed by the casual observer, but still, these inconspicuous manipulations can be revealed by physical faults that are disclosed through proper techniques and study.

To disclose that an insertion or addition has been made may involve an extensive study of the document as a whole. Many of its elements, which have been discussed in earlier sections, assume special importance. The lack of uniformity of ink; the work of more than one pen or typewriter; crowding, uneven margins, or unusual spacing of a modifying section if typewritten, evidence that the document has been removed and reinserted in the same or another machine; indication of more than one typewriter ribbon or a marked change in its condition if it is a fabric ribbon; evidence of the insertion of pages through study of the paper and fastening devices; sharp variation in handwriting; and any of a score of other factors individual to the problem at hand may point out the insertion. There is, however, one other sign that points conclusively to the fact that the document was not put together in normal order—evidence that the sequence of intersecting writing strokes or strokes across the folds or perforations in the paper is not in the logical sequence that would be consistent with the natural or alleged preparation of the document.

Sequence of Writing

Intersecting writing strokes may have distinctive patterns, depending upon the order of writing, the lapse of time between the two writings, the density of the two strokes, and the kind of inks, writing instruments, and paper used. With the binocular microscope or a hand magnifier aided by skillfully controlled light and photography, the true order of preparation may be revealed and demonstrated to a lay observer.

What appears to be the obvious solution may not always be the correct answer. For example, the line of deepest color usually appears on top even if it was written first. Careful study and testing is necessary before reaching a conclusion. Some of the more common criteria for determining sequence are considered in the following paragraphs.[13]

If we consider the intersection of two writing strokes or the intersection of writing and typewriting, the majority of problems are covered. Substantial, repeated intersections of two writings offer a higher probability of success than a single, indifferent intersection, such as a weak stroke crossing another or two lines barely touching one another, which only very infrequently can produce a clear indication of the order of writing.

---

[13]Linton Godown, "Sequence of Writing," *Journal of Criminal Law, Criminology and Police Science* 54 (1963): 101–109. This article is undoubtedly the best modern-day discussion on determining sequence of writing. Any worker confronted with such a problem will find it of definite help.

Fluid ink flows into the paper, and when such a line strikes another fresh fluid ink or other hydroscopic material, the second line tends to spread out or widen at the intersection (Figure 4.15). This condition is encountered with nib pen writing and at times with that of porous pens. If the first stroke is completely dry, the phenomenon is less apt to occur. When the first stroke contains a significant groove created by a stiff pen point or a roller pen, a relatively light second stroke may be found to narrow slightly or even to skip at the intersection with the groove. There is also the possibility with highly soluble dye inks that the second ink can dissolve a portion of the first line, spreading its ink beyond the edge of the original stroke.

Ball point pens with nonaqueous inks are rolled onto the paper. The ink does not flow. When two such pen strokes intersect, the grooved lines caused by pressure on the ball is the critical consideration in determining the order of writing. Interruption of the groove edges on one line would indicate that it was written first. If the first groove is deep, the second line may narrow slightly as it crosses or may show a microscopic skipping. This same phenomenon can occur when the ball point pen crosses a significantly grooved pencil stroke.

An additional means of studying the continuity of the edges of two intersecting ball point pen strokes involves lifting some of the ink at

Figure 4.15. A witness testified that he had signed on June 17 after the entry was made in a research chemist's notebook. His signature crossed the writing of a June 20 entry. The spreading of the dark ink into the light blue ink of the 20th entry established that the witness had not signed the book until June 20 at the earliest.

the point of intersection from the paper. Igoe and Reynolds suggest the following method for achieving such a lift.[14] The glossy side of Kromekote paper[15] is placed against an intersection in which the edge marks show more prominently, and the back of the paper is rubbed with a blunt point using even pressure. The resulting lift can show more clearly which of the two lines is continuous across the intersection. To improve the results with older ink lines, like those found on documents written several years before, Godown has proposed pretreatment of the Krometone paper with a dilute solution of thymol in alcohol.[16] The lift is then made by rubbing the back of the sheet with a warm tacking iron for about five seconds.

Pencil written intersections may contain evidence of continuous and interrupted striations or grooves in the two lines. Occasionally, the second line may drag particles of pigment from the first line, a condition more readily observed if the two strokes are of different colors. In fact, with any kind of intersection, if the second writing instrument drags particles of pigment or dyes from the crossed line, this is significant evidence that it was written last.

Several different considerations come into play when writing and typewriting intersect. With fluid ink crossing relatively fresh typewriting, there is a tendency for the water-based ink to be repelled by the oils and waxes found in the typewriter ink (Figure 4.16). As a result, small gaps or a slight narrowing of the fluid ink line can be observed. This same condition can occur when a fluid ink crosses a fresh ball point pen line. If there is a substantial interval of time between the preparation of the typewriting and the fluid ink writing, no repelling may be observed since the oily materials in the typewriting have completely dried out. Because of this complete lack of any repelling of the aqueous ink by the typewriting, it is suggested that the typewriting was prepared first, but it is not a sure indication of this fact. A rare phenomenon of the fluid ink spreading into completely dried typewriting has been reported. This contradictory action is due no doubt to the disturbance of the paper surface by the typewriting.

Ball point pen writing across typewriting can be recognized by the spectral reflection revealed by low-angle illumination or somewhat more readily by vertical illumination of the intersection.[17] The lack

---

[14]T. J. Igoe and B. L. Reynolds, "The Determination of Stroke Sequence Through a Lifting Process in Forensically Related Ball Point Pen Document Examination," *Forensic Science International* (in press).

[15]Kromekote paper is a high-gloss backing material used extensively for mounting lifted latent fingerprints.

[16]Linton Godown, "Recent Developments in Writing Sequence Determination," *Forensic Science International* (in press).

[17]Godown, "Recent Developments in Writing Sequence Determination."

Figure 4.16. The fluid ink of the handwritten notation was repelled by the very fresh, heavy typewritten line. This established that the typewriting was on the paper first. To some it might appear that the typewriting is continuous and must be over the handwriting, but this apparent solution is incorrect.

of such reflection constitutes strong evidence that the writing preceded the typewriting. If both the typewriting and the ball point pen writing emboss the paper, the condition of the edges of the embossing may assist in confirming the order of preparation. Again the lift-off technique can be employed using relatively weak, tacky, "removable" pressure adhesive. This material lifts the typewriting except when covered with writing at the intersection. The lifted image shows a continuous outline of the typewriting except when it is covered by ink. The presence of a break in the typewriting is a clear indication that the writing overlays the typewriting, but if there is no break at the intersection, then the opposite conclusion can be drawn.

A further indication that the writing is over the typewriting can be derived when the typewriting embosses the paper and the pen stroke shows a skipping at the center of the typewritten stroke where the pen failed to make contact with the paper in the deepest part of the embossing. This condition is often accompanied by damage to the edges of the typewritten stroke resulting from the pressure of the pen against the edge of the typewriting.

Paper Condition and Sequence

Writing across folds and perforations frequently leaves an accurate picture of the order of events and can well substantiate contentions of fraud or authenticity. Fluid ink strokes leave the clearest picture. The flow of such ink across a worn fold in the paper spreads discernibly into the adjacent paper fibers in a manner that immediately establishes that the writing followed the folding (Figure 4.17). A dried ink stroke that is subsequently bent or broken by a fold is not affected in this way. Instead it remains unchanged, or with deep folds, the ink film may contain microscopic breaks (Figure 4.18). Ball point pens may skip on the far side of a fold ridge or within the trough of a concave fold. There are times when ink is rubbed off the ball housing at a fold intersection (Figure 4.19).

The sequence of fluid ink writing and a perforation follow a similar pattern. When the perforations are put in the paper after the writing has been completed, both fluid and ball point pen ink strokes are

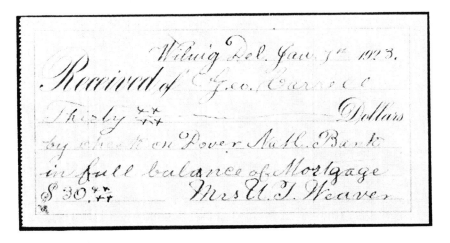

Figure 4.17. The entry "in full balance of Mortgage" was in dispute. Mrs. Weaver said it was not there when she signed.

The running of the fluid ink into the fold where the a of "balance" crossed shows that this line was entered after folding of the receipt. The M of "Mrs" did not run out, but in the enlarged portion (below) shows slight breaking of the ink stroke. This condition is consistent with writing before the folding, the breaking of the stroke due to wear at the point of folding. Note with both letters the condition reported occurs at points where the ink crosses the fold. *(From the files of Elbridge W. Stein.)*

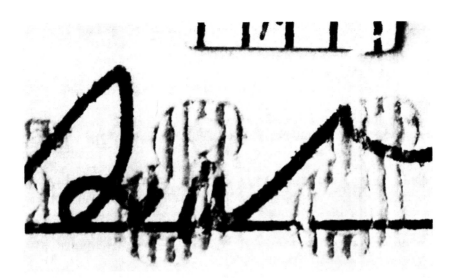

Figure 4.18. The impression of a misaligned check writer cut through part of the signature. Note where the ridges of the check writer impression broke some portions of the ink line, especially in the left-hand side of the first 8. Clearly it was applied after the check was signed and raised.

Figure 4.19. Ball pen lines written across a pronounced fold often deposit extra ink on the edges of the line, wiped from the housing as it strikes the raised paper area. The broadening can be followed by a skipping in the ink line after it crosses the fold. The condition shows most clearly in the heavier left-hand diagonal stroke.

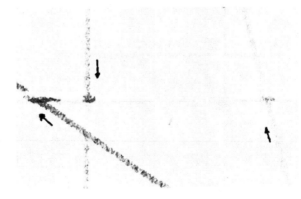

cleanly cut, but when the writer tries to write across a perforation, the fluid ink is very apt to flow along the cut edge (Figure 4.20). With a ball point pen, the ink does not flow, but the ball can catch in the perforation, staining the edges. Sometimes the crowding or twisting of the writing reveals the writer's effort to avoid the perforation entirely.

Pencil and typewriting strokes across folds and perforations may also leave evidence of sequence, but the demonstration of the facts is a more complex problem than with ink writing and may be subject to greater limitations. With each of these instruments, there is no ink that can flow into broken paper fibers. Still, typical differences in the continuity of the writing strokes or the ridge of a fold may allow definite conclusions, although not in every case. With these problems, as with all questions of sequence, experimentation under controlled conditions is often needed to verify that an apparent determination of sequence is the correct conclusion.

Under proper circumstances, sequence can be definitely established through these examinations, and the order is definitely fixed. The weight of this evidence can be great. When an unusual sequence of writing is established from the physical facts, it is not in itself positive proof of fraud. Rather, this physical evidence must be weighed in con-

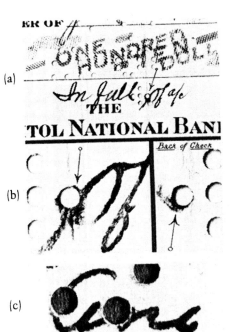

(a)

(b)

(c)

Figure 4.20. The check (a) bears the words "In full of a/c." The notation was added after the check had been processed through the bank. The running of the ink is clearly shown in the enlargement of the intersection of the word "of" and the bank cancellation hole (b). The fluid ink even ran through to the back of the check as shown on the right.

(c) The clean cut of a dried fluid ink line, which was also cut by bank cancellations. *(From the files of Elbridge W. Stein.)*

junction with the other testimony and facts in the case. The burden of proof generally shifts to those who oppose this new evidence, for it becomes their task to establish that this situation can exist without conflict with the intent or original purpose of the document.

Obliterated or Smeared-over Writing

Smeared-over writing—that is, the obliteration or blacking out of portions of writing by some opaque material—is seldom used for fraudulent purposes because of its obviousness. Nevertheless, from time to time such obliterations may be encountered in all types of documents. Many times the writer himself blots out writing simply by striking over it thoroughly with the same material with which the document is written. The anonymous letter writer may attempt to black out a printed return address on the only available envelope, and during war periods mail is censored in this manner.

These examples serve to illustrate the diversity of problems. Virtually each case has its own ramifications requiring various techniques and making difficult an accurate, generalized forecast as to the measure of success. The solution at best is a tedious process involving extensive experimentation, and it must be recognized that failures are to be encountered.

Successful decipherment or restoration depends principally upon the medium employed for the original writing and the covering material. Two possible methods of solution present themselves: (1) To penetrate the covering layer photographically so that the original writing lying beneath is thus revealed, and (2) to remove the obliterating material chemically or by some other means while the original writing remains untouched. A third rather infrequent method involves studying the impression from the original writing or typewriting that has not been destroyed by the obliterating action.

Photographic methods can succeed only if a difference in color or chemical composition exists between the original writing and the covering material. Separation may be effected with photographic filters of a color similar to the obliterating substances, but this attack breaks down completely when the covering is a true black. Transmitted light, infrared sensitive films, ultraviolet radiation, and oblique lighting to supplement photography with a filter may enhance the chance of success (Figure 4.21). As a general rule, if complete and accurate decipherment is to be achieved, the methods involve repeated attempts under slightly different conditions (Figure 4.22).

When photography fails, or is impractical, the obliterating material can sometimes be removed or weakened by chemical or mechanical means. Success depends upon whether the techniques employed affect

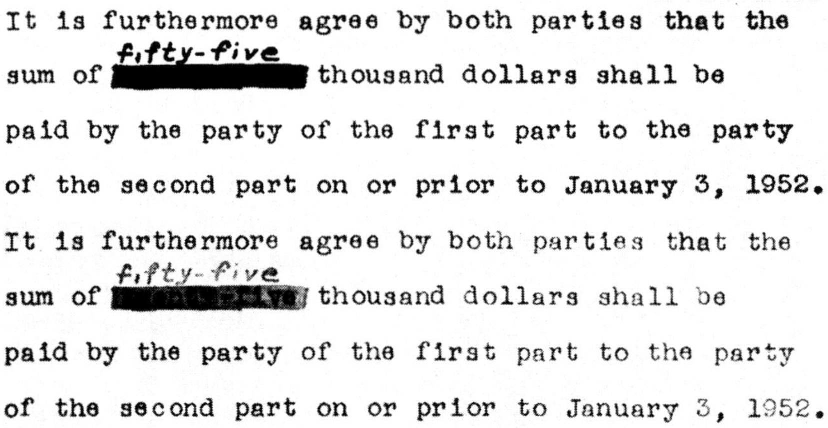

It is furthermore agree by both parties that the
sum of *fifty-five* ████████ thousand dollars shall be

paid by the party of the first part to the party

of the second part on or prior to January 3, 1952.

It is furthermore agree by both parties that the
sum of *fifty-five* ████████ thousand dollars shall be

paid by the party of the first part to the party

of the second part on or prior to January 3, 1952.

Figure 4.21. The upper portion shows heavy ink covering over the typewritten amount and the letters "fifty-five" above. Below, an infrared photograph penetrated the black writing ink, but not the typewriting, to reveal the original amount as "twenty-five."

only the obliterating substance, or at least have a more pronounced effect on it than the writing beneath. Blue-black or aniline inks obliterating carbon inks, pencil strokes covering inks, and many ink or pencil strokes hiding typewriting are combinations that lend themselves to these methods of attack. Ordinary erasers and common solvents of writing inks skillfully manipulated may achieve the desired

Figure 4.22. The date on a document (upper section) was obviously altered by a heavy overwriting.

The lower infrared photograph was made from the back of the document, revealing the 6 beneath the heavy inked 8. The ink could not be penetrated by photographing the face of the document.

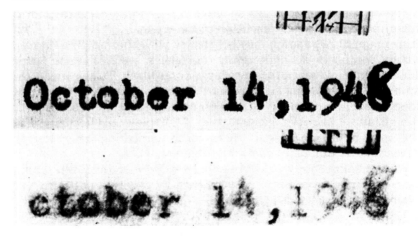

Figure 4.23. Two words were thoroughly obliterated first by covering with x's and then with n's. Decipherment was possible by studying those fragments of original typewriting that appeared above and below the line, followed by extensive microscopic study of strokes found between the projecting letters. Below is the typewritten decipherment, "handling of."

results. Thus, under favorable circumstances, this approach to the problem is successful, but as the combination of materials that are not susceptible to this treatment are numerous, success is far from universal.

One form of obliteration has rather widespread use today. This is the use of white-out in lieu of erasing especially with typewriting. One technique is to type through a correction ribbon or sheet covering the outline of the letters to be retrieved. Usually new typewriting is placed in the same area. The other technique is to use liquid white-out material, painting it over the area to be removed. Again new text can be written over the white-out. In both instances a careful inspection will reveal the obliteration. Normally the original material can be read by transmitted light or by photographing of the back of the sheet with infrared sensitive film and filters. Some of the white-out can be removed with proper solvent to weaken the cover and reveal the writing below, but solvents for some white-out material may attack typewriting ink, so only a limited amount of removal is generally advisable.

In very many cases the only hope is that the covering over may be faulty and some portions of the original writing may yet be discernible (Figures 4.23 and 4.24). These partial strokes or weak outlines of

Figure 4.24. A carefully prepared enlarged photograph of the date reveals that the original writing read "May 17, 1947," rather than "1949." The alteration was made by the same woman who made the one in Figure 4.22. Both were intended to win her lawsuit.

semiobliterated letters can be intensified and deciphered. All these obliterations by and large require a diversity of methods combining various techniques, experimentation, perseverance, and often a full measure of luck to assure ultimate success.

Overwritings and Insertions

Documents may be changed by overwriting words and portions of sentences or by insertion of a character, a word, a sentence, or more. At times it is necessary to attempt to determine what was originally written. In other instances it is necessary only to show that the changes were not made at the time of preparation of the document. Insertions in the form of interlineations may be very obvious, but if it can be shown that they were made with another writing instrument, by another writer, or on a different typewriter, it can go a long way toward attacking the value of the present version.

Insertions may be disclosed by differences in the writing material or differences in the handwriting. Crowding of the inserted material compared to surrounding writing suggests an addition. Microscopic study is used to detect differences in ink or writing instruments. Intersecting strokes may disclose the wrong sequence. Photography using filters, ultraviolet and infrared, is a useful tool. Most of the methods discussed in previous sections may come into play in these problems as well.

Overwriting that is not very obvious may be established by disclosing double strokes. Strokes that are not a part of the letters of the overwritten words assume significance. If there is enough writing, it may be possible to show that there are writing characteristics of someone other than the person who prepared the balance of the document (Figure 4.25).

Cases of this nature are not common. They are more often found in manipulation of accounting records and check frauds (Figure 4.26). Occasionally, they are incidental issues in document problems of entirely different kinds. They do, however, represent another way that documents can be changed, and despite the obvious appearance, changes of this nature will arise from time to time as evidence in the case of one party to a litigation. They must be accurately evaluated.

Whole pages may be inserted in a multiple-page document. Their detection often depends upon study of binding marks (such as staple holes if the pages are assembled in this way), the paper for kind and size, the pen and ink, the typewriting, or the pencils. Indentations on a following page may be the key. The appearance of the inserted page may not necessarily suggest the insertion, but interested parties will certainly become suspicious. It then becomes necessary to find the key elements that establish the facts.

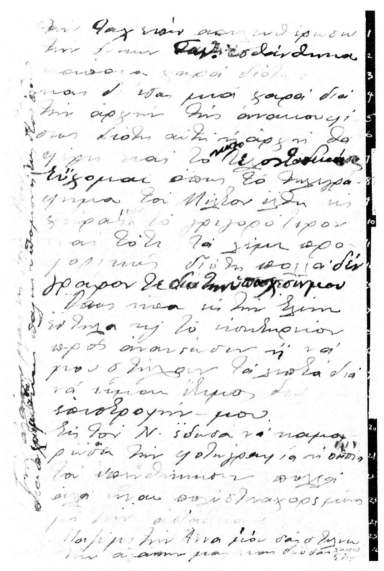

Figure 4.25. A page of a personal letter from an uncle to his niece, who was using it to prove that he had made promises of a dowry to her and her husband. Comparable alterations were made in almost every page of a series of lengthy letters, several from the uncle and several from his wife. In this instance the difference in ink revealed the changes, and where new words were inserted, there were differences in the handwriting.

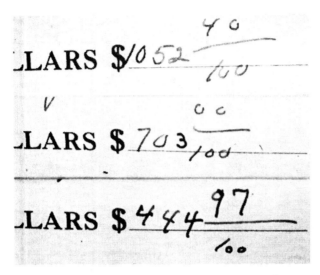

Figure 4.26. Raised amounts of checks revealed by differences in the color of the ink. Note 703.00 raised from 70.00. The check of Figure 4.18 was part of the evidence in the same case.

Altered Photocopies

Contemporary photocopies, such as Xeroxes, can be erased or sections deleted by liquid white-out material. Methods of demonstrating these changes follow those used with other documents. New matter can be inserted in the voided space by handwriting or typewriting. With the original photocopy, detection of the changes may be possible, but if the altered copy is recopied, the problem is seriously complicated. At this point the examiner is confronted with a fraudulent photocopy, a subject treated more in detail in Chapter 17.

Proof of an Unaltered Document

In the previous sections various techniques that may reveal alterations in documents were discussed. The question does arise, however, Is it possible to establish that a document has not been altered, and, if so, what procedures are necessary?

Proving that a paper is unaltered is a challenging problem.[18] It is an

---

[18]For a more detailed analysis, see Ordway Hilton, "Proof of an Unaltered Document," *Journal of Criminal Law, Criminology and Police Science* 49 (1959): 601–604.

important one, however, since it is incumbent on document examiners to be able to prove genuineness as well as fraud. This proof of genuineness is necessary to support the validity of certain disputed documents. Actually, the procedure involves not the application of any single test, but a consideration of all the applicable procedures to determine whether there has been an erasure, a substitution, or any other type of alteration in a document. In each instance, the findings must be that no significant alteration has occurred that in any way would change the intended purpose of contents of the document. It is the cumulative evidence that establishes that the document is unaltered.

Therefore, depending upon how the document was prepared, the examiner must apply those tests that are appropriate to establish that there has been no significant erasure, or that if there has been some minor erasure, it is clear that such an act was merely to correct an error, such as a misspelling, made in the preparation of the document. To accomplish this requires the application of every appropriate test that could disclose the presence of an erasure, and each must show negative results. It is the combination of these tests that supports the conclusion that the document contains no erasures.

By the same token, tests that may reveal additions to the document must be considered, such as those showing the use of more than one writing instrument, the addition of typewriting, or the insertion of material by an improper sequence of intersecting lines or lines with folds or perforations. With a handwritten document, was all the writing done with the same writing instrument and by the same writer, and is the document free from evidence of undue crowding of key material? Thus, in dealing with each specific page the examiner must be able to say that there is no evidence that a word, sentence, or paragraph had been added.

A further consideration in a multiple-page document, of course, is whether any pages may have been removed and others substituted, or new pages added into the document after execution. Such examinations, of course, involve consideration of the writing instrument, typewriter, paper, manner of binding, and the presence of writing impressions that may have resulted from preparation of material on the previous page. There are the problems of determining whether the entire document was prepared at one time in a continuous manner, which involve considering the margins on page after page, the spacing between lines, the manner of handling paragraphs, and if handwritten, whether there is an abrupt change in the quality of handwriting, which might suggest writing of some portion of the document under conditions different from the other. In this way the examiner should be able to show that no evidence is present that suggests or establishes that the preparation of any page is inconsistent with any other pages.

Actually, an unaltered document is one that contains no erasures, no additions, and no substituted pages. To establish this situation in a positive and definite manner involves considering a great number of factors. There may be some instances even after considering all the elements in which the examiner is unable to say positively that the document is unaltered, but he can certainly point to the preponderance of the evidence that is inconsistent with any change. Thus, the physical facts found within the document itself many times govern just how positively this question can be answered.

Conclusions

Regardless of how a document is altered—whether it is by erasing, by blotting out, or by insertion of new matter—it is vital to those who stand to be defrauded that all of the evidence contained within the document itself be brought to light. The extent to which this internal evidence can be extracted has been indicated, and the limitations frankly discussed. Despite occasional inadequacies, these techniques are more often potent tools by which fraud can be revealed, and in a number of problems, by which the facts can be set forth.

The need to establish that a document has not been altered may involve a complex study. There is no single, simple test. All potential tests for showing that something has been erased, added, or modified in anyway must be applied. When the combined results reveal no change, it can be stated that the document is unaltered.

5

Damaged Documents

Documents are susceptible to injury through carelessness, accident, or deliberate action. In the course of time a wide variety of questions may arise from these causes. Can a water-soaked document be restored or read? Can light-faded ink be intensified? How can stains be removed? Can torn scraps of paper be reconstructed into their original form? Are charred remains of important documents of any worth? How can we establish what they were and what they contained? These questions are diverse, but they have a single motivation, the desire or need to reclaim what appears to have been lost.

As a general rule little can be done to restore the document completely to its original condition, but even in what may appear to be a hopeless situation, the original contents can sometimes be accurately deciphered. This is particularly true in extreme cases like charred papers or serious water obliterations. Let us consider in more detail each of the questions that have been raised.

Damage and Obliteration by Water

One significant advantage of ball point pens is that the conventional inks for them are at most only slightly soluble in water. While in some cases the writing may become smeared or weakened when subjected to long water soaking, it is not entirely obliterated. Weak writing can be intensified photographically if necessary. Since the soaking process normally destroys or seriously weakens the writing impressions or embossing often encountered with this class of writing instrument, study or intensification of these traces cannot be of help if the ball point pen writing has been virtually obliterated.

Fluid inks, on the other hand, can be completely obliterated by soaking in water; fountain pen inks and inks of many felt or fiber tip pens are of this class. Floods, roof and plumbing leaks, and other causes of accidental water soaking of a document, especially when the document has remained in the water for an extended period of time, can remove most of the visible writing. However, with some fluid inks there are visible traces left in the paper. At times even the paper base is weakened or seriously damaged (Figure 5.1).

Proceeding on the assumption that the paper itself has not been seriously affected—for if it has, little could be done toward recovering the lost contents—partial decipherment and occasionally nearly complete restoration may be possible. The mode of attack and the probability of success depends to a large extent on the class of ink involved and the degree of obliteration. The techniques and limitations set forth in the earlier discussion of erased ink writing also apply to these problems. Well-oxidized blue-black fluid ink can to some extent withstand extended soaking, and reagents that combine with the iron residue can intensify the remaining writing. In most instances, dye inks are entirely lost, except for those that contain a fluorescent additive[1] (Figure 5.2). In these instances ultraviolet photography may allow extensive decipherment of the document (Figure 5.3).

Light-Faded Inks

Light affects various writing substances in different ways. Certain poorer quality synthetic dye inks and ball point pen inks may fade through long exposure to light, although most modern inks are relatively lightfast. Others, such as carbon and record typewriting inks, remain virtually unchanged. Therefore the length of exposure that brings about a given degree of fading is also closely associated with the particular dyes of the ink. The result of fading is not unlike a chemical erasure, and decipherment or restoration follows a procedure identical to that for treating erased writing (Figure 5.4). Unless completely obliterated, an extremely rare occurrence, some degree of decipherment is always possible.[2]

---

[1]In February 1955 the Shaeffer Ink Company added a fluorescent additive, RC 35, to their washable fluid inks. While erasing and water soaking destroyed the visible ink, it had little effect on the additive, which could be easily read under ultraviolet illumination.

[2]Fading of a synthetic dye writing ink to the point that it is completely obliterated is rare. The exposure time even in strong sunlight would at a minimum have to be several months or longer. This same condition holds true with ball pen inks.

An unknown accident victim was successfully identified by deciphering an obliterated tailor's label in his coat. In this case, wear and dirt caused the obliteration. M. Edwin O'Neill, "Restoration of Faded Writing—Identification of a Body by Means of a Tailor's Label," *Journal of Criminal Law and Criminology* 30 (1939): 420.

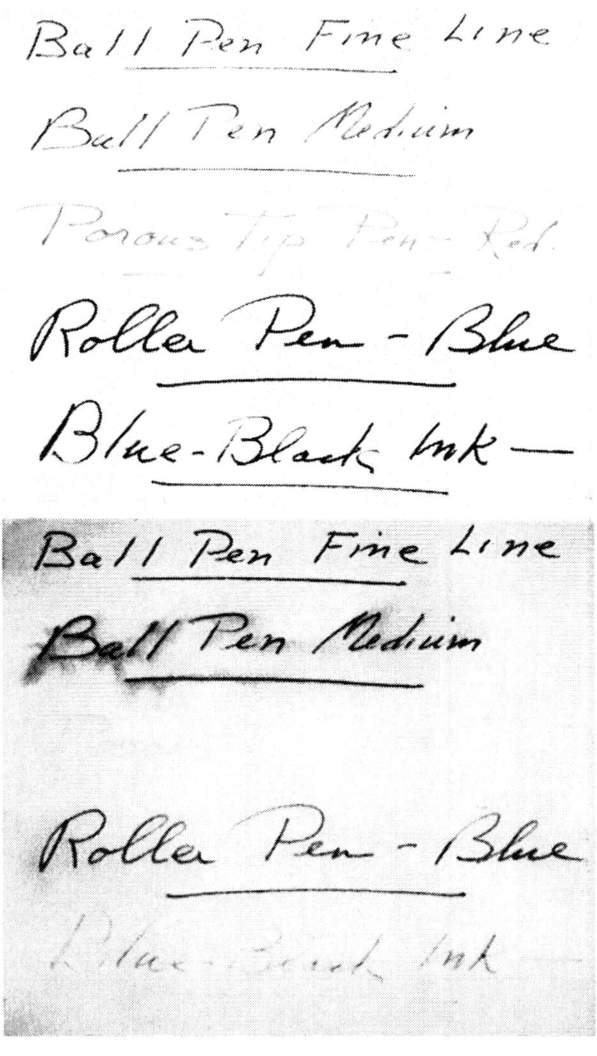

Figure 5.1. At top are shown several commonly used writing instruments as they were prepared for testing. Below is the effect on the ink of soaking for several hours in a pan of water. Some intensification of the writing was accomplished photographically. The first two ball point pen inks show that some ball point pen inks are more resistant to water than others. The porous tip pen ink was almost completely lost, as was the iron-based blue-black ink. The heavy stroke of the roller pen was weakened. The inks of these pens and porous tip pens are similar, but the heavier ink stroke of the roller writer probably affected the results.

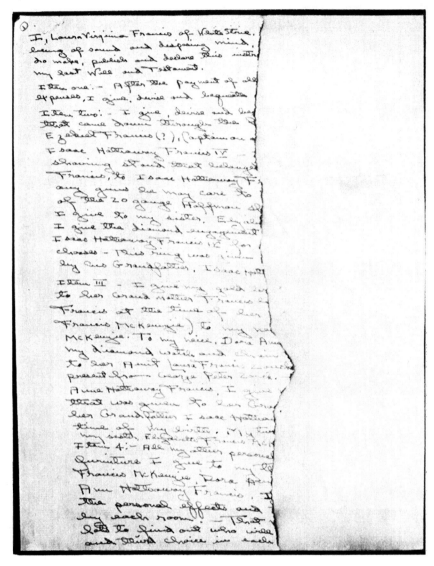

Figure 5.2. One of the pages of the will of Laura Virginia Francis as it was submitted for examination. It was written with green fountain pen ink. How the water obliteration of the right-hand side of the page had occurred was not known. The will had been found in the decedent's writing desk. All pages were damaged to the same degree and in the same area.

Figure 5.3. A portion of one page of the Francis will as it appeared under ultraviolet light. The will had been written with Sheaffer green ink with the fluorescent additive, RC 35. It was possible after extended study to decipher most of the original contents of this document. Decipherment of green washable ink would have been possible only with an ink containing a fluorescent additive.

Figure 5.4. At top is a portion of a testimonial scroll written with a black dye ink. The fading was the result of long exposure to daylight as it hung in the owner's office.

Below is the same area photographed under ultraviolet radiation. In this it was possible to decipher the entire contents and to restore the document.

Stained Documents

Documents may become accidentally stained or damaged by innumerable substances. Among the more common are inks, paints, greases, and oils. Many stains disfigure the document but leave it readable so that there is no particular need to eliminate them. Others obliterate portions, or seriously reduce the value of the document, making it necessary to remove or penetrate them. Certain stains can be removed by careful application of proper chemical reagents; others can be penetrated or eliminated in a photograph using techniques described in

Chapter 3 in connection with smeared-over writing. Of course, if chemicals are to be employed, the reagents must eliminate the staining material only without affecting the writing agent or leaving new stains.

A word of caution is in order at this point. If chemicals are applied to an important document, this should be done by a qualified document examiner or forensic chemist. Treatment by well-meaning amateurs or the use of "home remedies" can easily cause more serious, irreparable damage than the original stains. As a further precaution, the best possible photograph should be made of the document before any chemical treatment is undertaken. Thus, an accurate record of the document is available should the attempt to remove the stains cause further damage.

Torn Documents

Fragmentary bits of paper, the remnants of a torn document, need not be considered lost evidence. With patience and perseverance they can be reassembled and the document reconstructed. Experience with these problems is not always requisite, although it certainly has the advantage of pointing the way to shortcuts that speed the reassembling process.

The reconstructions simply consist of fitting together the numerous irregularly shaped pieces, not unlike solving a jigsaw puzzle. This is at best a slow and tedious procedure. Knowledge of how fragments tend to become grouped when papers are torn may be of assistance in reassembling, but this is possible only if the pieces are found bunched together and no previous attempt has been made to reassemble. In these instances the field investigator can be of greatest assistance by keeping the fragments together just as they were found.

The proof that parts were once a single whole is, as a rule, quite obvious once they are fitted together. When it becomes important, however, to establish without doubt that a single piece was torn from a document, a detailed study must be made of the serrations and projections along the torn edge, fitting the edges of the two pieces together very carefully.[3] Enlarged photographs and low-power microscopic study can establish conclusively that the two were actually once a whole. Obviously, the value of this evidence is greatly influenced by the facts surrounding the document being reconstructed, but to the police and law enforcement agencies in particular these techniques may frequently be of vital assistance (Figure 5.5).

---

[3]M. Edwin O'Neill, "Matching of a Torn One Dollar Note in a Robbery Case," *Journal of Criminal Law and Criminology* 30 (1940): 941–942.

Figure 5.5. Fragments of torn paper found in a stove during a police gambling raid were fitted together and identified as a policy slip. Study of the matching torn edges and the continuation of writing and folds across the tears established that the four fragments were part of the same original slip.

Charred Documents

Among the most phenomenal aspects of the field of document examination is the photographic decipherment of a charred document. When to all outward appearances the document is completely lost, when it is nothing but a black, charred sheet, it seems almost incredible that anyone should even propose that decipherment might be possible. Certainly it seems absurd to assert that a photographic copy can be made that has the appearance of one prepared prior to the charring. Yet research has disclosed a simple technique by which this can be done. A recently charred paper is placed between two unexposed photographic plates. The three are then tightly bound together to assure tight contact between them, and stowed away in a light-tight container for about 15 days.[4] At the end of this time the plates are unwrapped and developed in the normal way, producing a photographic negative of the original material.[5] Photographic prints from this negative have clarity and closely resemble a photograph made from the original document.

Other methods have been devised by various workers and include photographing with ultraviolet radiation, infrared films, and oblique or reflected light.[6] None of these methods holds any advantage over the contact photographic technique as far as the final decipherment is concerned, and some are inferior. Two chemical methods have been proposed, one using a chloral hydrate solution,[7] and the second a mixture of glycerine and alcohol.[8] Several of these methods may lead to a saving of time, and all can be used at any time after the document was charred. Unfortunately, though, results are not always certain. Nevertheless, with the variety of techniques available, charred documents as a rule can be successfully deciphered.[9]

Handling a charred document is very troublesome, and if done carelessly, can limit or preclude decipherment. The charred sheets are extremely brittle and easily break or crumble into small fragments. As long as the original sheet remains intact, and even if it breaks into several relatively large parts, there is a good chance that a satisfactory decipherment can be obtained, but once it is shattered into small bits there is little likelihood that the pieces can be reconstructed. Therefore, before attempting to handle a charred document, the inexperienced worker should study the section in Chapter 15 regarding the handling of this class of documents. Furthermore, it is always well to consult

---

[4]The period of 15 days must be considered as average, the exposure time varying from problem to problem and based upon slow-speed emulsions. Exposure of the charred documents to the photographic emulsion apparently slowly fogs the plate, but this fogging is retarded wherever the ink or other types of writing appear on the original document. See John F. Tyrrell, "The Decipherment of Charred Documents," *Journal of Criminal Law and Criminology* 30 (1939): 236–242; and Raymond Davis, "Action of Charred Paper on the Photographic Plate and a Method of Deciphering Charred Records," *Scientific Papers of the Bureau of Standards* 18 (1922): 445–450. Tyrrell advocates treating the charred document with an exposure to ultraviolet rays to improve the final results.

[5]A photographic positive is obtained when films are used instead of plates. (Tyrrell, "The Decipherment of Charred Documents.")

[6]Tyrrell, "The Decipherment of Charred Documents"; Julius Grant, "Decipherment of Charred Documents," *The Analyst* 67 (1941): 42–47.

[7]W. D. Taylor and J. J. Walls, " A New Method for the Decipherment of Charred Documents," *Nature (London)* 7 (1941): 417. Some workers, including David A. Black, "Decipherment of Charred Documents," *Journal of Criminal Law and Criminology* 38 (1948): 542–546, have reported indifferent results with this method.

[8]Black, "Decipherment of Charred Documents," pp. 542–546.

[9]For an excellent survey article, see Donald Doud, "Charred Documents, Their Handling and Decipherment," *Journal of Criminal Law, Criminology and Police Science* 43 (1953): 812–826. A. Lucas, *Forensic Chemistry and Scientific Criminal Investigation,* 4th ed. (London: Edward Arnold, 1946), pp. 126–131, describes methods of handling this very fragile evidence and surveys methods of decipherment.

a qualified document examiner or to seek the assistance of one who has had experience in handling charred papers.

Before leaving this subject we should consider briefly a second limiting factor, the element of time. Research shows that the best decipherments by the contact photographic method are obtained with documents that are treated very soon after charring. The field investigator, who generally determines when a problem is to be submitted to the laboratory, should keep this fact in mind so that unnecessary delay on his part does not hamper the technical work.

Conclusions

It is reassuring to know that steps can be taken to reconstruct or decipher a document that has been seriously damaged. Obviously, every precaution should be taken with important documents by keeping them in fire- and moisture-proof recepticles in order to prevent accidental damage, but these steps are not always carried out. For this reason, and because of the need for action after deliberate destruction, methods have been devised to salvage something from the wreckage.

6

Accidental Markings and Impressions on a Document

The preparation of a document represents a series of planned acts, but at times important elements become part of the document purely by chance and not through the premeditated design of either those who prepared the document or those who subsequently handled it. In this way latent fingerprints, writing offsets from some other document, embossings from writing strokes that are not part of the page in question, and traces of foreign matter with which the document has been in contact find their way onto it. More than likely their presence is entirely unknown to the document's author, but under propitious circumstances these chance markings and additions can play a significant role.

Latent Fingerprints

Latent (invisible) fingerprints are placed upon papers simply by handling and remain invisible until chemically developed. The ease with which they are added to a paper and their invisibility are definite assets, especially in criminal investigations. If it is possible to develop an identifiable print to be compared with those of a suspect, a very positive form of evidence may be forthcoming. With some types of criminal investigation, such as stolen checks cashed with a disguised, fraudulent endorsement, such a print can assume significant importance.

The most common method today of developing fingerprints on paper is the ninhydrin technique.[1] This reagent may develop older latent fingerprints for which other reagents are ineffective. Ninhydrin has a

---

[1] Andre A. Moenssens, *Fingerprint Techniques* (Philadelphia, Chilton, 1971), pp. 122–126.

serious drawback when the documents may need to be subjected to other types of examinations, such as the identification of signatures and writing or the determination of possible alterations and erasures. In the first place, the solution stains the document. With the usual method of preparing the ninhydrin solution, ball pen and some typewriter inks can be seriously weakened or obliterated. However, the solutions can be prepared using a nonpolar solution of ninhydrin in place of the usual polar solutions.[2] Damage to ink is minimized with this solution, but writing indentations and some trace evidence may still be lost. Therefore, with some types of document problems, there is a definite need to establish whether fingerprints should be searched for first or whether document examinations should be carried out.

There are other techniques for developing fingerprints on paper. Iodine fuming is commonly used and will develop very fresh prints on paper. It has the advantage that if no prints are developed other methods can subsequently be used, since the iodine stains will dissipate. In fact, the developed prints will fade and should be photographed promptly. When latent prints are several days old, iodine fuming is generally unsuccessful.

Another effective technique involves the use of silver nitrate solutions.[3] The entire document is soaked in silver nitrate, dried, and exposed to strong light. The prints appear as a black image.

Latent prints can also be developed with osmic acid fumes.[4] Osmic acid is toxic, so that the document must be treated under a fuming hood or with very good ventilation. The latent prints develop into a dark permanent impression. Again, each of these methods, like ninhydrin, seriously discolors the document and can preclude other kinds of examinations.

Moenssens points out that neither iodine, silver nitrate, nor ninhydrin is successful under all circumstances. He recommends in difficult cases using all three in the sequence iodine, ninhydrin, and silver nitrate, since the later tests are then not precluded by the earlier ones.[5]

There are those who suggest the use of special powders on the document in a dusting technique similar to that used in investigations at

---

[2]For details of procedure in preparing ninhydrin solutions and particularly for the preparation of a nonpolar ninhydrin solution, see David A. Crown, "The Development of Latent Fingerprints with Ninhydrin," *Journal of Criminal Law, Criminology and Police Science* 60 (1969): 258–264. A recently suggested method uses fluorisol as a solvent for ninhydrin: P. E. Blume, "The Ninhydrin Fluorisol Solution," *Identification News* 28 (1978): 6–7.

[3]The detailed methods of developing latent fingerprints on paper are thoroughly discussed by M. E. O'Neill, "Decipherment of Latent Fingerprints on Paper," *Journal of Criminal Law and Criminology* 28 (1937): 432–441.

[4]See O'Neill, "Decipherment of Latent Fingerprints," p. 439, and Moenssens, *Fingerprint Techniques*, p. 127.

[5]Moenssens, *Fingerprint Techniques*, p. 125.

the scene of a crime, but powders have been found to be less effective than the chemical techniques already discussed.

Whenever a document is to be treated for fingerprints, a top-quality, accurately scaled photograph should be made of it so that the handwriting and typewriting that appear on the document can be studied and identified if questions later arise. All treatments for the latent fingerprints on paper raise the risk of damaging or obscuring writing details, no matter how carefully performed.

The ease with which latent fingerprints can unconsciously be deposited on the paper presents a constant threat of the ultimate confusion or destruction of those left by the writer himself. Each person who handles the paper can leave his latent impressions. One or two of these may confuse the issue, and with repeated handling, the numerous prints may even obliterate the original ones. Therefore, because of this danger, as well as because of the constantly decreasing probability of development with older prints, papers that are to be treated for latent fingerprints should be handled as little as possible and with utmost care[6] and should be submitted for technical examination as soon as possible.

When fingerprints are developed, they may serve as a positive means of identification, but this potentiality remains unrealized many times because of circumstances surrounding the investigation. In the first place, it must be clearly understood that for the developed print to be of any value, it has to be a sharp, identifiable impression, not a fragmentary smudge or blur containing no clearcut pattern.[7] Fingerprints on a document may vary from fragments of a full print to two or three finger impressions. Seldom, if ever, are a complete set of prints from the ten fingers found, so that it is not possible to search a standard fingerprint file to identify the originator;[8] thus, until a set of finger-

---

[6]In handling a sheet of paper that may contain latent fingerprints, one should wear rubber gloves or the sheet should be picked up with tweezers or tongs. If neither is available, the document should be carefully gripped at the edges or corners. The document should immediately be placed in an envelope and delivered therein to the laboratory for treatment at the earliest moment. Transparent plastic envelopes are available in numerous sizes so that one may be selected in which the document can be opened out flat. In this way its contents can be studied without danger of destroying the latent prints.

[7]An identifiable fingerprint impression shows the ridge pattern clearly and is generally regarded as one containing ten or more points of identification. These points are a part of the ridge patterns reproduced in the impressions. The common identifying characteristics are forks, ending ridges, islands, and enclosures. See H. H. Wilder and B. Wentworth, *Personal Identification* (Boston: Richard G. Badger, 1918), or Moenssen, *Fingerprint Techniques*, for an authoritative discussion of fingerprint identification.

[8]The standard fingerprint identification files are cataloged by means of a formula derived from the patterns of all ten fingers. While a complete set of ten latent fingerprints can be checked against these files, no formula for entering the file can be determined from impressions of two or three fingers. Modern police departments also maintain single fingerprint files of certain types of serious criminal offenders, but this group is limited in number, so that the files are of little use in the more common anonymous letter problems.

prints can be taken from a particular suspect, developed latent prints have little immediate worth despite their high potential value.

Writing Offsets

When two papers come in contact with each other while the fluid ink on one is still damp, a writing offset may be produced on the other. Storage in damp condition can also produce offsets from water soluble inks. To decipher and interpret correctly what the offset represents stands as a challenge to those interested in determining the facts. The full force of this challenge can be best appreciated when it is realized that these traces are generally very slight fragments of writing. In some cases the offset proves after accurate decipherment to have only minor significance because of the particular circumstance of the case, but there can be instances in which the interpretation becomes forceful evidence linking two documents to a common source.

With weak traces, which are the general rule, writing offsets must be intensified by various means, and the image must be reversed, for an offset is always a mirror image. Different techniques of document photography combining control of filters, lighting, films, and developing procedures may intensify these slight traces, but it is far from an automatic process. Each problem requires protracted study and may require repetition of the same method with slight modification to achieve the best decipherment.

Impressed Writing

Fragments and traces of impressed writing—those small, virtually invisible indentations pressed into the paper by the force of writing on a sheet above—need only discovery and decipherment to assume their proper place in relation to the other elements of the document. Under favorable circumstances these hidden strokes can change the document entirely from harmless to incriminating evidence or from an anonymous to a definite source. The impressions are not confined to handwriting alone, but can just as well be indented typewritten characters in a former backing sheet (Figure 6.1) or on a sheet of carbon paper.[9] All originate in a similar way, and all are subject to the same methods of decipherment and interpretation.

Whenever two or more sheets of paper are stacked, traces of the writing executed on the top page tend to become embossed in the sheets below. The depth of these embossings, and thus the clarity of

---

[9]See "Carbon Paper" (Chapter 3) for further consideration of impressed writing on carbon sheets.

Figure 6.1. Impressed typewriting in a backing sheet revealed the contents of a compromising letter. Decipherment was achieved with a series of oblique light photographs. The salutation "My dearest Jinx" in an alleged business letter to a secretary had aroused the curiosity of the writer's wife.

the impressed writing, depends basically on the pressure of the writing strokes, the number of stacked sheets, the nature of the backing below the papers, the thickness and kind of paper, and the sharpness and firmness of the writing instrument. Depending on these factors, the amount of impressed writing may vary from virtually a whole document to a few weak fragments of letters or words, and its legibility from almost that of the original to a mere indecipherable presence. The sheet immediately below the page of writing obviously bears the clearest imprint, but impressions can occasionally be made out in the second and lower sheets (Figure 6.2).

Not all impressions can be deciphered. Weakness of the basic impression is a contributing factor, but it is not the only one to complicate the problem. Overlapping impressions from writing on several pages, all of which have lain over the sheet under investigation, can greatly restrict findings. The visible writing on the document itself may also interfere. The impressed writing is in reality a series of small grooves or creases that, when located in the same area as a slight crease or fold, makes reading difficult and may curtail the scope of the findings. Since these interfering folds and creases can be introduced with excessive handling of the document, every precaution must be taken to limit

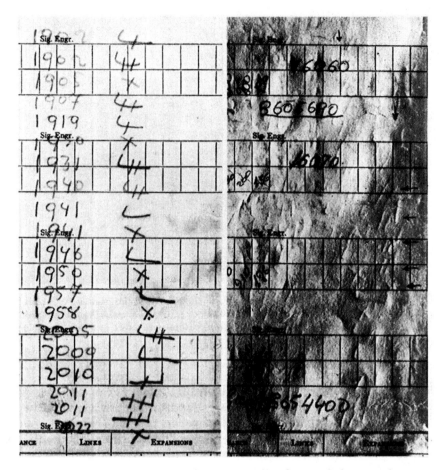

Figure 6.2. Writing indentations on the page preceding the record of suspected maneuvers of the ship that had cut a 20-ft gash in the side of another vessel (right-hand section above) led to proof that a page had been torn from the log and rewritten. The left-hand section shows a portion of the rewritten page with the highly suspicious entries 2011 and 2022, which indicate the engines were running full speed in reverse for 11 minutes, long enough for the ship concerned to have been backing away from the vessel it struck.

Indentations of the maneuvers shown from the suspected page are found in a column running through the last 0's of the pencil-written figures on the preceding page (indicated by an arrow at the top of the illustration). A series of maneuvering symbols is found to the right of this column indicated by a second vertical arrow and five horizontal ones.

handling and to prevent wrinkling or folding once the presence of these traces is discovered.[10]

---

[10]Any person handling documents suspected of containing impressed writing should be thoroughly familiar with the proper manner of handling of these documents, as set forth in Chapter 15.

At times the impressions can be clearly read by allowing light to strike obliquely from one side, but more generally the decipherment requires critical control of the side lighting combined with specialized photography not only to read the impressions but also to record and interpret them for the layman. Occasionally, especially with typewriting indentations, fuming with iodine may intensify the indentations. One examiner suggested transferring the impressions onto a sheet of transparent thermoplastic from which they can be read or photographed.[11]

A group of English forensic scientists has recently developed the equipment and technique for producing an electrostatic image of writing impressions. The document in question is covered with a polymer film held in tight contact, charged by a corona wire, and sprayed with a toner used in electrostatic copying to develop the image of the indented strokes. The image can be fixed by covering with a transparent adhesive plastic sheet or by photographing. The author's claim of superior results to oblique light photography has been substantiated by a number of other workers throughout the world.[12]

Foreign Traces

Small deposits or traces of many different substances may be found on documents and may aid in reconstructing their history. Many of these are placed there purely through chance contacts with foreign objects during the preparation and subsequent handling or storing of the document. Thus stains of a similar pattern running across several pages can help to show that they have been a unit for some time. Mold on paper is an indication of age. Carbon deposits in and around the outline of a signature cast strong suspicion on its genuineness (Figure 6.3).[13] With an anonymous letter, small traces of lipstick under the sealed flap or stamp point toward a woman writer. Paint, rust, grease, and many other stains are encountered from time to time in document examination. By learning what kind of stain is present, it may then be possible to arrive at its cause and significance.[14]

---

[11]The use of thermo-plastics to pick up writing impressions is described by Anthony Longhetti and P. L. Kirk "Restoration and Decipherment of Erasures and Obliterated or Indented Writing," *Journal of Criminal Law and Criminology* 41 (1950): 519–522.

[12]D. M. Ellen, D. J. Foster, and D. J. Morantz, "Use of Electrostatic Imaging in the Detection of Indented Impressions," *Forensic Science International* 15 (1980): 53–60.

[13]The significance of carbon deposits adjacent to the writing strokes of a signature suspected of being a traced forgery is discussed at length in conjunction with the detection of forgery in Chapter 9.

[14]In his decision denying a new trial in U. S. v. Hiss, 107 F. Supp. 128, 1952, Judge Goddard commented on the reported similarity between paint splatters on the wrapper of papers produced by Chambers and paint in the dumbwaiter shaft where, Chambers had testified, the papers were stored. This evidence was further proof of the authenticity of the documents and corroborated Chamber's testimony.

Figure 6.3. A photomicrograph reveals carbon deposits along the edge of an ink stroke in a forged signature. The heavy dark area running through the center of the illustration is the ink stroke. Here the fluid ink penetrated the paper and stained most of the fibers. Arrows point to some of the carbon fragments wedged into the microscopic crevices between intersecting paper fibers. The inert carbon did not penetrate these fibers. The limited amount of carbon present shows that the traced skeleton outline had been erased.

Conclusions

The fact that marks and traces have been deposited on a document by chance does not necessarily lessen their value; rather, circumstances peculiar to the particular problem are the controlling factors. Their recognition and identification through careful study and treatment, however, is essential if the investigator is to reveal facts that, weighed in relation to other aspects of the document, determine the true importance of the evidence.

7

Additional Clues
for the Investigator

The technical study of a document can assist the field investigator in directing his efforts. Although some of the findings considered in this chapter are only indicative, they can nevertheless be of assistance early in the investigation of the source of anonymous letters and other writings. The decipherment of illegible writing, facts derived from "blank" papers, and recognition of the development of secret inks may at times have high value. The problems arise infrequently, yet these special studies may reduce the work of the field investigator.

Indicative Information

Information derived from anonymous letters, even though not of sufficient force to serve as evidence in a court of law, may have unique value when properly employed by the investigator. The handwriting, its arrangement on the sheet, and the actual wording of the letter can help indicate the writer's nationality, degree of education, general age group, sex, and at times even occupation. These findings should not be confused with a graphological analysis of writing—character and personality reading based on the individual's handwriting, an art whose scientific basis is not clearly established. The characteristics under consideration are derived from the writing habits and styles of certain age, national, social, and occupational groups. This class of information must be regarded as at best an approximation and is fundamentally an investigative tool, not a proof of fact.

Writing systems are as nationalistic as languages. A person who received elementary education in a foreign country retains a foreign "accent" in his writing years after leaving that native land. Once in a while his children may acquire some of these characteristics through imitation. As a result, the presence of foreign writing characteristics is a strong indication of foreign background, and particularly of foreign education. Writing systems are very similar in some groups of countries, just as there are strong similarities among languages. As a consequence, while a writer may have a foreign influence in his writing indicative of an area such as central Europe, it may be difficult to designate exactly his country of origin (Figure 7.1).

In the United States there have been definite periods in which certain writing systems were taught.[1] The influence of the system on an individual's writing may serve as a fairly accurate gauge of his age. This influence must be interpreted loosely, since there is no sharp line of demarcation when one system stopped and another was adopted.

Feebleness due to age and immaturity in writing may under particular circumstances assist in estimating the writer's age, but here again these factors are subject to serious limitations. It is sometimes difficult to distinguish between immaturity and lack of education or writing experience and between the effects of serious illness and weakness due to age.

Determination of the writer's sex from handwriting is much more difficult than is generally recognized. Although certain handwriting contains strong indications of the writer's sex, some is completely void of any suggestions. Not all "masculine writing" belongs to men or all "feminine writing" to women. The great mass of writing shows little or no indication of the sex of its writer. The color of ink and paper, the phraseology, and the selection of words may reveal the writer's sex more clearly than the size, slant, or design of letters.

Certain occupations or professions tend to develop habits in writing. Elementary school teachers have for the most part neat, legible handwriting, closely imitating copybook style; draftsmen may reveal their occupation through their numeral styles or particular letter forms; many accountants have small, precise handwriting;[2] and other occupational groups also have writing peculiar to that profession or trade. These signs must of course be interpreted with caution because within each group there is the exceptional person who fails to conform, and many groups have no occupational habits.

Thus, no claim can be made that such a determination of nationality, age, sex, or occupation is infallible. At times apparently strong indi-

---

[1] A concise and accurate history of American writing systems is found in A. S. Osborn, *Questioned Documents*, 2nd ed. (Albany: Boyd, 1929), pp. 167–204. Since publication of this text, a manuscript style of handwriting has been introduced into the primary grades of some school systems and is undoubtably leaving its mark on the mature handwriting of those who have received this early training.

[2] See Osborn, *Questioned Documents*, p. 139.

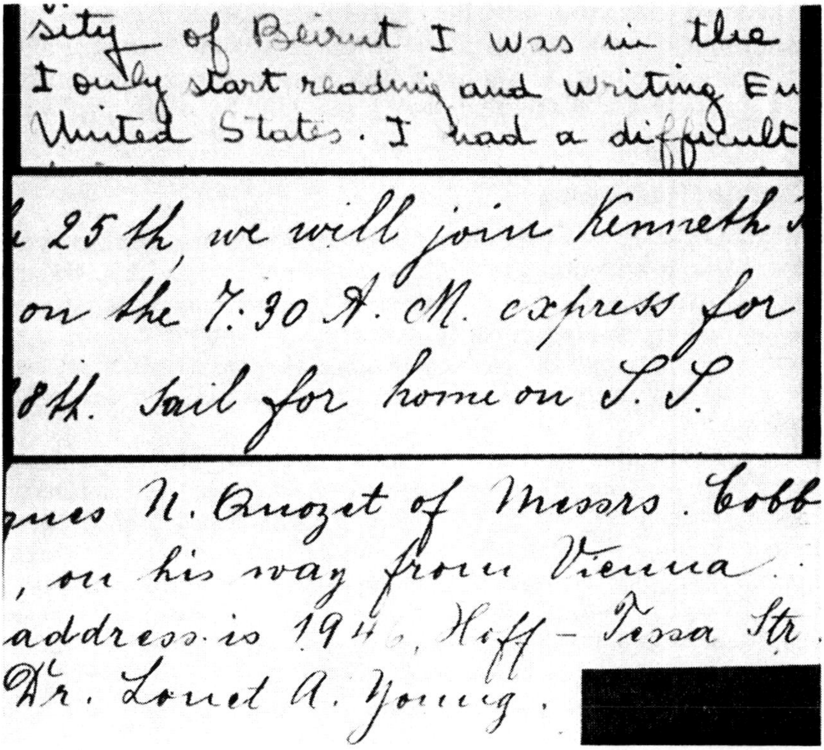

Figure 7.1. Writing systems of other countries use letters forms different from those in American writing.

The upper sample was prepared by a person educated in France. The a is a typical systematic form. The body of the letter is written continuously and is closed at the upper left by the pen swing back to the left in a counterclockwise direction. ("Was" in the first line is a clear example.) The connecting stroke to the following letter is a separate stroke starting at the upper right of the letter.

The central specimen is that of a German educated writer. The capital letter forms and the manner of crossing and connecting the t to the next letter are derived from typical patterns of German writing systems.

The lower handwriting was written by a person educated in Italy. The design of the e is characteristic of some European systems. The a is formed in the same manner as in the French writing and shows that some forms are common to writing systems of several neighboring countries.

Naturalized Americans who came to this country as adults generally retain foreign "accents" in their writing.

cations can be in error. Still, the information is better than none, and the document examiner can generally advise how much trust is to be placed in the findings. Coordinated with other information in the case, here is an added tool, one that has not generally been fully exploited.

Illegible Handwriting

Just what constitutes illegible writing varies with the opinion of the person who is attempting to read it and his familiarity with it. Writing that on first introduction is extremely illegible may after repeated association become merely difficult reading. Probably one of the most famous penmen was Horace Greeley, whose handwriting to many people is entirely without meaning yet to his associates conveyed its message.[3]

To read illegible specimens requires principally patience and perseverance. No special devices are available to assist, but familiarity with writing in general and the variant forms that are encountered from individual to individual may give inspiration as to the correct interpretation of the marks. The general context of continuous subject matter, such as a letter, may assist. Even illegible writing should make sense when deciphered. More carefully written specimens of the individual's writing may reveal further clues, but as a rule, extended study of the illegible specimen is the only mode of solution (Figure 7.2).

Blank Papers

At first the thought of a blank paper forming the basis of evidence or even serving as a lead in an investigation may seem preposterous. Yet these papers are not necessarily without content. A number of the factors discussed in earlier chapters are contained in a blank paper just as in any other document and need only be related to the problem at hand.

The importance of a blank paper depends on how it is involved in the case. Three common classes of information may be derived from this kind of document: the source of the paper, the identities of those who have handled it, and any hidden information it contains. Where the paper originated may be disclosed by its composition or watermark. A blank paper might have a torn, cut, or perforated edge that matches

---

[3]This and other illegible writing is discussed and illustrated by D. T. Ames, *Ames on Forgery* (New York: Ames-Rollinson, 1900), pp. 23–25.

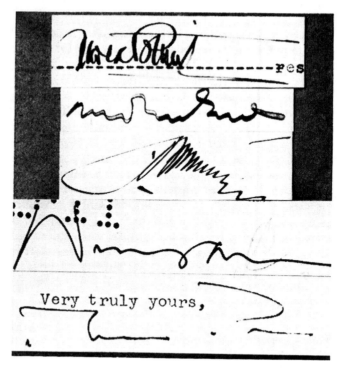

Figure 7.2. Many signatures assume varying degrees of illegibility. Five extreme examples are shown. Some writers consider it necessary to make their signature illegible to prevent forgery, but actually, the highly skillful, legible signature is by far more difficult to imitate.

The top signature played a central role in a will contest. Who was this witness? Despite extensive work by two document examiners and painstaking field investigation, no satisfactory solution could be found, and probate of the will was denied. The last signature to this exhibit was written by one of the attorneys who presented the problem.

the edge of a piece in the possession of a suspect. Papers that appear blank to the man on the street may actually contain latent fingerprints, secret inks (which will be discussed in the following section), inconspicuous writing offsets or stains, and erased, faded, or impressed writing. These elements when revealed give meaning and value to a "blank" paper and may even serve as physical evidence in a court of law.

Forewarned that a blank paper may contain evidence of as much importance as a written document, an alert investigator can be on the lookout for any unmarked paper and submit it for technical study whenever it would seem appropriate. Thus evidence and information that might otherwise be lost can be used effectively.

Secret Inks

Secret or invisible inks have been known since ancient times, and the basic materials for their manufacture range from such commonplace items as lemon juice and milk to very complex chemical preparations.[4] Some can be *developed*, that is, made visible, in a number of ways; others are compounded so that they can be read only after the paper has been treated with several specific solutions applied in a particular order. When the writing material is known to the recipient, the particular method of development or order of applying reagents may then be employed. When secret inks of unknown composition are suspected, this cannot be done, yet it may become important to know whether a suspected document contains secret ink writing and, if so, what the message is. Fortunately, the more common invisible inks employed today in all but espionage activities can usually be developed or otherwise deciphered by oblique lighting, ultraviolet light, iodine fumes, or one of several universal chemical developers.[5] There are inks that cannot be developed in these ways, but the methods are effective with the majority that are apt to be encountered in a criminal investigation or legal problem.

Ballot Frauds

Election frauds have been revealed and the guilty individuals brought to justice through the skills of the document examiner. In these problems his work can show how fraudulently marked ballots and tally sheets were prepared.[6]

Ballot-box stuffing is a well-known means of controlling elections. In doing this a few people must mark a large number of ballots. Generally, the ballots are not unstacked before being marked, with the result that impressions of marks from the top ballot are found on the one immediately below, an impossible condition when a voter marks his ballot legally and individually. The combination of the impressed mark, the pencil mark, and the similarity of a number of crossmarks

---

[4]D. N. Carvalho, *Forty Centuries of Inks* (New York: Banks Law Publ. Co., 1904), p. 135, refers to remarks of the Roman writers Ovid and Pliny concerning invisible inks. The first recorded use of secret inks in connection with military activities apparently occurred early in the American Revolution. S. C. Brown and E. W. Stein, "Benjamin Thompson and the First Secret-Ink Letter of the American Revolution," *Journal of Criminal Law and Criminology* 40 (1950): 627–636.

[5]A. Lucas, *Forensic Chemistry and Scientific Criminal Investigation*, 4th ed. (London: Arnold, 1946), pp. 99–105; C. A. Mitchell, *Documents and Their Scientific Examination*, reissue (London: Griffin, 1935), Chap. 8, pp. 153–165; and C. A. Mitchell and T. C. Hepworth, *Inks*, 4th ed. (London: Griffin, 1937), pp. 336–341.

[6]The technical methods for revealing election frauds have been set forth by Katherine Keeler, "A Study of Documentary Evidence in Election Frauds," *Journal of Criminal Law and Criminology* 25 (1934): 324–337, and "Documentary Evidence Involving an Election Dispute," *Journal of Criminal Law and Criminology* 27 (1936): 249–262.

in a set of suspicious ballots are all pieces of physical evidence that can prove the fraud.

A second technique is merely to manipulate the tally sheets by adding enough votes to ensure a candidate's election. Of course, the results then have no ballots to substantiate them, which could be established by an independent recount. A study of the tally sheets themselves may reveal the need for such action. A line of tallies marked in the course of regular count have an irregular appearance since the votes are individually recorded from each ballot, tabulating from top to bottom of the sheet opposite the candidates' names. When the time comes to supplement the actual count with a sufficient number of fictitious tallies to ensure victory, the marks are usually added consecutively across the line on which a candidate's name appears. The result is that these tallies have better alignment and a more uniform appearance. Because of these conditions, the false votes stand out from the authentic ones.

Conclusions

The effective development of a questioned document problem involves close cooperation between the field investigator and the document examiner. The problems discussed show how the examiner can assist the investigator with information derived from the physical evidence contained in the documents. The full and effective use of the examiner's findings, which are discussed in subsequent chapters, may only be possible through the teamwork of both parties.

III

DISCOVERY OF FACTS
BY COMPARISON
WITH KNOWN MATERIAL
THE NEED OF COMPARISON

While much can be learned from a study of the questioned document itself—analyzing completely all of its constituent parts—this generally is but a preliminary step. There are many more facts to be discovered. To accomplish this, detailed comparisons must be made between the questioned material and adequate, accurate standards or known specimens. Comparisons are necessary to establish the identity of the writer of disputed matter, to detect forgery or prove a signature genuine, to identify handlettering, or to trace typewriting and other mechanically written documents to their source. The details of solving all these problems vary, but each depends on one fundamental process—careful collation of the known and questioned specimens in order to establish definitely the facts regarding the identity or divergency of their source.

8

Identification of Handwriting

Writing is a conscious act. Still, through repeated use, the actual formation of each letter and word becomes almost automatic, so that the experienced writer concentrates most of his conscious thought on the subject matter rather than on the writing process itself. Thus, writing comes to be made up of innumerable subconscious, habitual patterns, which are as much a part of the individual as any of his personal habits or mannerisms. Writing is more, however, than a set of subconscious habits. It is a living, gradually changing part of the writer and is far from a mechanical reproduction prepared by the complex human mechanism of muscles and nerves that are called into play to produce it. It is influenced by a mental picture of copybook form, modified by individual taste and the writer's ability to imitate that which is in his mind. Physical and mental conditions at the time of writing may affect it. Whether it is a criterion of personality is debatable, but that it is individual to each and every person is an established fact. Therefore, it can be identified, and the identification is based on all the elements that combine to create the individuality.

The factors that identify any person's writing are numerous. Some are more important than others, but conditions surrounding the particular case determine those that are to be given the highest identifying value.

In a problem involving the authorship of handwriting, all characteristics of both the known and unknown specimens must be considered. Basic writing habits common to both must agree if all are the work of the same writer. A single significant difference between the two is a strong indication of two writers, unless this divergency can be logically accounted for by the facts surrounding the preparation of the specimens. Several repeated, fundamental dissimilarities establish without a doubt that two writings are not the work of a single person. Under no circumstances, however, can identity be established by one, two, or even several "unusual" characteristics. Rather, if two writings have been produced by one individual, there must always be a combination of a sufficient number of points of agreement without any fundamental dissimilarities that all chance of accidental coincidence is excluded. Identification rests therefore not alone on a similar combination of identifying attributes—a condition that always must be fulfilled—but also on a coexistant lack of basic divergencies between the questioned and standard writings.

Writing Forms and Qualities

What are the characteristics that serve as the basis of handwriting identification? In the eyes of most laymen letter form is highly prominent, but, while it is certainly worthy of consideration, it is not the entire picture. It might well be compared to the physical appearance of a person—definitely a means of recognition but not a complete description, for regardless of physical appearance each person has typical manners of action and speech that help to identify him. In describing handwriting the qualities of movement are even more essential to accurate identification.

Writing is far from a lifeless form. Every specimen reveals an animation individual to its writer and reflects the pen movements that have produced it. At one extreme is a smooth, continuous, rhythmic, rapidly executed writing, filled with grace and poise, and artistically shaded with points of emphasis, displaying a freedom of motion characteristic of a highly skilled penman (Figure 8.1, bottom). In direct contrast is a hesitant, interrupted, halting, laborious, slowly executed writing with an uncertain hand, showing irregularities typical of one to whom writing is a hard physical or mental task (Figure 8.1, top). There are still other qualities of writing movement. The strokes may be precise or careless, or they may be reworked or retouched in an effort to perfect and improve the legibility (Figure 8.2). Movement of the pen need not begin or terminate at the beginning or ending of a word. With some writers the pen is in motion when it first makes contact with the paper and continues after it is lifted, a condition that is shown in the writing itself. Examination of another class of writing reveals that the pen is carefully placed on the paper before any writing movement is undertaken and remains in contact until after the word was completed. The writing qualities of many, many writers lie between these extremes, and their handwriting displays various degrees and combinations of these qualities.

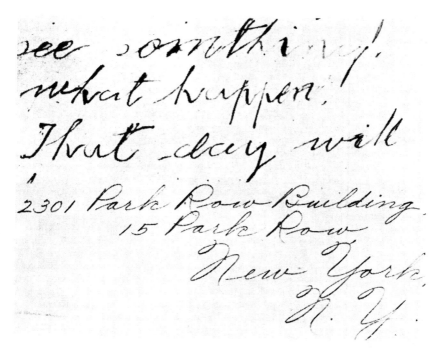

Figure 8.1. Two extremes in writing skills. The near illiterate's labored, clumsy writing (above) is contrasted with the skillful penmanship of a well-trained writer which is marked by freedom, uniformity, and clarity (below).

The animation in writing is closely related to the physical processes involved. Depending on the skill and training of the writer, as well as his natural inclinations, writing is executed by movement of the fingers, the wrist, and the arm, either individually or more generally in varying combinations. There is a relationship between the skill of the writer, the speed of writing, the actual form, and the manner of execution. The slow, measured writing of the beginner, involving a heavy pen pressure, is for the most part produced by unskilled finger movement alone; the rapid, smoothly flowing writing of the skilled penman is accomplished by arm movement tempered with unconscious finger impulses at points of shading or abrupt turns. All finger writing, of course, is not crude, nor is all arm-motion writing highly skilled. Moreover, most writing is not executed by one simple type of movement, for the average writer employs a combination of these movements to achieve his particular quality of writing.

Many writers have very personal habits in the way they hold and handle the writing instrument, which of course may affect the resulting writing. Most modern pens, particularly ball point and soft tip pens,

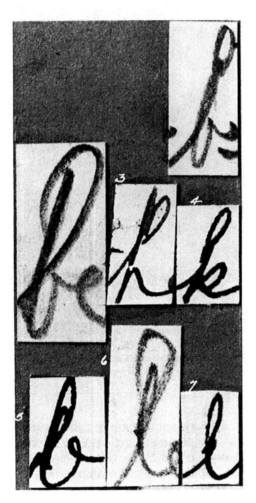

Figure 8.2. Habitual retouching of letters can serve as one point of identification. This writer confined his modifications for the most part to tall letters.

as well as the pencil, may not reveal clearcut evidence as to the angle that the pen makes with the paper and the line of writing; in contrast, the nib pen, especially the semiflexible-point fountain pen, reveals significantly different patterns of shading depending on how its point is held in relation to the paper.[1] With the latter writing instrument, one can recognize unusual habits of pen position, while with the former instruments the cause of the resulting individuality is not always clear.

Some attributes of form are influenced by the writing system that the writer learned; some are the result of individual taste. Handwriting

---

[1] See A. S. Osborn, *Questoned Documents*, 2nd ed. (Albany: Boyd, 1929), pp. 121–123.

is not an inherited trait, although personal skill or lack of coordination may be, but family similarities do sometimes exist in particular forms where one writer has imitated characteristics of another member of the family or even a respected friend or acquaintance. The letters may be angular or symmetrically rounded; they may be tall and slender, or short and squatty. The proportional size of various letters and parts of compound letters, such as k and g, vary among writers; the shapes may be either artistic or grotesque, and the letters may be crowded together or spread well apart depending upon the connecting strokes. Particular letters may be conventional or unusual in style; flourishes and ornamentations are common to some writing. Slant, which may vary between writers from backhand to a sharply inclined forehand slope, can be considered a further element of form. No study of letter form is complete without consideration of all these factors, for together they describe the form of the writing (Figure 8.3).

Figure 8.3. In establishing that the known writer prepared the questioned material, the smooth, uniform, rather skillful writing would be an important consideration. However, individual habits of form are equally important. Note the simplification of the inital f form, omitting the upper loop; the curved back of the h; and the use of the t crossing to connect to the following letter. Many others may be found in this exhibit.

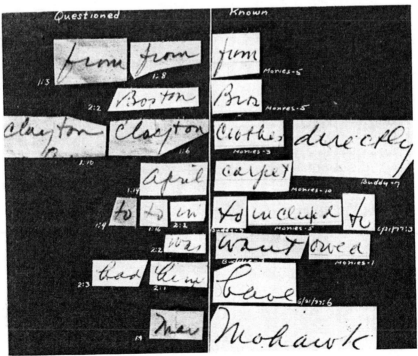

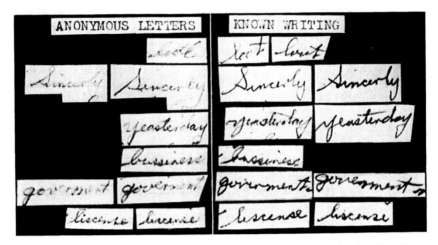

Figure 8.4. All elements of extended writing specimens can be considered in identifying the writer. In this instance the unusual spellings, which are repeated in both the known and questioned writing, together with the highly personalized writing itself, combine to make an impressive identification. The word "loot" in the first line is a misspelling of "lot."

Arrangement of Writing

Whenever identification involves an extended specimen of writing, many factors other than pure handwriting characteristics can and should be considered. The arrangement of the writing on the paper may be as individual as the writing itself. Margins, spacing, crowding, insertions, and alignment are personal habits. These factors come into play both with the use of printed forms, like checks,[2] and in letters or handwritten documents of other classes. Spelling, punctuation, phraseology, and grammar may further individualize the author (Figure 8.4). Every one of these factors can be personal and, if so, forms an important part of the identification of the writer.

Writing Variation

The identification of an unknown writing depends on the similarity between the writing habits manifest in it and in the standards, those specimens known to have been written by a particular person. In reach-

---

[2]Orville B. Livingston, "Bogus Check File Classification by Trademarks," *Journal of Criminal Law, Criminology and Police Science* 39 (1949): 783, considers a number of numeral arrangement factors in check writing.

ing this conclusion, consideration must be given to the writing variation. No two samples of writing prepared by anyone are identical in every detail, since variation is an integral part of natural writing. The amount and kind of variation differs among writers and in its way forms an important element in the identification. With some it is slight and occurs only in details; with others it covers a rather wide range (Figure 8.5). Variation is due principally to the lack of machinelike precision in the human body, but it is also accentuated by external factors, such as writing position, writing instrument, and care of execution.

Writing variation is also influenced by physical and mental conditions, such as fatigue, intoxication, drug use, illness, and nervousness. These several factors produce a varying degree of deterioration in the quality of writing, commensurable in its degree with the intensity of the cause. The advanced age of the writer and the quality of writing he prepares in the course of time may introduce greater variation between specimens written at widely separated dates.

Variation does not preclude identification of the writing. In fact, variation around the basic qualities of the handwriting forms an additional factor that serves to personalize and identify writing. Thus, handwriting can be most accurately identified when the standard and questioned specimens were written under comparable conditions. Establishing the source of writing, therefore, becomes a process of determining its fundamental qualities and habits together with an accurate range of variation through which the writing fluctuates. It is necessary to demonstrate that not only the unknown writing has the qualities and habits of the known writing, but also that the deviations from the basic patterns that occur in the unknown writing are such as can be predicted from the variations in the standards. All this presumes that the standards are truly representative of writing prepared

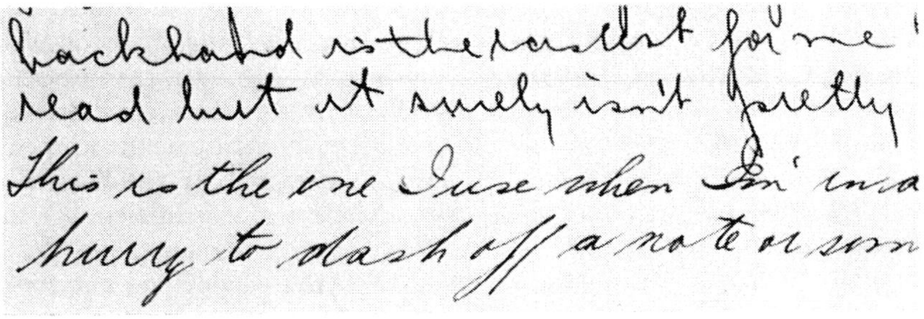

Figure 8.5. The sharp variation in slant is unusual, but is an example of the extreme variation that can be encountered occasionally.

under the conditions surrounding the execution of the questioned material.

Class and Individual Characteristics

All the factors that identify handwriting fall into two general and somewhat overlapping groups—class and individual characteristics. Class characteristics, as the name implies, are those common to a number of writers and may result from such influences as the writing system studied, family associations, trade training, and education. Individual characteristics are more or less peculiar to a specific writer. Class characteristics, of course, have little weight in identifying a writer, as it can readily be seen that there are others with these same writing traits. The most common error of the unqualified examiner is to describe an unusual characteristic as being individual when in fact it merely belongs to a writing system outside the sphere of his experience. Individual characteristics, on the other hand, constitute the backbone of an identification, but if two specimens of writing were not prepared by the same writer, this can be established through signficiant differences in either individual or class characteristics.

Identification in a Practical Situation

Only one person writes exactly in the same way as the writer of the disputed material. This premise is the cornerstone of every identification. In a practical situation, however, what are the essential requirements for an identification?

First, adequate specimens of known handwriting written under comparable conditions to the questioned must be available for study and comparison. These writings should establish two things—the person's individual writing attributes that correspond to those that make up the questioned specimens, and an accurate picture of the slight modifications which result from normal writing variations.

With these known specimens, what degree of agreement is necessary before it can be said that here certainly is the writer of the questioned document? Of course, the known and questioned writing must contain the same identifying elements. One has only to compare repeated words and letters in the known material, however, to realize that the disputed writing does not need to be a perfect duplicate of the known material to have been prepared by the same writer. Rather, the disputed writing must incorporate those personal habits and qualities of the known writing that have been treated in preceding paragraphs of this chapter. With due consideration for the writer's established range of variation, the habits and qualities of the known and unknown specimens must then agree. In other words, the questioned writing must be within the reach or writing scope of this person. When the same distinctive, personal writing characteristics are found in both the known and unknown writing in sufficient number that the likelihood of accidental coincidence is eliminated—and there are no basic or fundamental differences between the two sets of writing—then both must have been prepared by the same person.

The document examiner is occasionally asked how many points of identification are necessary to establish that two writings are by the same person. Such criteria have not been established, and probably could not be, because of the nature of handwriting identification. It involves not only factors of form that are subject to relatively easy count, but also the qualities of execution, freedom, movement, skill, emphasis, spacing, and the like that influence the entire writing and are not suspectible to tabulation.[3] As a consequence, the combination of a unique set of similarities coupled with the lack of significant basic writing differences must be used as the true basis for a positive identification.

Nonidentity of Writings

Writings of two different persons may be entirely dissimilar, or they may be very much alike but not identical. Although many writers have certain habits in common, each has developed personal peculiarities that mark his writing. These individualities, many of them in inconspicuous details, distinguish the writings of two persons who write very much alike.

Repeated small differences establish clearly that two specimens are the work of two individuals despite a great number of general similarities (Figure 8.6). Such problems cause the layman the most concern since the similarities may at times seem to outnumber the differences, and yet the fundamental, repeated differences are controlling. Everyone seems to appreciate that two writings are not by the same individual when there are a vast number of differences, but a few fundamental dissimilarities may not seem to lead to so positive a conclusion. Nevertheless, they do. If two writings are by a single person, then no fundamental differences should exist. Conversely, if there are any basic dissimilarities that cannot be accounted for by a logical, commonsense

---

[3]The problem is analyzed in depth in a paper presented at Royal Canadian Mounted Police Seminar No. 5, Questioned Documents in Crime Detection. See O. Hilton, "The Relationship of Mathematical Probability to the Handwriting Identification Problem," *Royal Canadian Mounted Police Seminar* No. 5 (Ottawa: Queen's Printer, 1960), pp. 121–128.

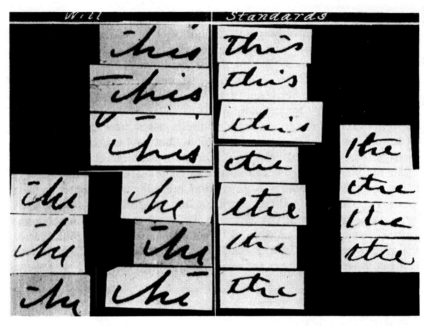

Figure 8.6. Proof that the testator did not write his holographic will rests upon the repetition of a series of small differences. In "this" and "the" from the will, the extremely short height of the t compared with following letters is unlike the t's of the testator's writing. His are proportionately taller when compared to other letters. The constantly repeated differences in this and a large number of other letters assumes importance and establishes that the will is not in the testator's handwriting. *(From the files of Elbridge W. Stein.)*

explanation, then the two writings must have been prepared by different writers.

Typical Problems Involving Writing Identification

The identification of general handwriting assumes importance under a diversity of circumstances. Despite the widespread use of the typewriter, completely handwritten documents are encountered in business and personal affairs. From time to time, questions arise as to who wrote a page or more of handwriting (Figure 8.7), or who wrote a few words that have been inserted in other material (Figure 8.8). It is surprising, moreover, that an individual will deny extensive writing he has prepared, and under these circumstances, it may be essential to establish what the facts are. Then there are instances when the writer who wrote the document is no longer available to identify it, and it becomes necessary to establish through comparision with his known writing that he did prepare it. If, on the other hand, someone is incorrectly accused of writing critical material, this misidentification can be corrected by proper study and comparison with his writing.

Important documents such as wills, receipts, agreements, contracts, notes and their drafts, and checks are many times wholly handwritten. They sometimes play a role in either civil or criminal litigation, possibly a controlling part, so that proof by expert testimony is important (Figure 8.9). In law enforcement and criminal prosecutions it is important to identify the writer of a ransom letter, bogus checks, or other handwritten documents, including less important anonymous letters (Figure 8.10). Accurate testimony on documents can substantially assist in the administration of justice.

Figure 8.7. The upper section shows a portion of a three-page letter written in 1776 in secret ink. It described in detail the patriot's military plans. *(The original letter is part of the University of Michigan's collection.)*

The comparison chart below is a key factor in identifying Benjamin Thompson, an American-born scientist, as the writer of the letter. The same modification of the Old English roundhand are found in the words from Thompson's writing and the letter. The design of the B, L, and W and the continuous writing as shown within the word "oppertunity", as well as its spelling, are significant individualities. A detailed report of the full investigation of this letter can be found in Sanborn C. Brown and Elbridge W. Stein, "Benjamin Thompson and the First Secret-Ink Letter of the American Revolution," *Journal of Criminal Law and Criminology* 40 (1950): 627–636. *(This illustration is used with the permission of the authors.)*

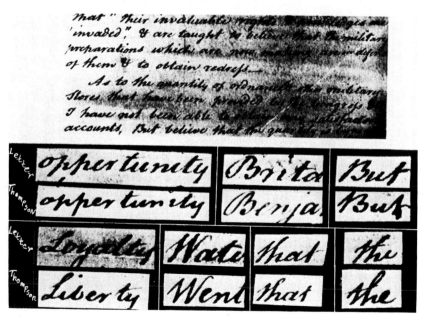

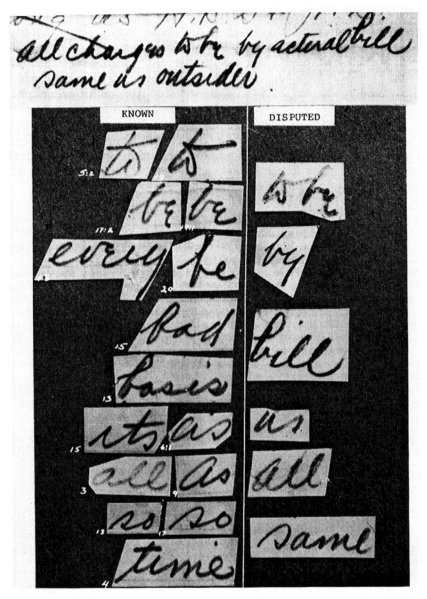

Figure 8.8. The two lines of handwriting at the top represent the entire insertion in a handwritten draft.

The chart below forms the means of identification of its writer. Of significance is the manner of writing the word "to" in an uninterrupted pattern, the slant of the Greek e, and the very sharp turn at the base of the b in "be" and "by." The freedom and writing skill are further similarities between the known writing and the insert.

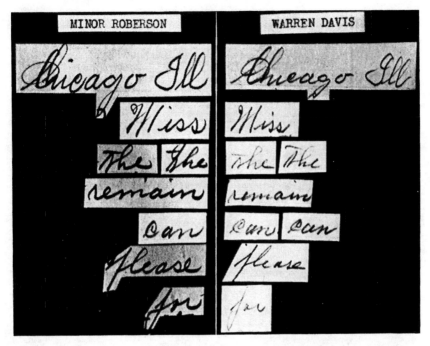

Figure 8.9. Roberson and Davis both filed unemployment applications and then wrote letters complaining because of the delay in approval. Neither could be easily located, and officials became suspicious. A comparison of the writing of these two men revealed a very comparable writing skill, similar slant, a like pattern of interruptions in words, and comparable individualized letter forms, with the conclusion that one person had used both names.

Holographic Wills

One of the most important identification problems involving extensive handwriting arises out of will problems. In many jurisdictions a holographic will is a valid instrument. By definition such a will does not require any witnesses. If a dispute arises about the authenticity of this document, the best proof is through the work of the document examiner who is able to study the entire document including its signature and to determine whether the decedent did in fact write the entire instrument. If holographic wills are drawn well before the time of death when the testator is still active and in sound health, the identification problem is not extremely complex. Of course, good specimens of known writing must be obtained for comparison purposes (Figure 8.11). There will be the occasional case, however, in which the decedent does not prepare a will until he has reached a very advanced age and may

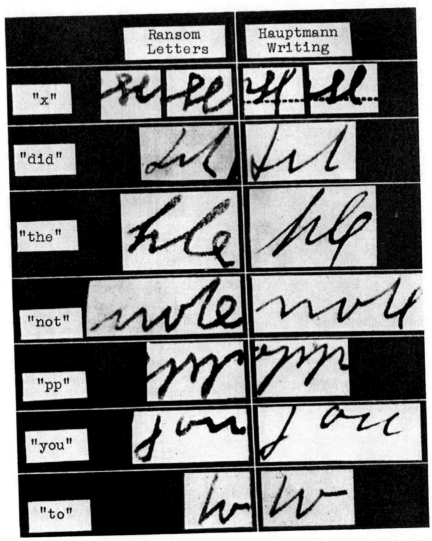

Figure 8.10. The highly personalized writing of Bruno Hauptmann was found in the ransom letters written in connection with the Lindbergh baby kidnapping. An invented form of the x, simplification of the t design ("tit" for "did") and y ("you"), and the double p written in Hauptmann's rugged manner of execution in combination with many other habits left no question that he wrote the ransom letters. *(From the files of Elbridge W. Stein.)*

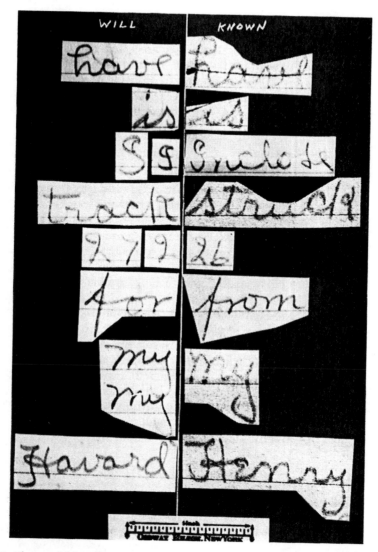

Figure 8.11. The proof that Sallie Keys wrote her holographic will is based in part upon the comparisons contained in this illustration. Her writing is clear and precise. Still, the forms are personal and agree with those of the will. Compare I, k (track), f, and H. The relative height of the m and y in "my" and of the tall letters to the a, o, and r is a further similarity. The combination of similarities is compelling evidence that the will is in her handwriting.

be in poor health or even on his deathbed. Under these circumstances, the will can contain a decidedly decrepit form of handwriting, and the limited comparable standards that are often part of these problems complicate the matter. Therefore, opinions may vary in their degree of certainty for a definite finding to probable or very probable results. Even such qualified opinions, together with other evidence, may assist in determining the authenticity or nongenuineness of the will.

Inhibiting Factors

Scientific examination of handwriting generally leads to definite findings. There are, nevertheless, restricting conditions that may prevent a document examiner from reaching a positive conclusion or may permit him to arrive at only a qualified opinion. Lack of a sufficient amount of known writing is the most common deficiency, but standards written under very different circumstances from the questioned material also limit the findings. Such standards might be a few scribbled notes to be compared with a holographic will. However, small bits of writing other than signatures,[4] especially inserts of a few words in either a near-copybook hand or very carelessly written, can cause a great deal of difficulty. A definite yes or no answer may also be precluded by wide differences between the dates of standard and disputed material, by an extremely hasty or careless bit of writing, or because a piece of writing was prepared during severe illness or under other adverse writing conditions. This is particularly true if no standards written under comparable conditions are available. These exceptional cases, however, make up a small minority compared to the great number of cases that yield clearcut conclusions.

Disguise

A disguised handwriting is one in which the person has made a deliberate attempt to remove or to modify all or some of his normal writing habits.[5] A favorite practice of the anonymous letter writer is to employ disguise to avoid detection. Perfect disguise, of course, would assure complete protection, but perfect disguise is itself extremely difficult. Although it is relatively simple to change one's writing habits suffi-

---

[4]Signatures, though short, tend to be more individual than other classes of writing, because of both the frequency and purpose of use. Furthermore, since signatures are used extensively, more and better than usual standards are available, and as a result a definite opinion can generally be reached.

[5]The discussion in this section presumes that the writer has produced a cursive or semicursive writing in this attempt rather than having lettered or handprinted the document. The latter class of writing is employed by some in hopes of hiding personal identity. While these tactics are usually unsuccessful, a full discussion of the handlettering problem must be reserved until Chapter 10.

ciently for one or two words to preclude identification, the task of maintaining an effective disguise grows more difficult with each additional word. When as much as a page of writing is disguised, it is generally true that the writer's normal habits are only partially veiled. Under these conditions the disguise may not be sufficient to prevent an identification, especially if a large quantity of known writing is at hand.[6]

Just why is disguise so difficult, and what is it that causes so many attempts to fail? To be successful the writer must carry out two difficult steps. First, he must have a thorough knowledge of the identifying details of his writing and the significance of each. This condition alone is seldom fulfilled. Assuming that it has been accomplished, however, for it is certainly within the reach of a clever individual who is willing to use every means at hand to avoid detection, then the second, more difficult step still lies ahead. This is the task of eliminating the identifying habits of his writing and adopting an entirely new set. Writing habits are very strong, and serious difficulties are encountered in any attempt to discard them. The usual result of these attempts is effectively to eliminate prominent characteristics but to leave numerous unconscious, but individual, writing traits. What is then believed to be an effective disguise actually is filled with these small but significant personal habits that may permit an identification of the writer (Figure 8.12).

Disguised writing has highly characteristic features that distinguish it from normal writing. It usually contains evidence of a conflict, the struggle between persistent, natural habits and the effort to suppress them. Consequently, it is less skillfully executed than the usual writing of the individual. Irregularities and inconsistencies tend to appear. Hesitation, variations in slant, odd and at times grotesque letter forms, patched up portions, and slowly drawn strokes are typical. The prominent features, such as capital letters and slant, generally undergo the most marked change, while the smaller, less prominent, though equally important, identifying factors retain their usual character.[7] All these facts bear consideration, for identification of disguised writing is pos-

---

[6]If over a period of time more than one document is prepared, the problem of maintaining consistent disguise is further complicated. Under these circumstances, if the writer retains a carbon copy of each disguise specimen, he may be able to write with some degree of consistency, but this amount of care is most unusual, and in all probability the total disguise will be inadequate.

[7]Elements of handwriting that are apt to undergo modification in attempting disguise are reported by June E. Downey, "Handwriting Disguise," *Journal of Applied Psychology*, 1 (1917): 368–379, as size, slant, pressure, form, alignment, continuity, connections, proportions, and the dot of the i.

John J. Harris, "Disguised Handwriting," *Journal of Criminal Law, Criminology and Police Science* 43 (1953): 685–689, reports on disguised writing experiments with 100 students. By far the majority failed effectively to disguise. The more common modes of disguise were change of slant, grotesque form, altered pictorial effect, and handlettering.

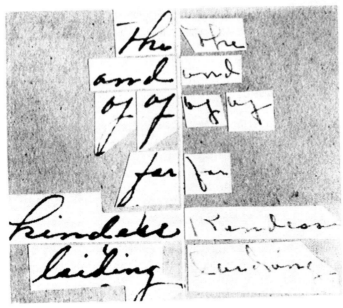

Figure 8.12. The personal writing habits of form and connections, modified only by a change of slant in an effort to disguise, together with the same misspellings combine to establish that one person prepared both writings. (The fact was tacitly admitted by the claimant's withdrawing his claim based on the disguised writing.)

sible only if the unnatural portions are recognized and properly evaluated, while the undisguised portions are used as the basis of the identification.

Disguise may be accomplished by writing with the opposite hand from that habitually used, i.e., so-called left-handed writing. It may be a very effective disguise as long as no standards of the wrong-handed writing are available. This method can sometimes be inferred from the relatively low writing skill. In criminal investigations, once a suspect is located, steps should be taken to obtain request writing executed with either hand.

There is a small group of penmen who write with almost the same ease and skill with either hand. These ambidextrous writings do not suggest disguise for each hand has been drilled to a degree of proficiency that removes all specimens from the class of wrong-handed writing. With each of these persons, writing with his right hand differs from that done with his left. Furthermore, he is generally known to have this unusual ability, and certainly he must have written extensively with each hand in order to acquire the skill. The problem then becomes one of procuring proper standards written with each hand for examination and comparison with the disputed matter.

Conclusions

Writing identification involves the discovery and study of all identifying characteristics; the differentiation between those that are typical and those that are abnormal or represent the unusual; recognition of those that are disguised or have been deliberately and consciously changed; and determination of the normal amount of writing variation common to the particular writer. If the unknown writing was executed without disguise, it must contain writing habits and qualities that the writer unconsciously employs. The similarities between the questioned and natural writing need not be identical in the sense that the two sets of writing can be matched or superimposed bit by bit; nor, on the other hand, can the differences between the disputed and standard writing far exceed the variation customarily found in the known writing. Finally, there must be sufficient individuality in both the known and unknown writing to establish beyond all doubt that the two sets of writing must have been the work of the same person.

Accurate identification of handwriting is an important part of the document examiner's work. It requires complete study of both the questioned and known writing. Ample and accurate known specimens are an essential part of this problem. Full understanding of the writer's ability and habits require both keen observation and careful analysis of what is observed. In every problem the search for differences must accompany the search for similarities, and, before one reaches an opinion of nonidentity, those apparent differences must be evaluated in the light of known and possible writing conditions in order to assure that they are not simply variables due to external factors. Unusual writing conditions, age, illness, and possible disguise are all factors which complicate some problems. In other words, the identification of handwriting is far from a simple or cursory operation.

9

Identification of Signatures and Detection of Forgery

When a person signs his name he is carrying out one of his most common writing acts. In time, the signature becomes highly individualized—often in a style quite distinct from that of the writer's other handwriting. How each person writes depends upon the combined effect of a number of factors. The near-illiterate produces a measured, plodding pattern, lacking in skill and freedom but nonetheless individual to the writer. With more advanced writers the entire makeup of the signature assumes greater skill, movement becomes less primitive and elementary, and many elements approximate to a greater or lesser degree the copybook writing that the individual studied. Just how he signs his name depends upon numerous factors such as muscular control, coordination, health, age, nervous temperament, the frequency at which he is called upon to write, and to some extent upon his personality.[1] While all of these factors are blended into the signature, the writer is not particularly conscious of them as he writes, and the same is true of all but the most prominent features of the finished product. Instead, through repetition he executes a semiautomatic for-

---

[1]The author realizes that the reference "personality" suggests a controversial issue. While the claims of such investigators as Robert Saudek, J. Crepieux-Jamin, or contemporary graphologists are open to debate, the reader must nonetheless realize that personal idiosyncrasies are at least to some extent responsible for the peculiar modification of copybook letter styles that occurs in almost everyone's writing. These personal styles of letter form may be compared to differences in dress preference, in mannerisms of speech and walk, and in other habits that are somewhat dependent on what can be loosely termed the personality of the individual. Just why they exist is not entirely known, but that they do come to be associated with the individual is beyond dispute. In a like manner, we associate to some extent the personal differences in handwriting as belonging to and dependent on the writer's personality. As examples of these characteristics, there are the artistic handwritings of certain artists or the rapid and possibly illegible writings of the overburdened business executive—extremes, of course.

mation of strokes, which tends to assume a consistent pattern, but always varying slightly from this ideal and from other specimens of his signature.

Genuine Signatures

The identification of signatures constitutes a specialized branch of handwriting examination. Fundamentally, the identification principles set forth for general handwriting remain unchanged, but certain factors must receive greater emphasis. Standards consisting of known signatures may contain elements not common to other classes of his writing. Furthermore, the identifying attributes that are given closest study in signature problems may not always receive the same special consideration in the identification of general writing.

How a signature is written controls in a large measure its identification. A signature is a combination of a rather limited number of letters. Because of its frequent use, it becomes with many persons almost automatic writing. With those who do not write as fluently, the measured, conscious writing act produces a more primitive writing movement, which of itself assumes identifying importance. Furthermore, in signature problems there is frequently a suspicion of forgery. Here again writing movement is a basic consideration, as discussed in the following sections. Thus, while the design of letters may be the eye-catching feature, the factors related to the execution of the signature are the cornerstones of accurate identification.

The skill of execution and the movement of the pen can be ascertained from a study of the signature itself. To do this, several factors, which, in combination fully describe the individual writing movement, must be analyzed: continuous writing or movement interrupted at intervals by either stops or actual pen lifts; the rhythmic or jerky pattern of writing; the shading and pen emphasis on particular strokes, as well as the overall writing pressure; the position of the pen; the speed of execution; the smoothly rounded, sharply curving or elliptical, or angular connecting strokes between letters and in turns of letters; the starting of the initial writing movement before or after the pen makes contact with the paper and the corresponding condition at the termination of the word or at interruption within words; and perhaps habitual retouchings. These qualities are dependent on how the writing instrument is moved—whether by action of the fingers, hand, or arm, or a combination of these—and also the developed writing skill or coordination.

What each writer strives for in signing his name is to reproduce a particular pattern. It contains the personal concepts of design, which when repeated time and again serve to distinguish his signature from all others. Thus, the elements that define the general form include the design of the letters and their slant; the relative size of capitals, single-space small letters, and those that project below the line or above the height of a single space; ornamentations and flourishes; simplifications of form; and the arrangement of different parts of the signature in respect to the balance of it. It is the combination of both classes of personal attributes, writing quality and form, that identifies the signature.

If a questioned signature agrees with the truly representative standards in all its identifying elements, then it must have been written by the same person (Figure 9.1). If, on the other hand, significant differences exist between the known and unknown signatures, they must be the work of two writers, but the differences between them have to be of a fundamental nature and not just the minor variations normally found between two signatures of any writer.

This natural variation between several signatures by the same writer plays an important role in an identification. No two specimens are absolutely identical. How much they vary from one another depends on the individual writer and the conditions under which each was written (Figure 9.2). It is because of normal variation that more than one known signature should be used to identify an unknown one. The process of identification requires that the known signatures establish accurately the extent of variation, and then it is necessary to ascertain whether the identifying qualities of the unknown signature fall within these limits. Thus, the identification of a signature consists not of matching it exactly with a particular known signature, but of determining that it contains the characteristics of and is written in the same way as the standards and also fits within the extremes of variation established by the collection of known signatures.

In the previous paragraph it was presumed that the variations encountered between a questioned and known signature are contained within the natural variations of the writer. This condition prevails in the majority of cases. However, another class of variation can be encountered, although rather infrequently. It may be termed an accidental or rare variation, applied to a divergency that occurs only in this signature, or if rare, then possibly in something like once in 100 or 200 specimens. A variation of this nature is most troublesome in signature problems, although it may also be encountered in general handwriting as well. There normally is no logical explanation for it, especially since the conditions under which virtually all signatures are made are at best only partially known. If only this divergency exists between a questioned signature and the known specimens, one may be justified in concluding that all are the work of one person, but at the same time one may be hard pressed to persuade someone who believes that the

Figure 9.1. Three distinct signature problems arose in connection with the Loretta A. Byrne will. Two of the three witnesses died before the testatrix, and it became necessary to prove not only Miss Byrne's signature but also the signatures of the two deceased witnesses, Kathryn R. Dawley and Florence Stewart.

The Byrne will signature is shown above two of the many authentic signatures of hers. All the qualities of execution and habits of form that make up her usual signature are combined in the will signature.

The signatures of the witnesses, Kathryn R. Dawley and Florence M. Stewart, appear together between two of Miss Dawley's and two of Miss Stewart's genuine signatures. Both of these women, like Miss Byrne, write a fluent, clear, distinctive signature, and there is absolutely no question as to the authenticity of these two witnesses' signatures.

Figure 9.2. All of the Galatio signatures were signed to payroll receipts by a single employee and show rather wide variations in his signature. Variation occurs in slant, size, alignment with the baseline, connections, and letter forms. The range of variation is unusually wide, but some variation is a part of all writing.

    The more variable a person's writing, the greater the number of known specimens required to define his habits accurately.

signature is a forgery that it is not. Nevertheless, under proper circumstances a single accidental variation does not of itself prove forgery.

Unusual Genuine Signatures

The principles for establishing that a signature is genuine or identifying its author were considered in the preceding section. The document examiner is usually confronted with signature problems in which the questioned signature can be presumed to be a normal or typical signature of the individual. With almost everyone such a signature appears on letters, applications, checks, legal documents, and other formally or semiformally signed papers. However, there are also problems that involve some special class of signatures and create rather unusual technical problems. The principles of identification or the proof of genuineness do not vary, but some elements of these signatures take on greater significance or create certain limitations. Since these problems occur from time to time in civil litigation, investigations, and even criminal trials, it is well to look at the particular factors involved. Any grouping of unusual signatures has to be arbitrary, and at this point let us consider especially receipt signatures, signatures written under the influence of alcohol or drugs, those written during severe illness, and those of elderly persons prepared during declining years of life.

Receipt Signatures

The term receipt signature encompasses a group of signatures that are hastily written under adverse writing conditions to acknowledge, for example, delivery of a parcel, registered mail, or merchandise. It is common to write such a signature with the paper resting against the wall, on a hand-held clipboard, or in any of a number of poor or unusual writing positions. Many do not consider the execution any more than a perfunctory operation, even to have to sign the receipt seeming to be an annoyance. The signatures are frequently dashed off in almost a scribble. Details of form are lost because of haste, lack of care, and

Figure 9.3. The receipt signature above shows a number of divergencies from the more formal Regan signature. With divergencies like those found here, it would be almost impossible to establish that the receipt was signed by the person who executed a number of signatures of the formal style.

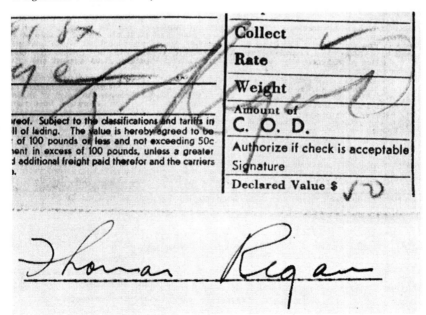

poor writing position. A series of these signatures does reveal some pattern of writing, but the variation from one to another may be great. Formal signatures may not tell much of what to expect in these specimens (Figure 9.3). Consequently, to answer the problem accurately, it is normally necessary to locate known signatures of the same class. These observations relate to many writers though not necessarily all, for a few people produce receipt signatures that are close to their regular signature forms. With a degenerate form of signature, the decision about genuineness often has to be made on a few typical forms in the signature together with the extreme freedom of writing and lack of legibility. Unlike a forgery, though, these signatures do not reveal any attempt to improve their defective elements. The only exception may be an occasionally freely written, not too accurate correction of a badly defective letter.

Signatures Influenced by Alcohol and Drugs

A person decidedly under the influence of alcohol or drugs may not sign his name in a normal fashion. Here, however, is a highly personal situation. Some of these impaired writers can produce almost normal writing even if their blood alcohol ratio is high; others find their writing coordination badly weakened and their signatures erratic and very sig-

Figure 9.4. The four bar checks were signed by the same person during an evening of drinking. Note the progressive loss of detail from the first (upper) to last (lower).

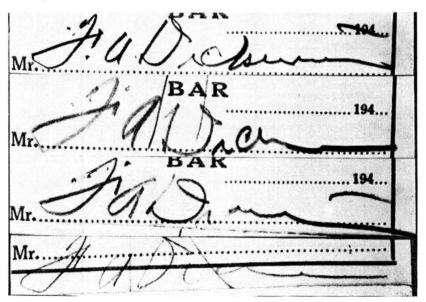

nificantly different from normal.[2] The same situation can occur with some drugs. The defects of the signatures are very different from the flaws of forgery, which are to be discussed in a subsequent section. In the extreme cases coordination suffers significantly with free movement and poor form (Figure 9.4). The pen seems to have staggered across the paper. With lower blood–alcohol ratios signatures tend to be spread out slightly and somewhat larger than normal. If some known writing under the influence of alcohol or drugs is available for comparison specimens, the document examiner's findings can be more extensive, more precise, and more accurate. Identification of the sig-

Figure 9.5. The top signature was written during a serious illness while the writer was confined to a hospital bed. The next two were written 9 months later, after recovery. While better than the first signature, they are not as fluent as the last two, which were written a year or so before the illness. Signatures written during illness may somewhat deteriorate, but there can be later recovery of original writing ability or at least some improvement after the period of illness with most writers.

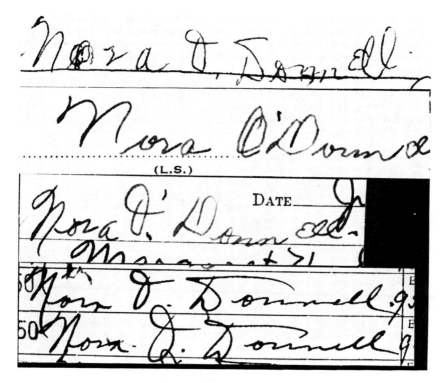

[2]A study of handwriting under various degrees of intoxication is reported on by O. Hilton, "A Study of the Influence of Alcohol on Handwriting," *Journal of Forensic Sciences* 14 (1969): 309–316.

nature can be made without these special standards, but the opinion becomes more persuasive when some of the known writing reflects a similar influence or deterioriation.

Illness and Old Age

Problems involving writing of seriously ill or very weak, elderly individuals lead to some similarities in the kind of signatures encountered. The weakened physical condition and the decline in ability to coordinate accurately are important factors that help to create a very much poorer quality of signatures compared to those of an earlier date. It must be recognized that with either serious illness or old age the decline affects both the design features of the signature and the writing skill and quality. Irregular strokes, poorly formed letters, poor alignment and letterspacing are among the factors found in this class of signatures[3] (Figure 9.5).

Figure 9.6. All four signatures were written by a woman who had suffered from palsy for a number of years. The first two were signed to checks in 1962. The others were signed in 1964, after the writer was using tranquilizers (Valium) for a period of time. Note the reduction of tremor and especially of the periodic long strokes that project beneath the baseline.

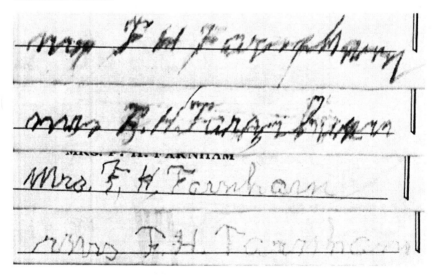

---

[3]The author has considered aspects of the problems of identifying writing during illness and of the elderly more in detail in earlier papers. See "Influence of Serious Illness on Handwriting Identification," *Postgraduate Medicine* 19 (1956): A-36–A-48; "Influence of Age and Illness on Handwriting: Identification Problems," *Forensic Science* 9 (1977): 161–172; "Considerations of the Writer's Health in Identifying Signatures and Detecting Forgery," *Journal of Forensic Sciences* 14 (1969): 157–166.

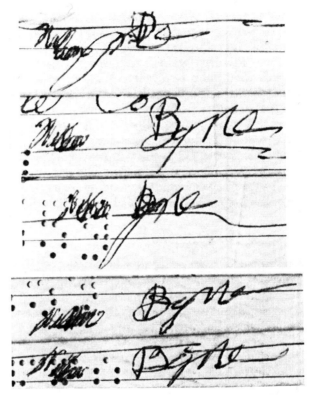

Figure 9.7. All signatures appeared on checks selected from a very large group covering a period of months. The first three were signed on the same day, several weeks before the last two. While the later signatures still show deterioration, they are an improvement over the earlier ones. There were other similar times of deterioration followed by slight improvement among later Byne signatures.

One quality of these signatures is the tremor of old age or weakness of illness which is found in some but not all of these signatures. This tremor or infirmity is accompanied by a corresponding decline in the design of the signature (Figure 9.6). Unlike receipt signatures, for example, poor design is accompanied by weakness in writing rather than a decline because of speed and lack of care.

A further typical quality of some of these signatures is the inability of the writer to get the signature started. There may be one or two false starts made up of weak, erratic strokes that have no connection with the final signature. By the same token, there may be points within the signature or near the end where suddenly the movement is free and relaxed. These typical endings may be a part of some but not all signatures by the same person.

Examiners familiar with writing of this kind may suspect that a poorly written signature was executed by an ill or aged writer, but contemporary specimens may be needed to prove genuineness. The problem involves again searching for signatures written under comparable conditions. Few will be found for a very sick person who writes only when absolutely necessary. With the elderly, there may be a gradual, extended, though not necessarily straight-line, deterioration toward the signature encountered. There will be within the pattern of deterioration occasional signatures of better quality than those immediately before. Often a few known specimens can be located (Figure 9.7), occasionally a good number, but the final judgment may depend on the examiner's experience and understanding of these problems in determining the authenticity of such a deteriorated signature.

Detection of Forgery

One important question, that of forgery, complicates signature identification and must be reckoned with in virtually every problem. A very small percentage of signatures in existence are forgeries, but since these are generally part of important documents or of papers that carry a monetary value, their detection is an absolute necessity. The qualities of forgery must be understood before a signature can be accurately identified, or else errors are certain to be made.

To imitate the signature of another person with fraudulent intent is to undertake an abnormal act that brings about in the individual a mental and physical conflict of serious proportion. While a sense of guilt, which doubtlessly varies among different persons, harasses the forger during the execution of the forgery, he is further subjected to other mental conflicts coupled with a difficult physical task. As everyone knows, the process of breaking even the simplest of habits requires intense concentration over an extended period of time. For some time, any relaxation of this mental alertness may result in a subconscious recurrence of the basic habit in at least a modified form. So also with a deliberate attempt to form a new habit; the act must be consciously repeated time and again.

Forgery involves a double process. The successful forger must discard all of his own writing habits—habits that for the most part are unconscious acts—and at the same time assume those unfamiliar characteristics of another writer.[4] Then, too, writing is not just one or two simple habits, but literally dozens, which vary in complexity, woven

---

[4]It is dubious that the usual forger is conscious of any but the most prominent characteristics of the writing he is forging. Analysis of most forgeries indicates that he neither comprehends nor appreciates the finer and more delicate features of the writing he is attempting to imitate.

together into an intricate pattern. Thus, the conscious mental task is enormous and involves as well the physical struggle of using a strange writing process in place of the well-founded, usual writing movements. It is little wonder, therefore, that truly successful forgeries are indeed rare.[5]

To attain his goal, a forger must employ one of two techniques to imitate a signature. Equipped with a genuine signature as a model, he may choose to imitate it freehand, or feeling that he lacks the requisite skill to accomplish this successfully, he may choose to trace his forgery from the model.[6]

A tracing can be produced in either of two ways. The first, which can best be termed the transmitted light process, is prepared by placing the spurious document immediately over the genuine signature, and while directing a strong light through the two papers from below or behind, tracing the outline that shows through the uppermost sheet. The second technique, which may be designated the carbon outline method, is completed in the following manner. A sheet of carbon paper is placed between the top sheet, which bears the genuine signature, and the fraudulent document below. Then the outline of the model signature is traced with a dry pen or sharp pointed instrument to give a carbon offset on the lower sheet, and this outline is subsequently covered over by retracing it with a suitable ink stroke.[7] Often when the ink stroke fails to cover the carbon outline completely, there is an attempt to erase the carbon outline. While passable forgeries may be prepared by any of these methods, each has its inherent faults and weaknesses that give it away.

Simulated Forgeries

Freehand imitations are generally the most skillful forgeries, although there are all grades of imitations, regardless of how they are prepared. If the forger is to produce a perfect freehand imitation, he must imitate

---

[5]A successful forgery need not be a perfect forgery, i.e., one in which all of the habits and qualities of the genuine signature are duplicated to such a degree of accuracy as to make it impossible to detect by any means that the signature is not genuine. Many forgeries, containing faults that under careful scrutiny would condemn the signatures, are successful in that they are skillfully enough done to pass unchallenged by unsuspecting persons, including even those who are directly affected by the forgeries.

[6]It is conceivable that the "model signature" might consist of a "mental recollection" or the forger's impression of the genuine signature. In principle the same process of determining the salient habits of the signature and reproducing them on paper would be employed as though the forger had an actual model signature at hand. In such a case the accuracy of reproduction, no doubt, would be reduced, and as a result the detection of the forgery more likely.

[7]An alternative, though less desirable, method includes impressing the outline of the signature on the document without a carbon sheet merely by tracing with a heavy pressure and "covering" this indented outline with an appropriate ink stroke. Likewise, the forgery may first be sketched in freehand with a light pencil stroke, which in turn is covered with an ink stroke.

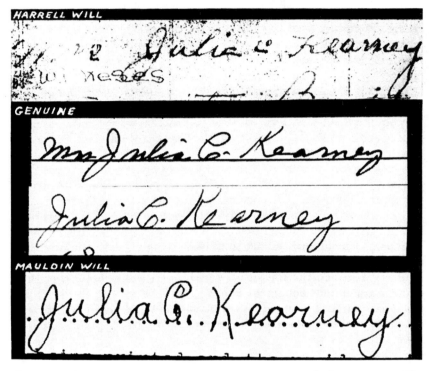

Figure 9.8. The two center signatures are genuine signatures of Julia C. Kearney. The upper signature was signed to an alleged will of Julia C. Kearney presented by one claimant, Mrs. Harrell. It is a poorly written, badly reworked forgery, characterized by overwritings and patchings. (Also see Figure 9.9.) Letter forms differ from those of the genuine Kearney signatures.

The lower signature is from a purported will brought forward by another claimant, Mrs. Mauldin. It is written without any significant attempt to imitate Mrs. Kearney's genuine signature. There are sharp difference in slant, in the relative size of small and capital letter, and in details of form.

all the habits and qualities of the authentic signatures while simultaneously discarding all conflicting elements of his own writing. He must discover from a detailed study of the model signature[8] that is to be imitated all its salient factors and must know enough about the corresponding characteristics of his own writing to be able to eliminate their influence in his final product. Finally, this process involves writ-

---

[8]Forgeries are generally made from a single model signature. This is a weakness in itself since only a partial picture of the writing habits to be imitated can be obtained. On more than one occasion the model has been defective in some manner or other, such as being inconsistent with the signatures of the alleged date of the document, with the result that even a good forgery is immediately subjected to rigorous scrutiny.

ing the signature in the same natural way as the authentic signature. Failure often results because the forger has only a superficial idea of a few characteristics of both his own writing and the writing to be simulated or because his skill as a penman fails to measure up to that of the person whose writing is being imitated. Even having circumvented all these pitfalls, the exacting task of execution, as we have already seen, leaves only a remote probability of success.

The forgery can generally be detected because of the inherent defects in how it is written (Figure 9.8). The normal signatures of the writer consist of a habitual speed of writing, firmness of stroke, pattern of shading and emphasis, degree of skill, fundamental muscular movement and coordination, rhythm, continuity, pen position, and freedom; a forgery is apt to differ from the genuine signature in any of these qualities. Hesitation, unnatural pen lifts, patching, tremor, uncertainty of movement as portrayed by abrupt changes in the direction of the line, and a stilted, drawn quality devoid of free, normal writing movements combine to reveal the true nature of a forgery (Figure 9.9). Many of these factors may exist in the genuine signatures of a particular writer, but if they do, a forgery of them is generally defective in the manner in which these qualities are imitated. It is of primary importance, therefore, to ascertain whether the variations between the known and unknown signatures are common to the normal writing habits of this person or point toward forgery. In the usual forgery, the signature tends to be a deliberate drawing in which emphasis is placed on the imitation of letter forms and design rather than on the move-

Figure 9.9. The left-hand section is an enlargement of the "arn" section of the Kearney signature to the Harrell will. The arrows indicate two separate strokes produced by the overwriting of this portion of the signature.

On the right-hand side are two enlarged portions of the y from the same signature. The arrows point to the splicing in the trough of the y and in the lower loop as well as to another double stroke. These and other fraudulent reworkings condemn this signature as a bungled forgery.

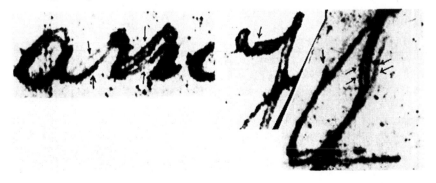

Figure 9.10. The guaranty signature at the bottom is a simulated forgery. Compared with the two genuine Wohl signatures the highly personal "Wo" connection is missing and the final ending of the l is short and blunt, lacking the typical free ending. The height of the "hl" compared to other letters is a further defect.

ment and writing qualities. With a forgery, therefore, significant differences in the mode of execution as compared with the standard signature stamp its fraudulent character (Figure 9.10). Regardless of the care taken in imitating the letter forms, variations in these characteristics are also apt to occur.[9]

Traced Forgeries

A tracing prepared by the transmitted-light technique has additional defects. Even with a strong light and thin paper, some of the less conspicuous details of the model signature are not clear to the imitator as he follows the outline, and with the usual weights of paper and

---

[9]Some persons believe that an acceptable forgery can be executed by writing it upside down, but this is far from the truth. With this kind of forgery, there is usually a sharp divergency from the genuine signatures in those qualities of writing such as shading and emphasis, pen position, and the like.

weaker light sources, even a greater number of details are omitted because of oversight. The actual forgery is produced not by a writing process but by drawing. Only the exceptional individual can with practice trace accurately with a fast, free pen movement. The faults of a freehand or simulated forgery are also found in tracings, but the typical traced forgery is drawn with a slow, measured stroke, which is usually filled with points of hesitation, uncertain movement, and sudden abrupt turns or jogs. This class of forgery typically contains a uniformly heavy stroke that lacks natural shading or pen emphasis common to natural writing. It is not unusual for the signature to display patchings and retouchings made in an effort to correct faulty letter forms. Retouchings may even be made with the pen moving in the direction opposite to natural writing. In addition to pen lifts or breaks followed by careful splicing, there may also be indications of the pen stopping in the course of a stroke but remaining on contact with the paper and then without a lift continuing on. The forger employs either method while he determines the proper course of the pen throughout the balance of a letter and into the next one.

A traced forgery prepared from a carbon outline is a crude imitation at best. Not only are the defects of tracing present, but they are emphasized by the double tracing process. This act gives two chances for errors and inaccuracies in following the outline. The presence of the carbon outline itself condemns the signature (Figure 9.11). This outline can be studied readily where the ink fails to cover it, a condition that is apt to occur at several points in the signature. With many inks, infrared photography will penetrate the covering ink and reveal the carbon outline (Figure 9.12). With the microscope and special photo-

Figure 9.11. Two forged signatures were traced from a common model signature. A carbon outline was first prepared, which caused the fuzzy halo effect around the signatures. The great similarity in size and design of the two signatures proves the common model.

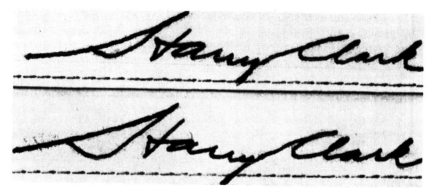

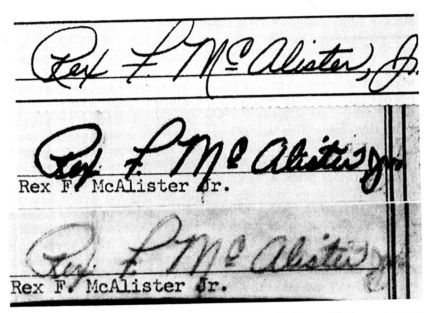

Figure 9.12. The upper signature is authentic, the second a forgery. The lower signature is an infrared photograph of the forgery, which reveals the original carbon outline.

graphs,[10] the difference in the quality of the ink stroke and carbon outline can be demonstrated. In an effort to remedy this defect, the forger may attempt to efface the carbon outline, especially any uncovered portions, by erasing with a soft rubber or artgum. The carbon deposits are persistent, and identifiable traces have been known to remain even after careful erasing. If the carbon is well removed, there may still remain a slight indentation from the pressure of tracing the original outline. Furthermore, the erasing may remove some ink as well or may dull it in a characteristic way. Photography, with carefully controlled side lighting, often reveals the presence of this impression and adds to the evidence of the fraud. It can be seen that each step in the preparation of a forgery introduces faults in the finished product that serve as the means to show the fraudulent nature of the signature and to establish how it was prepared.

Traced forgeries have been made with outlines other than a carbon outline. A very light pencil tracing, possibly using the transmitted-

---

[10]With a traced forgery in which a carbon outline was first made and then covered with ink, an infrared photograph may be very useful. Many inks are transparent to infrared radiation, that is, the ink writing is completely eliminated in an infrared photograph. This leaves the carbon outline clearly photographed, and the method of preparation is clear to the viewer. See O. Hilton, "Traced Forgeries and Infrared Photography," *International Criminal Police Review* 159 (1962): 195–197.

light process, can be made and easily corrected if necessary, and subsequently covered with an ink stroke. Forgeries have been created with a guide line consisting of a simple writing impression that the forger produces by tracing the genuine signature with sufficient writing pressure to produce the indentation. Such an outline is difficult to follow, and the end result may not be very accurate. There is no easy way to remove the indentations, and they wait to be revealed and interpreted. In another instance the outline of a forged signature followed along the pinholes in the paper. It appeared that these served as a guide for about the first half of the signature, but then strangely there was no guide for the second half.

In more than one instance, a forger has created two or more signatures by tracing the outline of a single model. The forgeries can be detected in part by the near coincidence and constant returning to the same outline of the two forgeries. For one important case, no model signature was located nor was there any outline around either signature, but the near identity of the signatures indicated clearly how the two forgeries had been prepared (Figure 9.13).

It is well to note that the mere presence of an outline around the signature or running along its entire course does not of itself establish forgery. This writer has examined a signature with a pencil outline interwoven with ink strokes. The ink signature had all the qualities of genuineness, but the outline lacked some of the writing freedom found in the genuine signature. When a Verifax copy was produced, only the decrepit outline appeared. It was ultimately ascertained that a secretary had applied the pencil outline when the copy machine did not record the original signature. She had been advised by salesmen of the machine to trace the signature in pencil in those instances when the original signature was lost. Thus, in this instance, there was a logical and provable explanation for an outline with a genuine signature. Walters and Flynn reported examining a signature with an apparent guideline running adjacent to much of the signature. The signatures had the quality of genuineness and in this instance it was found that the ink signature appeared on a photocopy made on a zinc oxide–coated paper. Experiments and research established that the plating of the socket of the ball point pen had been rubbed off on the paper by the abrasive action of the zinc oxide coating.[11] These examples show that the outline itself does not automatically prove forgery.

The model signature is of utmost importance in the investigation of a traced forgery. When a disputed signature is suspected of being a

[11]See Arthur Walters and William Flynn, "The Illusion of Traced Forgery on Zinc Oxide–Coated Photocopy Paper," *Journal of Police Science and Administration* 2 (1974): 376–380.

190

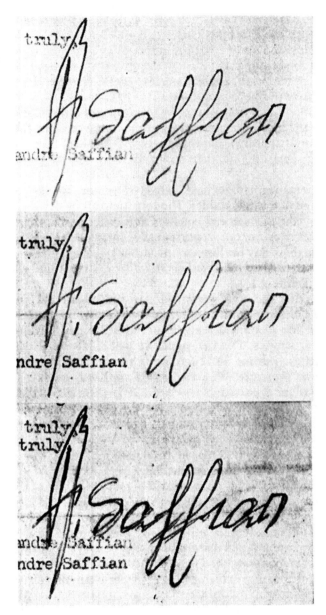

Figure 9.13. The two signatures were to the original and executed carbon copy of a letter. Both are forgeries prepared by placing the letter over a genuine signature and tracing the outline as seen through the paper. When they are superimposed (below) the two signatures keep returning to a common outline.

tracing, any genuine signature that may have been used as the model should be carefully examined to determine two facts. First, do the alleged model and tracing coincide sufficiently well to establish that the latter was traced from the former? Actually, a tracing and the model do not coincide exactly throughout, but when the strokes of the disputed signature wander away from those of the genuine, they invariably return to the common track, particularly at prominent points. Forgers fail to follow the outline exactly. When this condition exists between a signature that contains extensive indications of forgery and a genuine signature, the conclusion that the disputed signature was traced from this model is inescapable. The second condition establishing that a genuine signature served as a model for a traced forgery can be disclosed by an examination of the genuine signature. Often an indentation, closely paralleling the outline of the signature, results from pressure on the tracing instrument. Furthermore, traces of pencil strokes or pen scratches, when either instrument was used to make the carbon outline of the forgery, may be found around the model signature. Of course, forgery can be proved without locating the model signature, but locating and properly understanding its condition and importance leaves those who stand against the facts with little, if any, defense.

Spurious Signatures

When the forger has no genuine signature available, he may still attempt to commit the fraud with what can be best termed a *spurious signature*. Without endeavoring to simulate a person's writing, he merely writes the name in his own or a slightly modified handwriting, and contrives some means of passing the document for his personal gain before anyone recognizes the obvious fraud. (See Figure 9.8.) This is the technique of the check thief, the criminal who steals, endorses, and passes government or corporation checks, or who procures printed check forms, completes, and endorses them with fictitious signatures so as ultimately to pass them. With signatures of this class, the proof of nongenuineness is rather elementary once authentic signatures of the named person become available. Any similarities between the disputed and known signature are those of writing system or pure chance. Furthermore, the identity of the forger often can be effected by writing comparison, as will be seen later in this chapter.

Spouse's Imitations

One class of signatures encountered from time to time contains those of a husband written by his wife or those of a wife written by her husband. In many instances, these signatures cannot be considered forgeries, for often they are written with the knowledge and consent of the other party or with a certain unspoken, tacit understanding. Among such common signatures are endorsements to paychecks that are either negotiated at neighborhood stores or deposited in a joint bank account. The other partner merely forgets to sign the check or considers the procedure perfectly proper. The signatures frequently have only general imitated qualities. They may not be in the handwriting of the writer, but there is no real attempt to duplicate the other's signature except for a few prominent details.

Problems concerning these signatures may arise, however, after marriages dissolve. One spouse may have signed the other's signature on a loan, deed, or stock transfer with or without knowledge of the other partner. After the divorce or during settlement of property, despite previous understandings, controversies regarding the signatures require independent examinations. Signatures of this type also appear on election nominating petitions, and they are encountered from time to time among purported standards of the person whose name appears as the signer.

Determination of nongenuineness normally may not be difficult, especially with reliable standards. Careful study should reveal differences even with two writers whose signatures are not highly individualized and who have had their writing training in the same school system. Short names, similar writing, and some attempt to imitate again and again a prominent element or two leads to rather similar signatures in the eyes of a layman.[12] With such, the inconspicuous differences play a major role in establishing the authentic and nongenuine.

Forgery of Holographic Documents

So far, we have been concerned only with the forgery of signatures, which constitutes the great majority of forgery problems. However, from time to time, a forger finds it necessary to reach for a more difficult goal—the imitation of an entire handwritten or holographic document. Most such documents involve wills, especially in jurisdictions in which holographic wills that do not need a witness are legal. In recent years, however, there have been prominent cases, such as the nationally publicized controversy between legal representatives of the late Howard Hughes and the author Clifford Irving (1971–1972), which saw the production of several lengthy handwritten letters purporting

---

[12]John J. Harris, "How Much Do People Write Alike, A Study of Signatures," *Journal of Criminal Law, Criminology and Police Science* 48 (1958): 647–651, discusses examples of signatures of different writers that have many similar writing habits.

to have originated from Hughes.[13] In another, unrelated, case, the courts of Nevada in 1978 found an alleged three-page holographic will—this, too, of Howard Hughes—to be completely forged.

In forging a single signature only a limited amount of writing must be copied. With a lengthier completely handwritten document, the forger needs to imitate successfully pages of writing that consist of not one or two names, but a variety of words, numerals, and other writing habits forming part of the identification of extended writing specimens. This means that there are many more chances of making errors that can lead to detection. The chance of success is substantially reduced. Over the course of years some examiners have believed that a forger, while he may attempt to imitate more than a signature, will limit the production to the bare minimum, but as the Hughes–Irving conflict showed, this is not always the case. A great deal more than the bare minimum was written in that case.

In creating an extended document the forger has the same kind of problem as he does in disguising his handwriting. He needs simultaneously to discard his own well-developed, unconscious habits while he copies with the proper degree of freedom the habits of another writer. Such forgeries may well be marked with poor writing quality, unnatural interruptions, and other faults of execution. Of course, letter forms suffer as well. The forger is often handicapped by the limited amount of known writing at hand. All the difficulties accompanying a signature forgery will occur at frequent intervals throughout the document, so that the chance of successful imitation of an extended handwritten document is virtually nonexistent. Certainly the longer the document, the less chance there is of success and the greater the number of telltale faults in the finished product.[14]

Howard Hughes Forgeries

The two recent cases involving the forgeries of Howard Hughes's handwriting were not the first time that letters or extended handwritten documents of a prominent person were forged.[15] The Hughes cases are

---

[13]An illustrated article dealing with the problem of this case was prepared by R. A. Cabanne, "The Clifford Irving Hoax of the Howard Hughes Autobiography," *Journal of Forensic Sciences* 20 (1975): 5–17.

[14]The private papers of the poet Percy Bysshe Shelley contain extensive examples of forged holographic documents. An account of some of the failures of the forger can be found in Louis A. Waters' analysis of them reported by Robert M. Smith, M. M. Schlegel, T. G. Ehrsam, and L. A. Waters, *The Shelley Legend* (New York: Scribners, 1945), p. 100.

[15]In the 1880 presidential campaign an embarrassing letter was published, allegedly written by President Garfield to H. L. Morey of Lynn, Massachusetts. William Hagan, *A Treatise on Disputed Handwriting* (New York: Banks, 1894), pp. 220–224, discusses the faults of this fraudulent imitation of President Garfield's writing.

unique, though, for they involve the work of two different forgers attempting to imitate the same handwriting. They form an interesting contrast in the end result, for in many ways they not only fail to duplicate Hughes's writing but fail to suggest in a large measure that they are imitations of the same writing (Figure 9.14). Both are sufficiently unlike the model writing that each was declared nongenuine by several document examiners working independently.

Irving claimed that he had authority to write a biography of Howard Hughes. He produced six forged letters totaling 19 pages besides a number of signatures to various documents and checks.

Figure 9.14. The upper section is a portion of the Irving forgeries of Howard Hughes writing. The lower is an excerpt from the forged Hughes will. The discoloration around the writing was caused by the running of the ink. The document had the appearance of having been water soaked.

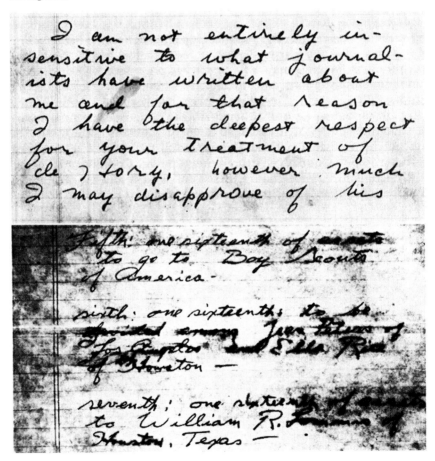

Irving produced writing that to a degree imitated Hughes's in freedom and form, but not without introducing differing details. Ultimately, study revealed some lack of freedom inconsistent with Hughes's writing. Still, before comparisons were made, the writing did not necessarily suggest forgery.

The brief illustrations included here do not exhaust the factors on which opinions of forgery rest, but they do show how different the results of the two attempts were.

Figure 9.15 shows several typical lines from Irving's imitations together with an excerpt from the Chester and Bill letter. The latter had been reproduced in color in the January 22, 1971, issue of *Life.* It served as an example of Hughes's writing for both forgers and the document examiners, and Irving in his confession of forgery indicated that it served him well. Close study reveals that Irving's forgery is not as freely written as Hughes's writing. Despite Hughes's many habitual interruptions, the forgeries tend to be somewhat less continuous. But it is details of form, repeated time and again, that differ from the way Hughes wrote. A typical example of several principal differences is displayed in Figure 9.16.

Figure 9.15. The upper section is from one of Irving's forged letters; the lower, genuine Hughes writing.

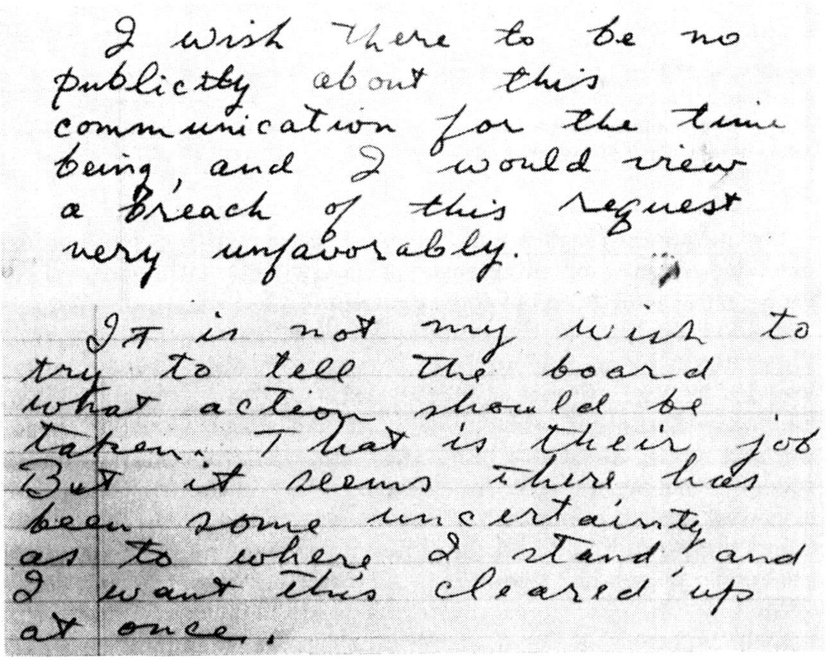
I wish there to be no publicity about this communication for the time being, and I would view a breach of this request very unfavorably.

It is not my wish to try to tell the board what action should be taken. That is their job But it seems there has been some uncertainty as to where I stand, and I want this cleared up at once.

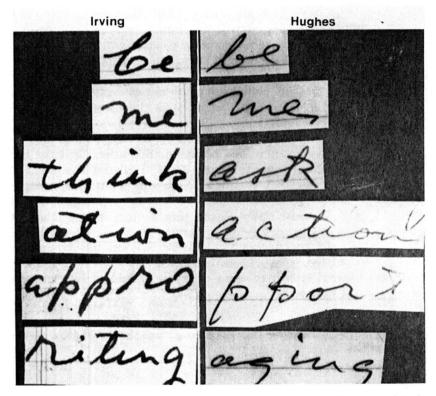

Figure 9.16. Defects of the Irving forgeries include: the consistent high start of the b; retracings at the base of the m rather than open turns; the k form; the open form of the o in the "on" combination; the continuous form of the p rather than the two-part Hughes form; and the upper enclosure of the g.

The purported Hughes will consisted of less writing, but was still extended, making up three pages of handwriting with signatures on each page as well as an envelope containing handwritten instructions.

A short analysis of the purported will appears in the next three illustrations. Figure 9.17 contains four lines from its second page surrounded by brief samples of Hughes's known writing. Above is a contemporary document, while below is another sample from the Chester and Bill letter, dated two years after the will. Unnatural hesitation occurs in the beginning stroke of the b of "be" in the will and unduly heavy strokes are found in "is." Both faults recur. Hidden pen lifts are found throughout the will, like the breaks between the u and c and the c and e in "spruce" (Figure 9.18). The overwriting of the downstroke of the t in "the" is a typical reworking of letters. Letter forms are only crudely imitated, as found in the c in "spruce" compared with the

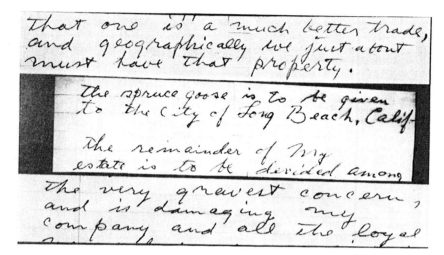

Figure 9.17. Comparison of four lines from the forged Hughes will in the center with writing of approximately the same date by Hughes (above) and his writing two years later (below).

Figure 9.18. An enlargement of two words from the forged will show "hidden" breaks between letters in "spruce," as indicated by arrows and the patching of the t. Both are typical, repeated faults of the will writing. Also note the difference in quality of execution compared with Hughes's writing below and the difference in the c design.

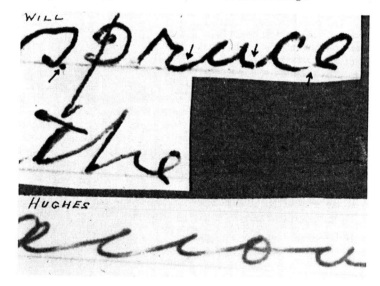

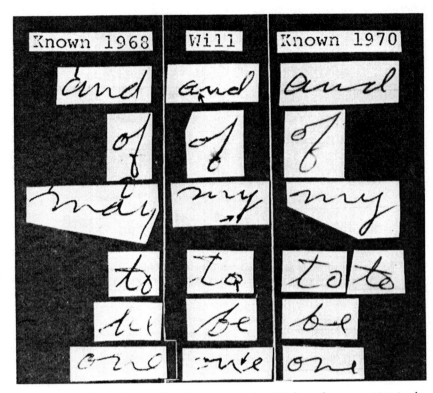

Figure 9.19. Defects of the will writing compared to Hughes's known writing in the outer columns include poorly written short, simple words. Also, the arrow indicates a small break between a and n in "and"; poorly formed letters in "of"; the addition of ending stroke (arrow) to y in "my"; the wrong direction of the ending of o, indicated by the arrow; the form of the beginning stroke and connection in "be"; and the form of n and e in "one." The words illustrated are almost automatically written by a writer like Hughes; the forgeries are not.

double c in Hughes's writing on the last line. Further examples appear in Figure 9.19. The will is clearly the work of an unskilled forger.

The task of copying pages of a person's handwriting in a perfectly natural way is virtually impossible. The skill of forgers varies, and their judgment of what should be important in producing an imitation is not necessarily the same. These factors and others were at play in both instances.

Forged Manuscripts and Autographs

A very specialized form of forgery comes into play in the manufacture of spurious ancient manuscripts and autographs. Here not only must the writing be imitated, but also the proper appearance of the paper's age, the correct ink and its aging, and other elements of the document must be considered.[16] Suspected ancient documents should be subjected to extensive critical study, including analysis of the paper, ink tests, examination to determine the kind of writing instrument used, writing identification, and a search for any signs of artificial aging of the document. Often the qualities of these forgeries are good compared with contemporary forgeries, but obvious errors such as steel pens instead of quill pens or dye inks instead of iron gall inks have been made. Despite the obstacles in the way of success, famous forgeries have been committed, and even today some rare documents in collections might be found practically worthless if subjected to these rigorous tests.

Identifying the Forger

One of the most difficult document problems is to establish from a study of the writing who prepared a forgery. Often, the question cannot be answered, since the process of forgery is in itself an excellent form

Figure 9.20. The upper "signature" is composed of letters selected from the defendant's general writing. Below is one of three fictitious signatures of a nonexistent person who completed a New York State business certificate. The law requires the true principals to sign the form.

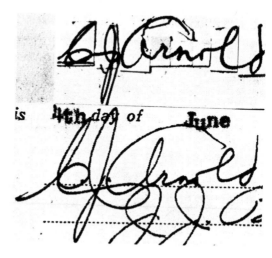

[16]One of the most extensive forgeries of rare documents was attempted by William Henry Ireland when in 1796 he brought forth a series of alleged manuscripts of William Shakespeare and contemporaries. These were first detected by Edmond Malone, *An Inquiry into the Authenticity of Certain Miscellaneous Papers and Legal Instruments* (London: Baldwin, 1796), and substantiated by the published confession of the forger himself: Ireland, *The Confession of William Henry Ireland* (London: Ellerton and Byworth, 1805).

of disguise. With only a fair imitation of the genuine signature, identification of the forger by means of his writing alone is the exception rather than the rule. Seldom do enough of the forger's own writing habits remain to serve as the basis for an identification. In rather rare instances, however, the forger may be identified by a number of his small but highly individual habits that occur in the simulated signature. Nevertheless, it must be understood that positive proof of his identity can never be based upon merely one or two similarities between his and the disputed writing.

With spurious or nonimitated signatures, especially those in which the writer did not attempt to change or disguise his natural writing, it is much easier to establish who prepared the signature (Figure 9.20). Here a serious difficulty is to collect adequate known writing upon which to base an opinion. A few of the forger's signatures will not do. A good quantity of his general handwriting is necessary. Once these specimens are available, however, the problem simply reverts to establishing the similarities between them and the disputed signature (Figure 9.21). Many times similarities can be pointed out letter by letter or by a combination of letters, but considering, of course, that the

Figure 9.21. The Anna Bosha signature was simply written on a form by an employee of the tax office to cover shortages. Below are writings of the employee-defendant that show strong similarities to the signature in question. The jury convicted the defendant of forgery.

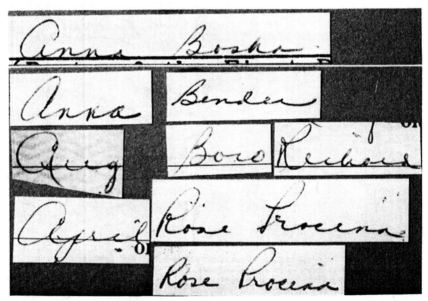

Figure 9.22. Identification of a forger using request signature included the unusual "catch" in the connecting stroke between the h and n, as indicated. The defendant willingly wrote "to prove his innocence."

forger writes with the required skill to have produced the questioned signature. At times there are cases in which a suspect can be asked to write the forged name and an identification made from these specimens[17] (Figure 9.22).

Summary

We have seen that a forgery may be prepared in several ways. For one to be successful to the extent that it prevents recognition under expert study, it must duplicate all the attributes of the authentic signatures to a degree that differences are few and can be attributed to chance or to the normal range of variation of the genuine signatures. Not only the form of letters but the qualities of writing movement must be accurately reproduced so that the problem involves imitating simultaneously a number of characteristics rather than each one singly. This task is at best extremely difficult. Thus, virtually all forged signatures

---

[17]This problem is discussed in more detail in O. Hilton, "Can the Forger Be Identified from His Handwriting," *Journal of Criminal Law, Criminology and Police Science* 43 (1952): 547–555.

contain typical faults and are only good enough to avoid detection at the initial time of use because no one is sufficiently suspicious to check them carefully. Therefore we find that when the forgery is challenged, certain typical faults are very likely to be present and can be detected with proper examination. Proof of forgery is based on these factors.

Assisted or Guided Signatures

In some instances, deathbed signatures, as well as those prepared during serious illness, are written with the assistance of another person. This aid may range from someone steadying the writer's hand or arm to a second writer actually guiding and more or less controlling the movement of the infirmed hand through the writing process. The former type of signature might best be termed an assisted signature, while the latter is often referred to as a guided signature.[18] However, the line of demarcation between the two types is difficult to draw, and it is not always clear from the resulting specimen just how much participation the second writer had. Even though the assistance is only in the form of support, it can introduce some constraint and suggested conflict in the writing.[19] When the assisting party guides the writing hand to such an extent that he is participating in the writing formation, characteristics foreign to the writer's usual habits can be introduced (Figure 9.23). Also, a signature often takes on an irregular appearance with pronounced evidence of conflict and uncoordinated movement brought about by the two writers trying to work in unison without previous practice. Guided and assisted signatures can legally validate a document, and consequently, because of the nature of the document and their abnormal appearance, serious disputes can arise concerning them.[20]

For the document examiner, the technical problems encountered in these signatures may become extremely difficult. Answers cannot always be as precise as with other types of signature problems. In the first place, assistance is necessary only when the writer has great difficulty in writing alone. In some instances, he first attempts to sign

---

[18]Dr. Edmond Locard divides the problem of guided handwriting into three classes: *assisted hand*, the writing of one who can hardly write due to physical condition but participates to some extent; *forced hand*, the writing of a person who is compelled by force to write against his will; and *inert hand*, the writing of one who merely holds the pen in his hand but is unable to participate at all. (See "The Inert Hand—A Rare Type of Forgery," *International Criminal Police Review* 45 (1951): 45–47). These distinctions are not attempted in this discussion.

[19]Also see Bobby G. Foley and James H. Kelly, "Guided Hand Signature Research," *Journal of Police Science and Administration* 5 (1977): 227–231.

[20]Osborn cites several cases dealing directly with the legal status of these signatures. See A. S. Osborn, *Questioned Documents*, 2nd ed. (Albany: Boyd, 1929), pp. 743–745.

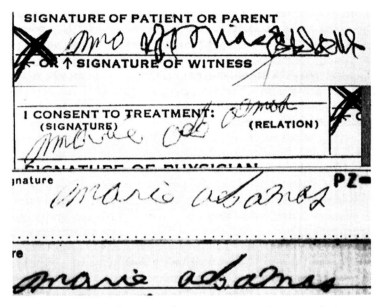

Figure 9.23. Marie Adams started to write the upper signature, but stopped after two letters. The signature that followed was assisted by an unknown hospital attendant. From some evidence in the case, it seemed very likely that the signature was completed with a reluctant Marie Adams.

unassisted and cannot complete the name. When the document contains evidence of such an attempt, this added evidence often aids the examiner in analyzing the completed signature. There is always the question of how much assistance was given. Was it simply steadying an infirmed hand or arm? Was there help in creating the writing? Was the writer so weak that the assisting signature is executed with the writer propped up in bed, a poor position even for a writer in good health. The testimony of those present and of the assisting person and the physical evidence within the document must be considered and weighed in combination. Unfortunately, there is seldom even one other signature available that was prepared in a similar manner with the same person assisting. If there is such a specimen, the question remains, Was the degree of assistance the same?

Many times a guided or assisted signature resembles a forgery, but the effect of restraint and conflict common to these two classes of signatures differs sufficiently to distinguish between them. Nevertheless, more than one allegedly guided signature has after proper examination been found to be a forgery.

The usual conflicting characteristics of a guided signature result from a combination of features. They include the strength and writing ability of the writer, the extent to which the assisting party participates in the writing act as well as the extent to which the primary writer participates, and the various physical conditions surrounding the actual execution,[21] such as the writer's and guider's position and the type of support for the document during execution. There may be an occasional guided signature that reveals little conflict but actually turns out to be the handwriting of the assisting party only slightly modified. Such a condition might well arise when a close member of the family is assisting the writer and the writer himself is almost unable to write at all. Under these circumstances, if he trusts the assisting party, he may merely hold the pen and relax completely, so that the guider must move the writer's hand and the pen in the execution of the signature. So it is when the writer merely touches the pen without even holding it, which in some jurisdictions may be accepted as a properly executed signature by the so-called writer. In these cases the examiner can probably say only that the signatures appear to have been written by the guider, and the court must ultimately decide the issue of genuineness on the basis of whether the assisting person's testimony appears truthful. The reader can appreciate that with this class of signatures, each problem is individual, and only the general rules set forth in this section can serve as a guide in determining how to evaluate the expert's opinion.

Identification of Initials and Illiterates's Marks

Initials and illiterates's marks can be considered special classes of signatures. The former are used often as shortened signatures in many classes of business activity; the latter are the only signatures available to the illiterate. Since disputes arise about both, further consideration of their identification is in order.

Initials

Most writers, and especially those who are called upon to initial documents from time to time, develop a personal manner of writing their initials.[22] Genuine specimens may be denied (Figure 9.24), and occasionally the initials of another person are imitated or forged (Figure 9.25). How the initials are written is generally the controlling factor. It may be possible to demonstrate the facts clearly, but occasionally

---

[21]Persifor Frazer, *Manual of the Study of Documents* (Philadelphia: Lippincott, 1894), p. 148, reproduces a series of experimental signatures involving assistance to the writer. While this represents only an experiment in which the two writers attempted to simulate a series of typical combinations of assistance, it gives some idea of what might be encountered in this type of problem.
[22]Nanette G. Galbraith, "Initials: A Question of Identity," *Forensic Science International* 18 (1981): 13–16.

Figure 9.24. The two disputed, denied initials were affixed to architectural drawings. The writer admitted all of the others. All initials are written freely as a unit, and all contain similar letter designs. The two denied are no exception and must be authentic.

Figure 9.25. The pair of initials appeared on a blueprint and are clearly written in imitation of the capital letters of the writer's signature. Both initials are slowly drawn with uncertain movement. Feldman in contrast writes a free rapid, firm signature. The hesitant execution marks the initials as a forgery.

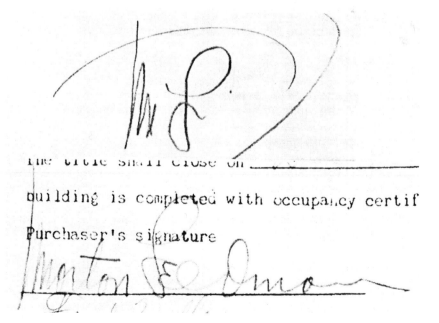

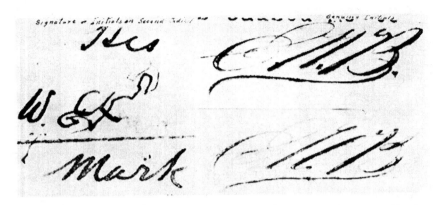

Figure 9.26. The combination of initials and a mark appeared on a document offered as a second codicil in the Browning estate. At the right are Mr. Browning's freely and skillfully written initials revealing his highly developed handwriting. The second codicil was executed on his deathbed. He had been unable to write when the document was brought to him at an earlier date. The quality of the mark, coupled with the inability even to initial the document, led to expert testimony that he lacked testamentary capacity at the time of execution. After similar medical testimony by doctors in attendance, the surrogate rejected the codicil on these grounds. *(Illustration from the files of Elbridge W. Stein.)*

the question cannot be fully resolved. Authentic initials are sometimes very difficult to locate, but are essential when the writer links them together in a unit in an individual way. If written separately, it may be possible to supplement a limited number of known initials with signatures to solve the problem. Basically, the small amount of writing makes the problem more difficult than signature investigations.

Cross Marks

Under the law, "his mark," properly witnessed, has been accepted as an illiterate's signature for generations.[23] On rare occasions a deathbed document is authenticated by a mark made by the dying person who under normal conditions would have signed his name (Figure 9.26). Usually, answers to questions about the authenticity of these marks can be ascertained from the attending witnesses, but at times the witnesses are not available or their reliability and integrity are in question. Under these circumstances the document examiner must endeavor to answer the questions.

While the mark is generally a simple cross, each may have some degree of individuality. In fact, two illiterates are unlikely to make

---

[23]See Tagiasco v. Molinari's Heirs, 9 La 512 (1836). Osborn cites the pertinent portion of the decision in *Questioned Documents*, 2nd ed., p. 944.

identical marks, but all who use this class of signature tend to develop a fixed pattern. The usual mark consists of but two or three strokes, and because of its simplicity is rather easily imitated. Often, though, the mark is made fraudulently without reference to a genuine one. Forged marks may also contain such common faults as improper sequence of strokes, greater skill of execution than the imitated writer is himself capable of, defective writing movement, too heavy or too light pen pressure, and a pen position that is inconsistent with the writer's habits. Though this kind of signature is simple, there are many elements to be considered in its identification. Naturally, many more marks are genuine than are forged, but all that are disputed must be carefully studied so that personal rights are properly protected.

Conclusions

The identification of a signature or proof of its genuineness assumes prominence in many legal controversies. It is not a rare event for an individual to deny having signed a document—a contract, deed, receipts, or virtually any class of paper (Figure 9.27). He may raise a cry of forgery; or he may only remark, "Well it looks like my signature, but I never signed that paper." If genuine, this fact must be established (Figure 9.28). Disputes over signatures may also arise when the writer has died or is not available to authenticate them (Figure 9.29). Possibly, there are no witnesses, or the witnesses themselves are dead. Still, the authenticity of the signature must be demonstrated. These conditions are encountered with contested wills or in claims against estates, in

Figure 9.27. In the course of trial a witness denied signing an agreement (top). When compared with his known signatures, one of which is shown below, it was very clear that the signature was genuine. There is the same freedom, smoothness, and continuity of movement, comparable writing skill, similar slant, and proportional size of compound letters, as well as the same personalized letter forms in all signatures examined.

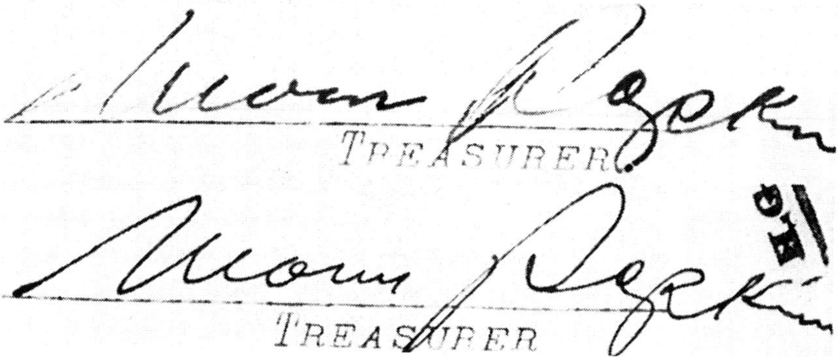

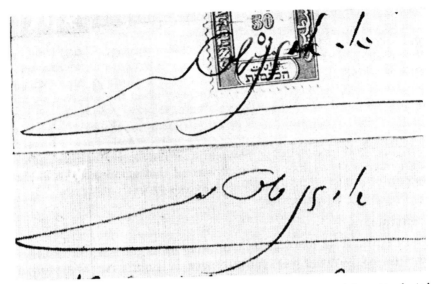

Figure 9.28. The upper signature was on a key document in a case, and the writer denied signing the paper. He did acknowledge a number of other signatures, including the second specimen. The Hebrew writing runs from right to left, and letters are normally written in a disconnected manner. The denied signature contains an initial to the right of the stamp, the balance is the surname. The standard shown does not have the initial; others did. The signatures are skillful, well-developed writing. The long free stroke of the letter near the center is individual, as are the two connected letters and the final three letters, which are slurred together at the beginning of the long free ending stroke that moves well to the left before swinging back under the entire signature. Clearly the denied signature is genuine.

Figure 9.29. The writer of the note signature was in Bulgaria and could not return to this country to testify. His signature consisted of a D (for "Doctor"), connected to the first letter of his last name and writing without lifting the pen into his first name. Except for the very apparent difference in size of writing the signatures are written in the same way, with the same writing qualities and similar design of letter. The signature is clearly authentic.

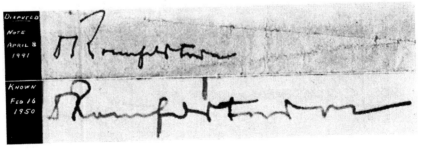

which almost any kind of legal document may figure. Because of a combination of circumstances, it becomes necessary to establish the genuineness of a signature through technical study, and at times to demonstrate the fact in court.

An opinion that a signature is a forgery is the alternative solution to many of these problems. Sometimes that conclusion is reached even though those interested in the document never suggest it or insist that it is highly improbable. Signatures to wills, deeds, notes, contracts, and checks are more frequently forged than signatures to other documents, but there is probably no class of document in which there has not at one time or other been a forgery. Scientific examination is generally the chief means of detecting these frauds.

Whether these questions can be accurately answered generally depends on how many authentic signatures are available. With a formally written signature in dispute, that is, one executed with normal writing care, a sufficient number of genuine signatures almost always permits a clearcut answer. If the disputed signature is written with little or no care, however, such as a hurried pencil-written receipt signature, there is somewhat less assurance that the opinion will be a definite one. Here the greatest difficulty is that genuine signatures written under similar conditions may be limited in number and hard to locate. The disputed signature may be so badly scrawled that it contains few identifying characteristics. Similar limitations may be encountered with signatures of the seriously ill or those of the infirm or aged. In such a case, only a qualified opinion can be given. Fortunately the vast number of disputed signatures are part of important papers, and the issue of their genuineness can be definitely determined through technical study.

10

Identification
of Handlettering
and Numerals

In the preceding chapters the identification of signatures and other handwriting has been considered. For some readers the general discussion of handwriting may appear to cover the identification of handlettering and numerals adequately. However, both classes of writing constitute a distinct form of handwriting. While both are significantly different in use, they have much in common, especially their mutual dissimiliarities to cursive handwriting.

Handlettering

Handlettering is a specialized class of writing that in one form or another has been used since man first invented an alphabet. All ancient manuscripts were prepared in a disconnected form of lettering, actually the only writing of that period. In fact, cursive handwriting is a rather modern development, belonging to the last few centuries, and, despite its widespread use, handlettering is still common. Persons engaged in various trades and professions regularly employ handlettering in their daily work,[1] and some schools training these workers teach formal lettering systems. In recent years most elementary schools start children printing disconnected letters before teaching them connected writing, and it is often assumed that those who never experienced this basic training can letter. Applications and all manner of other forms

---

[1] Some professions use handlettering almost exclusively. The work of draftsmen, architects, and engineers can be recognized as common examples. Millions of people see specimens of handlettering in daily comic strips and cartoons published in newspapers. While these are a large group of users, they represent only a portion of many modern-day applications of handlettering.

bear instructions: "Please print." Consequently, since various kinds of documents may contain handlettering, it is only natural that some questions will arise concerning the identity of the author of a particular specimen.

A pure lettering system, as opposed to other styles of handwriting, is one in which all characters are disconnected.[2] Numerous systems are taught and practiced, the principal differences being the class and forms of letters and variations in slant. In certain identification problems, consequently, there may be the influence of some basic system, although all lettering is modified by the individual writer. This condition certainly prevails with many whose primary education was based on the print–write method. Regardless of whether a person has ever had any formal instruction in lettering, practically everyone believes he is capable of printing or lettering. The result is that many specimens are highly individual and reflect no influence of formal training whatsoever, but rather are only a confusion of print styles with uppercase and lowercase letters mixed indiscriminately.

Most of the factors involved in the identification of handwriting apply to handlettering problems (Figure 10.1). The disconnected manner of writing causes details of form to assume somewhat greater importance than in the identification of connected-writing specimens, but how the lettering was executed should also be considered. These details include the number, direction, and sequence of strokes, slant, and the relative or proportional size of letters and of their several parts. Nevertheless, despite the more interrupted mode of execution, such writing qualities as pen emphasis and shading, skill, freedom, and rhythm are significantly individual and must be considered. Furthermore, handlettering identification is not complete without consideration of the qualities of movement, for example, the certainty or hesitancy in the writing movement, tremor or vigor, shading and pen emphasis, retracing and pen dragging, retouching, and the speed and manner of writing. Significant attention must be given to the continuity of the writing, that is, whether each letter is made as a connected, continuous whole or as several distinct separate strokes. Actually the elements of movement may readily distinguish between two similar but different specimens of handlettering. By the same token, two or more letters connected in a united group, which violates the basic disconnected feature of lettering, have identification value, but it must be recognized that with some writers connecting or not connecting

---

[2]The manuscript writing taught in elementary schools is disconnected penmanship closely resembling a pure lettering system. Subsequently, the child is shown how to connect these letters to write cursively. This early training undoubtedly influences some lettered specimens encountered in identification problems.

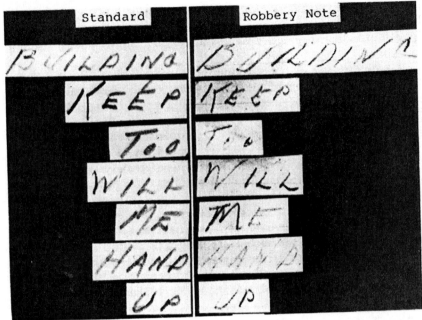

Figure 10.1. The writer of a robbery note is identified by his lettering. The writer used capital forms throughout, but certain letters were made taller as initial letters of a word: K, W, M, and T. The slant is similar. Compound letters like M and W are written continuously.

letters may only distinguish between informal or careless execution and more formal writing.

While an unusual combination of different letter styles and alternative forms may in itself point strongly toward the ultimate identification, it alone cannot establish positive identity. Final identification rests in large measure on the individual habits of design, including the size of letters compared to one another; curvature or angularity of strokes; the relationship between the parts of each letter; and artistic, conventional, or unique style. Furthermore, with extensive lettering, such as a page or more, some writers will revert to segments of cursive handwriting consisting of combinations of two or three letters or, on occasion, of full words (Figure 10.2). The accuracy of identification depends on careful and detailed collation of the known and unknown specimens and on consideration and evaluation of every aspect of letter form and quality of writing.

Variation naturally occurs in a series of lettered specimens by the same writer, just as with any form of writing. Consequently, the basic principles on which all writing identification is based can be extended with proper modification to handlettering problems. The conclusion

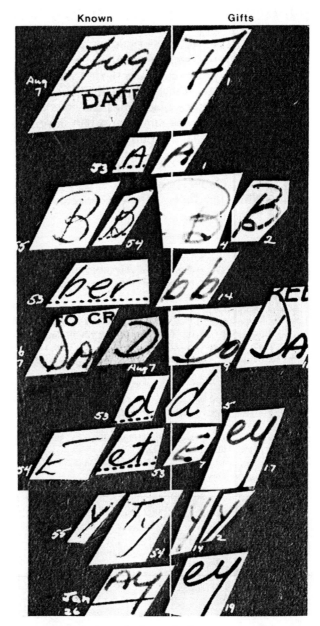

Figure 10.2. In a series of cards attached to gifts from a higher-up in a gambling ring, the lettering mixed capital and small letter forms with some connected, cursive writing. Note "et," "ey," and "d." Mixtures of this nature case often add to the convincing identification of a writer.

that a single writer prepared two sets of lettering is thus assured when all the habits of the disputed matter are found in the known specimens, while at the same time the existing variations between the representative known forms and the disputed lettering can be accounted for by the normal variation common to that individual's lettering. Furthermore a sufficient number of individual habits must be common to the two sets of specimens, questioned and standard, so that the likelihood of both coming from a common origin is so great that it becomes a virtual certainty. By the same token, fundamental differences, especially consistently repeated ones, establish that the two sets of lettering are by different writers (Figure 10.3).

In some circumstances, a person may attempt to disguise handlettering. While handlettering's disconnected nature facilitates success,

Figure 10.3. Four eyewitnesses identified the defendant, Christopher E. Balestrero, as the armed robber who had presented the robbery note. His lettering, prepared at the time of arrest (left column), and prior to the date of the crime (right column), is compared with that of the note.

Fundamental, repeated differences prove Balestrero did not write the note. He consistently forms his G in two distinct sections; the writer of the robbery note makes his in one continuous writing. The defendant's B's contain a careful retrace or loop as the center stroke and never degenerate into the form found in the note. The right-hand side of his R is made in a single writing, but in the robbery note the right leg of the R is a separate stroke.

A few days before the trial, another man, apprehended while committing an armed robbery, confessed to this particular crime as well. The handwriting findings were confirmed, and an innocent man exonerated.

A full story of the case appeared in *Life* (June 29, 1953), and a condensation was reprinted in *Reader's Digest* ("A Case of Identity," pp. 86–90, October 1953). Also see Ordway Hilton, "Handwriting Identification vs Eye Witness Identification," *Journal of Criminal Law, Criminology and Police Sicence* 45 (1954): 207–212, for a more detailed discussion of the case.

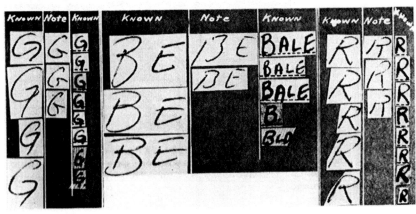

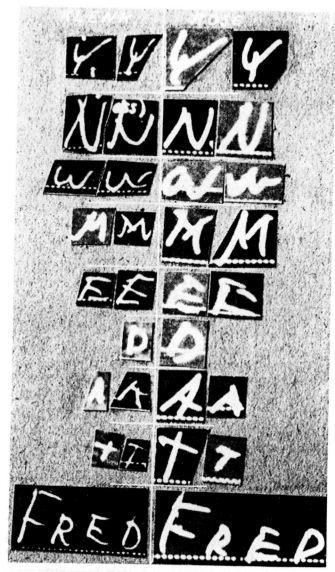

Figure 10.4. Comparison of lettering prepared by Klenk with a hotel registration by Rose established the alias. The rapid, broken, or stroke by stroke lettering (four separate strokes in the M) is found in both specimens. The same rugged execution, slant, and use of a larger capital F in "Fred" are part of the identification formula. (Circumstances surrounding the investigation required the use of photostatic copies only.)

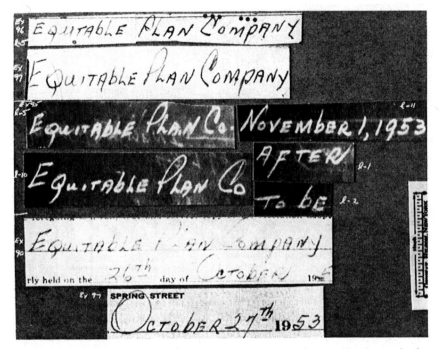

Figure 10.5. A series of different business documents was shown to be the work of a single writer. The lettering consists of a unique, consistent mixture of capital and small letters and the use of initial larger capitals where capitalization was needed.

especially with short passages, inconsistencies mark attempts to prepare extensive specimens in this way. Frequently, grotesque forms, undue attention to details, and abnormal writing qualities are among the telltale indications of disguise. If one is fully aware of the likelihood of disguise and has ample known lettering for comparison, the attempt is very apt to be recognized, and with proper comparison specimens, an identification ultimately effected.

Instead of handlettering being exempt from technical identification, as many believe, it is as highly individual as a person's cursive writing or signature and therefore is subject to identification.

The more handlettering is used today, the more frequently problems arise concerning its identification.[3] A number of these involve anon-

---

[3] James V. P. Conway has prepared an outstanding article dealing with these problems entitled, "The Identification of Handprinting," *Journal of Criminal Law, Criminology and Police Science* 45 (1955): 605–612. Included are three illustrated cases pointing up important considerations in these specialized questions.

ymous letters in which the writer has turned to lettering to hide his identity. Since many people feel that this step alone precludes detection, they make little attempt, if any, to disguise their handprinting. In more important matters, questions may also arise concerning the identification of lettering on hotel registrations (Figure 10.4), bank deposit slips, personnel forms, or any document on which the writer would be apt to print (Figure 10.5). At times the most difficult aspect of the investigation is to locate representative known specimens of lettering for comparison, since cursive writings are of very little assistance in handlettering problems. Once this is done, however, the findings generally are clear cut.

Numerals

The identification of numerals is closely related to that of handlettering. With both classes of writing, the examiner deals with a series of characters normally written in a disconnected manner. Because fewer characters are involved, problems involving only numerals may be more difficult than where handlettering is present, but they can be, and have been, effectively answered.

The numerals are only ten digits, but the questioned material is not always confined to these, even when no letters are involved. Various symbols are related to particular uses of numbers. Monetary amounts involve such symbols as the dollar sign ($) and the the manner of writing fractional amounts representing cents. If the material involves prices or stock items, symbols such as the number sign (#) and "at" (@) may be used when unit cost is involved. Other trades and professions combine numbers and symbols in numerical records. Decimal points and slashes (diagonal strokes) are common adjuncts. The elements of numeral identification can certainly be extended to include these special symbols as well.

Three fundamental factors are involved in the identification of numerals, factors that are basic to every writing identification: form, writing quality or movement, and variation. When a specimen of numerals is the work of one writer, a unique combination of these factors will be present and will form the basis of a positive identification. Fundamental differences in either form or movement are the means of distinguishing numerals prepared by different individuals.

Identification of numerals rests not only on their basic design; it also involves the complete analysis of the subordinate factors of design. These factors include initial and ending strokes, ornamentation, any simplification of design, overall slant, and the interrelationship of component parts of compound digits, which are usually all but the 1 and 0. In this phase of the examination one must consider the size of one

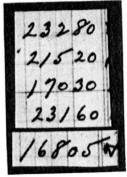

Figure 10.6. A writer uses smaller zeros than any of his other numerals. The sample was taken from work of a bookkeeper.

part compared to the others, the slant of enclosures or individual strokes compared to the digit as a whole or to other parts, the angles between intersecting strokes, whether the parts are connected by small loops or retracings, and whether individual strokes are straight lines or some form of curves. Are certain digits consistently small or larger than others? (See Figure 10.6.) The numerals 6, 8, 9, and 0 may contain elongated ovals or nearly round enclosures. Some have distinctive means of closing or failing to close these areas completely. Thus, while a particular digit may be very clearly formed, it may still have distinct characteristics. The numerals of some writers may be so highly individualized as to be difficult to read.

Besides their relative size, further individuality may be displayed by the positioning of multiple-digit numbers. Their spacing may be distinctive, and what is more often encountered, these may be a particular pattern of alignment, especially in fractions and monetary units. Some writers consistently place cent units above the line, and an underscore or lack of underscore is a further individual habit.[4] Thus, a personalized use of digits further identifies the writer.

Numeral design has individual aspects but is influenced by formal training. A writer normally derives his personalized manner of writing numbers from the system he was taught in school. Writers educated in the United States may write numbers with an "accent" different from that of writers taught in Europe. Architects, engineers, and draftsmen have been taught a second numeral system, which they use professionally. Yet all of these writers develop individual habits that, while reflecting some aspects of their original training, distinguish their writing from others'.

---

[4]The various possible ways of writing amounts on check form the basis of filing fraudulent checks. See Orville B. Livingston, "Bogus Check File Classified by Trademarks," *Journal of Criminal Law, Criminology and Police Science* 39 (1948): 782–789.

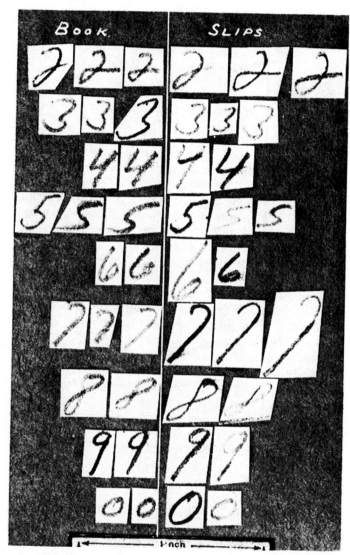

Figure 10.7. The writer of gambling slips was identified by numerals in a record book. Factors in the identification include the greater slant of the 8's than other digits and its overlapping closure, the pronounced rounding of the turn in the 7's, the variable forms of the 5's, and the rapid, open form of the center stroke of the 3's.

Figure 10.8. A writer consistently connects "30" and "20."

Individuality goes beyond form, however. The manner of writing numbers is reflected in the end product. With the disconnected execution of characters, it is not always as easy to evaluate skill, writing speed, and freedom of execution as it is with continuous connected writing. These factors and others that combine to characterize writing quality, however, can and must be assessed. Writing skill can distinguish between two sets of rather similar numerals. The smoothness of strokes, freedom of execution, and evidence of automatic or labored production, coupled of course with the preciseness of design, are factors in evaluating skill.

Other factors of execution include shading or its absence, symmetrically curved or angular strokes (Figure 10.7), careless or precise execution, the start and end of strokes, and the direction in which the strokes are written.

Finally, although each digit should be made separately, some writers habitually or frequently join certain pairs (Figure 10.8). How is this accomplished? When the digits are written separately, there may still be drag lines that characterize the work of some individuals. Thus numeral identification involves a number of factors that in a large measure account for the individuality of the end product.

Variation

All forms of a person's handwriting contain variation. Numerals are no exception. Two aspects should be considered: variation due to relative care and speed of execution, and variation in form. These two elements may not be entirely unrelated, but they can be considered separately.

Hastily, carelessly written numbers normally vary from those written in a more formal manner. Furthermore, lack of care can introduce greater variation from one writing of a number to the next. It can cause decline in the accuracy of form so that details do not agree exactly with those found in more carefully written numbers. Even formal, very carefully written specimens contain elements of variation. When several examples of the same digit are compared, they will not agree

Figure 10.9. The work of a bookkeeper who prepared part or all of bid sheets for three companies is identified by her numerals. The work of the other person is shown in Figure 10.10. This writer has two form of her 4's, which can be recognized by the formation of the turn at the left corner, a distinctive top stroke of the 7's, and very narrow elongated forms of 8 compared to the rounded forms of the 3.

222

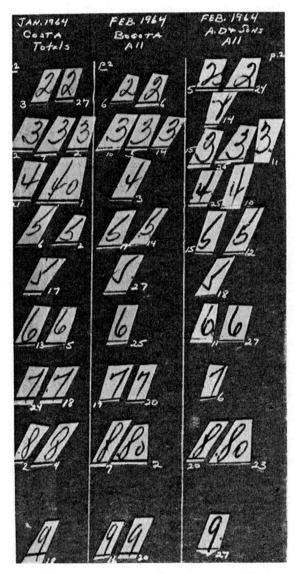

Figure 10.10. The work of this bookkeeper can be distinguished easily from her partner's (Figure 10.9) by the occasional use of an alternate, imprecise form of 5 and by the small 0 compared to other digits. The low left-hand closure of the 8 is highly personal. The work of both writers can be individually identified, but in searching through a quantity of bid sheets it was very helpful to be able to have easy recognition factors for each writer.

entirely. How they vary from one writing to the next defines the limit of variation, so that with a truly representative set of known specimens any number written by an individual will fall within the limits established by the variables of the known examples.

Variation in form may consist of alternative forms of the same numeral or simply rather wide modifications of the same basic form. The alternative forms are quite common with some writers. For example, at times the writer may make a slight retrace or definite stop at the end of the initial downstroke of a 5 before swinging off to the right to form the lower curving section. On the other hand, he may have examples of this same number made in a curving form resembling a printed S. This latter form will undoubtedly be more common to his more carelessly written numbers, but some writers use the forms almost interchangeably. Similar alternative forms may be found in other digits as well. Whenever there is more than one design of a numeral and both designs occur in the known and unknown writing, we have as a consequence more than ten digit designs to be considered in making the identification.[5]

Normally, problems involving the identity of the writer of numerals concern accounting records (Figures 10.9 and 10.10), stock records, bank deposit slips, engineering drawings, and logs relating to time, distances, and similar data. In criminal matters, the keeper of gambling records may be identified by means of his numeral writing. Problems of this class are not as frequent as other writing problems, but one must not forget that numerals encountered in other writing problems can add to the final identification.

Conclusions

These two specialized forms of handwriting, handlettering and numerals, may stand alone as a means of identifying the writing of an individual. In other problems each can strengthen cursive handwriting identifications. The methods of identification are no different from those for handwriting in general except for necessary modifications due to the interrupted, character by character method of writing. Individuality in handlettering and numerals forms the basis of identifications that are as convincing as those of signatures or cursive handwriting. Important document cases involving lettering or numerals only have been successfully completed.

---

[5]This discussion is a condensation of O. Hilton, "Identification of Numerals," *International Criminal Police Review* 241 (1970): 245–250. Readers desiring more information on this subject are referred to that article.

11

Typewriting Identification

In Chapter 3 it was pointed out that all typewriting is not the same, but rather each specimen may in certain instances indicate the manufacturer and the period in which the machine was built. By comparing a disputed specimen of typewriting with the work of specific typewriters, we can extend the analysis to identify the particular machine on which the disputed matter was written. In fact, this identification is possible without ever seeing the machine itself or determining when and where it was made. The basis of this identification is the individuality of every typewriter.

It is often said that a typewriter prints with machinelike precision, but let us pause for a moment to consider the full meaning of the phrase "machinelike precision." While it has come to imply extreme regularity, this precision differs under various conditions, the degree of variation encountered depending on the particular mechanism. The adjustments and tolerances of a typewriter are not so fine that it is impossible to distinguish differences in the work of some new machines. It must be recognized, however, that with present-day manufacturing and the more modern machines, such as the single element and electronic typewriters, tolerances have been reduced compared with those of manufacturing processes of former years. Use of a typewriter, as of any mechanical instrument, causes wear and damage to the working parts, which in time lead to the appearance of individual defects or writing pecularities in the work of every machine.

Actually, the identification of a particular typewriter from its work is established by a combination of factors. The type size and type style or font is the first, basic factor. Large numbers of machines generally make up this fundamental grouping, but at the same time there are a number of type sizes produced by every manufacturer as well as several different fonts within each type size. Then the final factor is the particular combination of the imperfections or defects shown in the typewriting together with the properly writing characters. All these factors together individualize a particular machine and establish its identification. A basic difference in any one of the factors considered—type size, type design, a particular defect, or a specific character's printing properly rather than with defect—can establish that a document was prepared on some machine other than the one under consideration (See Figure 11.1).

Identification of a typewriter is a function of its operating characteristics. That means that identification of a typebar machine must involve a set of operating characteristics different from those of a single element, type ball machine, such as the IBM Selectric, or again of an electronic single element, type wheel typewriter, such as the Xerox 800. Nevertheless, the same kind of peculiarities are sought in all problems, although their frequency and importance differ with each class of machine.

There is a further consideration in typewriting identification: Many of the identifying characteristics develop with use. Thus, with a new machine just off the assembly line, there may be very few individual typing characteristics, but gradually, over the years as the machine is used, other defects or pecularities will develop. There is no way of forecasting when defects will change in a machine, and many of them are persistent over a long time. For example, if the type metal itself becomes damaged, this defect will persist, while other kinds of defects can be corrected by readjustment of the machine, even though such corrections are rather infrequent. Let us first consider the basic defects that may occur and then see how these may be encountered in each class of machine.

A number of different kinds of identifying defects are normally encountered in an identification problem. One group relates to the letters and characters and how they print (printing defects). A second group

Figure 11.1. Page 4 was typewritten on a different machine than pages 1–3. The lack of a serif on the center stroke of the m, page 4, is a design difference of the second machine.

Page 1	Page 2	Page 3	Page 4

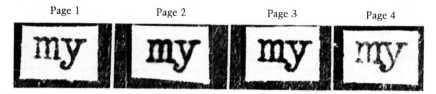

pertains to other operations of the machine (machine defects). There are elements of variation in typewriters that can be recognized from their work, and finally there are some transitory defects. Each group will be discussed more in detail, for there are subgroups or elements within each class of defects.

Printing Defects

Traditionally, the defects or peculiarities found in the type impressions of work from the machine have been the chief basis for identification. They may be divided into two basic classes—alignment defects and typeface defects.

A typewriter is designed so that each character prints an even, uniform impression resting on or across an imaginary baseline and opti-

Figure 11.2. The upper sections show an example of horizontal malalignment. If the r printed properly, it would be spaced equidistant from the two e's.

Below, the N and n are out of alignment vertically, printing above the baseline established by the i, e, and other letters on the machine. The photograph was made under a glass typewriter test plate.

Figure 11.3. The i leans 4° to the left of vertical, as shown by this photograph under a special typewriting protractor. The horizontal lines of the test plate are carefully set parallel to the line of typewriting so that the vertical lines measure the number of degrees of twist.

Figure 11.4. All the characters in this exhibit write off-their-feet, that is, too heavy in one portion of the impression. The darker area is at the top of the t and S, at the bottom of the a, on the left-hand side of the m and M, on the right-hand side of the h. With the 2, d, o, and y, the character prints the heaviest at one corner.

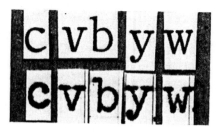

Figure 11.5. The upper line is from a modern shaded typefont. The wider, heavier part of the impression is due to the design of the type font. In contrast the lower line is a specimen of standard pica type in which all strokes of the letter are the same width and the shaded appearance is due to improper typeface alignment.

Figure 11.6. The condition of rebound appears in both letters above. It is characteristic of some manual typebar machines. In the case of the D, the second or rebound printing is found to the right of the principal (heavier) impression; with the A, it is slightly above and to the left of the heavier impression.

cally centered within a designated space or unit along that line. That is the ideal, but in practice the alignment is not always perfect. Some characters print above or below the proper position or to the right or left of it (Figure 11.2); others are twisted on their axis so as to lean away from the proper slant (Figure 11.3); still others are "off their feet," which means that the typefaces strike the paper surface unevenly so that one edge or corner gives a heavier or darker impression than other

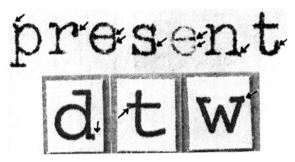

Figure 11.7. The six letters that make up the word "present" each contain a typeface defect. They are indicated by arrows. The upper left serif of the p is partially broken off. Impressions were made through a worn fabric ribbon.

Below are three letters from a machine with contemporary typefaces. The impressions are through a carbon film ribbon and show very subtle typeface damage. The lower serif of the d is slightly worn. The t-crossing has a small chip, as does the right serif of the w. Fine defects of this nature would be obscured by even a high-grade fabric ribbon.

parts of the letter, rather than the uniformly inked impression of a properly typewritten letter (Figure 11.4). Certain contemporary shaded type fonts contain many letters with some portions wider than others, which makes it rather difficult though not impossible to recognize letters that print "off their feet" (Figure 11.5). At times a letter may consistently print appreciably too heavy or too light or may rebound, printing two impressions not quite superimposed (Figure 11.6). The foregoing individualities are commonly referred to as *alignment defects.*

The *typeface defects,* on the other hand, consist of actual breaks in the impression, resulting from chips or bumps in the type metal, and dented or irregular outlines of letters caused by damage to the typeface itself (Figure 11.7). In both classes, the defects may be slight, requiring careful examination under magnification or, in the case of malalignment, aided by alignment test plates. With a thorough and detailed study, each kind of defect can be discovered.

Machine Defects

Occasionally, other operational peculiarities of a typewriter may assist in an identification. The following are some of these more infrequent defects: a consistently slight variation from the designed spacing between letters or lines; slippage of the paper so that successive lines are not parallel; skipping of a space after certain letters; improper working of the ribbon, which affects the printed impression (Figure 11.8); and irregular left margins or the stacking of letters on the right due to

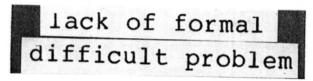

Figure 11.8. The improper action of the typewriter ribbon caused the top of the l in "lack" to fail to print.

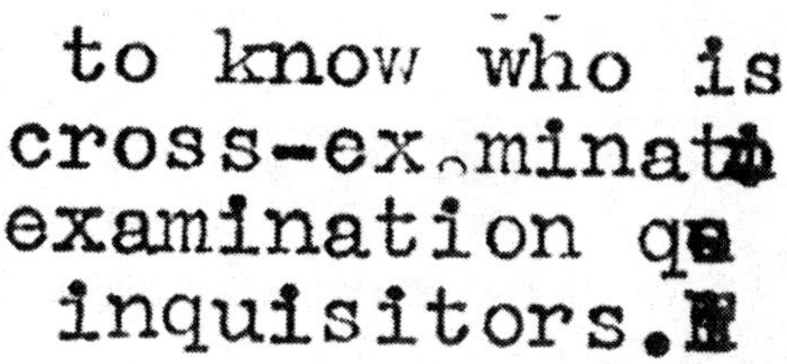

> to know who is
> cross-ex.minat
> examination q
> inquisitors.

Figure 11.9. The typewriting of the last three lines in this specimen shows stacked type along the right-hand margin because of the improper functioning of the margin stop. If repeated throughout a series of specimens, this condition can assist in identifying the machine.

defective operation of the margin stops (Figure 11.9). If any one of these repeats with regularity throughout a series of specimens, it can certainly be considered an identifying pecularity of the machine.

Variation

Although variation in the work of the same typewriter occurs to a much lesser degree than in a person's handwriting, repeated impressions of the same character may not reflect the same evidence of defects in each impression. The kind and amount of variation common to any one machine are governed by several factors: the condition of the machine in general, especially the play in moving parts of older machines; the rough surface of a worn platen (roller) in particular; the amount of ink on the ribbon; the manner in which the keys are struck, i.e., uniformly or not particularly with a manual typewriter; the weight of the impression; and unpredictable variables.[1]

Variation is more apt to influence alignment defects, but it also affects certain typeface defects as well (Figure 11.10). Irregular type-

---

[1]See O. Hilton, "The Influence of Variation on Typewriting Identification," *Journal of Criminal Law, Criminology and Police Science* 50 (1959): 420–425.

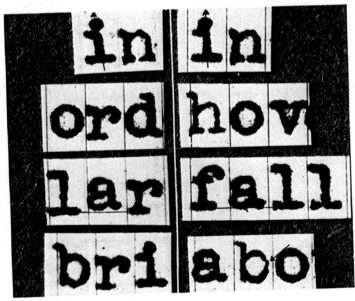

Figure 11.10. The words shown in the two columns are all from the same machine and show some of its variable factors. The i prints both twisted and properly, the o to the left and then to the right, the a high and on the line, and the b left and more nearly centered. (The weak or apparent broken portion of this letter indicated by the arrow, is due to a ribbon flaw.)

Figure 11.11. Variable impressions of the l as they appeared on a copy of a will. The lower left-hand side of the base stroke appears very short in specimens 3 and 14 and substantially longer in 7 and 9.

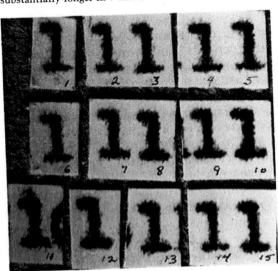

writing rhythm, especially on a manual machine, may cause variation in the position of successive printings of the same letter. More often, however, letters off their feet appear to print normally when struck heavily, and slightly battered and damaged typefaces may print without any apparent defect if the impression is well inked through a fabric ribbon. In both instances lighter impressions of these letters show their defective character clearly.

With some machines, successive impressions of certain letters show recurring variations—not just an occasional abnormal printing due to chance (Figure 11.11). Thus, variation may be the explanation for the occasional abnormal impression. It may be explainable by such things as substantially different ribbon inking or it may, when repeated often enough, play a role in the ultimate identification. Under any circumstances it must be considered in any identification.

Transitory Defects

Besides these relatively *permanent* defects,[2] such *transitory* factors as dirty typefaces and worn fabric ribbon may under favorable conditions assist in the identification. Since typefaces become filled in various ways, standard specimens executed at approximately the same date as the questioned material may well contain valuable points of identification based on this factor. Cleaning of the faces, however, immediately destroys these points of identification, and a new pattern is soon begun. Thus, if the standard and disputed matter were prepared at widely different dates, a different pattern of clogged typefaces cannot contradict a positive identification based upon a similar combination of alignment and typeface defects.

The condition of the fabric ribbon may play a part in an identification, but its limitations nearly parallel those encountered with clogged typefaces. Principally because of the transitory nature of these factors, however, differences in them may indicate only different dates of execution, whereas to establish that a particular machine was not used means that the standard and questioned material must contain different patterns of permanent defects.

---

[2]We speak of certain alignment and typeface defects as identifying the machine, a statement that may imply that these are constant throughout its life. Instead, just as a person's handwriting develops through use, so the identifying characteristics of a typewriter are acquired. Over a long time these defects undergo changes—new defects appear and the old ones become exaggerated or modified. Consequently, the individualities of a typewriter are representative of that machine at a given instant. (In practice this instant extends over a definite span of time—weeks, months, or even years, depending on the use to which the machine is put.)

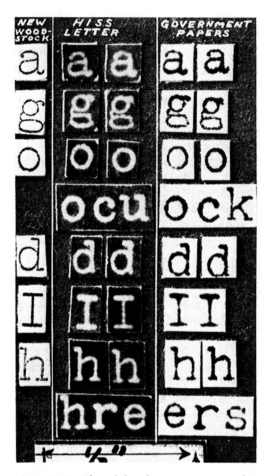

Figure 11.12. The exhibit shows a comparison between typewriting prepared on Alger Hiss's personal Woodstock typewriter (center) with that of copies of classified government paper which Whitaker Chambers testified he had received from Hiss (right). The extreme left-hand column shows new Woodstock type used on machines of the same age-model as the Hiss typewriter.

The photostat of the Hiss letter was written on his letterhead to an insurance company and bore his signature. The problem was submitted by investigators of the House Un-American Activities Committee (80th Congress).

The Hiss typewriter wrote in a highly individual manner and contained typefaces that were used for only a short time by the Woodstock company. The defects illustrated are only a few found in the typewriting of over 60 pages of copies of government papers. Defects in common to the questioned and known documents included the a printing heavy on the bottom, the flattening of the right side of the lower enclosure of the g, the o heavy on the right, the c typing low, and the double defect of the d, heavy at the top with the lower left serif damaged.

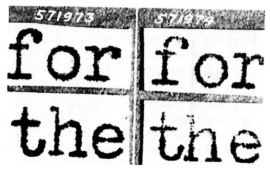

Figure 11.13. Work from two Remington Noiseless typewriters bearing consecutive serial numbers, 571973 and 571974, show different typewriting pecularities. 571973's f prints too heavy on the upper right portion, while the other prints light along the top of the f. The "he" combination is spread wider apart in the right-hand example than in the left. These machines had had little use when the specimens were taken.

Basis of Identification

The ultimate identification rests on the accumulation of evidence within the known and disputed typewriting. Three basic conditions common to both the standard and disputed matter establish the identity of the source—the same size type,[3] the identical typeface design, and a similar combination of defective and correctly writing letters and characters (Figure 11.12). On the other hand, divergence in any one of these conditions indicates that the questioned work was not prepared on a known typewriter (Figure 11.13).

Typebar Machine

All the defects discussed in previous paragraphs will be encountered in the examination of typewriting from the standard typebar machine. The typebar machine represents the original method of producing typewriting and throughout the years has been improved and modified until today the electric office typewriter is an excellent, rapid typing unit. Typebar machines are manufactured for office use in both electric and manual model, although today in this country electric typewriters predominate and are manufactured by numerous companies throughout the world.

---

[3]All manufacturers furnish several sizes of type fonts. The most popular are pica (10 characters per inch) and elite (12 characters per inch). Smaller and larger type sizes range from 6 to 16 characters per inch.

The manual machine, which was the original development in the typewriter, consists of a series of mechanical linkages from the type key to the actual typebar, which throws a typeface against the ribbon and paper. The modern machine contains two typefaces on each typebar, a capital and a lowercase letter or a numeral and another character, as indicated on the keyboard. Thus, there is some relationship in certain types of defects between the two characters on a single typebar. The change from capital to lowercase letter is accomplished by the action of a shift key, which either moves the basket or segment of type up and down or moves the carriage unit up and down to position the upper or lower section of the typeblock for printing.

The electric typewriter using the typebar action operates in much the same way except that the actual typebar movement is activated by means of an electrically driven power roller or other motor-driven device rather than directly by the stroke of the key and the force imparted by the typist. Electric machine work may be somewhat more uniform than manual typewriting unless in poor repair, but with a highly experienced typist using a manual machine, it may be difficult to distinguish the work of the manual machine from that of an electric typewriter.

The portable typewriter is another subclass of the typebar machine. The engineering of these machines is diferent from that of the standard office models, but, except that the construction is lighter, since machine weight should be low, the action is similar. Both manual and electric portables have been developed. In many instances, especially with the low-price models, which are not as well built as the more expensive models and may not contain several of the operating features of the more expensive models, work of the portable typewriter may be much more erratic. Variation especially depends in large measure on how sturdy and refined the manufacturing features of the machine are. Low-cost portable typewriters are engineered without some features that assure more uniformly productive work, and the machine cannot have the frame strength that is found in the heavier portable models or office machine. Consequently, alignment variations from one typing of a character to another may be much greater. Other defects also may be more extensive.

In recent years, several companies have developed an intermediate model electric typewriter. These compact machines are not intended to be portable, but are designed for office and home use where the volume of typewriting is moderate. In size and weight they fall between the large of deluxe portables and the standard office machine. Here again, while they are well engineered, they will deteriorate somewhat more rapidly than the top-line, well-built office machines, especially after extensive use. However, examiners would be hard pressed in many instances to recognize the work of these machines as opposed to standard electric office models.

With all typebar machines, one can expect to find slight alignment defects and some other defects early in the history of the machines.

Proportional Spacing Typewriting

In the 1940s and early 1950s, IBM developed and successfully marketed the first proportional spacing typewriter, which was known as the Executive. The distinctive characteristic of this machine is that each letter on the machine no longer occupies the same horizontal space, which had been typical of all typewriters previously developed. Instead, letters are built on a basic escapement unit of $1/32$ or $1/36$ in. depending upon the font. Individual letters occupy 2, 3, 4, or 5 units, that is, letters are not necessarily the same in width. Thus, the type fonts resemble printing. Depending on the particular font, letters such as i, e, f, j, and t would usually occupy two units of space, a great bulk of the lowercase letters such as a, o, e, n, h, and k occupy three units and w and m occupy four or five units. Capital letters for the most part are wider than their corresponding lowercase letters. However, no letter occupies more than five units and none less than two.[4] The machine uses a typebar action.

During the 1950s, other companies manufactured competitive machines in this country. Remington Rand followed IBM in proportional spacing typewriting using both the $1/32$ and $1/36$ in. escapement. Underwood introduced a differential spacing machine, a different concept, which used a basic escapement of $1/10$ in. with provision for narrow letters to occupy only $1/2$ unit and wide letters $1\frac{1}{2}$ units. All these machines were electric typewriters.

For a short period of time, the Italian firm Olivetti produced a manual proportional spacing machine with highly distinctive type design, but in more recent years this has been superseded by their electric proportional spacing machine using the standard $1/32$ and $1/36$ in. escapement.

Two other European companies, Olympia and Hermes, entered the proportional spacing field in more recent years, but the latter ended production in 1974. While proportional spacing typewriting was extremely popular, especially for executive correspondence in the Amer-

---

[4]O. Hilton, "Problems in the Identification of Proportional Spacing Typewriting," *Journal of Forensic Sciences* 3 (1958): 263–287.

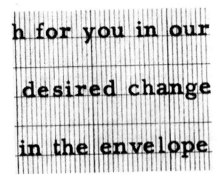

Figure 11.14. An example of IBM Modern type under an alignment plate shows that the i and l each occupy two units of space while the o, r, e, and s among other letters occupy three units. Three units is the more common size, but some letters need four or five units.

ican business world and to some extent in the legal field, the development of the single element typewriter and its wide selection of typing fonts appears to have superseded the proportional spacing typewriting. Manufacture of most typebar units has been phased out.

Work of proportional spacing typewriters can be identified, and the same defects of other typebar machines will be found to occur in their work. The typefaces develop individual defects. Particularly with IBM, which has dominated the field, the typefaces are found to contain much broken type after the machines have been used for a period of time. Most of the type fonts are made up of shaded type, that is to say, some portions of the outline of letters are slightly wider than other portions. This characteristic may make it somewhat difficult to recognize letters printing an uneven impression, but it must be understood that these defects are just as common with proportional spacing typefaces as with other typebar machines. Because of the variety of letter widths, it is necessary to use a type of alignment test plate different from that used for standard typewriting (Figure 11.14), and the most practical one developed appears to be that ruled with lines spaced equal to the basic unit escapement.[5]

With these modifications in examination typewriting identification of a proportional spacing machine parallels exactly the procedures for identifying any typebar typewriter. The final identification rests on the same combination of type design and type size together with a unique combination of defective and nondefective letters and characters appearing in both the known and questioned typewriting (Figure 11.15).

---

[5]The test plate developed by the writer has been accepted as a standard tool. See O. Hilton, "A Test Plate for Proportional Spacing Typewriter Examination," *Journal of Criminal Law, Criminology, and Police Science* 47 (1956): 257–259.

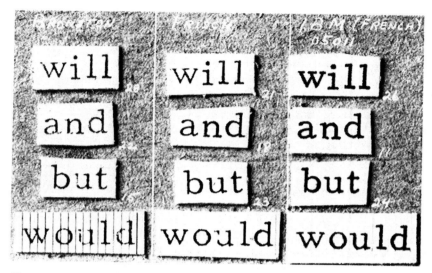

Figure 11.15. Two letters allegedly taken from the files of two different individuals were typewritten on the same machine, rented by the plaintiff who produced the letters. The i prints below the baseline; the n has a damaged lower left serif; and the u prints to the left of the centered position, as does the w. These and other defects establish the identity.

Single Element Type Ball Machines

With the introduction of the IBM Selectric typewriter in 1961, an entirely new class of typewriters was encountered. This group has become known as the type ball or single element typewriter. Until 1974 the Selectric was the only type ball machine available, but since then several other companies have produced their versions. Remington Rand, which shares certain patent rights with IBM, is building a machine very similar to the Selectric. In 1979 Silver Seiko of Japan introduced the Silver Reed 223C type ball machine. Elements or type balls are interchangeable among the three makes. Adler and Triumph (Germany, 1974) and Royal (1975), an American company manufacturing in Germany, make up the second group of interrelated machines with interchangeable type balls (cores). Facit of Sweden also began distribution in 1975 of the first type ball machine that could handle more than 88 characters. Hermes (Switzerland) and Olympia (Germany) combined in the development of a fourth version of this class of machine with type balls (spheres) of their own design. Olivetti (1975) introduced a unique single element machine with a very different element and its own type designs. At the same time they produced the first portable single element typewriter. In 1978 production of this portable was moved to the SCM factory in the United States, and both companies are marketing the machine under their own trade names. While the type design is typically Olivetti, the machine uses a type element unlike the office Olivetti or any other type ball machine. In 1978 Brother (Japan) introduced its Select-O-Riter and then the Correct-O-Riter in which yet another pattern of character arrangement is found on the element. Each make, except where noted, uses a type element individual to that machine, but several of these elements incorporate identical type design since the same supplier manufactures the elements.[6] This series of type ball machines was brought about by the great popularity and widespread use of the Selectric typewriter throughout the world.

The single element typewriter creates a completely new typing unit with a corresponding distictive identification problem. Considering the Selectric typewriter as a prototype of all type ball machines, the document examiner no longer identifies a particular typewriter but instead identifies a particular typing unit.[7] All the type elements are interchangeable among machines of the same manufacturer, which means that several different type balls, including those of different type design, can be used on a single typing unit or each of these balls can be used on any of several units. The identification is influenced by both the particular element or ball used and by the particular typing unit on which it is operated. Thus, a change of combination of these two parts of the typing assembly creates a new and distinctive identification problem.

Consequently, the first step in present-day typewriting identification is to determine whether the material was prepared on a single element type ball machine or some other class of typewriter.[8] For the most part, the type ball machines have distinctive type design, different from typebar machines. IBM Selectric pica fonts, which are among the most common, are distinctive, and other companies use type designs slightly different from those found on any typebar machines. Normally, the type ball unit does not emboss the paper as do the typebar or type

---

[6]IBM manufactures all its own typeballs in this country and in Europe. There are slight design differences in the same fonts manufactured in the two plants. Caracters S.A. of Switzerland is the other principal manufacturer, which supplies all other machine manufacturers except Olivetti, which designs its own elements. Several companies supplied by Caracters S.A. have virtually identical fonts even though their elements may not be interchangeable.

[7]O. Hilton, "Identification of the Work from an IBM Selectric Typewriter," *Journal of Forensic Sciences* 7 (1962): 286–302.

[8]O. Hilton, "Some Practical Suggestions for Examining Writing from the Selectric Typewriter," *Journal of Police Science and Administration* 3 (1975): 59–65. Corrected photographs appear in 3 (1975): 249–50. The paper is a good working guide for those who are confronted with the identification of work from a single element type ball machine.

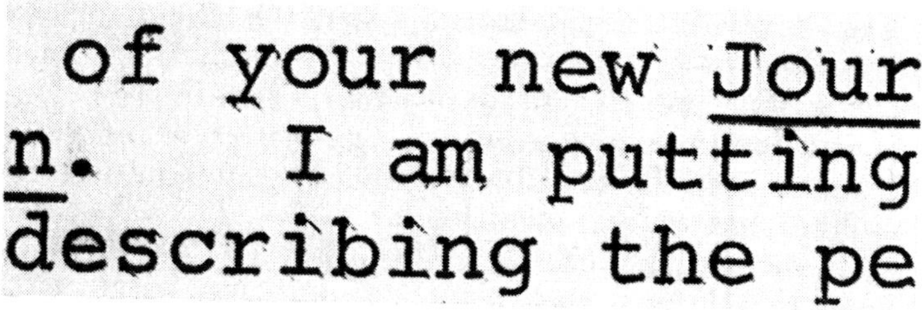

of your new Jour
n. I am putting
describing the pe

Figure 11.16. The light, diagonal, hairline strokes appearing in several letters are encountered with type ball machines. When present, it is a strong indication of the single element typewriter.

wheel units. The work of some type ball machines contains slight hairlike drag lines that help to distinguish them from other kinds of typewriters (Figure 11.16). Probably the most common suggestion that the document was written on a type ball typewriter is the marked uniformity of the typewriting. Only the electronic typewriter approaches this uniformly written copy.

To understand the identification of a single element unit better, it is well to know how the machine operates. The surface of the type ball is divided into two hemispheres. In one are located all the lowercase letters, numerals, and other characters that type when the shift key is not depressed. To print the capital letters and other characters on the keyboard, the shift key is depressed, rotating the element 180° to present the opposite hemisphere to the paper. The action of the shift key is entirely a typing-unit function.

The typefaces on the IBM Selectric element are arranged in 4 horizontal rows of letters and characters in each hemisphere and 11 vertical columns. The same arrangement holds for Remington and Silver Reed and for the Adler–Royal group. Prior to typing any character, the element is positioned with the top row and the middle column centered in printing position. With the IBM Selectric, Remington, and Silver Reed, the letter z occupies this rest position. In order to type a particular letter, three rapid movements are necessary. The ball must rotate so that the proper column is centered. It must tilt so that the proper row is centered. This combination of actions moves a particular character into position to type, and then the third action causes the ball to move forward and strike the ribbon to print the character on the paper. Immediately following the printing action, the typeball returns to its rest position. The entire cycle is completed in a fraction of a second.

Accurate alignment of a character does not result simply from the rotation and tilt action but is accomplished by means of two detents or knife edges operating in the center of notches in the machine itself for tilt or baseline alignment and around the base of the type element for rotation or left–right alignment. Some machines other than the Selectric have modified means of achieving the final detent action, but the end results involve a similar combination of actions. Thus, one alignment depends basically on the machine and the other on both the machines and the type element.

This means that 22 characters in one row may have identical baseline alignment relative to the other characters since baseline alignment of each depends on the same detent notch action. Similarly four characters in a single vertical column of any given rotation are controlled by the positioning of the detent in the same notch on the type element,

Figure 11.17. A comparison of typewriting from two documents establishes that both were written on the same Selectric system. The alignment defects with these machines are slight but when repeated are sufficient to identify. Observe the slight left position of the w in line 1 and the b also left, a single Selectric defect resulting from the same mechanical cause. Other independent defects include the i, slightly right; the s and T to the left.

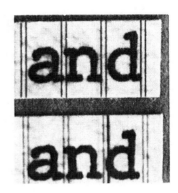

Figure 11.18. The upper "and" occurred near the left-hand margin, the lower near the right. The alignment grid was not realigned and shows that this machine was underspacing slightly. This machine defect is a significant identification factor.

and all four should have the same left–right alignment. Consequently, we find that there is a direct correlation between alignment defects found among the several characters on the element, whereas with the typebar machine, the only alignment correlation is found in the two characters that are combined on a particular type block, usually the capital and lowercase letter. With the single element machines, this is not the case with the capital and lowercase letter, since the centering detent acts in a different notch for the two letters (Figure 11.17). In all cases, however, alignment defects are measured in small increments and compared to this class of defects with typebar machines of earlier days might be considered as almost nonexistent. With single element typewriters they must be recognized as definite identifying factors.

Certain typing unit defects are to be found in the occasional identification problem. They are not unlike machine defects found in typebar machines. The more common of these is a consistent unit spacing that is slightly less than or greater than $1/10$ in. with pica escapement. This results in all letters on the left-hand side of the page aligning differently than those in the middle or on the right-hand side (Figure 11.18). Very occasionally a left-hand margin stop malfunctions, producing an irregular margin (Figure 11.19). A change of type element does not modify these defects.

Typeface defects are extremely rare, although they may be found occasionally because slight casting faults in manufacturing are not detected[9] or possibly from damage to the element, most likely when it is not on the machine. This condition is true of the Selectric typewriter and all others using plated elements that are aligned by detents

---

[9]A. G. Leslie, "Identification of the Single Element Typewriter and Type Element, Part 1—Type Element," *Canadian Society of Forensic Science Journal* 10 (1977): 87–101.

Figure 11.19. The occasional left-hand margin defect occurred in several documents prepared on a Selectric unit. The defect adds to the identification, some of the factors of which are shown in Figure 11.18.

operating away from the immediate area of the typeface itself. During the Selectric development, IBM found that unplated, plastic elements wore more rapidly than IBM was willing to accept. Consequently, IBM developed a plastic plating process to increase the life of an element. Most of their machines and those of other manufacturers are under service contracts that provide for replacement of worn elements, thus eliminating defective elements upon discovery by the service representative. Leslie reports significant damage to letter outlines on Olivetti Lexikon 90C models (office machines) caused by a defective detent that operates adjacent to letters.[10] Furthermore, Olivetti, SCM, and Brother use unplated plastic elements exclusively, which may show typeface wear more readily with use, but document examiners have not reported such findings to date (1980).

With other single element typewriters, the same factors are at work although the positioning of letters and characters is different on a number of the type elements (Table 1). Thus the interrelationship between certain letters would differ depending on the arrangement of the letters over the face of the element. With some machines there are more columns of letters, as in the Facit ball, or more rows of type, as

---

[10]Leslie, "Identification of the Single Element Typewriter and Type Element, Part 1—Type Element," discusses and illustrates damage to typefaces on the Olivetti Lexikon 90C, pp. 97–99.

used by Olivetti and SCM for their portable machines, than are found on the Selectric element.

The Olivetti office machine differs significantly in its mechanical arrangement and type element from the machines of its competitors. However, the action is similar and letter selection depends on twist and rotation. The axis of the ball mount is at a right angle to that of other machines so that the twisting action is right and left rather than the up or down tilt of all other machines. Rotation, while in a vertical rather than a horizontal plane, completes the letter selection. Consequently, in identification problems there is again an interrelationship between groups of letters because fine alignment of right and left positioning or of baseline adjustment is controlled by the same mechanical devices for several characters rather than a single one. Thus with all single element machines, the correlation between defects of several letters must be considered in the identification formula.

Proportional Spacing Single Element Machines

In 1972 IBM released its Mag Card Executive Typewriter as part of its Mag Card word processing units. It was the first proportional spacing machine to be developed around the single element concept. The input/output typing unit can be used as part of the word processing system, using the memory cards or other available memory system, or as an individual typewriter.

Olivetti released its version of a single element proportional spacing typewriter following IBM and Xerox (discussed in the following section). Its fundamental design follows the distinctive characteristics of the standard Olivetti single element office machine with the element rotation and twist at right angles to that of the other type ball machines. The configuration of the type element differs from all other single element machines, and type fonts are of a distinctive Olivetti design.

The identification problem for these machines follows the same pattern as for standard single element machines. However, in the case of the proportional spacing machine, the spacing of letters and characters varies so as to produce finished typing that is comparable to traditional printing. The IBM letterspacing is built on a series of units—the basic escapement being $1/72$ in. Narrow letters space four units; the majority of letters and characters space six units; some capitals and lowercase letters require seven units; the majority of capitals space eight units; and the m and w in both capital and lowercase form require nine units. Letters are arranged in columns and rows around the ball as on other type ball machines. Thus, the identification problem represents the combined features of the type ball and earlier proportional spacing machines.

Table 1. Arrangement of Letters and Characters on Type Balls

Position of typefaces shown left and right of center are the positions as viewed on the ball itself. Rotation values to the left of center in each diagram represent the number of right rotation spaces required to print characters in that column. All machines return to rest position at center of upper row.

```
5  4  3  2  1  0  1  2  3  4  5        Rotation

9  0  6  5  2  z  4  8  7  3  1

b  h  k  e  n  t  l  c  d  u  x        IBM — also Remington

w  s  i  '  .  ½  o  a  r  v  m        and Silver Reed

-  y  q  p  =  j  /  ,  ;  f  g
```

```
5  4  3  2  1  0  1  2  3  4  5        Rotation

t  f  d  z  q  y  '  p  o  i  j

g  r  e  w  a  b  ½  ;  l  k  u        Adler and Royal

v  c  x  s  2  h  =  .  ,  m  n

6  5  4  3  1  7  /  -  0  9  8
```

```
6  5  4  3  2  1  1  2  3  4  5  6     Rotation

½     '  n  v  u  t  r  e  3  2  1

;  =  th k  h  l  d  s  x  4  ,  9     Facit

]  ¶  w  b  o  i  c  m  f  .  5  0

y  -  z  j  g  p  8  7  6  a  /  q
```

```
6  5  4  3  2  1  1  2  3  4  5  6     Rotation

z  f  g  u  n  e  t  l  v  /  ½

y  w  p  d  r  s  i  q  j  ;  '  =     Hermes and Olympia

k  b  c  h  o  a  .  m  x  0  3  ¶

2  4  ,  5  6  7     8  ±  -  9  1
```

Table 1 (*continued*)

5	4	3	2	1	0	1	2	3	4	5	Rotation
/	9	0	;	8	2	3	4	7	5	6	
½	k	o	=	u	a	s	d	b	c	t	Brother Correct-O-Riter
'	m	1	.	n	*l*	w	e	h	r	v	Select-O-Riter
-	i	,	p	j	q	z	x	y	f	g	

4	3	2	1	0	1	2	3	4	Rotation
3	k	c	a	o	i	z	/	1	
=	9	h	r	e	t	m	f	4	Olivetti portable and
8	0	v	l	n	s	u	5	'	SCM portable
,	;	.	b	x	d	2	w	7	Note: Machines use 5 tilt
	j	p	q	g	-	6	y	½	positions

All of the above type elements rotate 180° when the shift key is depressed. The capital letters and those characters combined with the numerals and other characters typed as lowercase letters are in the corresponding position on the type ball to the lowercase equivalent.

The Olivetti Lexikon 90, their office model, is a distinctively different type ball machine. The element is mounted with its axis at a 90° angle to the axis of other type ball machines. Thus the equivalent of the tilt function is achieved by right and left movement along the axis mount in six steps, and rotation consists of eight units. Furthermore the positions of uppercase and lowercase letters are not the same on the two hemispheres. Consequently, both are charted below.

Lowercase						Uppercase						
3	2	1	1	2	3	3	2	1	1	2	3	tilt
¨	z	2	y	k	4	!	[	_	Z	H	%	
′	f	*l*	x	b	9	"	V	J	U	R	&	
'	r	1	3	m	½	:	T	L	C	B	K	
-	e	i	j	d	g	,	A	C	S	E	Q	
,	o	t	a	p	0	.	P	I	O	M	X	
.	n	c	u	h	6	/	?	Y	ç	N	$	
;	s	v	w	q	8	+	*	(	#	D	@	
/	]	=	5	z	è	^	F	)	¢	W	¼	

The Electronic Typewriter

The electronic typewriter represents the latest advance in typewriter design. These machines have been developed as a unit of various high-speed word processing systems. In 1974 Xerox introduced its word processor using an electronically controlled type wheel typewriter or printer. The type wheel concept had been developed by Diablo, now a wholly owned subsidiary of Xerox. In 1978 QYX released its electronic memory typewriter built around the type wheel concept, a single unit machine, almost as compact as the standard electric typewriter, but capable of text-editing functions with its more complex units.[11] Both machines type a paper copy as the material is entered into the memory and can be used independently as a typewriter by simply cancelling the input to the memory. The same machine, as an output unit, produces the final edited, stored material working directly and auto-matically from the memory. The memory may consist of magnetic tapes, disks, or solid state chips. Olivetti's electronic typewriter does not make an original copy but, like a number of word processors, uses a video screen to display the material as it is typed, edited, and finally either stored or printed through a separate type wheel output unit.

A few months prior to the release of the QYX typewriter, IBM re-leased an electronic typewriter using the type ball concept. It is a substantial improvement over the Selectric typewriter and uses a type ball with additional characters and different character arrangements than the Selectric (Table 2). Royal also produces a type ball electronic typewriter. Both machines type a hard (paper) copy original and can be used directly as a typewriter, bypassing the memory system.

With electronic typewriters there are few mechanical actions. For each make of machine the type wheels or the type balls are inter-changeable, and the manufacturers supply a number of different fonts that use either 10 or 12 pitch escapement as well as proportional spac-ing type styles. Most manufacturers design their machines to use all three classes of type interchangeably. The spacing change may be ac-complished automatically when one of the type styles is inserted in the machine or may require that the operator set the typing mode manually.

The machines differ from even the most advanced electric type-

---

[11]Mid-1978 saw the start of electronic typewriter production with the release of the IBM and QYX machines. The electronic typewriter has characteristics and features described in this text, but can be distinguished from other typewriters and from word processors by the fact that it is a compact desk-top machine with memory features similar to word processing units. Four machines (available in mid-1980) have been checked by this writer and are included in the section. Willoughby Ann Webster, "What to Consider When Selecting Text-Editing Equipment," *American Bar Association Journal* 67 (January 1981): 45–49, adds the following recently released electronic memory typewriters to the list: Adler-Royal, A. B. Dick, Olympia, and Savin, all unchecked by this writer.

Table 2. IBM Electronic Typewriter Element

Location of letters and characters on the face of the type element. Note position of typefaces differs from Selectric type balls. (See Table 1.)

```
6  5  4  3  2  1  1  2  3  4  5  6    Rotation

z  2  7  5  2  0  6  4  8  9  3  /

;  '  i  s  t  e  c  b  k  u  §  =

v  m  w  d  o  r  n  a  x  h  ½  ±

-  1  .  j  q  p  y  f  l  g  ]  ,


Z  3  &  %  @  )  ¢  $  *  (  #  ?

:  "  I  S  T  E  C  B  K  U  ¶  +

V  M  W  D  O  R  N  A  X  H  ¼  °

_  !  .  J  Q  P  Y  F  L  G  [  '
```

writers in that there are no mechanical linkages of any kind between the type key and the printing of the character. Instead the action is accomplished and controlled electronically. When typing automatically the type wheel machines are faster than type ball machines. They make up the great majority of typing units in word processing systems.

With all electronic typewriters the letterspacing, letter selection, basic alignment, line spacing, and ribbon action are all controlled within the basic electronic unit, that is, the typewriter itself. They are directed by means of microprocessors and movements are handled by solenoids and sophisticated electric motors. With the type wheel machine the actual typing is achieved, after the typeface has been properly positioned, by a plunger striking the back of the typeface, causing it to press the ribbon against the paper. The type wheel is the portion of the unit most apt to develop individuality or defects and for the document examiner appears to be the principal source of identification factors. The faces can become worn and the spokes of the wheel twisted or bent to create slight alignment or printing defects. Each spoke contains a single letter or character so that there is no relationship between defects developed in connection with a particular spoke and its character and any other character. Engineers who know the electronic functioning of these machines consider that there is only a slight chance of machine defects occurring. Still, defects may occur in some form

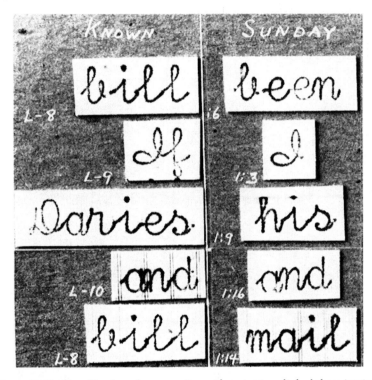

Figure 11.20. Identification of a typewriter with script type linked three incriminating letters to one party of a lawsuit. The type is designed to have letters joined together.

from time to time. Since the machines are virtually all under some type of service contract, however, upon recognition of any malfunctioning of the electronic system, most defects are reported and corrected promptly. Thus these defects would most likely be of a very temporary nature. At this writing, document examiners have had very limited experience with these machines, especially ones that have seen extensive use, so that all identification factors probably have not been recognized. As with the type ball machine, however, tolerances are very close, and the document examiner may need to establish more precise methods than have been necessary with earlier models of typewriters, especially typebar machines.

Identification Problems

Since the typewriter enjoys widespread use in virtually all offices as well as in many homes, all kinds of documents are typewritten. Any one of these may be challenged under the right circumstances. Ques-

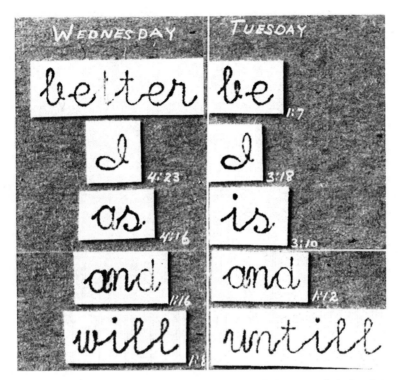

"bi" does not. The I prints heavy in the lower left, and there is a slight break in the ending stroke of the s. Among other defects the n prints to the left.

---

tions regarding typewritten material arise frequently in connection with every class of document—wills, agreements, deeds, business and personal letters, bills or statements, and the like (Figures 11.20 and 11.21).

The most common question raised is whether a particular typewriter was used to prepare a questioned document. With proper standards these questions can often be definitely resolved. The amount of known typewriting from a single element typewriter generally has to be more extensive than that from a typebar machine. Not only can it be established and demonstrated that a different machine was used to prepare one or more pages of the document, but, if necessary, the work of both typewriters can be identified. There have been cases in which only a few words have been inserted with a second typebar machine, in which event it may be easier to prove the insertion than to identify the second machine. Unless the insertion is made with a highly individualized typewriter, two or three words may not permit the identification of

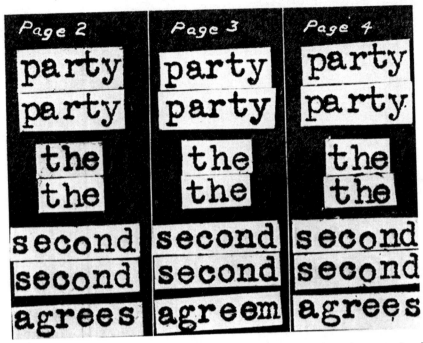

Figure 11.21. Page 3 of a document was written on a different machine than pages 2 and 4. Spacing between "par" and "the" differs. The baseline alignment of the o is a further difference.

the machine used, and this would be particularly true when dealing with a single element typewriter. In all these problems, however, it may be more difficult to locate the particular machine used and to procure proper specimens than to make the final identification.

Identification of the Typist

Identification of the typewriter employed may not always satisfy the needs of an investigation so that a further query is raised as to the possibility of establishing who operated the machine. A question of this nature is difficult because of the standardized methods of typewriting and a tendency for many modern machines to turn out uniform work despite variation in the operators' techniques. A great number of individualities upon which an identification might be based is thus eliminated by the way the typewriter operates. Thus, the single element machine, the electronic typewriter, and modern electric office machines all tend to produce uniform work despite irregularities in operation that would be recorded by a manual typewriter. Conditions surrounding the particular case generally decide the question. At times a quantity of rather distinct personal habits appear in the disputed document by which it is possible to identify the typist, but it is more common to find only slight, if any, individuality in the matter under investigation.

The training of the typist and his mode of procedure have much to do with the work done and the possibility of identification. In general the self-taught, "hunt-and-peck" or two-finger operators tend to have definite traits by which their work can be recognized, while those who have been thoroughly instructed in modern touch typewriting techniques have fewer and less prominent personal habits. A study of the work of a large group of operators who have been thoroughly trained in the same typewriting methods nevertheless may still reveal some personal habits. Obviously, typist identification becomes more likely as these personal habits increase in number and take on a more individual character.

The factors by which a typist can be identified are almost as varied as the habits of the individuals concerned. Some depend on personal preferences; some are repetitious errors. The more valuable identification points are irregularities in alignment resulting from improper use of the shift key and the stacking or partial stacking of particular letter combinations, factors more common to typebar machines, especially manual models, and the habitual tendency to interchange or transpose letters in common words. A greater number of these personal habits are present in the work of a typist of limited skill, but one should not expect all to appear except when a manual typebar machine is used. Well-trained operators generally make only a few of these errors. Contrary to popular belief, variation in touch and rhythm does not show up noticeably in the written work from even manual machines and probably not at all with single element typewriters, and seldom can any definite pattern be discovered. With all typists, however, consideration of the habits of arrangement, punctuation, capitalization, choice of alternative or optional symbols, spelling, hyphenation, phraseology, mode of correction, stenographic signatures, and presence of overtypings may point out an individual.

While there are many details in the specimen from which identification can be made, because of rather standardized training in arranging material on the paper, most of these habits are common to a large group of typists. Many are susceptible to imitation or deliberate disguise. Furthermore, those representing errors in operation are not constantly repeated with each writing so that extended specimens must be available if any pattern of error and frequency of occurrence is to be established. These observations indicate that identification of a typist must be based on extensive disputed specimens in which the personal habits are repeated with sufficient regularity to ensure a correct identification. It can be conservatively stated that if the group of potential suspects is virtually unlimited and the work is that of an average or better skilled operator, and today this includes a rather large percentage of the population, investigations to identify a typist generally lead only to qualified results.

When, by other facts peculiar to the investigation, the suspected typist is known to be one of a small group, the task of identifying him from his work becomes simpler, and in general the results are more encouraging. Under these circumstances, regardless of the kind or the commonness of habits, those found in the disputed typewriting and in the work of only one of the group point accusingly toward this individual while completely eliminating the others. In this instance one of a limited group is identified by those habits that in combination are peculiar to him alone. The conditions of the problem have therefore altered the basic probability factors and requirements.

Identification by Typewriter Ribbon

There are occasions in cases involving typewritten documents in which it is possible to examine the typewriter suspected of writing the document. If the machine is equipped with a single-use film ribbon, and many modern typewriters today are, it can serve as a means of establishing that the machine typed a recent document.

Carbon ribbons consist of a carbon-wax coating on a polyethelene base. The blow of the type striking the ribbon causes most of the coating to be deposited on the paper, leaving a clear outline of the letter on the tape. Since the ribbon passes through the machine only once, there remains a readable outline of every letter typed, and with a properly working ribbon feed, no overlap of the letters occurs. The contents can be read by viewing the ribbon with light behind it or by holding it close to a white background (Figure 11.22).

In machines in which the fresh ribbon is fed from the right, interpretation of the material on the ribbon is not difficult. Spacing must be provided by the reader, but otherwise words read normally and all punctuation is present. Some typewriter ribbons, however, feed from the left, so that all of the words are spelled backward and interpretation is more difficult. Nevertheless, it is possible in either instance to match up the message between the ribbon and the document to establish whether the document was typed on the machine.

In making these examinations additional evidence can be developed if there are typographical errors in the document, even if the errors have been corrected (Figure 11.23). If they were corrected as made, both

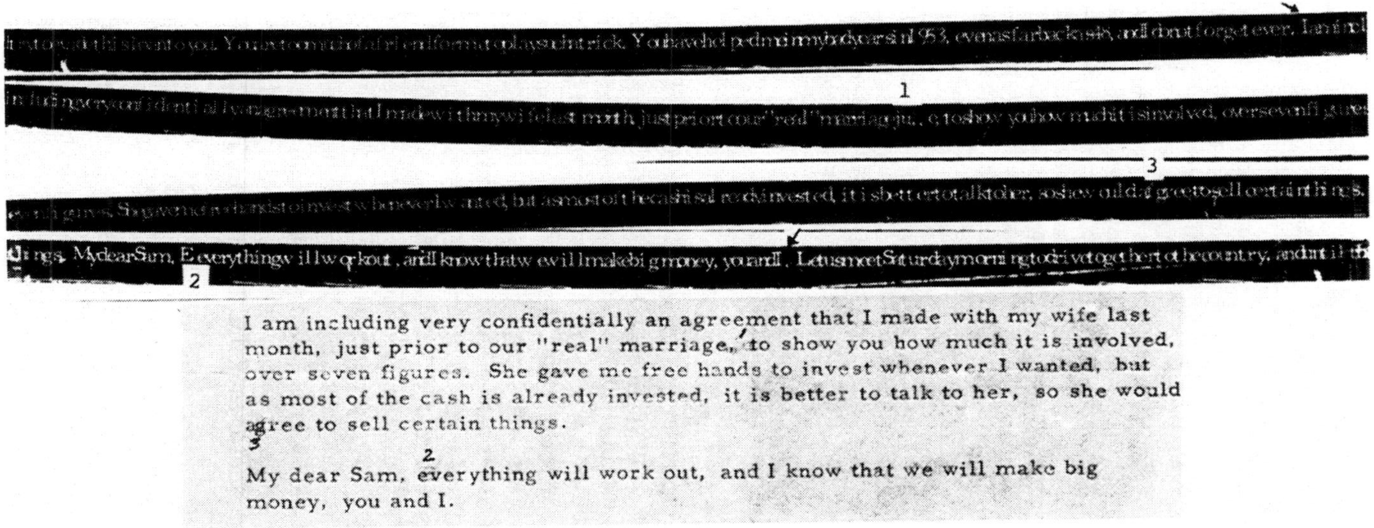

I am including very confidentially an agreement that I made with my wife last month, just prior to our "real" marriage, to show you how much it is involved. She gave me free hands to invest whenever I wanted, but as most of the cash is already invested, it is better to talk to her, so she would agree to sell certain things.

My dear Sam, everything will work out, and I know that we will make big money, you and I.

Figure 11.22. A portion of the typewriting ribbon used to type a disputed letter dated several years earlier appears above the corresponding section of the letter. The actual text of the section shown is found on the ribbon between the arrows. Three typing errors occurred in this section of the letter and are numbered to correspond to the enlarged words in Figure 11.23. The ribbon had been removed from the typewriter a few weeks before the hearing, and it was possible to demonstrate that the letter was typed with this ribbon and therefore was a complete fabrication.

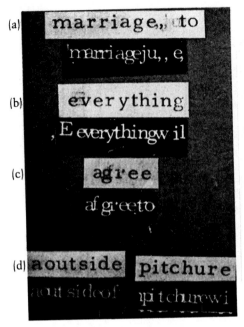

Figure 11.23. Three typographical errors that had been corrected in a fraudulent letter and two misspellings established in part that the ribbon had been used to type the letter. (a) The comma following "marriage" is surrounded by two erased commas in the finished letter and the erased letters "ju." The ribbon shows the typing of these characters after "marriage" and also a second typing of the e, which apparently had been erased in making the corrections. (b) An erased E had been typed first and corrected by the present typing. (c) "agree" had been started "af" and erased. The ribbon feed with this machine was working improperly causing the letters to run together on the ribbon.

the error and the correction will appear in the ribbon.[12] If the corrections and errors can be developed on the original document, very convincing evidence is established. With a correcting typewriter equipped with a lift-off ribbon or a white-out tape, these too can be examined and related to the corrections on the paper.

These techniques are not applicable to fabric ribbons, which are reused a number of times before the ribbon becomes exhausted. As the ribbon moves back and forth from end to end, the imprint of letters are stacked on it as it is reused. Bicolor ribbons may show outlines of letters that have been used on one color a number of times and then typed on the second color, especially when the second one is lighter than the first.[13] Likewise the IBM Tech III ribbon, which partially overlaps five strokes before the area of the ribbon is exhausted, cannot be used for these studies. These ribbons move slowly through the machine once and do not rewind, but the imprints are badly scrambled by the overtyping.

---

[12]O. Hilton, "Identifying the Typewriter Ribbon Used to Write a Letter, A Case Study Employing New Techniques," *Journal of Criminal Law, Criminology and Police Science* 63 (1972): 137–42.
[13]W. Hofmann, "Certain Aspects of Evidence Provided by Writing in Connection with Crime Detection," paper presented at the Seventh International Meeting of Forensic Sciences, Zurich, Switzerland, 1975. Also, John F. McCarthy, personal correspondence.

Forgery of a Typewriter

The building or modifying of a typewriter that will exactly duplicate the work of another machine is an extremely complicated and difficult task, as well as a costly one. Every one of the 84 or more characters must be accurately designed to agree with the age and model of the copied type. They must also be accurately adjusted and damaged so the machine writes with the same combination of correct and incorrect character impressions as the typewriter being imitated. No alien defects can be present. Since the individual peculiarities in the work of each typewriter are caused by wear, adjustment, or chance accidental injuries to the typefaces and moving parts, one can begin to realize the complexity and difficulties of this problem of typewriter imitation or forgery. Slight differences in the degree of wear in pivots or bearings of the typebars and associated mechanisms introduce variable defects that are not readily recognized or controlled. In fact, the forging of a typewriter is much like forging a signature. Failure stems from the fact that the forger is unable to introduce the more delicate details and the many variations of the authentic machine into the work of the attempted forgery.

Three times in connection with criminal trials there have been reported attempts to build a duplicate ("forged") typewriter. The first effort took place in 1911 in the matter of People of the State of New York v. Risley.[14] Only two words were in issue, "the same," which had been inserted in a document with Risley's typewriter, but the errors committed in doctoring the second machine in an attempt to duplicate these two words were clearly pointed out by expert testimony. At best, it was inaccurate observation and unskilled workmanship that caused the failure.[15]

The work in a second case was undertaken sometime in 1950, and the matter was disposed of only in July 1952. It was a part of the defense action for Alger Hiss in U.S. v. Alger Hiss. Affidavits discussing the machine were presented in the U.S. District Court, Southern District of New York, in an argument for a new trial following Hiss's conviction in January 1950. The mechanic who undertook this forgery described in a popular magazine the steps and extensive work he took to try to achieve his goal. However, despite the mechanic's public claims of success, U.S. District Judge H. W. Goddard, who heard the arguments for a new trial, ruled specifically that the machine was not a perfect

---

[14]214 N.Y. 75, 108 N.E. 200 (1915).

[15]William J. Kinsley, who testified in the Risley case, describes the problem in a privately printed booklet, *Typewriting Identification*. The account was reprinted from *The Typewriter World*, New York (dates are not given).

duplicate,[16] this in the face of the fact that there was available ample time, extensive financial resources, a fully equipped shop, and an experienced mechanic to achieve the desired end.

The efforts in this attempt at typewriter forgery were far more extensive and thorough than in the Risley case. Not only did the mechanic take over a year to complete his work, but he consulted and received critical assistance from others who had experience in typewriting identification. The consensus of published reports and informal statements of those who have examined the work of this adjusted machine is that it is a good, but not perfect, forgery. When compared with the work from the original typewriter, there is poor duplication of its less obvious identifying details. This fault is common to every other attempted good forgery, regardless of whether it was prepared by handwriting or other means.

A third attempt at forgery to come to the attention of the writer involved an effort to modify one machine so that it produced work exactly like that of a second. This effort differed from the others in that parts of the machine to be copied, actually the segment or typebar assembly, were removed from it and put in the other machine. The forgery was a hurried manipulation of the two machines carried out in the course of an extended trial in hope to prove the authenticity of several letters and to discredit or destroy the proof of fraud by the prosecution's document examiner.[17]

Expert testimony on typewriting identification, together with data concerning the purchase of typewriters, established that key documents, all dated in 1967, were written on two machines, one that was available at that time and a second that was not put in use until mid-

---

[16]The decision deals with all phases of the defense's claims of newly discovered evidence. Concerning the duplication of the typewriter, Judge Goddard writes in part: "Defendant's supposition—it is only conjecture with absolutely no evidence to support it—is that Chambers constructed the alleged duplicate typewriter from the typewritten characters in the Hiss letters, or that it was done for him by some Communist friends. The defense argues that it was made to use in his answer to the libel suit brought against him by Hiss and was constructed in the three months between the time of the Congressional hearing in August 1948 and November 17, 1948, when the documents were produced by him. If this be so, it would mean that he constructed in three months a machine that has taken the defense's several experts at least one year to produce and that still falls short of being a perfect duplication."

This supposition that the documents were "manufactured" in 1948 fails not only on the typewriting evidence but also on the condition of the Chambers documents themselves, and especially the paper they were wrapped in. When first submitted for technical examination on November 20, 1948, it was noted that this wrapper had all the characteristics of a container that had remained unprotected in dead storage for several years. There was no sign of artificial aging. Chambers had stated that the documents had been hidden in his brother-in-law's dumbwaiter shaft since the time of his break with the Communist Party in 1938. Judge Goddard in his decision also refers to government expert's affidavits further confirming the natural aging. The affidavit discussed the similarity of the paint splatters on the wrapper and in the dumbwaiter shaft. (U.S. v. Hiss, 107 F. Supp. 128, 1952.)

[17]A more detailed discussion of the typewriting testimony and manipulation can be found in O. Hilton, "The Effect of Interchanging Segments Between Two Typewriters: A Unique Criminal Defense Defeated," *Journal of Forensic Sciences* 19 (1974): 841–851.

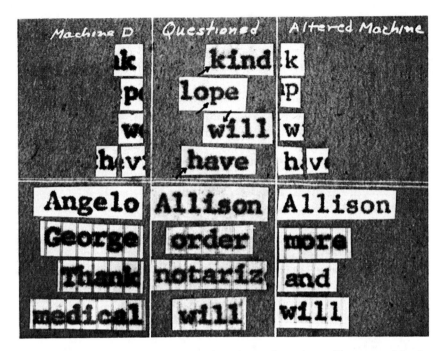

Figure 11.24. In the upper section are four damaged typefaces that appeared in the questioned document and letters written on machine D. These typefaces were found on the altered machine when it was introduced in evidence at the trial. Below are some of the alignment differences between the altered machine and the questioned letter, which are not differences between the typewriting of machine D and the questioned letter.

In the questioned letter the n of "Allison" prints an even impression; on the altered machine the impression is much lighter on the left than on the right. Below in "and" from the work of the altered machine the ruled test plate emphasizes the twisted condition of the letter which can also be recognized in "Allison." The n of "notarized" in the questioned letter is not twisted. The staff of the r in "more" leans to the left as well, but in machine D and the questioned letter it is parallel to the vertical ruled lines. "will" from the altered machine's work shows the l's printing to the right in the ruled space, but not in the other two columns. The broken type confirmed that the segment had been taken from machine D and put in the other machine, but alignment of the type had been disturbed and not corrected so that the altered machine could not duplicate the typewriting of the questioned material.

1969. From a list of machines by serial numbers and their dates of purchase, plus extensive standards prepared in the office, it was possible to pinpoint the actual machine that wrote each document without having direct access to the machines themselves.

In rebuttal the defense introduced the older machine (C) in evidence. Its serial number agreed with the one is use in the office in 1967. As produced it contained all the damaged typefaces of the 1969 machine

(D), and a defense expert testified that its work was identical to the documents that the prosecution had established were typed on machine D. This testimony could be demonstrated to be incorrect by careful comparison of work from the machine and the letters (Figure 11.24). There were a number of different alignment and other defects, but since the prosecutor and his expert recognized that the machine had been tampered with, a factory engineer was consulted. He established and testified that the style of typebars on it had not been manufactured at the time that machine C had been built but were developed after the date of the document. The prosecution subpoenaed machine D. It was found to contain typebars that had been discontinued at least a year before it was manufactured. Furthermore, despite its relative newness and being under a service contract, it was in very poor state of repair. The typefaces contained the broken type of machine C, the typebars were of the style used on machine C, and there were other abnormalities that established that the two segments had been interchanged. Attempted typewriter forgery or duplication failed again.

The problem of a forged typewriter is a very rare one. Even if its difficulties and numerous complexities have so far apparently precluded success (none has been reported), and may very well do so in future attempts, one cannot say that because of known past failures no future attempts will be made. With human ego such as it is there are bound to be others in the years to come who in spite of these failures may feel that they are the ones who can successfully complete the task.

Disguised Typewriting

Attempts to disguise typewriting are rather infrequent. In part this may be because many people do not realize that typewriting can be identified, but it is also undoubtedly because methods of disguise usually involve serious tampering with or manipulation of the typewriter itself. Gayet of the Lyon Police Laboratory in France has reported on two such attempts, and these represent the only published information on cases involving attempted disguise.[18] In both instances he was still successful in identifying the typewriter. The most extensive disguise reported involved filing the typefaces of every character on the machine after an anonymous letter had been written. This action might achieve success under the right circumstances, but once such an act appears likely, examination of the machine itself will reveal what has been

---

[18]Jean Gayet, "Efforts at Disguise in Typewritten Documents," *Journal of Criminal Law, Criminology and Police Science* 46 (1956): 867.

done. Earlier specimens of typewriting from it can then be referred to for identification purposes if the disputed material was typewritten before the manipulation. Disguised typewriting requires careful analysis so that the disguise can be recognized and proper steps taken so that the machine can be identified. If the first step is accomplished, the second may then be possible.

12

Other Mechanical Impressions, Including Check Writers and Printing Identifications

Today there are numerous record-making office and business machines. In varying degrees, depending upon their use, questions may arise about the source and authenticity of each class of record. Since the document examiner's proficiency in typewriting and handwriting identification is known, he is the logical person to be called upon to answer the question at hand. Several classes of such records are considered in this chapter, but no attempt is made to include an exhaustive survey of potential problems from these numerous sources.

Check Writers and Check-Writing Units

Various devices have been developed for the preparation and protection of checks. Certain of these instruments are basically security devices, while others have been designed to handle the vast volume of check writing common to daily business activities. In the former class are check writers, rather commonly referred to as check protectors, and signature plates; in the latter class are several types of accounting machines and computer systems that incorporate check-preparing facilities. Each can lead to identification problems and other document questions.

In regard to check writers the most common question is, Did this check writer print the fraudulent check? These identifications are encountered most frequently in criminal investigations, but occasionally they are involved in civil litigation. We have already seen in Chapter 3 that the make of check writer can be determined from its work, but it is more important that the individual machine can be identified.[1]

---

[1]An illustrated discussion of the principles of identifying the make of a check writer and the individual instrument appeared in "Check Writers," *Bulletin of the New York State Police* 15 (1950):

(continued)

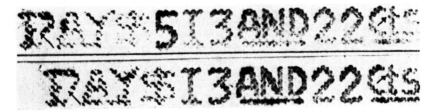

Figure 12.1. Two check writer specimens are clearly the work of one machine. Among the defects which individualize this writer are the uneven impressions such as 2 printing slightly heavier at the top than at the bottom, breaks in the outline of the P and t (arrows), and the I printing lighter than the following 3.

Two basic conditions must exist for the suspected check writer to have written a disputed check. Besides the requirement that the design of numerals and letters on the check must agree with those of the suspected check protector (i.e., that both must have the same class characteristic), it is also necessary that the individual defects or peculiarities of the disputed impression occur in the work of the suspected machine. With most check writers, the characters and numerals do not print a solid impression. Rather, the face of the character is made up of a number of ribs or dots that imprint the amount and at the same time perforate or shred the paper. The process of manufacturing the actual printing face creates individuality in the form of slight variations in the printing surfaces of a series of the same characters. Use may wear or cause damage to the printing surface and further individualize the outline. Besides these slight differences in form, not all letters and numerals necessarily print with the same intensity, especially when the impression is weakly inked. Another type of defect is an uneven impression—a character writing heavier in one area than in others (Figure 12.1). It is the combination of defective and nondefective characteristics on a particular check protector that individualizes its work and makes possible its segregation from all other check protectors.

Signature plates, which print a facsimile signature, are generally designed with some background pattern as part of the signature unit as a security measure (Figure 12.2). Thus, the determination of whether a particular plate was used to sign a check requires study of both the signature design and the surrounding pattern printing. Since the latter

---

footnote[1] continued
3–7. A further and more extensive analysis is to be found in David J. Purtell, "The Identification of Checkwriters," *Journal of Criminal Law, Criminology and Police Science* 45 (1954): 229–235. James T. Miller, "Role of Check Protector Identification in Law Enforcement—Exemplar and Comparison Problems," *Journal of Police Science and Administration* 3 (1975): 259–266, not only discusses identification but also makes suggestions on how to prepare the best comparison specimens from a suspected writer.

Figure 12.2. In many machines a check signature plate imprint contains not only the signature but also a distinctive background design, which in this case is a combination of dots and slightly wavy lines.

is a distinctive part of the plate, it too must match. Forgery of these signatures may be rare, but certainly not beyond the realm of probability. On the other hand, in some instances it may be very important to establish clearly that a particular signature plate is the one that was imprinted on the check in dispute.

Accounting or bookkeeping machines have been developed that can be programmed to write checks and to enter them into the permanent accounting records. With use a particular unit produces work that is individualized and can be distinguished from the work of other machines of the same manufacture, as can be done with a typewriter. Problems involving the work of these machines are infrequent. When they do arise, the examiner probably needs to inspect the machine itself and to study how the work of the particular model is printed in order to recognize the elements in a questioned check that can be specifically related to an individual unit (Figure 12.3). He is then able to distinguish what information on the check was made by the machine in question and what was produced by other office devices. The imprint of symbols, numbers, words, or individual letters each can become distinctive through use so that any one of them prints in an individual manner. With machines of this type, it is important to know what parts of each imprint are made by an individual typeface and what parts are made from a unit of several letters or characters. For example, the abbreviations of the month may constitute a solid block of type, but the digits of the amount of the check are printed by individual typefaces. Furthermore, with some machines repetition of some data on the check and the stub may have been printed by the same type units. It is important for all concerned to understand that the work can be identified, and it may be significant to know what information on the check is automatically recorded in other records.

Adding-Machine Tapes and Cash-Register Receipts

There is an extensive variety of record printing office and business machines in common use. While the old-fashioned adding machine has in large measure been replaced by electronic calculators, many of which produce a printed record, their records and those of other ac-

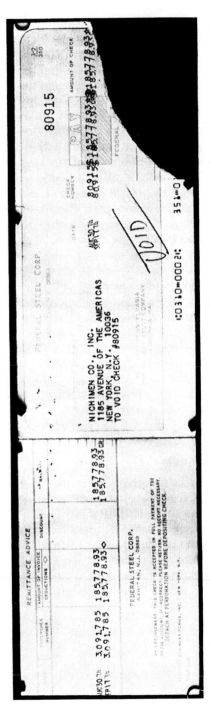

Figure 12.3. A check and its remittance device were prepared on an NCR check-writing or accounting machine. The machine contains a date imprinting device, various columns of digits that record accounting numbers and amounts, and a typewriter section that inserts the payee's name and address. All is printed on the check, and the machine also prepares a record for the accounting department. Machines of this type can be programmed for other kinds of work as well.

counting devices become questioned from time to time. The printed records from these machines frequently can be identified as coming from a particular unit by the simple process of comparison of its work with the questioned records. Numeral and symbol designs of a particular make or model of adding machine or calculator may be distinctive, and as a machine is used, the quality of the printed copy may deteriorate in a distinctive manner. Identification depends on knowledge of how the record is printed since the machine's construction determines the interrelationship of character imprints within a column and in different columns of figures. The work of the suspected machine must be studied to locate individual characteristics similar in nature to typewriting and other mechanical printing. This type of case is encountered rather infrequently in the document examiner's day-to-day work, but his knowledge of identification requirements and of other comparable machines prepares him for identifying this class of material.

The numerous kinds of cash registers and computer printouts used in recording purchases, both for cash and for credit, represent an ever-changing field of identification for the document examiner. The older devices are mechanically operated machines activated either by hand or by an electric motor, while the newer devices are much more complex mechanisms. In addition to printing a record for the customer, many are connected to computer storage units in which the information is deposited. Again, the design of the type found in the printed record, its individual peculiarities or defects, and the general operation of the machine all have bearing on whether a particular slip or record can be individualized and the source identified.[2]

Other Recording Machines

Occasional problems have arisen involving printed records from scales (Figure 12.4) or meters such as those attached to delivery trucks for oil (Figure 12.5), gasoline, and other bulk liquids.[3] In fact, the many specialized record-making devices available rarely come into controversy and involve the services of the document examiner. It has been shown in one matter that the source of stamped metal plates can be established by the same techniques as those applied to more conventional documents.[4]

---

[2]Also see J. Warren, "Cash Register and Cash Adding Machine Identification," *Royal Canadian Mounted Police Seminar* No. 5 (Ottawa: Queen's Printer, 1958) pp. 89–99.
[3]O. Hilton, "Individualizing Oil Delivery Imprints," *Journal of Forensic Sciences* 21 (1976): 213–217.
[4]Maureen A. Casey and Arthur R. Paholke, "A Dual View to Identifying Metal Stamped Impressions," *Journal of Police Science and Administration* 3 (1975): 177–182.

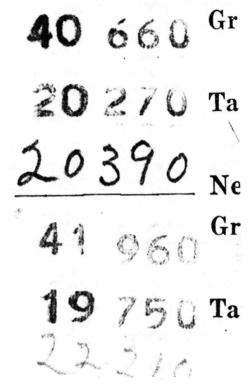

Figure 12.4. Two weight tickets recorded by the scales. The two tickets were printed on different scales, as can be seen from the design of the numerals. Compare 40 660 with 41 960, especially the 6 and 0.

Figure 12.5. Two oil delivery slips prepared by the same printer. Very small breaks in the type metal of the 7 and 9 are indicated by arrows and are among the factors that individualize these printouts.

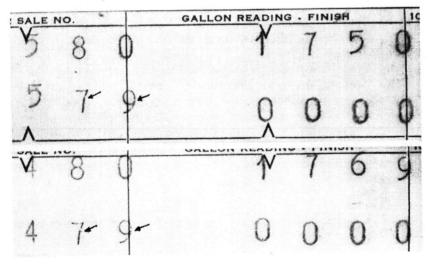

Computer Printouts

The widespread application of computer techniques in the business world today has seen the continued development of units that produce printouts of the data stored and processed by computers. These units range from modified typewriters of the single element design to specialized high-speed printers using metal typefaces, thermal printing devices, ink jet printers, and laser printers. Each class of printer has its own identification problem, but with every type, some degree of individuality develops through use.

More and more, the document examiner undoubtedly will be confronted with problems involving the work of these machines. Those using metal and plastic typefaces represent the kind of problems closely related to typewriting identification (Figure 12.6). The nonimpact classes, that is, ink jet, thermal, and laser printers, have been developed more recently and represent the latest identification challenge to those who are called upon to identify documents.[5]

Time Clocks and Date Stamps

Time clocks are widely used in factories and businesses in which employees are paid on an hourly rate. They are also used in parking lots and various security posts where in and out time checking is needed. Details of design and operation differ among units, but basically the printing is clock controlled and stamps an impression on paper or a card through an inked ribbon. Individual machines may be identified through their records, but problems also arise concerning altered records. The penetrating nature of the ink driven into the paper by the stamping action makes erasing very difficult, and the results of an attempt are fairly obvious. Touching up the figures with ink, even ball pen ink, can be recognized under careful visual examination, especially under moderate magnification since the ink strokes react differently on paper (Figure 12.7).

Many date stamps used in offices produce an impression similar to that of a time stamp except that no hour or minute record appears. The machines are generally hand set and print from metal or rubber type. In addition to machine identification, it may be possible when the typefaces print through a ribbon to verify the date on a disputed document by examining evidence of the ribbon's degree of wear. Of course, nondisputed imprints are needed to form a sound basis of judgment in such cases.

---

[5]A. G. Leslie and T. A. Simpson, "Identification of Printout Devices," *Forensic Science International* (in press).

```
WILLIAMSON  MUSIC  INC                    2617*
WILLIS  MUSIC  CO                            8*
WITMARK  M  &  SONS                       3480*
WOOD  B  F  MUSIC  CO                        18*
WORDS  &  MUSIC  INC                        341*
WORLD  MUSIC  INC                          133*
YANKEE  MUSIC  PUB  CORP                      2*

       WILLIAMSON
  ●                              2891      100
                                 3652      100
                                 4225      200
  ●                              4709      200

       WOODWARD
  ●

       YANKEE
  ●                               943       20
                                  944       20
                                  945       20
  ●                               946       20
```

Figure 12.6. The two records are from a punch card accounting machine. It was suspected that they may have been both run on the same unit, but the type style established that they were not.

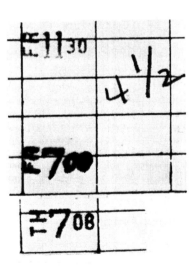

Figure 12.7. An altered time clock impression is revealed by a microscopic study of the 7 00 recording. Here the solid ink strokes obscure the ribbon imprint, which can be seen in a stamped impression.

Figure 12.8. The small fragment of black printing shown at the upper right appeared on a thin layer of salmon-colored paper, which was adhering to a piece of cellophane tape. Police investigating an armed robbery and killing discovered the fragment stuck to the bottom of a suitcase. One of the participants in his confession of the crime stated that this suitcase had been used to carry the money taken in the robbery of a *Reader's Digest* truck. One of the armed guards had been killed during the commission of the crime.

The question was raised, Could this fragment have been torn from the face of a subscription card like the one shown below? A comparison of the printing with the printing in the upper right hand corner of the certificate appears in Figure 12.9.

Printed Matter

Printed material, regardless of the method by which it is prepared, can be identified; that is, forms or other types of printed material can be compared with known specimens from particular sources to establish where they were produced.[6]

---

[6]Lucile Lacy, "Modern Printing Processes," *Journal of Criminal Law, Criminology and Police Science* 47 (1957): 730–736. A. M. Headrick, "A Review of the Printing and Duplicating Processes," *Royal Mounted Police Seminar* No. 5 (Ottawa: Queen's Printer, 1958) pp. 101–120. Jan Beck, "Printed Matter as Questioned Documents," *Journal of Forensic Sciences* 12 (1967): 82–101.

Figure 12.9. The three words in the left panel appear in the upper right corner of the subscription card (Figure 12.8). The printing on the small fragment from the suitcase is in the right section. Along the right-hand side, the edge of the fragment had been folded back and stuck to the tape in that position. The triangle on the extreme right shows the printing from the back. It can be seen dimly in the photograph of the face as an inverted comma between the o and the w.

Proof that the fragment came from one of these certificates rests on the following factors. The color of the paper stock matches the certificate. The wording corresponds to that of the section shown. The design of type is identical. In printing the word "now" the type was spread in order to justify the right margin, while the next two lines were set solid with no extra space between letters. Finally, the distance between the first and second line of printing is the same (measurements to ½₅₀ in.).

The technical testimony formed one link in the chain of evidence connecting the receipt of the money at the *Reader's Digest* office and the armed robbery. Several employees testified that occasionally bills were received fastened to the card by tape. Obviously, in separating one, a portion of the surface of the card was torn away and the tape remained attached to the bill until it was placed in the suitcase during the holdup. After hearing all this and other evidence, the jury found the defendants guilty.

This chain of substantiating evidence took on even greater significance after the United States Supreme Court handed down its decision in the case [Stein v. New York, 346 U. S. 156 (1953)]. In ruling on the admissibility of the confession, the Court held the conviction supportable by other evidence and would stand even though the confession had been coerced. Without this chain of evidence the Court might well have decided that the confession was untrustworthy.

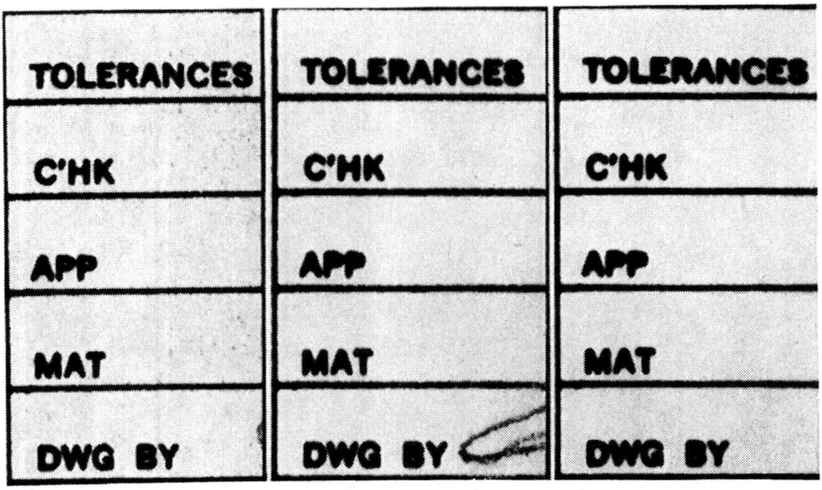

Figure 12.10. Determination of whether the center form was part of the same run as the left printing or the right can be made by considering the condition of the small enclosures within the letters. All the material was prepared by offset printing. In the left sample the R, P, and B have small white centers to the enclosures. In the right specimen they are closed up, indicating that in rerunning the forms a plate was made by photographing a sample from an earlier run. The center, questioned specimen matches the right-hand (later) printing in this respect.

Identification of all types of printing, especially when it is of traditional printing type style, can be accomplished by consideration of the design (font) of type, the spacing between letters, words, lines, and sections of the copy; the malalignment of letters; defective or damaged typefaces or uneven type impressions; and actual printing errors (Figures 12.8 and 12.9). If the material is produced by letterpress, each letter represents a separate type unit and may contain some identifying factor. If the material is set by offset, the various letter impressions come from a common source, but, of course, there is always the slight variation possible in the imprinting of one impression compared to another. By studying the combination of these various factors, it is possible to say whether two identical texts were produced by the same type or plate.

It is always possible to reproduce the same subject matter by a second printing. If there is a lapse of time between the two, it may mean that the original was reset if letterpress was used, or the original copy was prepared again if offset methods were employed. A second production of this nature may produce slight variants that will distinguish between the two printings.

With offset material it is also possible to prepare a new printing plate from any clear copy of the original printing. If it is done with great care, it may be difficult to distinguish between the two runs, but if the quality control in making the second plate is low, there may be some broadening of the type impression, a loss in sharpness of details noticeable in the partial closing of small open areas of enclosures, and other flaws in the printed material that did not appear in the original copy (Figure 12.10). These factors make it possible to distinguish between two different printings of the identical form. One must always approach such a conclusion with caution if one has only a limited number of examples of printing from the first run because with poor

Figure 12.11. Was the disputed accounting sheet ruled in the same order as the 1952 sheet? Comparison of the horizontal rulings shows that while the bottom line and the fourth one above are equally spaced, the two intermediate lines do not intersect exactly. In the setting of the ruling pens to make these forms there is allowance for slight variation from one setup to another in many plants, and differences such as those shown will separate different runs.

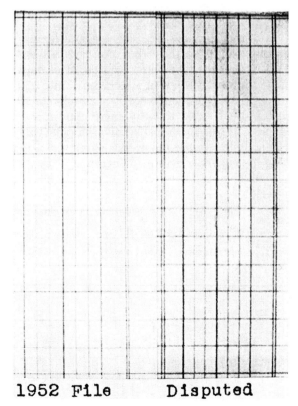

1952 File   Disputed

press work somewhat similar flaws can occur in the course of a single run.[7] Depending on the nature of the case at hand, any of these findings may assist in establishing accurate conclusions in the case.

When law-enforcement officers are investigating the source of questioned printing, particularly anonymous handbills or illegal forms,[8] the type employed may be found standing or the offset plate located. If so, several proofs should be pulled immediately to serve as comparison standards, and it is appropriate to impound the type or plate, whenever possible, for future evidence and for actual technical examination. In lieu of this evidence, proof sheets kept by the printer should be searched for.

Ruled forms in which there may be more than one color ruling, such as bookkeeping and accounting forms, are generally produced on ruling machines. These machines are equipped with a series of adjustable pens, each of which can be loaded with its own ink supply. To rule a particular form pens are set at a designated position to produce the series of lines. Some may be adjusted to write an intermittent line. Several ink colors can be loaded in different ruling pens so that all vertical or all horizontal rulings can be made at one time despite the presence of more than one color of ink.

In setting the pens it is common practice not to control the individual setting exactly so that when the pens are again set up to produce the same form on another run their position may vary by a small fraction of an inch from the former setting. Thus, it is very likely that rulings made at different times will not match exactly. It is also possible that forms ruled some months apart may contain ink colors that differ slightly in tint as well. These variable factors can assume importance when there is a suspicion that some parts of a series of dated records may have been added or rewritten at a later date (Figure 12.11).

----

[7]John E. Cogol, *Photo-Offset Fundamentals* (Bloomington: McKnight, 1973), Chapter 19, pp. 381–389.

[8]A report of a criminal investigation and prosecution involving lottery tickets is described by Lieut. S. S. Smith, "Lotteries," *Journal of Criminal Law and Criminology* 38 (1948): 658–669. Lieut. Smith shows on p. 668 the basis of identification of the plates from which the tickets were printed.

13

Age of a Document

The document examiner is often asked to determine when a document was prepared. Many of these questions are set within a short time period, such as whether the document was prepared five months ago or three years ago. Questions of this type have definite limitations, are extremely complex, and generally cannot be answered directly. However, there can be data in a document revealed by examination that allow an estimate of its age. This chapter deals with a number of the possibilities and limitations encountered.

Dating may be accomplished by one of several techniques. The materials that make up a document may tell something of the earliest possible date of preparation. In some instances, the condition of the material may shed some light on the likely age of the document. This leads to the second means of dating, that is, the change that may have occurred in some constituent of the document, a change that has come about after the original preparation. Another technique involves comparison with known undisputed material, that is, by comparing it with a series of documents prepared with the same typewriter or pen and ink or paper, for example, and fitting the document in question into such an established framework. Finally, documents have been dated by means of chance impressions or marks found on them. Despite the number of techniques, each has rather limited possibilities and these will be considered in the following sections.

The most successful results in questions of dating a document are proofs that the alleged date is wrong. Any part of the document that can be established not to be as old as the date on the document serves as the basis of the opinion. An attempt to substantiate the authenticity of the date, however, generally does not lead to definite findings. Even when all factors concerning the document are consistent with the date, the best determination generally is that it could have been prepared on its date or, more definitely, within a time span that includes the date. To find from the physical factors involved that the date of the document is the only possible time of preparation is extremely unusual. Time spans may range from a few days or weeks in an occasional problem to months or years. Unfortunately in some instances, this range may include the conflicting claims of all parties interested in the document.

Dating by Materials

The usual document is made up of writing with pen and ink, pencil, or typewriter on paper. These factors together with stamps, printed forms, letterheads, and other constituents of the document may contain information that establishes the earliest possible time of use.

Paper

The materials that make up paper contain information about when the paper was first manufactured.[1] The fiber content and the various other materials, such as the substances for coating, loading, or brighteners, all have first dates of use. Any study of the paper on the basis of formulation requires two factors in order to produce any significant date. First, the manufacturer of the paper must be known, and this cannot always be ascertained. Second, the manufacturer must have records in its plant or archives that disclose when certain combinations of materials were first introduced. Occasionally, this information can be developed and is of value, but many times it fails because the manufacturer cannot be identified or it is found that his records are incomplete.

A common method of determining the source of paper and its possible time of manufacture involves the watermark, part of better grades of writing and typewriting papers. Today only a few of these watermarks include a dating code that allows the manufacturer to determine the year in which the paper was made. Records are generally available about when a brand of paper, designated by the watermark, was first placed on the market, but most brands have been sold for a number of years. Documents have been dated or the dates proven fraudulent by changes in design of the watermark (Figure 13.1) or by the flaws in a particular mark. Here again, success depends on the accuracy of the

---

[1]Also refer to Julius Grant, *Books and Documents* (London: Grafton, 1937), Chapter 2.

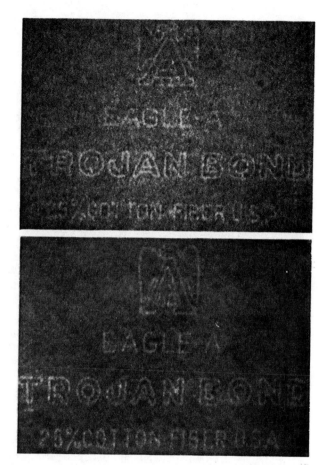

Figure 13.1. Trojan Bond paper before (top) and after (bottom) the change in its watermark in 1976.

plant records. Since the watermark can be displayed in photographs, the dating information can be demonstrated effectively to all concerned.

Writing Inks

During the 20th century a number of new chemicals have been developed and made a part of older writing inks. New classes of inks suitable for the changes in pens have also become available. Each may be identified from examination of the written strokes and may establish the earliest date at which the writing could have been executed. Unfortunately for current problems, these changes have not occurred yearly or at any regular interval, but fraudulent documents may still be detected from time to time by the presence of ink that is inconsistent with the document's date.

When the ball point pen was first introduced in the 1940s, an entirely new kind of writing ink appeared.[2] These pens depend on an oil-based ink rather than the fluid, water-based inks that had been used for fountain and dip pens up to that time. Thus, the combination of a new writing instrument with a distinctive character and a new ink meant that documents with these characteristics could not have been written prior to the mid-1940s. In 1952 inks with polyethylene glycol base began replacing the oil-based inks in ball point pens, adding another date for inks.[3]

During the modern history of fluid inks, numerous dyes were developed and adapted to some of these inks, but most dye materials as a class at least were synthesized in the latter part of the 19th century.[4] In this century, though, alkaline water-based inks, as opposed to acid inks, were introduced.[5]

The introduction of the relatively fine-point porous tip pen, commonly referred to as the fiber tip pen, came early in the 1960s. A broader-tipped felt marker of course has been available for some time, but used inks of a different composition. Without chemical testing, though, it would be difficult to differentiate between these inks on paper in order to use this criterion as a means of dating a document.

During the mid-1970s, rare-earth elements were added to some inks in order to tag them. Detection of these elements in the ink permits dating within a range of a year or two since the plan is to change the elements periodically. By the same token, chromatography, which permits detailed analysis of the ink's dyes, when related to reference collections of inks can be utilized to establish the earliest date of use. At the present time, however, the most extensive reference collections are maintained exclusively in federal law-enforcement laboratories and

---

[2]Ball point pens were first sold in the United States on October 30, 1945, but had been manufactured in Argentina as early as 1943. See note 2, Chapter 3, for further historical data.

[3]Wilson R. Harrison, *Suspect Documents* (New York: Praeger, 1958), p. 217. A. H. Witte, "Examination and Identification of Inks," in *Methods of Forensic Science*, Vol. 2 (Frank Lundquist, Ed.) [New York: Wiley (Interscience), 1963] places the date as 1950 (p. 66).

[4]William E. Hagan, *A Treatise on Disputed Handwriting* (New York, Banks, 1894) discusses the Davis will case, in which an 1866 will had been written with nigrosine ink, which was "discovered about 1870." Also, on the Gordon will case, he noted that a red ink interlineation had been "made from eosine, something which was not known, and had not been discovered until some years subsequent to the time when this so-called original draft . . . had been made."

[5]Harrison, *Suspect Documents*, reports early patents in 1927, but that Parker's Superchrome Ink with copper and vanadium compounds dates from 1949.

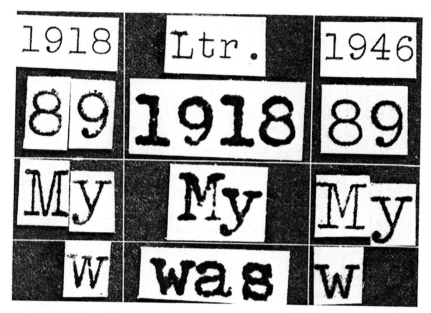

Figure 13.2. A letter dated in 1918 was brought forward in a claim against an estate. It had been written on a Remington typewriter. The designs of the M and w are not like these letters on a 1918 machine, and in fact it was not until 1946 that the change in these letters was made. Clearly the letter could not have been typed in 1918.

are not available to parties in civil litigation.[6] Actually, these reference specimens are most helpful in proving that a document could not have been written on a certain date because the ink was not then available.

Typewriting

Typewriting study may lead to more productive dating findings than other parts of the document. As has been pointed out in Chapter 3, the design of type may tell something of the manufacturer, and each design has a specific date of introduction (Figure 13.2). Thus, with proper reference material, it is possible to establish whether the type design was available when the document was allegedly prepared (Figure 13.3). This information does not determine when the document was written, but it has established that a document could not have been prepared on the date it bears.

---

[6]The Bureau of Alcohol, Tobacco, and Firearms, Department of Treasury, Ball Pen Ink Library is described in D. A. Crown, R. L. Brunelle, and A. A. Cantu, "The Parameters of Ballpen Ink Examination," *Journal of Forensic Sciences* 21 (1976): 917–922.

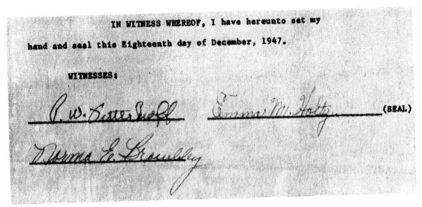

Figure 13.3. A will dated in 1947 was typewritten with a machine equipped with Underwood Esteem type, first released in March 1958.

Photocopies

Determination of the type of photocopy establishes the earliest date at which it could have been made. For example, a document bearing a date in the early 1950s could not have been photocopied at the time of preparation with one of the three common photocopying techniques now available—the Xerox or other plain-paper copying methods; the direct electrostatic method with zinc oxide paper; or the dual spectrum copy developed by 3M.[7] A similar situation with a 1943 document would hold for copying methods introduced in the late 1940s and 1950s, all of which are virtually obsolete today.[8] This information does not mean that the document itself could not have been in existence then, but it would disprove the claim that the photocopy was made when the original was first executed.

Printed Matter

Documents prepared on letterhead paper or on printed forms frequently contain information regarding the earliest date at which they could have been prepared. Printed forms may contain a code indicating the

[7]The Revolution in Office Copying, Part 1, "*Chemical and Engineering News* (July 13, 1964): 115–129, and "Part II" (July 20, 1964): 84–94, discuss the development of office copying machines and methods. Reported are dates of introduction: Xerox (Transfer Electrostatic Process) Model 914 in March 1960; Apeco, December 1961, the first direct electrostatic process machine using zinc oxide paper; and 3M Dual Spectrum Copier in October 1963.

[8]Three methods were introduced and widely used during this period: the diffusion transfer process, first commercially available in Germany as Blitzkopie, an Agfa product, in late 1949, and introduced in the United States by Remington Rand as Transcopy in 1952; the gelatin transfer process, Verifax, developed by Eastman Kodak and released in early 1952; and the thermographic process, Thermo-Fax, released by 3M Corporation in January 1950. "Revolution in Office Copying, Part 1," pp. 115–129.

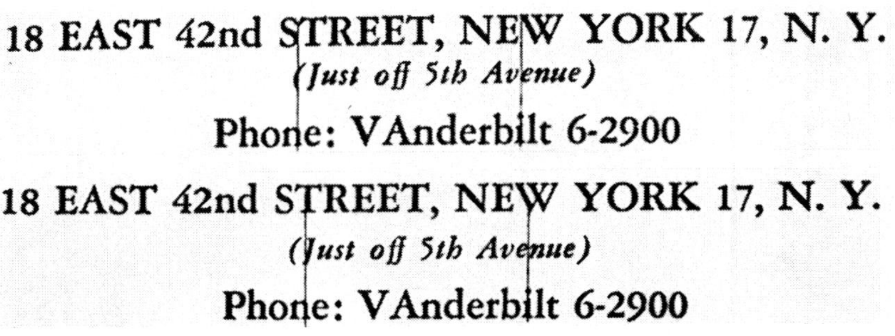

18 EAST 42nd STREET, NEW YORK 17, N. Y.
(Just off 5th Avenue)
Phone: VAnderbilt 6-2900

18 EAST 42nd STREET, NEW YORK 17, N. Y.
(Just off 5th Avenue)
Phone: VAnderbilt 6-2900

Figure 13.4. The top letterhead bore an undisputed 1947 date, the lower, 1948. There are slight differences in the arrangement of the two printings as indicated by the ruled lines. In addition the spacing between the first and second lines differs by $\frac{1}{16}$ in. The information helped to authenticate the date of a disputed document.

date of printing. Changes in design or wording create dating data (Figure 13.4). Telephone numbers, area codes, addresses, postal zones and ZIP codes, and design of and information on letterhead related to the individual or business establishment concerned may be inconsistent with the date on a fraudulent document. Many times this information is overlooked when it could prove clearly that the document was not prepared on its date.

Paper

With knowledge of the manufacturer of a questioned sheet of paper and samples of the same brand whose dates of manufacture are undisputed, it is possible to subject all sheets to a series of chemical, microscopic, and chromatographic tests. Matching the questioned document with certain dated specimens establishes a presumptive time of manufacture. The tests involve cutting samples from the paper and destroying or modifying these samples.

Miscellaneous Items

Every part of a document has dating value. Thus hand stamps, binding material (staples, paper clips, et.), company logos (Figure 13.5), postage stamps on mailing envelopes with indistinct postmarks, indented writing, perforations, or canceling devices each have dates of introduction. In brief, a document's date can be verified only if all its elements were available at the date of preparation, while any item in its makeup that was not available at the alleged date establishes definitely that the date is incorrect.

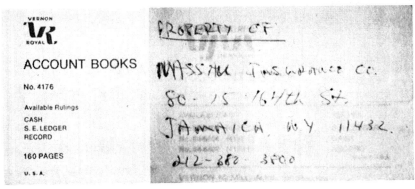

Figure 13.5. The right-hand section shows an infrared photograph of a label in the front inside cover of a bound record book containing a log of distribution of insurance forms for December 1975 and for 1976. The weak outline of the logo of Vernon McMillan, Inc., was first printed in record books sold in April or May 1977. The company had been formed by a corporate merger of Vernon Royal and McMillan Book. The left-hand section shows the logo and inside printing of a bound record book that was available in 1975 and 1976. The logo and other revealed printing proved the claim that the book contained day-to-day records made on their dates was false.

Dating by Changes in Materials

Writing Inks

Although many people believe that writing inks can be dated, that is, that the document examiner can determine how long the ink has been on the paper, this is seldom possible. Some change must have occurred in the ink after it dried on the paper for dating to be possible. Few inks undergo reliable, measurable modifications after they have dried.

A complicating factor even with inks that do undergo change after the original writing is how the writings have been stored. Documents kept in files and those left on a table or desk top for long periods of time age differently. Heat and humidity can affect the rate of change. For example, some dye inks which are not entirely light fast, fade when exposed to sunlight or daylight over a period of time, but the same inks stored in a file may maintain its original color for a number of years.

With the iron-based fluid writing inks, which prior to the mid-1950s had widespread use, a change occurs in the early weeks or occasionally months after deposit on the paper. There is a significant oxidation that causes darkening of the ink, rapid at first, but definitely slowing in a few days or weeks. The change is measurable over a period of time. The rate of change serves as an estimation of how long the writing has been on the paper.[9] A very rapid change indicates the age of the writing to be a few days or at best a week and a few days, while very slight changes over a period of several months would indicate that the writing had been on the paper anywhere from a few weeks to a few months, depending on how it had been stored. After approximately six months, and in many instances even less, the change becomes so slight that it can no longer be measured.

Other types of inks do not undergo such oxidation. Included in this group are the dye inks used with fountain and other nib pens, the fluid inks of porous tip pens, and the ink used in the ball point pen. To date, no other chemical change has been observed, except in those few cases in which the dyes fade after extended exposure to light. Few inks today do fade, except under extended exposure to strong light, and it would be the unusual document that was so carelessly stored.

A method was proposed some years ago for testing inks of this latter group for age indication. Most fluid inks contain either chlorides or sulphates as one of their constituents. It has been found that these ions migrate or spread out from the line of writing gradually. Measurement of the amount of migration from the line or writing has been used as an estimate of age, but the test requires cutting a significant portion of the ink stroke from the paper and subjecting it to a series of chemical tests that would destroy or alter most of the ink writing tested.[10] The test is complicated by the temperature and humidity conditions in which the document had been stored. Often factors of this nature cannot be readily ascertained. The method has never enjoyed widespread use in this country, because of its destructive nature and limited accuracy.

Paper

The age of paper sometimes becomes highly significant, particularly in the investigation of old documents and ancient manuscripts. It must be clearly understood that paper cannot be dated within narrow limits of time, but as it ages, its appearance and physical properties change. These changes are the work of time and the elements. Man cannot accurately reproduce them by an accelerated method, although there are always those willing to try. Simulation of the discoloration due to age is seldom correct in its detail and may be grotesque and clumsy. How the paper was stored and the material from which it was made

---

[9]C. A. Michell, *Documents and Their Scientific Examination* (London: Griffin, 1935), pp. 61–65.

[10]A. H. Witte, "The Examination and Identification of Inks," in *Methods of Forensic Science*, Vol. 2 (Frank Lundquist, ed.) [New York: Wiley (Interscience), 1963], pp. 69–75.

influence the rate of discoloration. Cheap woodpulp paper, such as newsprint, may start to discolor along the edges within a year or two even when stored in a closed file, but rag paper of a high quality may be very old before there is any sign of discoloration.

Extreme aging of paper or of some inks, particularly iron-based inks, can occur over a period of 10, 20, or 30 years. Tests of this nature are not particularly accurate in the sense that one can say this ink must be at least 10 years old or this paper must be at least 20 years old because of its condition. We have seen with both materials that the condition is dependent on storage and handling and also on the manufacturing processes and materials. In other words, all these tests can give some general estimates, but certainly cannot refute a particular date as opposed to one a few years earlier or later.

Pencils

Pencil writing does not undergo any change whatsoever after it is on the paper, and consequently does not provide a means by which any estimate of date can be made from examination of the writing stroke itself.

Dating by Comparison

Inks

With certain types of document problems, inks can be dated by comparison with other writing prepared around the date in question. This procedure has some utility with ball point pen inks since each pen contains its own ink supply.

If it is possible to assemble a large quantity of material of undisputed dates it may be possible to match the questioned ink with one of the pens and inks used by the writer during the period. The method is far from a conclusive confirmation of the date of writing, but depending on the factors involved in the controversy may at times assume great significance.

This latter situation would be particularly true, for example, if one ink was used for a few months and the writing quality of the pen was consistent with the questioned material as well. Examinations of this type are most helpful in determining whether certain questioned entries in a diary were written on their dates or at some other time. If the entry in question fails to match any writing of that particular period, this raises a strong supposition that it was added at some later date. On the other hand, if it is consistent with all that surrounds it, this goes a long way toward substantiating its authenticity.

When the questioned ink fails to match any ink used around its date, the presumption arises that the date of the document is not correct. However, the presumption is only as strong as the undisputed material is truly representative of the period. In other words, if the undisputed material can be shown to be representative of all writing prepared during the interval of time in question, the proof is relatively strong. A few check signatures, for example, would hardly establish a full picture of the inks used by the writer. On the other hand, if the document is claimed to have been signed in the writer's office and a quantity of correspondence, important documents, and checks of the period served as the comparison material, the proof should be more convincing. One can see that this dating method depends to a very large extent on the circumstances surrounding the document in question, as well as on the comparison materials.

Typewriting

Comparative techniques with typewriting are extremely useful in dating documents. The gradual deterioration of a typewriter, especially a typebar machine, permits the document examiner to study its work over a period of months or years, and to establish when new defects or changes in previous defects first occurred.[11] The period in which the same defects are present in the known and questioned documents establishes when the questioned material must have been prepared (Figure 13.6). Changes may not occur more frequently than every few years, or may occur within a few weeks of each other (Figure 13.7). Each typewriter is individual. However, when a particular defect shows for the first time, a document containing that defect must have been prepared after that date. Breaks or damage to typefaces are important elements in this type of dating problem, but alignment defects can also be used in narrower periods of time (Figure 13.8). Changes in variable defects may help in establishing the period in which the document must have been prepared (Figure 13.9), but all these criteria represent a time span of weeks or months, sometimes even years, during which the document may have been prepared.[12]

Narrower dating periods may be achieved by studying the gradual deterioration as a fabric ribbon is used. Thus the depth of impression, that is, the darkness of the type impression, forms the basis of com-

---

[11]George G. Swett, "Dating of Typewriting," *Journal of Criminal Law, Criminology and Police Science* 50 (1959): 86–88.

[12]O. Hilton, "Dating of Typewriting by Analysis of Variable Defects," *Journal of Criminal Law, Criminology and Police Science* 51 (1960): 373–377.

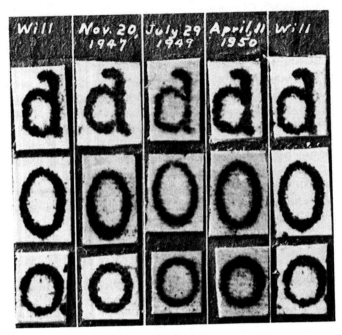

Figure 13.6. The will from which the letters of the two outside columns were taken was dated August 20, 1947. The condition of the three typefaces shown above showed that it was not written at that time. The flattened condition of the left side of the d resulted from actual damage to the type metal, and the damage did not occur until about July 1949. The 0 printed heavier on the right-hand side, a condition first observed in the known specimens in July 1946, and the small o was without defect until the April 1950 specimen, when the letter typed heavier on the upper right as it did on the will. These physical facts established the fraudulent quality of the will despite its genuine signature.

parison. Newer ribbons print a dark, heavily inked impression; worn ribbons, a very dull weak impression. The decline from fresh to worn is gradual and assists with age estimates (Figure 13.10). At the same time, the impressions of the type strokes are broader at first and become rather fine and narrow toward the end of the ribbon's life. These conditions, when properly documented by undisputed dated typewriting, may permit an opinion that the document in question was prepared within a span of one or two weeks, or even less, depending on the extent of use of the machine.

In much the same way, the cleanliness of the typefaces may also assist in short-term dating. The amount of fouling found in small enclosures of frequently used letters builds up gradually when the operator fails to clean typefaces regularly. When the date in question falls

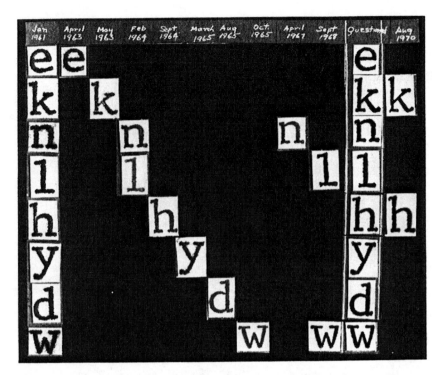

Figure 13.7. New dating factors occurred in a series of typewritten documents between 1961 and 1970. On each date shown at least one new defect was revealed. April 1963, the ending stroke of the e is damaged; May 1963, the lower left serif of the k; February 1964, the lower left serif of the n and the left side of the base stroke of the l; September 1964, the lower left serif of the h; March 1965, the left serif of the y, which in later specimens became more prominent; August 1965, the lower serif of the d; October 1965, the right serif of the w is chipped; April 1965, the upper serif of the n is now damaged; September 1968, the upper left projection of the l is damaged and the right serif of the w is now completely off. These letters and a number of others show the same defects as those in the letter. The further damage to the k and h in the August 1970 specimen shows that the questioned document was typed before the last date. The plaintiff who first said that the document was prepared in 1961 or 1962 now says it was prepared in September 1968.

within a short time span, ribbon wear and improperly cleaned characters may help to pinpoint the most likely date (Figure 13.11).

At present, most of these techniques have failed to produce comparable results with material prepared on single element units. Defects are much more subtle and more limited, which means, as is true of the identification, the techniques must be refined and studied further before they are successfully adapted to this class of typewriters.

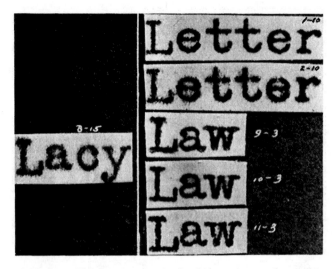

Figure 13.8. The deterioration in the shift motion on the machine during the course of a year shows that the questioned material "Lacy" was prepared no earlier than the October–November period.

Handwriting and Signatures

Changes do occur in the handwriting of individuals (Figure 13.12). In a great number of instances the change is a gradual evolution (Figure 13.13), and it is difficult to set a date before which a particular habit or quality of writing will be found. Still, documents have been dated, and signatures and entire documents proved to be fraudulent, because the writing habits were not in keeping with the date.

Age deterioration is often a progressive change, but once it is a part of the handwriting, it is inconsistent with the writing of one or two years before. Illness and accidents can sharply affect handwriting, and the change may take place on a particular day or in a particular week (Figure 13.14). With recovery, there are instances in which there is a

Figure 13.9. Changes in the variation pattern of a typewriter shows that page 10 was typewritten later in the machine's history than page 9, e's were clearly printing heavier on the top than the bottom when page 10 was written (the specimens below the white lines). This was consistent with other testimony that a revision had been made in page 10 seven months after the main portion was prepared. Other documents from the office confirmed the change in pattern of variation in this period. (See footnote 11.) *(Illustration reprinted from the Journal of Criminal Law, Criminology and Police Science.)*

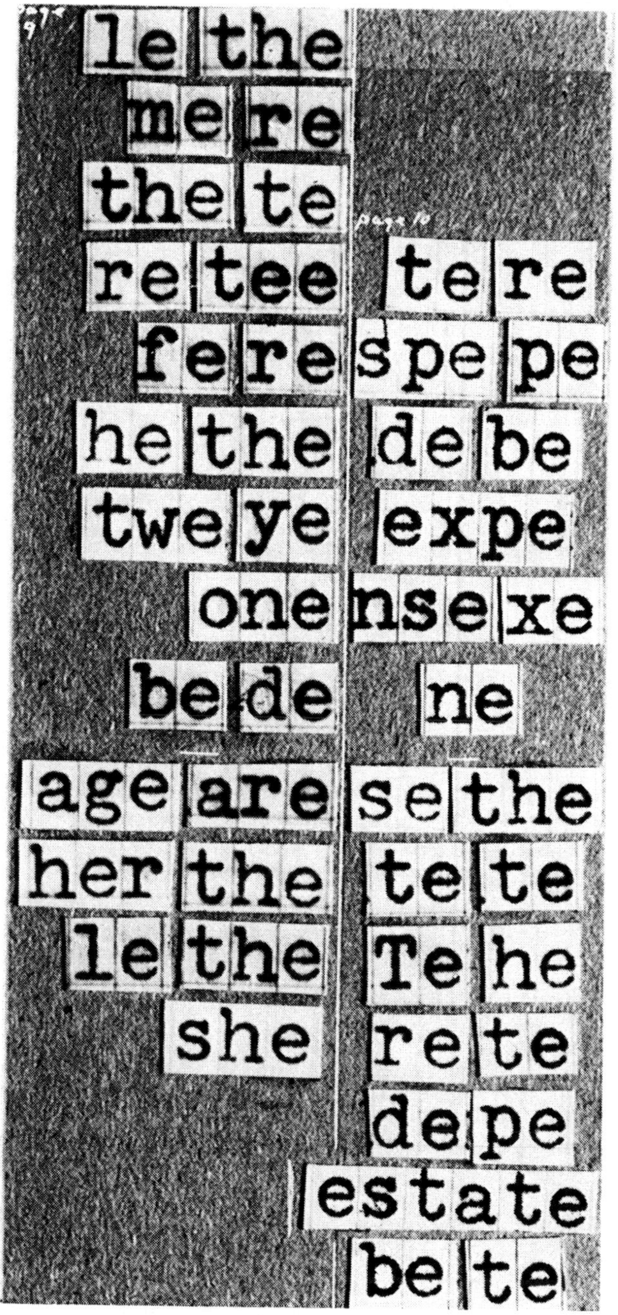

le the
me re
the te
re tee te re
fe re spe pe
he the de be
twe ye expe
one nse xe
be de ne
age are se the
her the te te
le the Te he
she re te
de pe
estate
be te

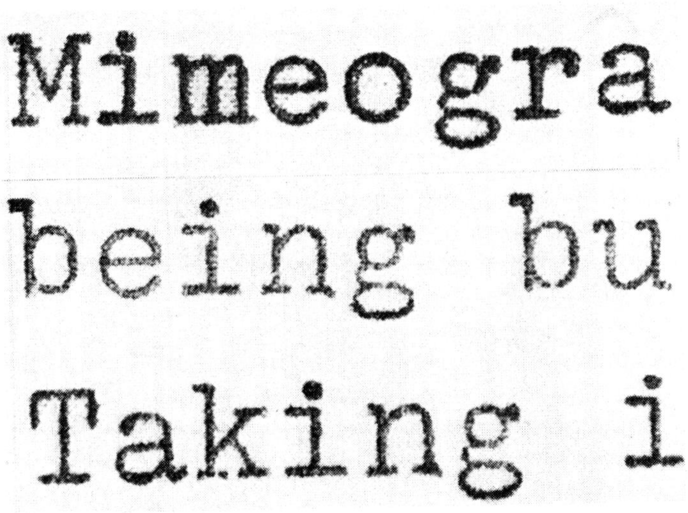

Figure 13.10. A party to a litigation stated that an undated document had been prepared by a public stenographer during his April visit to the city. His opponents believed that it had not been prepared until July of the same year when he returned for a second conference. Typewriting from the office of the public stenographer in April and July showed that her July typewriter ribbon matched the document and that the April typewriting had been prepared with a much newer ribbon, which wrote a darker, heavier impression.

Figure 13.11. One of the questions raised in connection with a suspected letter was, Could it have been prepared on its date, August 29, 1946? The typewriting of August 25 showed a similar pattern of filled typefaces, d, p, and b, which helped to establish that the two documents were written around the same time.

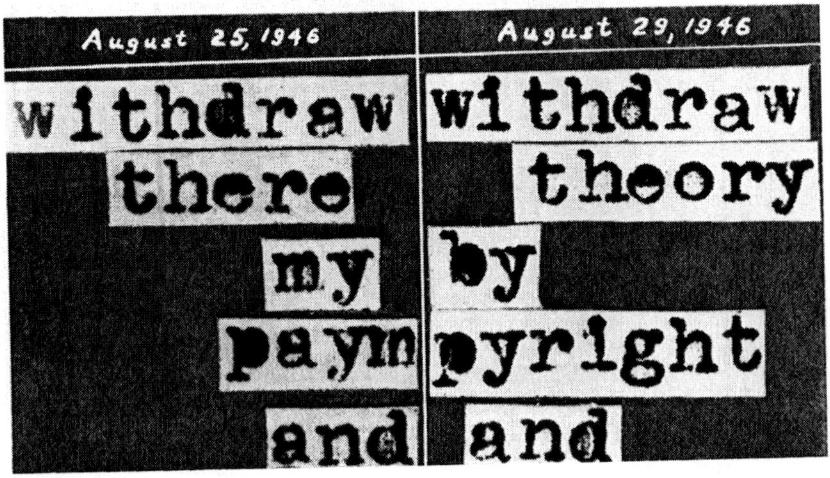

Figure 13.12. The very distinctive change in G. E. Tarbell's signature made during the two year period between late 1928 and 1930 was brought about by decline in his health and vision. It served as a means of verifying the dates in a series of disputed notes.

residual effect, but often none is apparent, so that the period of deterioration in the writing is clearly bracketed.

Changes in handwriting of mature writers are generally very slight and cover periods of years.[13] Therefore in the majority of cases, consideration of the handwriting is not a useful tool for dating documents. This generality is no reason, however, to ignore the possibility. Dates on documents have been disproved by the handwriting on them, and

---

[13]David J. Purtell, "Dating a Signature," *Forensic Science International* 15 (1980): 243–248.

290

Figure 13.13. The design of the S in the fraudulent Saffian signature of August 17, 1957 (center, unmarked) was inconsistent with the S-design of that date. The design of the S of the forged signature was consistently used after March 1958, and the earliest example occurred on a check of December 1957. The wrong design was a significant, but not the only, defect of the forgery.

in certain instances changes in handwriting have helped to authenticate the date, despite the fact that it is a somewhat unusual situation.

Printing

Among legal decisions can be found a few important cases in which the ultimate verdict rested in a large measure on evidence derived from a study of a form or certificate printed from a lithographic, engraved, or other type of plate.[14] In most of these matters the problem has been to determine when the certificate was first printed exactly like the contested document. A fraudulent claim in the estate of Ella Virginia von Echtzel Wendel was defeated in part by proof that a marriage certificate offered in evidence was not printed until at least 37 years after its date[15] (Figure 13.15). As can be seen from this case, details of the printing can be extremely important (Figure 13.16). The key to the solution of a problem may be found in the design of the letters and ornamentations, the exact size of the printed area of the document or injuries and breaks in the typefaces. When a particular plate has been reprinted periodically, its pattern of wear and deterioration can through careful comparison of several printings establish when the contested document was printed.

Dating by Chance Marks

Occasionally, in the history of a document it is possible to establish that some small offset of ink or writing or other chance mark must have been deposited after a specific date. Folds, embossings, binding marks, and postmark impressions appearing in the document can have dating value. Furthermore, these marks, folds, and other chance ad-

---

[14]In the Oliver will case the position of the tail of a comma, remaining after the printer's code had been cut from the document, established that the form had been printed subsequent to the date of the will. See A. S. Osborn, *Questioned Documents,* 2nd ed. (Albany: Boyd, 1929), illustration at p. 486.

[15]A brief discussion of the case appears in Elbridge W. Stein, "Proof of Handwriting and Typewriting," *Journal of Criminal Law and Criminology* 31 (1941): 641–642. Stein wrote a somewhat longer account of the case and the document evidence in a privately published pamphlet, *The Wendel Case.* Arthur Garfield Hays, *City Lawyer* (New York: Simon and Schuster, 1942), Chapter 12, pp. 289–336, as one of the trial attorneys, relates his account of the famous case.

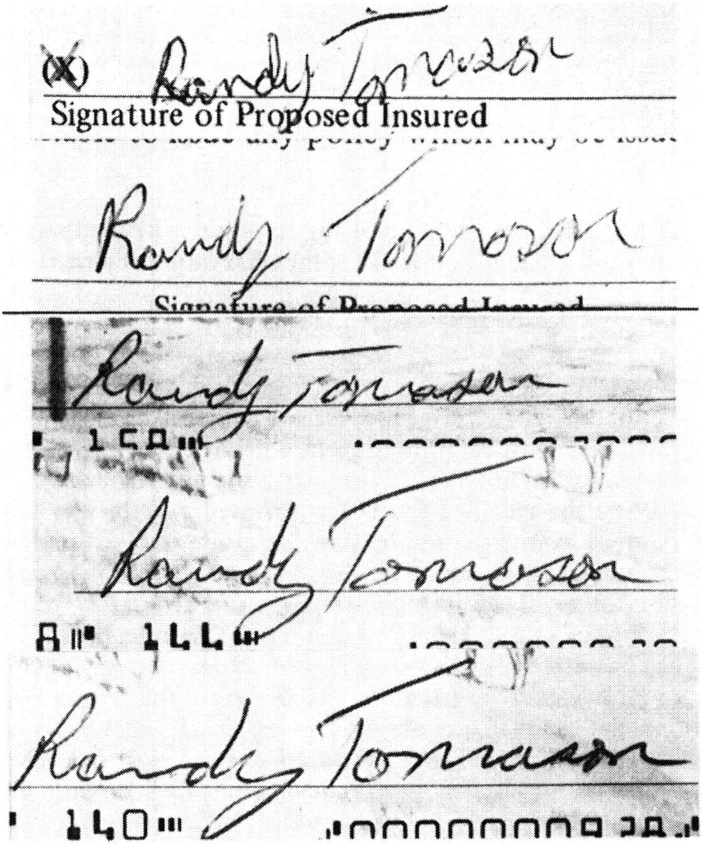

292

Figure 13.14. The two upper signatures appeared on two parts of an insurance application form dated October 20, 1977. The other three signatures are from a group of known check signatures dated earlier in October and September.

Tomason worked on October 20 as a truck driver transporting ore from a mine to town. In the afternoon he had taken time off to drive a distance to his home, picking up the mail from the post office box en route. It was claimed that he executed the insurance application, which was in this mail, while home and had returned to work that evening. During the evening run he was forced off the road, his truck and trailer jackknifed, and he was very seriously injured. He did not regain consciousness at the hospital until the next day (October 21) when the doctor stated he would have been able to write despite a body cast. He died of the injuries on October 23.

From a comparison of the two application signatures with the known check signatures, it was concluded that the signature was not written prior to the accident when Tomason was in good health, but because of the deteriorated quality of writing, must have been written after he regained consciousness in the hospital on October 21.

Figure 13.15. This certificate was the most important document in Thomas Patrick Morris's claim that he was the nephew of Ella Virginia von Echtzel Wendel and sole heir to her $40,000,000 estate (New York County, New York, 1931). Some of the evidence contained in the certificate which established its date of printing appears in Figure 13.16. *(From the files of Elbridge W. Stein.)*

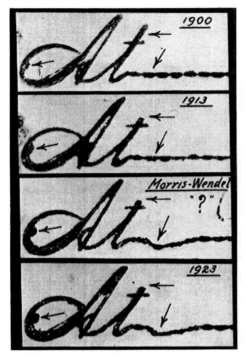

Figure 13.16. Comparison of printing defects in the plate which produced the Morris–Wendel certificate (Figure 13.15) with three dated printings from the same plate established its earliest date of printing as 1923. This fact showed that the certificate of June 11, 1876, was a forgery. The top of the staff of the t had been broken off between 1900 and 1913. The ruled line following the "At" had been bent between the 1913 printing and the 1923 printing. Other defects confirmed this dating.

The surrogate declared the document to be a forgery. Morris was subsequently tried and convicted of conspiracy to defraud the Wendel estate and sentenced to three years imprisonment. *(From the files of Elbridge W. Stein.)*

ditions can be useful in establishing when different parts of a document were prepared relative to one another. As a result, these factors standing alone have little value, but when related to claims and statements of opposing parties, they may assist in establishing the most probable date of preparation among those put forth in claims and counterclaims.

Combination of Factors

A single element of a document can raise a strong suspicion that its date is incorrect, but is insufficient to form positive proof. However, two or three factors of this nature in combination may form clear evidence that the alleged date is not the true one. In this respect consider for the moment the pattern of staple holes shown in Figure 3.34 and the printer's code in Figure 3.28. They were actually part of the same will. The legal back was stapled to the will and had the same pattern of holes as some of the pages, but fewer than the signature page, which was dated in 1929. The code indicated that the back was printed in early 1931. The staple holes established that the back was first used when the last changes in the will had been made, sometime after early 1931 and definitely after the date of execution. The surrogate ruled the will was invalid. In this case both factors in combination were necessary to establish the time of change. Thus dating of a document may rest on either a single element or a series of elements contained within the document. In other instances external evidence, that is, facts clearly proven by other evidence in the case, in combination with evidence found in the document may be necessary to date it correctly.

Conclusions

There are no automatic or universal ways of verifying the disputed date of a document, but the various techniques discussed in this chapter have under appropriate circumstances resolved the question at hand. Not every document can be dated by laboratory techniques. To establish from the document itself that it was prepared on a specific date is a rare accomplishment, possible only under a unique set of circumstances provided by other factors in the case. Far more often, when any dating is possible, it must be established within a time bracket—not before one date and not after a later one. It is such evidence that the examiner strives to reveal from the conditions and material that surround and make up the document at hand.

IV

THE ATTORNEY-INVESTIGATOR'S ROLE IN A QUESTIONED DOCUMENT PROBLEM

Up to this point the primary consideration has been a study of the questioned material itself. The scope of information that might be derived from it and the limitations that were imposed on the findings were examined. It was found that only by comparison with specimens from known sources could many questions be positively answered. These standards, upon which the identification is based, were assumed to exist in proper form, but unless this is true, very definite restrictions are imposed upon the findings of even the most highly qualified examiner.

The preparation and collection of standards represent a phase of the document investigation that is rarely the responsibility of the document examiner. The attorney, investigator, or some other person interested in the questioned document is generally called upon to select these specimens, and often he is not fully aware of the scope of the problem at hand. He may believe that forgery can be disclosed by comparing the questioned writing with *any* genuine signature, or that an anonymous letter writer can be identified from a scrap of writing consisting of but a few hastily written words. Unfortunately this meager evidence would hardly serve as a sound basis for an opinion.

Assembling authentic specimens to serve as the basis of comparison is a task of the utmost importance. Inadequate and improperly prepared standards limit the findings more often than any other single factor. In order to correct this situation, a detailed analysis of the requirements for an adequate set of standards is set forth in the following chapters.

Carelessness or lack of knowledge of the effects of mishandling documents has at times led to the destruction or damage of important physical evidence. Consequently, anyone investigating questioned document problems should have knowledge of the best way to handle these important papers in order to minimize the chance of damage.

In addition, there is another decision the investigator or attorney may have to make. He will encounter situations in which it is not possible to submit the original papers to the document examiner. How should copies be prepared so that the examiner's study is least inhibited? There are several choices, and they need to be carefully analyzed.

14

Preparation and Collection
of Handwriting Standards

The accuracy of handwriting opinions depends on the accuracy of the known writing. Writing standards may be defined as specimens that tell how a person writes. To obtain such writing sounds like a simple operation, but actually it may be one of the most complex and difficult steps in the whole writing investigation.

What are the basic requirements for proper writing standards? They must show how the individual writes and most especially how he would produce the material in question under similar conditions to those in which the questioned writing was prepared. These specimens certainly must contain enough appropriately prepared material to indicate not only the individual writing habits of the author but also the usual variation in these habits from one writing to the next. They need not necessarily contain all the innumerable identifying characteristics of the person's writing, only those that should be found in material exactly like that in dispute.

Two classes of specimens can be relied upon to fulfill these requirements. One consists of writing executed from day to day in the course of business, social, or personal affairs. These specimens may be referred to as *collected standards*. The second class consists of material written at the request of an attorney or investigator for the sole purpose of comparison with the questioned documents, material commonly known as *request* or *dictated standards*. The problems encountered in assembling collected or request standards differ in a number of ways, so each class will be treated separately.

Collected Standards

The most important single factor in assembling good standards is the amount of writing, but other factors influence the usefulness of collected standards. The principal points to consider are

1. the amount of writing available,
2. the similarity of subject matter,
3. the relative dates of the disputed and standard writing,
4. the conditions under which both questioned and known specimens were prepared, and
5. the type of writing instrument and paper used.

Amount of Standard Writing

The importance of an adequate amount of writing has already been emphasized as the keystone of good writing standards. There is a common belief that a writer can be postively identified from only one or two of his signatures. Unfortunately, this is far from the truth. Normal writing variation alone generally makes this impossible (Figure 14.1). Only with a quantity of material, therefore, can all the writing characteristics of an individual and the variations that usually occur from specimen to specimen be accurately determined.

That everyone does not sign his name or write any combination of words in exactly the same way twice is one of the more complicating elements of handwriting identification. This natural variation must be revealed by the known writing. Variation in writing is a personal factor—it is not the same for each individual either in extent or nature. Besides, it can be influenced by the conditions under which the writing was done. Here is the reason that no hard and fast rule can be set for a minimum number of signatures or a minimum amount of general handwriting.

With many problems, 10 or 20 signatures should constitute an adequate sample, but there are a certain number of cases that may require 30, 40, or even more signatures in order to accurately reveal the writer's habits, ability, and range of variation. Actually it is poor policy for the investigator to be satisfied with the bare minimum when just a few additional specimens can greatly fortify the findings.

The minimum amount of writing necessary to identify the author of a handwritten document or an anonymous letter likewise varies. As a working minimum, four or five pages of carefully selected continuous, natural writing usually prove satisfactory. Regardless of these suggestions, though, a person submitting a problem should always strive to obtain as large a quantity of handwriting as possible rather than merely to fulfill minimum requirements.

Similarity of Subject Matter

The best set of standards not only contains a quantity of writing but also includes an ample amount of the same general type of material

Figure 14.1. In a signature problem in which approximately 120 known signatures were submitted, it was found that the writer used an alternate form of the R only infrequently. Here are portions of the first 14 signatures in order of date of writing. The alternative form appears for the first time in the 14th signature (bottom right). Among the entire group, this form occurs in only six signatures.

Unusual characteristics occasionally play an important role in handwriting identification, and it is for this reason that numerous standards should always be collected.

as that in dispute. Thus, if a signature is questioned, standard signatures should be collected; if a check is believed to be fraudulent, genuine canceled checks should be procured; if an account entry is challenged, other entries serve as the best standards; if the authorship of any anonymous letter is to be established, letters and pages of connected writing should be gathered for purposes of comparison. The reasons for these choices become obvious with brief consideration of the various factors involved.

A person's signature, because of both its frequency of use and the nature of its employment (to represent the writer in business and personal affairs), tends to become more individual than any other combination of letters that he writes. By way of illustration, the reader undoubtedly recalls several unusual signature styles of acquaintances, signatures that differ radically from the remainder of the person's writing. In some countries signatures customarily are so stylized that they bear virtually no relationship to the person's general handwriting and may hardly hint at the spelling of the name. Obviously, in these instances only genuine signatures are of value in passing upon the authenticity of one in question, but even when the writer's signature appears very much like the rest of his writing, there may be small details peculiar to his signature alone.

In collecting signature standards one must also consider the use for which each specimen was written. Some writers have two or more distinctive styles for particular purposes. For example, one variety may be used on checks and legal documents and a second for correspondence (Figure 14.2). Some individuals are consistent in their use of a specific signature style, while others may be entirely inconsistent. Furthermore, there may be serious divergences between formally written signatures—those on deeds, contracts, and wills for example—and informal or somewhat unimportant signatures, such as those used to receipt for a delivery or to sign for a small purchase of gasoline. Therefore there is a need to obtain numerous signatures employed for the same

Figure 14.2. These two signatures were used by the same person to sign a check (above) and the letter (below) that enclosed the check. Some writers regularly employ two or more distinctive signature styles.

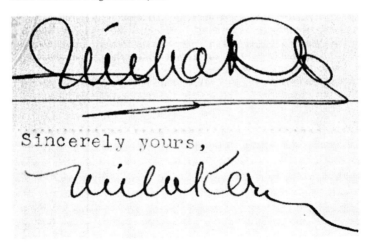

purpose as the one in question and, whenever possible, it is desirable to include those appearing on other classes of documents (Figure 14.3). Only with such a set of standards can it be readily determined whether the writer employs more than one style of signature and, if so, what relationship the questioned specimen bears to any one of them.

Principally because of the limited number of writing characteristics common to signatures, but also because of differences in many instances between them and the remainder of the person's writing, signatures make poor standards for comparison with other types of disputed writing. In these latter cases standards made up of letters, reports, and other handwritten documents provide for more extensive and

Figure 14.3. The need to collect signatures used for more than one purpose is illustrated by this case. The upper two signature represent the style used on all of Mann's checks. Her experts used only check signatures and concluded, as she claimed, that a deed signature was not written by her.

Below are other signatures and writings of her name that were available to the holder of the deed. These explained the differences between the deed signature and the check signatures, and the court found in part because of these other signatures that she had signed the document.

proper study of the problem. Similarity between the subject matter of the standard and disputed writing greatly assists in the identification. The document examiner needs to compare like things. A general analysis of what is needed to compare with the questioned writing may, for example, reveal a great number of capital letters combined with lowercase letters suggesting that known material, such as an address book, would produce good comparison writing. Contrariwise, these same standards may be of relatively little value in identifying the writer of a letter or holographic will, just as hastily written notes are poor standards for comparison with formal writing. Thus thought must be given to the selection of the kind of general handwriting to be collected.

Relative Date of Preparation

In previous discussions of handwriting identification it was pointed out that over the course of years a person's writing may undergo gradual change just as his physical appearance does. The rate and nature of change varies from individual to individual (Figure 14.4). It depends on

Figure 14.4. The very sharp, abrupt, and unusual change in signature design and execution was completed by this writer within a period of two years. After writing his signature for years like the first example, between 1928 and 1930 he completely remodeled it to the form of the last specimen. A few signatures were found like the center example, but only on documents dated between 1928 and 1930.

Pronounced changes in signature style of mature writers are somewhat rare, but slight modifications may be encountered more often. It is therefore always well to obtain some authentic signatures written near the date of the questioned one.

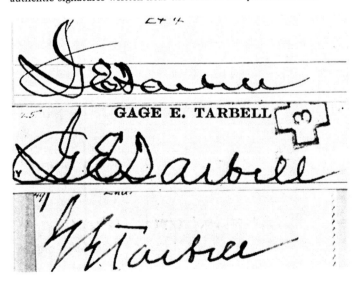

Figure 14.5. A very decided decline in this writer's signature occurred within a period of less than seven months. In August she was seriously ill and only a few months away from death. No subsequent signature specimens showed any return to the vigor and skill of the February writing.

such factors as how often and how much he writes, his age, his writing skill, and his mental and physical condition. Writing of a middle-aged person in good health, for example, may change very little from year to year, but during a severe illness, it may deteriorate sharply only to return to its original vigor as he gains strength (Figure 14.5).

An infirm signature may have been written immediately after a serious accident or operation when it was believed essential to execute the particular document. During a severe illness one is not apt to do much writing so that there may be only a limited number of comparable signatures written if in fact any exist at all. In such a case the date of preparation is extremely significant.

Normally in the case of a typical adult basic writing habits change gradually. Therefore, material written two or three years before or after the disputed writing serve as satisfactory standards, but as the lapse of years between the date of standards and questioned material becomes greater, the standards have a tendency to be less representative. Consequently, an effort should always be made to procure some specimens written near in date to the disputed matter.

Writing Conditions

The conditions under which writing was prepared may affect its value for comparison purposes. Haste, lack of care, or unnatural writing position—for example, resting the paper on the knee—introduce variations that may make the specimens entirely unsuited for comparison with carefully written material. In the case of illness, writing in bed in a somewhat awkward position may introduce variables in addition

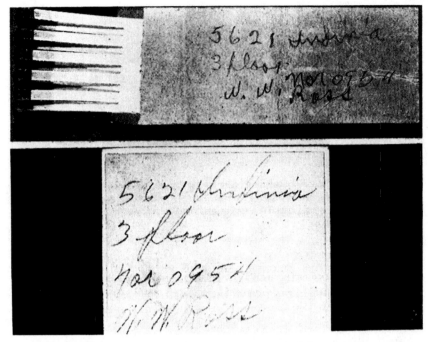

Figure 14.6. The writing in the match cover was prepared while standing on a moving elevated train with the cover held in the left hand. The same person wrote the other specimen seated at a table. The unusual writing conditions introduced restraint in the first example. Note how the longer strokes are shortened in the l and d as well as in the lower loop of the f.

to those produced by the writer's physical condition. Other noticeable variations can be caused by writing on a rough or irregular surface, or in a moving vehicle (Figure 14.6). Illegible receipt signatures and hastily written notes are common classes of specimens that reflect qualities typical of the conditions under which they were written (Figure 9.3).

No writing prepared under such unusual conditions should be depended on exclusively for comparison with writing done under more normal circumstances, although they may often serve as valuable supplements. Brief investigation into the conditions under which a document was written can indicate something of its appropriateness as a standard in the current problem.

Writing Instruments and Paper

Since the identification of handwriting depends on consideration of all its elements, the kind of writing instrument used for a particular sample may have some influence on its usefulness as a standard. Pen and

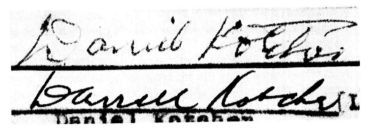

Figure 14.7. The rather poorly written upper signature was written with a ball point pen. Below is the writer's typical signature, smoothly and freely executed with a fountain pen. These writings were executed at a date when the ball point pen was a new writing instrument. In addition to the pen's writing somewhat defectively, it was an unfamilar writing instrument for this person, and he experienced difficulty in using it. Certainly the first signature would hardly be a satisfactory standard by which to judge the genuineness of signatures written with a more familar writing instrument.

ink writing contains certain identifying characteristics that are not fully revealed in pencil specimens, while a change in the style of nib pen (for example, from a flexible to a stiff point) may also introduce writing variations.[1] Furthermore, the reader must remember that a ball point pen produces writing that is not completely comparable to work of a nib or fountain pen, and is in effect a distinctive class of writing instrument (Figure 14.7). In addition the porous tip pen produces writing strokes that have still other slightly different characteristics.

The composition, size, shape, and ruling of paper may measurably affect the writing. If the reader has ever written with a fountain pen on poor grade, unsized paper, he knows the difficulties encountered and the blurred strokes that so often follow, results not obtained when writing on high-grade, bond paper. Likewise, many writers adjust the size of their signature to some degree to the space allowed for signing. Besides, standards on ruled forms permit consideration of how the individual habitually arranges his writing in relation to the printed baseline. Each element may assist in reaching a more accurate solution to some problems. Standards prepared with comparable writing instruments and on appropriate paper or forms help to provide the examiner with the most useful material. It may be possible to reach an accurate conclusion, and the examiner often does, with standards that were not prepared with similar pens or pencils or on paper exactly like

---

[1]Popkess and Moore report the following experience regarding the influence on handwriting resulting from a change of writing instruments: "An interesting fact disclosed by experiments over a number of years in Nottingham, however, in which persons were required to fill in three handwriting cards with broad, medium, and fine pens respectively was that unconsciously the writer held the pen in such a way as to write with almost equal thickness in each case" [A. Popkess and J. Moore, "Handwriting Classification," *Police Journal (England)* 18 (1945): 44]. These findings are not in keeping with those of this writer but may represent tendencies with some penmen.

the questioned document in composition, size, shape, and ruling, but we are looking for the very best standards upon which he can base his opinion, not just what will do. There are some few cases every year in which less than ideal standards seriously restrict the findings. Thoroughness on the part of the investigator from the start means consideration of each limiting factor and elimination of them whenever possible.

Sources of Standards

Writing is a part of the daily life of practically everyone. Consequently, the potential sources of writing standards are numerous, and those who frequently investigate handwriting cases soon develop a comprehensive list of sources for standards. Many who are confronted with a handwriting problem have had little or no experience, however, with this type of investigation and will undoubtedly find the following suggestions of assistance.

Among the possible sources of signature standards are canceled checks; traveler's checks; signature cards for savings, checking, and charge accounts and safe deposit boxes; signed receipts for telegrams, special delivery or registered letters, express and store packages; business and personal letters; credit and loan applications and cards; sales and charge slips; leases, mortgages, agreements, bills of sale, contracts, deeds, notes, stock certificates and transfers, and other legal or business documents; partnership and incorporation forms on file with government agencies; court records and affidavits, such as naturalization papers, bankruptcy proceedings, divorce papers, probated wills and estate files, powers of attorney, answers; passports; marriage license affidavits; driver, automobile, chauffeur, and other types of licenses and license applications; applications for gas, electricity, water, and telephone services; loan applications and notes and receipts; tax returns or affidavits; insurance applications, records, and beneficiary forms; employment applications and records; records from currency exchanges, check-cashing agencies, and pawn shops; voter's registrations, petitions, and polling lists; hospital records; time sheets, payrolls, pay receipts, and personnel forms; union and trade-association files; relief, unemployment, and social security, medicare, and old-age compensation records; signatures for certain drug narcotic and poison purchases; hotel and motel registrations; church, charitable organizations, club, and professional-society records; veteran and military records; fingerprint records; and in the case of younger persons, board of education or university class cards and records.[2]

---

[2]As a further guide to sources of handwriting specimens see A. S. Osborn, *Problem of Proof,* 2nd ed. (Newark: Essex, 1926), pp. 342–344.

In investigations of handwriting other than signatures—for example, an anonymous letter or holographic will—these same sources may disclose writing of the proper class. Other specimens of writing very often can be obtained from acquaintances, business associates, or correspondents.[3] If the suspect has recently filed a telegram, it may be possible to obtain a photographic copy of the original form. Business reports, records, and letters furnish other excellent sources of standards, as do personnel forms and applications for employment and club membership. In fact, any association or activity, either business or social, in which the person is interested and active is a potential source of specimens of his handwriting.

Verifications of Standards

It is absolutely essential to verify who wrote the standards. No matter how logical the assumption may be, the investigator should not merely assume that the suspect prepared the writing; by careful checking he should establish it as a fact. The importance of this is revealed in the following case history. In a problem of ascertaining whether a group of employees individually signed affidavits, several endorsed paychecks were submitted as standards. Some endorsements and affidavit signatures failed to agree, but before the study was completed signatures written in the presence of a personnel officer were requested. These personnel form signatures revealed that one employee had not been endorsing his paychecks (Figure 14.8), but he signed the affidavit. A serious error might have been made if the examiner had relied on the assumption that the endorsement on the paycheck was genuine, although such an assumption may be well warranted for most purposes. In another case involving a denied signature, standards written over a period of several months established that the same writer had executed the denied signature. Further investigation shortly before trial disclosed that an employee, rather than the suspect himself, had signed all the standards as well as the denied signature. Before any standard can be used in court, it must be proven by competent evidence. Such proof should be established by interviews before submitting the documents to an expert for his use.

Standards should be verified through a detailed field investigation and by obtaining specimens written in the presence of reliable witnesses. Careful questioning of those bringing forth the standards, and

---

[3]Correspondence carried on by Roland B. Molineux was used extensively by the state in the famous trial in 1899 of Molineux for the murder of Katherine J. Adams. For a brief description of the trial and the handwriting evidence involved, see D. T. Ames, *Ames on Forgery* (New York: Ames-Rollinson, 1900), pp. 216–236. A more detailed account of the case appeared in *The Molineux Case* (Samuel Klaus, ed.) (1929).

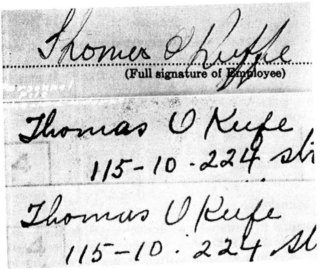

Figure 14.8. All three signatures were believed to have been written by an employee, O'Keefe, but only the upper signature from his personnel file could be verified as authentic. It was on a document known to have been signed in the company office. The two endorsements (below) to paychecks had been cashed in food stores, apparently by some other member of his family. Obviously, an assumption that the check endorsements were written by O'Keefe would have lead to serious error in the opinion regarding any disputed signature.

if possible the writer himself, can serve as a means of authentication. Writing used for different purposes, prepared at various times and under diverse circumstances, permit technical cross-checking and verification. Standards are the cornerstone of the examination of disputed writings, and no identification can be more accurate than the standards that support it.

Request Standards

Despite the vast potential sources of handwriting standards, circumstances do arise under which it is difficult, or perhaps impossible, to obtain an adequate set of collected standards at the moment at which they are needed. These circumstances are most common to criminal investigations, although they are by no means confined exclusively to these cases. Therefore, if the suspected person is available and willing, a set of request or dictated standards can be secured.

The conditions under which these standards are prepared make it imperative that certain precautions be observed so that their comparison value is not impaired:

1. The material must be dictated to the writer.
2. The dictated text must be carefully selected.
3. An adequate amount of writing must be included.
4. Some portion of the dictation should be repeated, preferably three times.
5. Writing instruments and paper should be similar to those used in preparing the disputed document.
6. The dictation should be interrupted at intervals.
7. Normal writing conditions should be arranged.

It must be recognized that the guidelines can lead to serviceable standards at best—standards that can identify the actual writer and, one hopes, can eliminate all who did not write the material in question. Request specimens normally are not completely representative of the full range of a writer's habits, but they should, if well controlled, tell a great deal about his writing habits. Experienced document examiners recognize the shortcomings of these specimens, especially that they tell only a limited amount about a writer's habits. For this reason, while identification may be impossible with a particular writer, elimination may be unwise. Apparent differences can be brought about by disguise, nervousness during preparation, or simply the restricted scope of the specimens written at a particular time and with the knowledge that the results are to be used for comparison purposes. On the other hand, if the standards compare favorably with the disputed material, t⌐ fact that they do not fully reveal the writer's habits does not preclude or restrict an identification established by them.

Dictation of Material

Dictation has been found to produce the most representative request standards. In dictating, however, the text must be read to the writer without suggestions as to the arrangement of material, spelling, punctuation, capitalization, or other points that may cause him to disguise or modify his natural writing habits.

The manner of dictation has much to do with the ultimate value of the standards. If the subject matter is continuous, as with a letter, the rate of dictation should be gauged so that the person writes continuously rather than intermittently. The initial speed of dictation should be set so that he is not rushed, but subsequent specimens ought to be taken at several different writing rates, with some portion written hurriedly. Only in this manner can his normal range of writing variation be even approximately reproduced in the request specimens. Rapid dictation prevents a suspect from furnishing only his best or neatest writing, which is often as undesirable as poorly written spec-

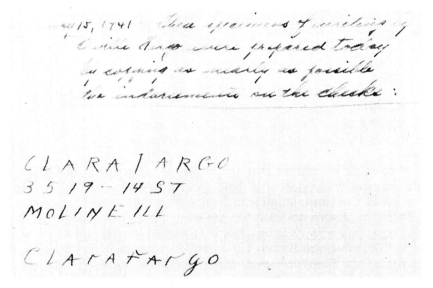

Figure 14.9. The notation above these request standards indicates that the suspect was told to copy "as nearly as possible the endorsements on the checks." They were the first specimens taken. This procedure produces writing that is utterly worthless for comparison with the questioned material and in this case may have influenced all subsequent specimens prepared by the writer (see Figure 14.10). Proper request standards should always be written from dictation and never by copying the questioned document.

imens, since the quality of the disputed material generally lies between these extremes.

Furthermore, if the writer attempts to modify or disguise his specimens, a more rapid rate of dictation lessens his chances of success. Here it is well to observe that many near-illiterates can write only very slowly, focusing their main attention on the formation of each letter. One who attempts disguise may write in a similar manner. Thus, upon first impression, the natural manner of writing of the near-illiterate may suggest disguise, but throughout extensive specimens his writing characteristics will be consistent. On the other hand, a mass of extended specimens prepared with unpracticed disguise lacks such uniformity, and the numerous inconsistencies reveal its true nature.[4]

Request standards obtained by any means other than dictation, for example, by having a person copy typewritten, handwritten, or printed matter, do not lead to as satisfactory results (Figures 14.9 and 14.10).

---

[4]Hardless suggests that in addition to dictating the material it is well to time the writing and record the time consumed in preparing the specimen. This procedure is especially appropriate if the suspect is attempting to disguise. [Charles Hardless, *The Identification of Handwriting and The Detection of Forgery* (Calcutta: Hardless, 1912), p. 191.]

Figure 14.10. These signatures constituted a portion of the request signatures prepared by the suspect after he had been instructed to copy the disputed endorsements (see Figure 14.9). Both endorsements were handlettered. How much of the lettering is actual disguise and how much represents the writer's true lettering could not be determined by these standards. No other specimens were available to serve as a means of verification. It was certainly fortunate that the investigator who had these standards written carefully labeled each sheet so that the document examiner knew the circumstances under which they were taken. The information tells much about their reliability.

By allowing the writer to use a prepared copy, the manner of arrangement, as well as the correct spelling and punctuation, is indicated, and these individual characteristics, which might otherwise be helpful for identification purposes, are lost. Furthermore, a person who must copy from a script alternately reads and writes and produces discontinuous specimens. Since each page of writing contains numerous stops and starts, the standards may lack the writer's personal freedom and rhythm. Obviously, carefully conducted dictation eliminates these pitfalls.

Selection of Text

The request standards may be based upon any of three types of text:

1. the contents of the disputed document;
2. some similar material, which contains many of the same words, phrases, and letter combinations; or
3. a standardized form that includes all the letters of the alphabet and a number of the more commonly used words.

Whenever the suspect has at least partial knowledge of the contents of the questioned document—and this is a common condition—there is no serious objection to dictating it. In fact, there are advantages to this procedure that make it superior to the others. In so doing the investigator is relieved of any need to prepare special material for dictation, while the document examiner is greatly aided by being able to compare the same conbination of words and letters in both the standard and questioned writing.

Occasionally, however, it may be desirable not to disclose the contents of the disputed document to the person who is furnishing the comparison specimens.[5] Experience has shown that in these instances the preferable procedure is to dictate material that is similar to the disputed writing, such as a continuous text for comparison with anonymous letters, or specimen checks and receipts for standards to compare with disputed checks. In selecting this material, as many words and letter combinations from the disputed matter as possible should be included, making sure that any misspelled words or unusual uses of capitals or punctuation found in the questioned specimens are included in the dictated material.

Probably the least successful matter for request specimens is the standardized or form dictation, such as "the quick brown fox jumps over the lazy dog." More elaborate texts that include all uppercase and lowercase letters of necessity contain unusual and unfamiliar words or names. Consequently, even though the dictation is repeated several times, the resulting standards tend to lack the freedom of the person's normal writing. There are times, however, when form dictations, such as those developed by Osborn,[6] prove valuable, and anyone who frequently investigates handwriting problems would do well to become familiar with one or more of these forms.[7]

---

[5]There are some differences of opinion among document examiners about the material that should be dictated. Quirke, in a discussion of the preparation of standards, suggests that this second type of request standard, a specially prepared dictation, should be used in all cases. He further advises that these dictations be prepared as follows: The first part, consisting of short elementary words, should be read to the suspect prior to the actual dictation; the second portion, containing words and phrases from the anonymous letter, but not actually the letter, should be dictated without prior reading; and the final portion should consist of common words of some length. He further suggests careful observation of the suspect during the entire dictation in an effort to discover any indications of guilt. For a more detailed discussion of his proposed technique, see A. J. Quirke, *Forged, Anonymous and Suspect Documents* (London:Routledge, 1930), pp. 233–235.

[6]A. S. Osborn, *Questioned Documents*, 2nd ed. (Albany: Boyd, 1929), p. 34; *Problems of Proof*, 2nd ed., pp. 346–347.

[7]Purtell, while a staff member of the Chicago Police Crime Laboratory, developed standardized forms for preparing request writing in criminal investigations in the Chicago area. He discusses the concept of his forms in David J. Purtell, "Handwriting Standard Forms," *Journal of Criminal Law, Criminology and Police Science* 54 (1963): 522–528. With similar research, law-enforcement investigators can develop other forms suitable for their area. Of course several federal law enforcement units have also developed forms for their investigative units.

The reader should not infer from this discussion that only one type of dictation should be used with each subject. On the contrary, more representative standards can often be prepared by using two or even all three classes of texts. These combinations can be employed to best advantage when the disputed writing is brief. Otherwise, merely using the disputed subject matter would require extensive repetition in order to secure sufficient material for adequate standards. Yet this technique may have equal advantages with more lengthy disputed writing, for a change of subject matter—such as from that in question to some unrelated material—may cause the writer to relax and thus introduce more of his typical writing variations into the standards.

Under certain conditions, particularly in criminal investigations, request standards may be obtained without resorting to dictation. When a suspected writer is apprehended, he generally attempts to explain away any action that might incriminate him. The alert investigator will see that the suspect writes out his statements. While composing such an explanation, he generally centers his efforts upon furnishing a logical excuse for his suspicious actions and gives little thought to the actual execution of the writing. Thus, these written statements represent a good sample of his normal writing.

A person who is to supervise the preparation of dictated standards should always have full knowledge of the questioned material. If not, he will have to restrict his request specimens to a generalized form; even then, there may be the danger of not getting the right kind of standards. This writer has experienced situations in which a field investigator was asked to obtain writing specimens from a suspect and was told only something about the contents of the questioned document. He admitted afterward that he had never seen the document. He obtained a relatively good set of specimens in the connected handwriting of the individual, only to find when he was shown the questioned material that it had all been handlettered. Consequently, his writing specimens were of very little assistance. Key factors such as capitalization, spelling, and the importance of certain words within the questioned material may not be fully apparent until the field investigator has seen or discussed the questioned material with those who know more about the case or about the problems of the document examiner.

Amount of Material

It is extremely difficult with request standards to obtain a truly representative picture of the usual variation in an individual's writing. Even under the most favorable circumstances it requires the preparation of extensive specimens. The great majority of request specimens are deficient simply because they do not reveal the variation that is part of the suspect's normal handwriting.

Two factors, nervousness and deliberate disguise, frequently curtail normal writing variation. The initial portion of request standards furnished by a writer who has had no part in the preparation of a disputed document may well reflect nervous tension. This nervousness may be instilled at least in part by the accusation or suspicion of having prepared the disputed document, or merely because the writer knows that the specimen is to be compared with other writing. This nervousness, however, may disappear when the dictation is continued at length, so that subsequent writing may tend to assume a more natural character. On the other hand, many guilty individuals deliberately attempt to disguise their writing in order to avoid detection. Fortunately, only the exceptional can continue an unpracticed disguise throughout several pages. Therefore, if we are to make sure that the request specimens begin to portray the natural writing variation of the individual and are free from the effects of nervousness or deliberate disguise, it is necessary to have the writer furnish at least five or six pages of continuous handwriting or 20 or more signatures, each written on a separate sheet of paper.

The most common defect of request specimens is the failure to have the person write enough. At times this is because the investigator does not know how much writing is needed for good standards, but often it is merely because the investigator finds this time consuming, which it is, and believes that other aspects of the investigation are more important. However, if identification of the writer is to be accomplished, extensive standards should be prepared.

Repetition

Regardless of the type of subject matter employed, the value of the standards is increased by some repetition. In the course of dictation a page of writing should be repeated at least three times. It should preferably be taken from the questioned material. Repetition allows the writer to become familiar with the subject matter and helps him to write more freely and naturally. At the same time it serves as an effective means of discouraging disguise. At times the guilty writer, realizing that he cannot continuously reproduce the modifications of his first specimen, abandons the attempt altogether. If, on the other hand, he continues his efforts in this direction, marked variation between successive specimens should appear. Upon detection of these inconsistencies, additional and more extensive writing, including still further repetition of previous material, must be obtained. In this way attempted disguise could be more readily detected and with enough request writing, even in extreme cases, some specimens should ultimately be obtained free from disguise.

Writing Instruments and Paper

The influence of the writing instrument and paper can be readily controlled with request standards. It is necessary only to furnish the writer with a pen or pencil similar to the one used in the questioned document (Figure 14.11). At the same time paper should be selected with the same physical characteristics and ruling as the disputed sample, trimming it, if necessary, to the proper size and shape (Figure 14.12). With this preparation personal habits affected by writing materials are less apt to be excluded from the request specimens.

When the questioned writing is in ink, it is important to recognize what kind of pen was used. "Pen" is an inclusive or general term, and we have seen in earlier chapters that there are several classes with substantially different writing characteristics. Today the ball point pen is the most common and the most popular. It rolls ink on the paper with a nonflexible ball. Some different writing characteristics are revealed with a nib pen or a fountain pen using fluid ink, especially if there is some flexibility of the point. Finally, there are porous tip pens, generally producing wider strokes than other instruments, strokes that can hide details that would otherwise be present. Not every writer can write with equal ease with each instrument, and if one class of pen has been used for all questioned writing, then this kind of pen should be used for the request standards.

Figure 14.11. The upper signature displays the writer's usual writing skill when using a pencil. The lower specimens are his best efforts using a pen, apparently a less familiar writing instrument. There are some writers, especially those of limited ability, who seldom write with a pen and do so with difficulty.

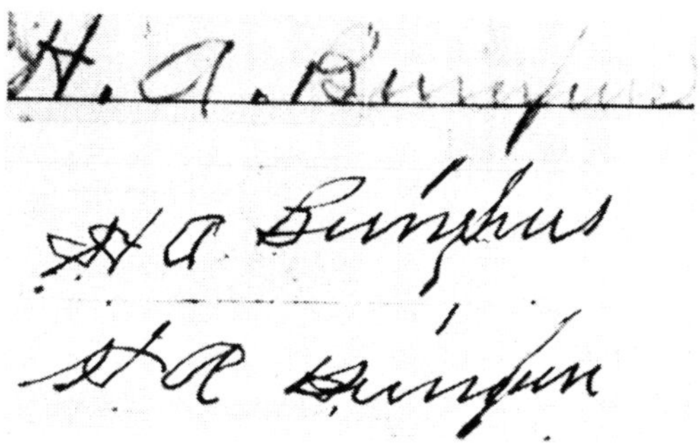

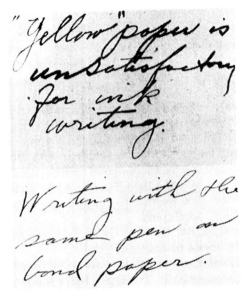

Figure 14.12. Not all papers are designed for writing with fluid ink. The same writer prepared both specimens with the same pen. The upper example is on an unsized paper, which absorbs fluid ink as a blotter does, causing the feathering and heavy flow. The paper below is a grade manufactured for ink writing. In preparing request specimens the paper should be selected with care.

Interruption of Dictation

Breaking dictation up by a rest period or two is good procedure. Writing fatigue brought about by the preparation of extensive specimens may be eliminated and disguise may likewise be discouraged or rendered ineffective. If all completed specimens are removed from the writer's view during these pauses and his attention is focused on other matters, consistent disguise becomes more difficult, since after such a rest period, the writer's recollection of details of disguise can be less vivid. Finally, interruptions aid in introducing more natural writing variation into request specimens than is to be found in the same amount of continuous writing.

Except when interruptions represent pauses in which the investigator talks with the suspect and does not apparently discontinue the session, there is a danger of being unable to get the writer to resume writing. With the break of several hours or a day, he may refuse to write any more, maintaining that he has already furnished writing specimens. This possible situation must be kept in mind whenever a break is taken in the preparation of request specimens (Figure 14.13).

Writing Conditions

The writer should be allowed to be seated comfortably at a desk or table. However, the questioned specimens may be known to have been written under less normal conditions, such as while the writer was

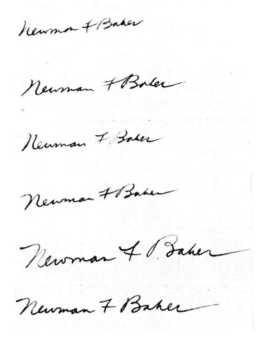

Figure 14.13. Request specimens that are more representative can be obtained on two or more occasions than at one continuous session. These six signatures, prepared for use in a testing experiment, were written on two separate days, the first four at one sitting, the other two several days later. Each is written on an individual index card. More pronounced variation occurs between the sets than between the individual signatures of either set. Note particularly the variation in size between the writing on two different days, and, more important, that the writer connected his middle initial with the surname in the first four signatures, but not in the last two. Representative variations such as these should be included in accurate standards.

standing, resting the paper against the wall, as many receipts are signed. Under these circumstances the suspect should be asked to execute some supplementary standards in a similar position. When the exact writing conditions are unknown but the writing suggests some abnormal writing position, specimens should be taken in several different ways, for example, standing and resting the document on a high counter or bending over a table; writing with the paper on a clipboard held in the hand or on a pad resting on his knee, in addition to the normal writing while seated at a table. An exact record of how each specimen is written should be made. Thus, with a combination of standards prepared under common and unusual writing conditions, the effect of these changes can be fully studied.

Special Considerations for Request Signatures

By far the most troublesome problem with request writing is obtaining a satisfactory set of signature standards. Since the amount of writing involved is small even when a large number of signatures are prepared, the effects of nervousness or deliberate disguise may not be entirely eliminated. Request signatures, too, have a tendency to be more uniform than signatures written from day to day. For this reason, they fail to show fully how the person usually signs his name.

Several techniques help to correct these faults. Increasing the amount of writing and at the same time introducing different subject matter tend to improve the standards. With signatures this can be best accomplished by interspersing other writing. Instead of executing a set of signatures alone, the writer might fill out 20 or 30 specimen checks or receipts, each of which contains his signature as either the maker or the endorser or both.

Another scheme, especially effective when a person has written a fictitious name in his natural handwriting, a situation common in police investigations of fraudulent checks, is to include among the standards a number of similar names together with the fictitious one. Following such a technique, if the fictitious name was "Joseph Martin," several variations, such as "Joseph Harts," "Rudolph Martin," and "Stephen Marvin," could be added.

When circumstances permit, an excellent procedure is to have the writer prepare portions of the standards on different days. In this way the request signatures tend to be more like those written from day to day. This procedure need not be confined to signatures, as it is equally effective in increasing the representativeness of any writing and should be employed whenever possible.[8]

The most common fault of request signatures is their failure to contain a representative amount of writing variation. Every effort must be made to overcome this deficiency. To achieve this end, each specimen should be written on a separate sheet of paper similar to the questioned document. The shift of writing position accompanying each change of paper tends to introduce slight variations that are not generally encountered in a series of signatures executed on a single sheet. In fact, ten signatures written one after the other on a single sheet often have less value than two or three signatures written on separate occasions.

---

[8]Brewester advocates obtaining request signatures on three different days. See F. Brewester, *Contested Documents and Forgeries* (Calcutta: The Book Co., 1932), p. 438. Caution must be exercised in delaying completion of the standards over a period of two or more days. It is not unheard of for the suspect, especially if guilty, to refuse to write upon a later occasion, claiming that he has furnished sufficient material at the first session.

With the request standards a preliminary examination is often made to evaluate the various specimens submitted. To assist in this problem, each sheet of writing should be numbered, and accurate notes should be made on how the specimens were written, when the dictation was interrupted, which sections were written at rapid or slow rate, and, if the specimens were not all prepared on the same date, the date and conditions under which each was compiled. These notes, particularly when disguise has been attempted, greatly assist in segregating the abnormal standards.

Combination of Request and Collected Standards

There is no reason that request and collected standards cannot be used simultaneously. In fact, under certain conditions the two classes of specimens must be resorted to in order to obtain an adequate and accurate set of standards. Whenever there is a suspicion that the effects

Figure 14.14. The last four signatures are from a series of request specimens which the writer, Carl Edelson, wrote on a single sheet. The first appeared on a business letter, which he admitted signing. The difference in execution is very significant and illustrates the advantage of supplementing request specimen with signatures written in the course of daily affairs. In addition the request signatures in this case would very likely have shown more natural variation if each had been written on a separate sheet rather than all on one page.

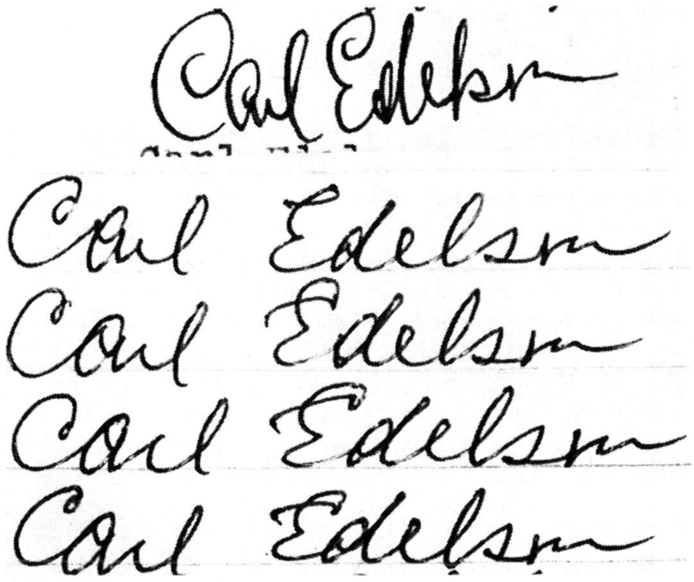

of deliberate disguise have not been and cannot be completely eliminated from request standards, the standards must be supplemented by collected specimens. This procedure need not be limited to cases of suspected disguise, however, for even rather limited collected standards are useful adjuncts to a complete set of request writing (Figure 14.14).

In some instances even the most thorough and exhaustive search for material results in inadequate collected standards. To supplement these effectively with request writing usually requires that a complete set of dictated standards be made up. Only by such a procedure can one be sure that the latter specimens are representative.

Standards for Special Problems

The document examiner is called upon to identify or to prove fraudulent abnormal signatures of writers as well as normal or usual signatures. Problems of this type include signatures written under the influence of alcohol or drugs (both those used for treatment of illness and those used in drug-abuse situations), during serious illness or near death, and during times when the writer is elderly and weak. There are also signatures for receipt of delivery of packages and mail as well as signatures to charge slips for gasoline or merchandise. Appropriate standards are generally needed to answer these questions since each questioned signature prepared under any one of these situations may have abnormal qualities.[9]

Intoxication

Excessive consumption of alcohol produces different effects on different writers. Some individuals have far greater tolerance than others and can consume large quantities of alcohol before their signature is affected. In the earlier stages of alcohol consumption, the signatures of an individual may be only slightly affected, generally showing a slightly larger and slightly less accurately written signature, but as more alcohol is consumed there may be further deterioration in the writing. Lack of accurate coordination may lead to inferior design and poor writing alignment. The overall writing skill may decline even though the writer is still striving to execute a normal signature. Signatures begin to take on the appearance of a lack of care and may ultimately in some instances assume "a drunken stagger." Successive

---

[9]Several of the following subsections are based on discussions by O. Hilton, "A Further Look at Writing Standards," *Journal of Criminal Law, Criminology and Police Science* 56 (1965): 382–389.

signatures wander away from the normal design and even from the design of the immediately preceding signature in somewhat unpredictable ways. In other words, variations become great. Successive specimens written during the same night of drinking, e.g., signing club chits for successive rounds of drinks, may vary greatly in many identifying elements (Figure 9.4). What we are concerned with in this discussion is not the extent that alcohol affects writing, but how to obtain comparable specimens that can be used effectively in accurately identifying a signature that clearly reflects the influence of alcohol.

In these problems the task of obtaining known specimens may be less difficult than with other classes of abnormal signatures. A writer who may have signed a questioned document under the influence of alcohol probably has signed others on similar occasions. In most cases, especially those involving heavy drinkers, proper investigation uncovers a number of signatures showing various evidences of intoxication. Again, the wider range of variation requires more authentic specimens, and as many specimens as possible should be "intoxicated" rather than "sober" signatures.

Standards for these problems consist almost exclusively of material collected from various sources. Request specimens (or any specimens, for that matter, written when the writer is not drinking) may have only limited supplementary value. Of course, if the writer is apprehended in a criminal investigation while intoxicated and can be persuaded to write a number of specimens, signatures so prepared should be of value. Seldom in a case involving a questioned signature written under the influence of alcohol is it possible to obtain request specimens with the suspect intoxicated. No cases have been reported in which a suspect was permitted to drink during the preparation of standards until he became sufficiently drunk to prepare appropriate specimens of writing.

In passing, it should be observed that the use of drugs and, once in a while, physical disability from other causes produce symptoms suggesting intoxication. These symptoms may be reflected in the writing. On the other hand, the writing of sufferers from palsy or Parkinson's disease may be improved by properly prescribed medication.

Age Deterioration

Very difficult problems may be encountered with signatures that have seriously deteriorated due to the writer's age or to terminal illness. Of these, the deathbed signature is particularly perplexing since the deterioration may have been rapid with little or no forewarning in earlier signatures. With decrepit signatures of an aged writer, the decline normally occurs gradually over a period of months or years. More known specimens revealing writing weaknesses are therefore available than with deathbed signatures.

Writing of this nature is characterized by a lack of fluency in execution and inaccuracy and inconsistency in details of form. It is not as good writing as earlier signatures by the same person. Study of a series of signatures by an infirm writer reveals much greater variation from signature to signature than was typical of vigorous signatures of earlier years. The inconsistency of these signatures, which in some cases is very prominent, complicates the problem. In order to reach the most accurate conclusions, two or three times the normal number of signatures may be needed, and they must be closer in date to the signature in question than in the usual case. Although a sufficient number of signatures may have been executed, it is often hard to locate them.

We are confronted with the same identification problem with the deathbed signature, since a dying person signs his name only for the most urgent reasons. Often available genuine signatures are almost as suspect as the deathbed signature, since circumstances surrounding their preparation are so like those surrounding the questioned signature. (For example, at the time all specimens were written, the writer was being cared for by the one member of the family who is strongly favored by a disputed will.) Because of the very small number of signatures comparable to the deathbed signature, it is virtually essential that all be studied; it is still likely that the total signature production will be far too few.

Adequate standards for these problems must include as many signatures written during the period of decline as can be obtained. There is advantage in supplementing them by earlier, more vigorous signatures, even though they are not representative of the questioned period. These specimens do give the examiner some idea of the basic model the writer is attempting to duplicate. When a large group of infirm signatures, say at least 25, can be obtained, reasonably accurate solutions can be reached. Usually far fewer signatures are located. Then there must be serious "leaning on experience" to judge whether the questioned signature would digress from the standards in the way that it seems to. The fewer infirm signatures there are for study, the more unanswered divergences between the known and questioned signature will remain. Opinions rendered must frequently be treated most cautiously and conservatively in order to minimize errors.

Sickbed Signatures

Infirm signatures written on a sickbed, as opposed to deathbed signatures, represent badly deteriorated signatures of a writer who subsequently regains some or all of his writing vigor. A signature of this kind may have been written immediately after a serious accident or operation when it was believed essential to execute the particular document. Periods of illness, especially severe illness, are not times when one is apt to do much writing, and so there may be only limited numbers of signatures written. Therefore the right kinds of standards are extremely difficult to locate, if they exist at all.

The question of a writer's weakened condition is normally complicated by his being propped up in a bed or at times under worse writing conditions. The writing position, as much as the physical weakness, leads to a low-quality signature. These factors must be considered in collecting standards and examining the case.

Sickbed signatures, like most of these special signature cases we are considering, can most effectively be solved with more signatures than in the general run of cases. Unfortunately, the writer may never have executed a sufficient number of signatures while sick to satisfy the true needs of the examiner. In fact, the questioned signature may be the only example written during the illness. Writing at request after recovery does not help much if the person has completely regained his writing vigor. In some instances, the person may have gone through a long recovery period during which he did some writing and the quality of the signatures are below his preillness or postrecovery vigor. These specimens can be of help in giving some idea of how his signature declined and are certainly better than having to depend exclusively on his normal specimens.

Receipt Signatures

The carelessly written receipt signature really represents a special class of erratic signatures. It has a lack of consistency compared to other receipt signatures and to formal specimens of the writer. With the same writer under other conditions, his signature is undoubtedly more uniform and certainly superior in form and execution.

With a questioned receipt signature, one is never quite sure of the conditions under which it was prepared. It could have been signed against a rough plaster wall, reflecting both the irregularities of the writing surface and the poor writing position. It could have been signed with the paper attached to a clipboard held in the hand. It could have been signed with the paper resting on the knee or in the other hand and with no support for the writing hand. To complicate the problem further, the writer may have been in a hurry or annoyed at having to sign at all. With the scrawled receipt signature, it is obvious that he has taken very little care. When these receipt signatures are compared with formal signatures, the divergences can be shocking. The scrawled, almost illegible receipt signature may bear little relationship to signatures on checks, letters, or legal documents. If the signature is denied, the layman is sure at a glance that it must be forgery.

With problems of this nature, the only signatures of real value are other receipt signatures. In most cases, 15 or 20 formally written signatures add almost nothing to the picture. Request signatures may be of little value since they are usually written with care, which is very likely to be the case if the receipt signature is denied. The search for additional signatures of comparable nature may be long and difficult since this class of signature is not generally preserved for long periods of time. They are, however, essential if an accurate conclusion is to be reached. Certainly, if trial demonstration becomes necessary, adequate, comparable receipt signatures are almost mandatory for the most convincing demonstration.

Charge Signatures

Signatures appearing on charge and credit slips may be more poorly written specimens than those on checks, letters, and legal papers. There are exceptional writers who produce their usual signature on these forms, but many do not. When the signatures do deteriorate or are modified, the change may be slight or rather pronounced, although they are seldom in a class with receipt signatures. In every problem of this kind, it is well to consider the signature as possibly presenting an exceptional problem and to proceed accordingly.

This class of signature is influenced by the writing conditions and the document on which it is produced. Most charge slips are limited in size, with a relatively confined space to sign in. Writers with long signatures are forced to condense or crowd their writing. Names may be replaced by initials. With gasoline charges and fuel deliveries, the document may be on a clipboard signed in cramped or unnatural writing positions and under adverse weather conditions that may affect the writer's hand muscles. In retail stores writing conditions may not be much better. The slip may have been signed on a crowded counter with little or no arm support or limited support for the document itself. These conditions can certainly influence the signature produced.

Whenever these problems arise, it is well to seek some known signatures on similar documents. Copies of charge or credit signatures may be difficult to obtain except when the same company concerned can provide other undisputed purchases. Nevertheless, a collection of appropriate signatures is not impossible. Ideally, a large quantity should be collected, although as few as three or four with a large supply of more formal signatures can suggest the variables that may be expected in this class of signature. It is always true, however, that the best opinions rest on an adequate set of comparable signatures.

Standards Prepared Under Cross-examination

From time to time handwriting identification problems arise unexpectedly in the course of trial.[10] The most common circumstance finds a witness denying that he has signed or written a document. It may then be very important to show that the writing was prepared by the witness if only as a means of impeaching his testimony.

These unexpected courtroom denials require that known writing samples be obtained with the least possible delay. One way is to have the witness write while under cross-examination, but such a procedure must of course be considered an emergency step. If there is any opportunity whatsoever to collect other specimens that can be proven by independent testimony, this should be done.

When, however, the witness is required to write under cross-examination, it is absolutely imperative that he does it in such a way as to produce truly representative specimens. In many instances this may be the only writing available for study. It is best to assume when obtaining cross-examination writing that no other writing will be available. Too often, this is the case.

Writing in the courtroom is actually a special form of request standards. Consequently, all the factors considered in connection with them must now be brought into play.

For the most useful courtroom standards, the witness should be seated at a table rather than in the witness box. With the court's permission, the witness should be asked to step down from the box to the counsel table, where he will encounter more usual writing conditions. Few witness boxes are designed to allow one to write freely and naturally.

The attorney must select the proper writing instruments and paper and have the witness prepare each specimen on a different sheet rather than write a series of signatures on one page. It is never a bad idea to have the witness write with his own pen or pencil if it matches the denied writing instrument well.

The greatest weakness of writing prepared in this manner is that it is often of far too limited amount to allow a thorough and complete study of the problem. There is no value in having the witness merely sign his name once if he has denied a signature. Rather, a number of signatures are required. The amount of writing should correspond to the quantities suggested for comparable classes of request standards.

If the document was written a number of years before trial, the specimens made during trial may not form a very satisfactory standard.

---

[10]The discussion in this section is based on O. Hilton, "Procuring Handwriting Specimens During Cross-Examination," *Connecticut Bar Journal* 28 (1954):168–172.

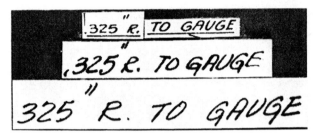

Figure 14.15. The upper line of numerals and letters appeared on an engineering drawing on which the witness testified he had worked. Under cross-examination his assertion was severely challenged, and he was asked to furnish the samples shown below. The material in dispute had been prepared 15 years earlier, and the witness stated immediately after completing the specimens that he had changed his G's about 10 years before by the addition of the final downstroke. Therefore, because of this statement and especially the wide difference in dates, the cross-examination writing was not fully satisfactory.

Changes in the witness's writing may have occurred during this lapse of time so that it will be necessary to have standards contemporary to the denied material to resolve the question accurately (Figure 14.15).

While the witness is under cross-examination, he should of course be asked if he has with him any documents containing his handwriting or signature. Almost everyone carries a driver's license, identification cards, or memoranda that contain his writing. It may be well to start the cross-examination by asking for this material. These papers should be marked in evidence, as should all specimens written by him in the courtroom, and the witness interrogated very carefully about exactly what portions of them are in his handwriting. In this way there can be no later issue when this writing is compared with the denied material.

Handlettered Standards

The mode of procedure and the principles involved in the collection of handlettered standards closely parallel those for handwriting. Since the requirements for adequate standards are the same as with handwriting, the various steps in the preparation of both collected and request standards just discussed apply.

Handlettering is used more frequently in daily life than is generally realized. Few people, except those who letter professionally (draftsmen, architects, engineers, and illustrators, for example) prepare any extended specimens in this manner, but many applications, questionnaires, and other forms require portions to be printed. Lettering is used from time to time to prepare more legible addresses on envelopes and to write postal cards or even entire letters. While it may seem difficult to locate the equivalent of three of four pages of continuous lettering, this may be accomplished with the exercise of a little diligence, particularly with individuals active in the business world and with many younger people who learned to print before they learned to write and resort to it from time to time.

It is true, nevertheless, that with many individuals the potential supply of collected standards is more frequently limited in handlettering problems than in cases involving suspected handwriting. Consequently, we must turn to request standards. Specimens must be naturally lettered and reflect the style of printing habitually used by the writer. Clearly, no instructions should be given to "print only capitals," "print small letters and caps," or the like. After several pages have been prepared, if it is suspected that the style of lettering being employed is different from the writer's usual habit, he should then be instructed to use a specific type of lettering. This fact should be noted on the specimen so written. The absence of particular individual letter form, however, does not mean that the writer should be instructed to make a certain type of e, for example. This procedure will only destroy the value of the standards and prove nothing about how the writer usually letters.

Each of the factors discussed in connection with handwritten request standards must be closely observed, but the amount of request lettering necessary for adequate standards becomes by far the most important consideration. In all instances sufficient material should be procured to ensure that the specimens are free from disguise or nervous restraint and at the same time contain those usual variations so typical of the individual's normal lettering. On the average, five or six pages of request material should produce satisfactory specimens.

Because of the disconnected execution, disguise in handlettering can remain undetected in more instances than with handwriting. In order to prevent this and to check upon the request standards so as to be able to discount the unrepresentative portions, some collected specimens should be provided as a supplement. With these latter samples comparison between the two classes of standards serves as a guide in determining the writer's true habits.

Conclusions

To build an adequate set of standards requires perseverance and painstaking care. It is not sufficient simply to include enough material to show what the individual's writing looks like. The standards must represent as fully as possible his writing at different times and under varying conditions, but it definitely should show how he wrote at the time of the questioned writing.

To obtain request writing one cannot merely furnish a suspect with paper and pen and ask him to write a few lines. One must thoughtfully select the material to be dictated, supervise the suspect while he writes in order to minimize disguise, and simultaneously keep in mind all the various factors discussed above.

Rather than pick up the first two canceled checks that are at hand, the best collected standards are gathered only after exhaustive searches, checking all possible sources of writing while being constantly aware of those conditions that enhance or detract from the usefulness of any piece of writing. The quality of the standards determines largely the extent and accuracy of the ultimate opinion. It is only through diligence on the part of the person collecting them that they are free from defects and fully serve their intended purpose.

The importance of accurate standards cannot be overemphasized. Every year a number of indefinite conclusions are reached in cases in which better standards would have meant a positive identification or elimination of a suspected writer. This situation is illustrated time and again where the original standards are inadequate, but after one or more indefinite reports and conferences between the field investigator and the document examiner, sufficient representative writing is obtained. It is then possible to determine the facts.

15

Typewriting Standards

Accurate typewriting identification rests largely on the quality of the standards. When these are correctly prepared, an exhaustive study can be made of a typewriting problem. Just what constitutes proper standards is not always thoroughly understood by the layman, many of whom believe that an opinion can be based on almost any piece of typewritten material. This view, of course, is erroneous.

Chapter 11 studied two distinct typewriting problems: the identification of the machine and the identification of its operator. With good standards a definite conclusion can in most instances be reached in the first class of problems. The identification of the operator, however, is not always possible, in part depending on the class of machine used. Under the most advantageous conditions unless a rather long document is in dispute and a great quantity of well-selected standards can be located, the findings are meager with many modern electric typebar machines; certainly with single element units, positive identification is virtually impossible. With every kind of typewriting problem, however, the standards must fulfill rather exact requirements.

Standards for Machine Identification

What must typewriting standards reveal? In this answer is to be found their basic attributes. To identify the work of a typewriter, one must discover those individualities or operating defects that are peculiar to it. They must exist in sufficient number that it is probable for only one machine to have this combination of defective and nondefective characters. Obviously, then, typewriting standards must include enough correctly prepared material to reveal accurately all the identifying characteristics of the suspected machine that would be found in the questioned document if it had been written on this typewriter. These characteristics embrace not only the defects that repeat consistently from specimen to specimen, but also those that do not necessarily appear with each printing of a character. Standards for the latter identifying characteristics must not only show their occurrence but must accurately reveal the frequency and condition under which they are repeated.

Typewriting standards for machine identification may be divided into two classes, depending on the purpose of original preparation. The first consists of material written on the machine in question in the course of business or private affairs. These specimens may be referred to as *collected standards*. The second class comprises matter written on the suspected machine by the investigator himself or by some other person at his direction, specifically for comparison with the questioned document. These latter specimens may be designated as *prepared standards*. For the purpose of identifying the particular machine either class of standards serves equally well, and as long as they are contemporary with the disputed document, they may be used interchangeably.

In Chapter 11 it was pointed out that there are significant differences in identifying the work of a typebar machine and the work of a single element unit, of either the type ball or type wheel class. The requirements for preparing or collecting typewriting standards for the identification of a single element unit are more rigid than those for typebar machine identification, although the same considerations underlie both. The basic requirements for good standard to identify a typebar machine will now be discussed. The additional or special considerations for single element typewriters will then be analyzed.

Merely to gather together a few pieces of typewriting or to run off an impression of the entire keyboard does not ensure satisfactory standards (Figure 15.1). Generally, no positive identification is possible, although some typebar machines may be eliminated. Instead, the following factors warrant careful attention:

1. the amount of material;
2. the similarity of disputed and standard text;
3. the relative dates of execution of questioned and standard material;
4. variable factors dependent on
   a. paper,
   b. kind of backing,
   c. ribbon condition,
   d. cleanliness of the type faces,

   and with manual and some electric type bar machines,

   e. operator's "touch."

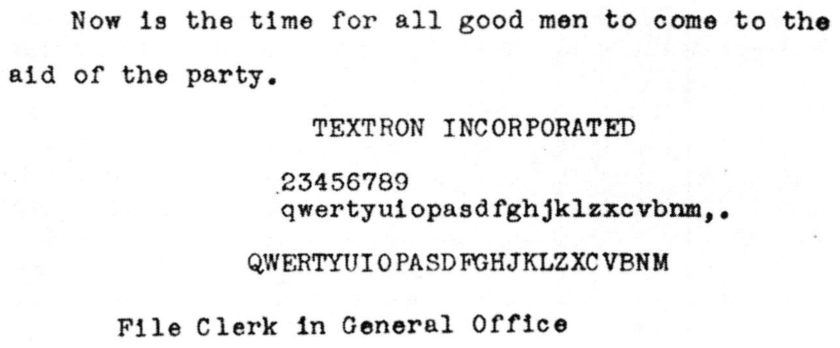

```
Now is the time for all good men to come to the

aid of the party.
```

TEXTRON INCORPORATED

```
.23456789
qwertyuiopasdfghjklzxcvbnm,.
```

QWERTYUIOPASDFGHJKLZXCVBNM

```
File Clerk in General Office
```

Figure 15.1. This specimen, which many people would consider an adequate typewriting standard, prevents a full and complete study of the machine's work. While all the letters and numerals appear, their lack of repetition precludes any accurate determination of slight but significant defects or of variables that might be present in the work of the machine. Generally, two or three pages of continuous typewriting should be obtained as a minimum.

All these factors affect the value of both collected and prepared standards and are to be considered in detail. Through understanding their influence, the quality and accuracy of the standards can be more fully controlled.

Amount of Material

The amount of typewritten material is the primary consideration for adequate standards. A large quantity makes possible a thorough study of the machine's work. Then too, wide dissimilarity in the contents of the questioned and standard documents or lack of opportunity to control closely the variable factors listed above may be compensated for to some extent. This does not mean that the best standards can be obtained merely through quantity, but certainly an important step is taken in the right direction when ample material is assembled.

With every page of continuous typewriting, virtually all the letters and many of the other characters on the keyboard appear at least once. Naturally, the more common letters, which because of their frequent use are apt to contain identifying defects, are found repeated time and again. Thus, if extensive standards are procured, not only do the defective typefaces appear in them a number of times, but also each of the more common ones is repeated with sufficient frequency to indicate accurately the degree of variation present in them. In this respect at least, these specimens approximate the basic requirement for correct standards.

Just how much known material should be gathered may depend on the particular case and on the state of repair of the typewriter. Two or three letter-size sheets of single-spaced typewriting should in general serve as a good working minimum, although special problems may require a greater amount of material. This can well be the case in identifying a suspected machine if the disputed matter is very brief. Then very extensive standards from the right machine establish with certainty that the relatively few points of identification belong to this typewriter. On the other hand, with prepared standards exactly duplicating and repeating the questioned material several times, an identification may be effected with more limited specimens, but in these circumstances the questioned material needs to be near in date to the prepared standards.

Similarity of Text

The need for the questioned and standard text to be as much alike as possible stems from the basic identification rule that similar things must be compared. Standards that exactly duplicate the disputed document represent of course the most useful specimens. This condition can be readily achieved with prepared standards, but with collected specimens it is seldom possible. The alternative is to select known material that was used for a purpose comparable to the disputed in order that many of the same combinations of letters and words are more likely to be found. For example, personal correspondence contains a sprinkling of capitals and numerals among a great mass of lowercase letters. The phraseology is informal and may contain colloquialisms and slang. In contrast, business letters may be more carefully worded and sometimes filled with stilted phrasing. Check forms and financial records may be made up of a larger proportion of numerals and capitals, and sometimes checks are entirely without the use of lowercase letters. Thus it is apparent that the text of the disputed document may warrant critical consideration.

Rather than starting out indiscriminately, the first step in gathering collected standards is to analyze carefully the subject matter, phraseology, and contents of the questioned document. This study entails an initial effort on the part of the investigator, but often it eliminates subsequent delays and unnecessary backtracking to procure the comparable specimens. Casually compiled standards may fail to serve their intended purpose simply because of gross dissimilarity between their contents and that of the disputed matter.

The person procuring prepared standards has a simple task, for he merely has to make several exact copies of the questioned document on each suspected typewriter (Figure 15.2). If conditions make it ill-advised to copy the questioned document exactly—the watchful curiosity of a suspected individual can at times create this situation—it

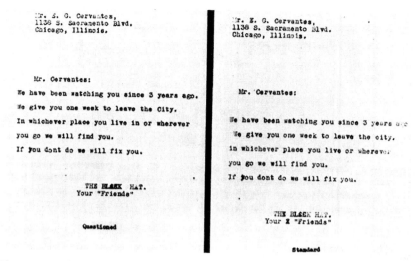

Figure 15.2. The standard specimen in this case was made directly from the suspected typewriter. The investigator made an exact copy of the anonymous letter, even duplicating the strikeovers. It served as a very satisfactory standard in the investigation.

may be necessary to employ a composed text that closely parallels the questioned but at the same time does not reveal its exact contents. Under either condition, however, the subject matter of the prepared standards can be accurately controlled.

Relative Dates of Execution

Since, especially with typebar machines, individual defects that identify typewriting develop and change as the machine is used, some may be altered during the long lapse of time between the preparation of the questioned and standard material. In order to minimize this danger the best procedure is to select standards written near the date of the disputed matter, preferably some immediately before and after. Such specimens should be sought in every investigation.

This ideal procedure cannot always be followed. How long a period can elapse between the writing of disputed and standard matter without seriously impairing the accuracy of the standards? The interval may depend on the make of typewriter, how much it is used, the frequency of overhaul, the skill and typewriting habits of its operators, and the effects of accidental damage (Figure 15.3).

In the great majority of problems several months can elapse without influence on the identification, and with some machines the interval

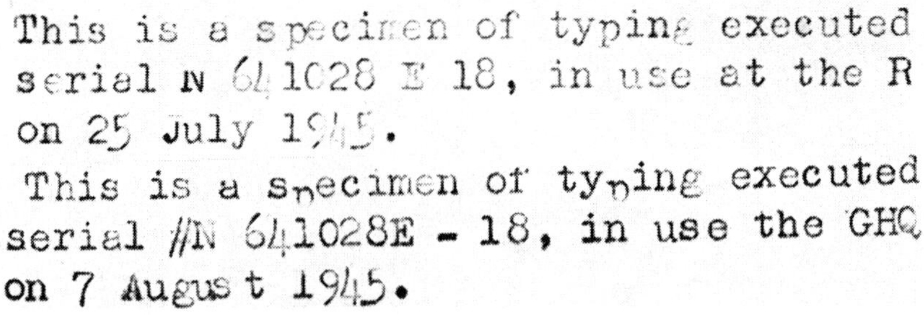

This is a specimen of typing executed
serial N 641028 E 18, in use at the R
on 25 July 1945.
This is a specimen of typing executed
serial #N 641028E - 18, in use the GHQ
on 7 August 1945.

Figure 15.3. These two specimens were prepared on the same typewriter on the dates indicated. The type block containing the p became unsoldered and had slipped badly out of position about August 7. With these standards available it would be possible to make an accurate estimate of when during July and August a document was typewritten.

can be extended to several years. As the difference in date becomes greater, additional specimens creating a straddle allow the examiner to evaluate divergences between the known and questioned. However, an occasional disputed paper is found that was written immediately after the appearance of a new identifying defect, a condition that lessens the value of all known specimens prepared previously. These facts must always be kept in mind when selecting standards.

When the date of a document must be established from the work of the typewriter on which it was written, a large number of specimens covering the entire period during which the document might have been prepared is particularly necessary. These standards may show a progressive deterioration in a machine or the sudden appearance of one key defect. Definite dating of the disputed document is then possible.

Variable Factors

The three factors just discussed are essential to all typewriting standards, but other variables—the paper, backing material, ribbon condition, cleanliness of the typefaces, and the operator's "touch"—may also influence a typewritten specimen. They are of lesser importance than the factors already discussed, and often identifications can be made even though they are completely disregarded. Nevertheless, situations do arise when any one of them may substantially restrict the findings. At times, in special problems, one of these factors may strongly affect the ultimate solution. Consequently, the effect of each variable factor should be recognized and, if possible, controlled when assembling standards.

Paper

Of all the characteristics of paper, the surface texture has the greatest influence on typewriting specimens. A rough paper may lead to irregular impressions, particularly with fabric ribbons when letters contain slight typeface breaks or print off their feet. Both classes of defects have significant identification value, and for this reason, a paper with a decided surface texture should be avoided.

Actually, selection of special varieties of paper for standards is necessary only in the exceptional case, for most typewritten documents are on typewriter paper, which has a relatively smooth surface and reproduces the type impression clearly. Therefore, within this rather wide range of papers, selection need not be too exact. From time to time, disputed typewriting is done on paper with greater surface texture, such as a linen-finished sheet. Then it is well to find or prepare a portion of the standards written on the same class of paper, but some specimens should always be prepared on regular typewriter paper.

Backing Material

What is beneath the paper may influence the quality of the typewritten matter and the identification of the machine.

The platen, around which the paper rolls, is a cylindrical, smooth, hard rubber surface of fixed diameter. With long use it hardens and becomes rough and pitted. In this state the typeface strikes an irregular surface, causing the typewriting to appear more defective. Upon first inspection numerous chipped and broken typefaces may seem to be present. Closer study, however, reveals that these apparent defects do not repeat consistently. When these conditions prevail, the amount of standard typewriting must be increased so that each apparent defect may be carefully evaluated (Figure 15.4).

With a machine with a worn platen, the insertion of several backing sheets behind the original smooths and softens the writing surface and leads to more uniform and useful standards. This step is always advisable before typewriting some of the specimens on an old deteriorated machine.[1]

---

[1]When the platen has become badly worn between the writing of the questioned document and the standards, this procedure is essential for the best and most comparable specimens. If standards taken in the ordinary manner appear much more irregular at first glance than the disputed typewriting, then additional typewriting should be made with backing sheets. It is always likely, however, that the machine has developed new identifying defects during this period, and some control specimens must be collected from material nearer to the date of the disputed matter. Only in this way are the most accurate standards obtained.

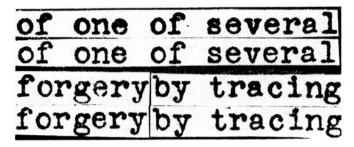

Figure 15.4. The upper line of each pair of phrases was typewritten on a machine with an old, badly pitted platen; the lower line, immediately after a new one had been installed. No other changes had been made on the machine. There is somewhat more variation between several impressions of a given letter, for example, the g or e, in the typewriting against the worn platen than in that against the new. With a machine with a badly worn platen it is always useful to take one specimen, properly identified, with a backing sheet that will compensate in part for the irregular surface.

The typewritten impressions on the original or ribbon copy may be affected by the number of carbon copies prepared with it. First, several second sheets and carbon papers appreciably increase the platen diameter, causing the typefaces to strike with different force and with a slight change in the angle of incidence. At the same time, these additional sheets soften the surface upon which the typefaces hit so that the original copy is more or less embossed (Figure 15.5). Whenever five or six copies are made simultaneously, these conditions combine to produce a deeper inked original with some modification of less pronounced defects. All of this means that knowing exactly the number of carbon copies prepared with a disputed original leads to a better selection of standards.

Figure 15.5. The back of a letter reveals intense embossing that resulted from a combination of several backing sheets or carbon copies. Typewriting from the same machine without this soft backing would show little or no embossing. (The photograph of the back of the sheet was made using oblique lighting to intensify the embossing.)

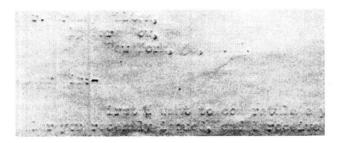

Figure 15.6. Two specimens were prepared on the same typewriter—one with a nearly exhausted ribbon, the other with a fresh fabric ribbon. The slight battering of the upturn of the t can be clearly seen in the weaker inked impression (arrow) but is completely obscured by the heavier inking of the fresh ribbon.

Some operators consistently use one or more blank sheets as backing when writing an original or original and single carbon. The effect is similar to what has just been discussed. Armed with this knowledge, the alert investigator can locate or prepare the best standards. A simple procedure to follow when there is a question about whether backing sheets were used or several carbon copies were made is to hold the questioned sheet reverse side up at eye level with light coming from the far side toward the viewer. Embossing will be apparent if present. Known typewriting can be selected by its similar appearance.

Ribbon Condition

Ribbon condition is a factor to consider when the typewriter is equipped with a fabric ribbon. Replacing a worn fabric ribbon with a fresh one makes a pronounced change on the typewritten copy. The lightly colored, ribbed letter impressions from an exhausted ribbon tend to emphasize slight defects, while the heavy, well-inked, solid outlines from a new ribbon are likely to obscure them (Figure 15.6). For this reason, it is difficult to compare accurately the details of heavily inked and weak impressions. Therefore, the depth of inking in the questioned typewriting should be carefully observed, and, if there is a sharp difference between it and the available standards, other, more comparable material should be sought.[2]

The apparent condition of a fabric ribbon is an excellent criterion for estimating the date of a document within the life of a ribbon. From the time the ribbon is first put into use until it is finally discarded, there is a gradual but consistent deterioration. Therefore if documents written during the life of a particular ribbon are assembled, it may be

---

[2]When prepared standards are procured, one set should always be taken with the ribbon currently in use. If the inking differs decidedly from the questioned material, additional standards should be prepared with a ribbon that more nearly duplicates the disputed material.

possible through study of the ribbon condition, fitting it into the appropriate place in the deterioration pattern, to establish the date of the disputed document with relative precision or to show positively that it could not have been prepared when alleged. To reach such a conclusion, however, may require an extensive collection of dated typewriting.

Today more and more typewriters in business activities are equipped with carbon film ribbons. Each one of these ribbons is typed on only once. All impressions are relatively uniformly inked and the problem of ribbon condition is not present. However, carbon film ribbons do have different inking characteristics, and a collection of standards from the same machine may show different intensity of inking at different dates according to the kind of ribbon being used.

Cleanliness of Typefaces

Typefaces must be regularly cleaned to keep them from becoming filled or clogged with dirt, ink, and other accumulations. If this is not done, they may reach such a state that this filling is reproduced in the printed impression with the center of the letters shaded or solid black. With infrequently used office machines, and more often with privately owned typewriters, a number of documents may be written with the typefaces in need of cleaning. If these conditions exist in the questioned matter and are also reproduced in the standards, we have supplementary identifying characteristics as well as a means of establishing the date of the disputed document.

For the most part, collected standards of approximately the same date must be sought.[3] The only exception is when the suspected machine is located shortly after the questioned document was written, as might be the case in an investigation of anonymous letters. If the typewriter has not been cleaned since the questioned document was typed, prepared standards should contain the same variable characteristics.

In the event that the typefaces of a suspected machine are found badly clogged, the following procedure will produce the best prepared standards. As a safety measure, these steps should always be carried out regardless of the condition of the typefaces in the questioned document. An *adequate* amount of typewriting should first be taken with

---

[3]The time interval between the preparation of standard and questioned material depends largely on how much the machine is used. Since the accumulation is gradual, it may remain almost unchanged for several days or weeks, or possibly even longer, when the typewriter is used only infrequently. On the other hand, this evidence can be completely destroyed at any time simply by cleaning the typefaces.

the machine in the exact condition in which it is found. It is essential that these specimens, showing the dirty typefaces, should contain an ample amount of material, for subsequent steps will make it impossible to supplement them. Next, the typefaces should be thoroughly cleaned and a second set of standards taken. If the typefaces were originally badly clogged, the latter specimens will reveal more clearly the permanent identifying defects. The resulting standards show exactly the condition of the machine at the time they were taken and also permit a full study of its work.

"Touch" of the Operator

The typist's "touch" has the most pronounced effect on typewriting from a manual machine, far less on modern electric typewriters. This discussion will first consider the former, more significant case.

The operator's "touch" varies from person to person. With the highly skilled it is uniform both in force and rhythm, and the work of several skillful operators may at best show only the slightest differences. With the less skillful, however, the typewriter is operated erratically. The latter group of operators produces typewriting characterized by differences in the inked impression of certain letters, irregular spacing, or variation in the baseline because of the improper use of the shift key and at times because of the manner in which a key is struck. These irregularities can lessen the value of limited standards, but as a rule, if a large amount of typewriting is found, the fact that several different people prepared the documents does not seriously detract from their comparison value.

It is practically impossible to imitate another's touch that is very different from one's own. Whenever questioned typewriting is affected by personal touch, standards should be sought that were written by the writer of the questioned material. This procedure not only may assist in the machine identification but may also make possible at least a partial identification of the operator.

In recent years a mechanical adjustment has been built into typewriters, especially electric machines, by which the operator can alter the key tension to suit his individual taste or the work at hand. The extent to which the adjustment is used depends on the individual operator. Many never change it at all; others vary the setting in accordance with the work at hand and particularly with the number of carbon copies to be cut. A change in the tension setting may be reflected in a different depth of impression and may also modify the operator's touch. This factor is particularly important with electric machines, but should be considered when preparing standards on any kind of typewriter. Since the typebar of electric machines is activated by means of a motor-driven mechanism and some are designed to prevent stacking of type, the influence of the operator's touch is minimized.

Special Standards from Suspected Machines

Whenever the suspected machine is available and the date of the disputed document is not too remote, special supplementary standards ought to be prepared. With a manual machine these specimens should be made up of from six to ten repeated impressions of each character, the first struck very heavily, each successive stroke lighter than the preceding, and the last barely printed (Figure 15.7). With an electric machine keyboard, specimens should be taken at different pressure settings. With a fabric ribbon a set should be made both through the ribbon and then by setting the ribbon-activating device on "stencil," typing directly through carbon paper. With a letter off-its-feet, one showing more than average variation between impressions, or a character with a slight typeface defect, these specimens are extremely valuable.

Whenever prepared standards are executed on a suspected typewriter, they should be dated and carefully identified. Every typewriter bears a distinctive serial number assigned at the factory. Each manufacturer locates the number at a different place on the frame, sometimes not even using the same location for each model, but generally it is to be found adjacent to the type basket, under the carriage, or on the back of the machine. With a machine situated in a large office, its serial number permits positive relocation if additional standards must be prepared at a later date. Failure to include this identifying data can cause confusion or serious trouble at the time of a court trial.

Figure 15.7. These impressions were made with a manual typewriter by striking each key repeatedly with slightly varying force. Specimens typed in this manner are particularly useful because many questioned documents prepared on this kind of typewriter contain some examples of letters struck with unusually heavy or light touch. A standard made this way allows study of how a heavy, average, light, and very light impression of each letter prints from the machine in question.

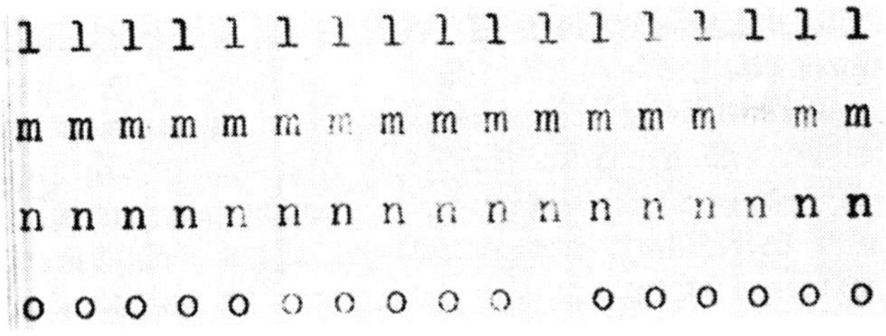

If the typewriter can be made available for the document examiner to inspect its typefaces, he should be given the opportunity. An examination of the typefaces assists in correctly interpreting borderline points; and first-hand knowledge of the mechanical repair of the machine and of the condition of the platen is at times very important. When the questioned document was prepared very recently, the opportunity to examine the ribbon may reveal further evidence of value.[4]

Single Element Standards

As we have seen in earlier chapters, the modern single element typewriter presents special identification problems. The identification is based on much more subtle defects than are encountered in the average typebar machine identification. Consequently, these problems require careful control of the standards together with a large quantity of known typewriting.

A particular problem that is distinctive to this class of typewriter is the ability of the typist or operator to interchange parts within the system and in many cases to make the change in the course of preparing a single page of typewriting. Both the type ball machine (the IBM Selectric and similar units) and the type wheel machine can use a number of different typefaces. The interchange is very simple. It does not even require removing the document from the typewriter. On many of these machines, either through automatic recognition by the machine itself or by a change activated by the typist, the escapement can be modified. Thus the typewriter is capable of typing both pica and elite escapements, that is, in the United States, 10 and 12 characters to the inch, and with some of the more sophisticated machines proportional spacing as well. If the machine is part of a word-processing unit, it is possible to produce automatically a finished document with justified right and left margins. (Justification means that each margin appears as a straight line as on the printed page.) Further, different types of ribbons, fabric ribbons and either correcting or standard carbon-film ribbons, can be inserted on the same machine, again at any time. This latter exchange of ribbon is also possible on some modern typebar machines, but it is almost standard with all single element typewriters. Each of these factors should be considered when preparing standards from a single element machine.

It is well to look at some of these problems in more depth.

---

[4]See O. Hilton, "Identifying the Typewriter Ribbon Used to Write a Letter—A Case Study Employing New Techniques," *Journal of Criminal Law, Criminology and Police Science* 63 (1972): 140–141.

Amount of Material

Several pages of typewriting may well be needed for the examiner to establish a complete identification pattern of a single element typewriter. The full quantity depends in a large measure on the problem at hand. However, from three to four pages of typewriting would normally be the minimum amount desired. Identifications can be and have been made on less known material, but there have been other cases in which this minimum amount has not been adequate. It should be clearly understood that with a single element typewriter typing all of the letters on the keyboard and one or two brief standardized sentences represents an absolutely worthless standard, except to establish that a different type font was being used when the questioned material was prepared.

In collecting typewriting standards from single element typewriters, the investigator or attorney must be certain that the standards he submits are all from the same typing unit if more than one unit is available from a single office. It may well require some checking on the practices within the office. If there is doubt about whether all the papers were typed on the same single-element machine, the examiner should so be informed and should be given some idea about the number of machines that might have been used. Thus, he can treat each specimen as probably coming from a different machine and only after he has verified that several specimens contain the same significant identifying pattern can he depend on these as coming from a single source. Under these circumstances, however, a larger than usual amount of typewriting should be gathered.

Matching Type Font and Ribbon

If the typewriting collected from a particular office or single source reveals typewriting prepared with more than one type design, either more than one single element typewriter is indicated or the operator has available more than one type ball or wheel. It then becomes necessary to select a particular type design from several available. The investigator may need to consult with the expert to determine the font used for the questioned material and the key to recognize it among the available typewriting. Single element typewriters depend on two units to complete a particular system. One is the typing unit itself, that is, the basic machine, and the other is type ball or type wheel used on it. A change of either produces a new typing system, which very probably has different typing characteristics from the former system.

A change in the kind of ribbon may not affect the usefulness of the standard in many cases, but carbon film and fabric ribbons, even of the best grade, do not necessarily reproduce the identifying characteristics on a machine in exactly the same way. Carbon film ribbons print the sharpest impressions and often reveal very fine typeface defects that are partially hidden when a fabric ribbon is employed. Therefore it is well to endeavor to obtain some typewriting from the known sources typed through the same kind of ribbon. If none can be readily located, it could suggest that the known source is not the machine that prepared the questioned material, but this conclusion has to be carefully checked out by thorough investigation. It is not an automatic indication of a different machine, as it would be with older typebar machines.

Prepared Specimens

When an investigator or attorney is planning to have typewriting prepared on a single element machine specifically for the purpose of identifying the machine, certain preliminary steps should be taken. First, it is well to determine if more than one machine is available at the known or suspected source. If so, some inquiry should be made as to the habits of the operators who use the various machines. For example, does a particular typist always use the same unit? Or, because of the nature of the office work, does anyone use any of several different machines? In other words, would the typist's initials definitely establish that the typewriting came from one particular unit?

Also, it is necessary to know whether all machines are equipped with the same font of type. Are any other fonts available? If only one font is available, is one type element kept with a single typing unit or are these switched around from time to time? Would the nature of the questioned document suggest that the person preparing it might modify a system by changing the type element? The answers to these questions can well establish how prepared specimens are to be typed.

The subject matter for these specimens can follow the same patterns as for typebar machines.

Before the preparation of any material from a particular typing unit, the serial number should be determined. For simple cataloging of specimens from several machines, each may be given a definite designating number or letter. The investigator would then do well to mark within the type ball or at the center of the type wheel found on the machine this same designating number of letter. This procedure enables one to come back later and locate the units that were together. If there is knowledge or suspicion that typing elements are exchanged between different typing units, then specimens need to be made with different combinations of typing units and elements. For example, if the typing units are designated A, B, and C and the original elements in each are marked with the same letter, then, besides specimens of machine A with element A, one also needs specimens from machine A with element B and so on. The problem becomes extensive, and specimens must be carefully cataloged.

It is also well to know in advance the kind of ribbon used to type the questioned document and to prepare each specimen with the same class of ribbon. A new ribbon cartridge can be inserted if necessary.

Following these procedures, an adequate set of specimens can be developed.

Summary

The factors that influence the usefulness and adequacy of typewriting standards have been considered in detail. Some of them are fundamental to all standards; others are of concern only in particular cases, and except in these instances, if overlooked, may not seriously limit the standards' value. Overlooking even the most variable factors, however, is not recommended at any time. What may appear to the investigator as a relatively simple problem, may after thorough technical study develop along lines not originally anticipated. The neglected steps could then limit the findings. Care and thoroughness are always essential in the assembling of the best typewriter standards. These specimens are the cornerstone upon which the ultimate identification must rest.

Standards to Identify the Operator

Indentification of the operator of a typewriter rests on his personal typewriting habits and errors. His work is individualized by such factors as irregular impressions, stacked and transposed letters, malalignment caused by improper use of the shift key or irregular striking of the keys, the arrangement of material on the paper, punctuation, and unconventional use of characters and symbols. Any standards from which he is to be identified must contain evidence of his habits in their usual manner of occurrence. A second prime requirement for successful identification is a large amount of known material to compare with a lengthy questioned document. The need for a large quantity of normally typewritten material is so great that it is virtually the sole requirement.

Every problem is itself individual. The necessary quantity of standards is influenced both by the class of material involved, e.g., letters, forms, and checks, and by the operator's skill and the kind of typewriter used, i.e., manual, electric typebar, or single element. Unlike for handwriting identification, in which skill does not have a bearing on how much known writing is needed, the more skillful the operator is, the greater is quantity of typewritten material necessary to identify him. It must be remembered that skillful operators turn out very uniform work even on manual typewriters. While it should be borne in mind that there are instances in which it is impossible under any conditions to identify him positively, the cases that lead to successful conclusions depend primarily upon extensive standards,[5] much more extensive than are necessary to identify the machine itself.

Collected standards alone have sufficient reliability to be used in this kind of problem. The ease with which deliberate disguise can be introduced into prepared standards rules them out as all but a last resort. On the other hand, this danger of disguise, especially in such factors as arrangement, punctuation, and spelling is not present in collected specimens, nor would deliberate typewriting errors be apt to be made a part of specimens executed in the course of daily affairs.

With modern typewriters, especially electric and single element machines, identification of the operator rests on far fewer factors than with manual machines. Some of the more useful factors are eliminated by the way the electric typebar machine is constructed. In the first place, whereas a poorly struck key on a manual machine can be reflected in the imprint obtained, with the electric typewriter when the typebar mechanism is released by striking the key, the force of driving the typebace against the paper is accomplished by the motor-driven mechanism. Thus, impressions are more uniform. Furthermore, on some machines, the mechanical construction eliminates or limits stacked and partially stacked type. Depressing the shift key moves the basket through the complete shift, eliminating a partial shift and the corresponding vertical malalignment of capitals, which can occur in manual typewriters.

With the single element machine, there are even fewer mechanical linkages and all of the selection of the letter, activating it to type and changing from lowercase to capital is accomplished by the machine mechanism itself without any regard to how the particular key is struck or the shift is activated. With both classes of typewriters, typist identification is limited to transposed letters, the arrangement of the material on the paper, punctuations margins and indentations, and any unconventional use of characters and symbols. The manner of operating the machine is rather successfully veiled by the motor-driven, mechanical elements of these machines. Thus, any hope of identification rests on a very large quantity of typewriting prepared from day to day, generally a collection of a substantial number of documents.

---

[5]An excellent rule to follow is to consult with the document examiner prior to collecting standards to ascertain what matter and how much should be sought. If, subsequently, there is any doubt as to the adequacy of the standards at hand, further consultation is clearly in order.

Conclusions

Regardless of how the questioned document was prepared —handwritten, handlettered, or typewritten—proper standards are the foundation of the identification. These specimens must therefore contain all the identifying characteristics and at the same time must be in sufficient volume and of a quality to disclose the usual variations common to the typewriter. Unless these conditions are fulfilled, findings may not be entirely accurate and may be limited in their scope. The additional time and thought necessary to obtain correct standards may only be slightly more than that required to pick up a few scraps of typewriting. The end results, however, will more than adequately compensate for the greater effort.

16

Care, Handling, and Preservation of Documents

The improper or careless handling of a disputed document can lead to serious curtailment of certain technical examinations. Most frequently this condition is brought about by ignorance of the consequences of mishandling. Just the simple act of removing and replacing a letter in its envelope repeatedly can cause noticeable deterioration. An understanding of the factors involved and a few precautions are actually all that is necessary to deliver a document to the laboratory in the same condition as when it was discovered.

The care, handling, and preservation of documents can be discussed adequately by setting forth certain positive rules of action in the form of "DOs" and listing several admonitions in the form of "DON'Ts." There is no special treatment necessary for a disputed document that should not be accorded any important paper, but it is surprising how often a field investigator or someone else complicates the problem because he has not observed just ordinary commonsense rules and precautions.

DOs

1. Keep documents unfolded in protective envelopes.
2. Take disputed papers to the document examiner's laboratory at the first opportunity.
3. If storage is necessary, keep the document in a dry place away from excessive heat and strong light.

DON'Ts

1. Do not handle disputed papers excessively or carry them in a pocket for a long time.

2. Do not mark disputed documents (either by consciously writing on or by pointing at them with writing instruments or dividers).
3. Do not mutilate or damage by repeated refolding, creasing, cutting, tearing, or punching for filing purposes.
4. Do not allow anyone except qualified specialists to make chemical or other tests; do not treat or dust for latent fingerprints before consulting a document examiner.

A disputed document that is important enough to be subjected to scientific study certainly deserves better than average care. Yet only normal care generally keeps a paper in good condition and prevents damage or deterioration between the time that it first comes under suspicion and when it is turned over to the document examiner. Before leaving this subject it may be well to comment briefly on the various suggestions listed above so that the reader can better appreciate the pitfalls that are present.[1]

Protective Envelopes

The most useful and effective protective covering for a disputed document is a transparent plastic envelope. This kind of envelope can usually be purchased commercially or can easily be made from sheets of clear plastic to a size sufficient to accommodate any flat and unfolded paper. With such a cover the document can be completely examined by witnesses and others who may have occasion to refer to it, and at the same time it is protected from dirt, wear, and stains occasioned by handling. Thus, after an extended investigation and trial, it will be in virtually the same condition as when discovered.

As an alternative, a large, heavy manila or kraft envelope or folder can be used. Again, the document should be laid flat, unfolded so as to prevent wear along folds. If a nontransparent envelope is used, it should be carefully labeled both for convenience and to eliminate unnecessary handling. This kind of envelope makes a poor permanent substitute for a transparent one because the document is not easily examined, but protection by any sort of envelope preserves the document and reduces the chance of damage.

Early Submission for Examination

With many classes of problems a suspected document ought to be thoroughly examined as soon as practicable after it is discovered. These

---

[1]Those readers who investigate questioned document problems from time to time undoubtedly will find it of value to read the thorough treatment of this subject found in A. S. Osborn, *Questioned Document*, 2nd ed. (Albany: Boyd, 1929), Chapter III.

problems have been specifically discussed in earlier chapters. Nothing is gained in any instance by delaying. Early submission means that there is less danger of the document being in a different condition than when found or questioned, and there is less danger of damage or wear through handling. It is also well to remember that many document examinations entail considerable time, and proper preparation for trial is always time consuming. Information gained from a laboratory examination may reveal unsuspected facts that could alter the course of the entire investigation. Consider as an example the change occasioned by the discovery that a signature suspected of being an imitated forgery was actually genuine but was on a paper that had been cut from another document. That discovery obviously redirects the emphasis of the pretrial investigation, and if learned well in advance of the trial date, ample time is available for proper development of all leads to defend against the fraud. This is but one possibility, and many others could be added to illustrate why submitting the document for examination upon its discovery may be the wisest course.

Proper Storage

Once a document is disputed it is seldom stored or filed for long, but important documents are very often kept for years. Some of these may be challenged long after they were prepared, and poor storage conditions may have caused the document to deteriorate seriously. Very moist or humid atmosphere, excessive heat, and strong light accelerate the normal effects of aging, bringing about changes in a relatively short time (Figure 16.1). Under these conditions it is entirely possible that even though there is no apparent effect from exposure to moisture, heat, or light, the document has undergone microscopic changes. The best storage conditions for important papers should be maintained in order to preserve them in their original condition for as long as possible, and a disputed document must naturally be protected from abnormally bad storage conditions.

Figure 16.1. The very faded countersignature on a traveler's check had been written with green ball point pen ink. Some writing inks are not lightfast, and even moderate exposure to strong light causes serious fading.

Avoid Excessive Handling

Repeated handling of a document can actually wear it out. In this way a paper becomes dirty, frayed, and stained. Folds are deepened and finally broken by repeated opening and refolding. Long before the document shows a marked deterioration, microscopic changes have occurred that may influence or interfere with a technical examination. Pencil writing and carbon copies of typewriting are common examples of documents that are subject to smearing and obliteration by undue and careless handling. The time in which the deterioration occurs can be surprisingly short, and one must be constantly on guard to prevent it.

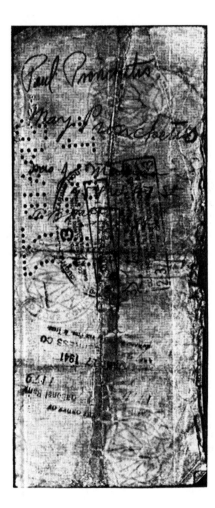

Figure 16.2. The worn condition of a check resulted from its being carried around loose in the investigator's pocket for several weeks. When he took it out, he stated that he had been hoping to get it to the examiner for some time. If it had been placed in an envelope, much of the fraying and wrinkling would have been prevented.

A person engaged in a field investigation of a disputed document may without thinking fold the paper and place it unprotected in his pocket. A few days in his pocket, where papers and other contents are frequently being changed, can almost wear a document out (Figure 16.2). Rubbing against pocket contents and the lining, along with body heat and perspiration, combine to cause the deterioration. In a great number of instances a photograph or a good quality photocopy can serve as well as the original in this phase of the work, and the substitution assures that the original is not damaged.

Certain problems require that the document receive greater than normal care. This is certainly true if the paper is suspected of containing erasures or traces of impressed writing. Even moderate handling may further obliterate partially erased writing, may soil or stain the surface of the paper so as to hinder restoration, may destroy some of the minute indentations upon which the decipherment of erased pencil or impressed writing is dependent, and may leave deposits that develop into smudges when chemicals are used in the attempted restoration.

Do Not Mark

Interfering marks may result either from someone's deliberately writing on the paper or from those unconscious strokes and smudges placed there by someone's pointing at the document with a pen, pencil, pair of dividers, or eraser. Both must be avoided.

Investigators frequently initial papers for identification, but this practice should be kept to an absolute minimum or eliminated completely. If initials are placed on a document, they should be marked inconspicuously in a back corner where they do not interfere with any elements that could possibly be the subject of examination. A far better method is to make accurate notes of the pertinent contents of a document by which it can subsequently be clearly identified. Whenever there is suspicion of erasures or alterations, or a possibility of writing traces being impressed in the paper, the document should not be marked for identification or in any other way. Writing on it may seriously interfere with these technical examinations.

It would seem unnecessary to state that no extraneous writing should be placed on a paper that may either become disputed or serve as a writing standard, but from time to time police and other investigators present papers containing writing and notes placed on them during the investigation. In legal proceedings an alert trial attorney would very likely be able to exclude from evidence papers so defaced.

Personal writing habits must never be circled or underlined on the original document in order to call attention to them (Figure 16.3). Some individuals, especially those unfamiliar with the technical investiga-

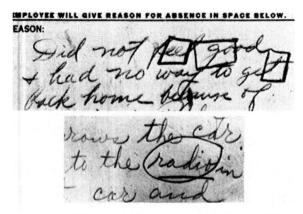

Figure 16.3. These examples are typical of objectionable marking of documents before submitting them for technical study. A qualified document examiner hardly needs this guidance from an interested party. Besides, the marking may raise serious questions about whether the examination was truly scientific and unbiased.

Figure 16.4. In this further example of objectionable markings on a document, only the purchaser's signature on this sales slip was in question. The party submitting the problem felt it necessary not only to circle the questioned signature, but to strike out other portions of the document. This defacing action could seriously curtail a full investigation of the case if it subsequently became important to identify the clerk's writing on the slip.

The proper method of indicating what handwriting is in dispute is by an accompanying letter describing the writing by its location and substance.

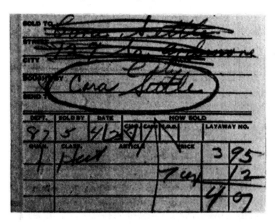

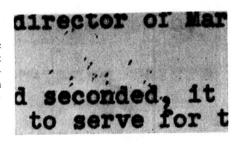

Figure 16.5. The small pencil dots were unconsciously made while pointing out the contents of the document. Microscopic deposits arising from such causes have occasionally brought suspicion on an absolutely authentic paper.

tion of documents and court procedures, mark a document in this manner while making their own preliminary examinations. This kind of marking may not only weaken the value of the document as legal evidence but also occasionally damages the physical evidence contained in it (Figure 16.4).

Marks or blemishes may be made part of a document without anyone realizing it. These defacements most commonly result from the use of pens and pencils as pointers (Figure 16.5), but a pair of dividers or a dirty eraser tip used in the same way may also scuff or mar the paper. Whenever an inked pen or a pencil strikes the paper a mark is left; the sharp points of dividers can scratch or pierce the paper; and the soiled eraser may leave smudges. These disturbances are merely microscopic, but microscopic evidence in a document can at times assume importance. Occasionally, these marks may interfere with some phase of the examination, or perhaps they may cast suspicion on an otherwise genuine document. In any event it is best not to use these instruments as pointers.

Merely rubbing the fingers against a document may also bring about similar harmful results. If pencil writing is rubbed with the fingertips, it can be smudged; fingers damp with perspiration may even blur certain classes of writing inks. Smudge marks or fingerprints may be left on the paper. The best safeguard against all these sources of damage is to keep the document in a transparent envelope.

Do Not Fold, Cut, or Tear

Wear occasioned by the refolding of a paper a number of times has already been discussed, but new folds placed in a disputed document can also hinder certain technical examinations. Deep folds make it more difficult to prepare oblique-light photographs or to examine the document with this type of illumination. A fresh fold made in an area that contains a suspicious detail restricts proper study. Furthermore, a new fold refolded a number of times can lead to the same wear as

Figure 16.6. All of the check except the body writing had been cut away so that only one person's writing remained. Without the signature and other information on the check, it would be extremely difficult for the person who wrote it to testify regarding its preparation and thus to prove it as a standard in any trial of the matter.

might be found along the original folds. It was for these reasons that it was recommended earlier that disputed papers should be kept open and flat.

Deliberate tearing of a questioned document is a very infrequent act, but occasionally parts of a disputed paper are cut out in order to conceal the identity of persons referred to in it or parts of the subject matter (Figure 16.6). A competent document examiner is very likely to refuse to examine a paper in this condition. Moreover, it is almost certain that the document will have little value in subsequent legal proceedings. Document examiners are called upon to make technical investigations of many confidential papers and would consider it highly unethical to disclose their contents to any unauthorized person. If the individual submitting the problem does not feel free to give the document examiner all the facts that may have a bearing on the disputed papers or are contained in it, he should not submit the problem at all.

If in the course of an investigation a disputed document becomes torn, its repair should be left to the document examiner. He is best

Figure 16.7. In punching the paper for filing, one letter of the signature was completely removed, even though the signature had a direct bearing upon the investigation.

Figure 16.8. Banks using perforating canceling devices may mutilate the endorsement. In this case it was the key to the dispute.

able to mend it so that subsequent technical examinations are restricted as little as possible. Pasting the torn fragments to some sort of backing is very objectionable. This procedure prevents examination by means of transmitted light or of the back of the paper itself. Both studies are of importance in certain classes of problems.

When a document is punched for filing, or as a means of cancellation, one must be careful not to cut away any of its important details (Figure 16.7 and 16.8). Once it has become questioned, it should not be punched at all, nor should it be filed on an old-fashioned spindle. All parts of the document are of potential importance, and sometimes apparently blank areas contain controlling physical evidence. Until it is known that a disputed document does not contain these hidden facts, it is far safer to file it in a way in which no new holes are made in it.

Do Not Allow "Amateur" Testing

Chemical and other tests on a document require extensive knowledge of the methods and possible pitfalls. Valuable evidence may be destroyed by the testing of an "amateur expert." A problem involving erased pencil writing was submitted in which a friend of the client had darkened the paper with the side of a pencil lead in an effort to intensify the indentations of the original writing. The results were unsatisfactory. The volunteer had then carefully erased most of the newly added graphite. This very thorough erasing simultaneously removed practically all fragments of the original writing. There was no way to tell if the original erasing had been incomplete, but when submitted the document showed the effects of extensive rubbing, and there was very little graphite on its surface. Infrared photography was consequently ruled out, and the ultimate findings were fragmentary. Many questioned document problems are extremely difficult to solve under the best of conditions, and when complicated by mistreatment of the document through unreliable or improperly applied tests a solution may become impossible.

With anonymous letters, and occasionally with other classes of documents, one of the first thoughts is to treat for latent fingerprints. If nothing else is to be investigated about the document, then there is no reason for not making this test immediately, but even treatment that fails to disclose any fingerprints can prevent further technical

Figure 16.9. A pencil-written robbery note was almost completely obscured by the heavy coating of fingerprint powder, and no identifiable prints were developed. Fingerprint powders are generally unsatisfactory for developing prints on paper, especially with inexpensive tablet sheets. Since fine writing details are obscured by the powder, in this instance there was a question as to whether the handlettering could be accurately identified.

Regardless of the method used, latent fingerprints on paper should never be treated until the document has been accurately photographed.

investigations of the document (Figure 16.9). It is far better to consult first with a competent document examiner who can advise on the chances of success for developing latent fingerprints based upon the facts surrounding the document and a preliminary examination of it. If it seems advisable to make this attempt,[2] accurate photographs should first be prepared so that other technical examinations may subsequently be carried out.

Charred Documents

Charred documents, because of their extremely fragile nature, must be handled as little as possible. Even transporting them to the laboratory requires extraordinary care. With forethought and caution, however, they can be brought from a distant fire scene to the laboratory. Two instances are reported in which charred papers were transported from the Philippines to Los Angeles.[3] When documents of this kind are discovered, much is to be gained by discussing all aspects of the question with a qualified document examiner before any attempt is made to move the material to his laboratory.

Whenever possible, the charred documents should be moved in the container in which they are found. If the fragments are not packed tightly, lightweight absorbent cotton may be used as padding.[4] Jarring of the box must be kept to a minimum if it cannot be entirely eliminated. When the fragments must be transferred to another container, this should be done by an experienced person. No attempt should be made to unfold the burnt papers or to flatten curled sheets. When finally packaged in a sturdy container, the fragments must be held firmly, without crushing, to prevent movement or shifting. Decipherment of a charred document that has been shattered into small fragments is almost impossible. Therefore every precaution must taken in handling and transporting the charred residue in order to prevent the large pieces from becoming badly broken.[5]

---

[2]A concise discussion of fingerprint identification that deals specifically with the question of latent fingerprints is to be found in Andre A. Moenssens, *Fingerprint Techniques* (Philadelphia: Chilton, 1971), Chapter 4.

[3]See David A. Black, "Decipherment of Charred Documents," *Journal of Criminal Law and Criminology* 38 (1948): 542.

[4]Black, "Decipherment of Charred Documents," p. 543.

[5]The handling of burnt papers found in a stove or grate is discussed by Hans Gross, *Criminal Investigation* (translated by John Adams and J. C. Adams) (Madras: Krishnamachari, 1906), pp. 478–482.

A further discussion of the problem of handling charred documents is to be found in Donald Doud, "Charred Documents, Their Handling and Decipherment," *Journal of Criminal Law and Criminology* 43 (1953): 812–826.

Conclusions

How a document is handled or cared for may have a bearing on what can be determined from a technical examination. The discussions in this chapter have been presented in order to prevent the destruction of important evidence through mishandling. It is hoped that when the reader understands how physical evidence in a document can be destroyed or weakened, fewer cases will be encountered in which lack of care or knowledge has worked against science and justice.

17

Reproduction of Documents

It is not always possible to submit original papers to the document examiner's laboratory for technical study, so it often becomes essential to make reproductions of them. Should they be photographed, photocopied, or copied by some other process? Which method provides the best reproduction for such an examination? Since each process gives different results, the question should be seriously considered. Reproductions can be made that permit certain classes of examination, but not all methods will achieve the same ends. A good copy should show the maximum of writing details, but merely employing the best method does not necessarily ensure satisfactory results. The person making the copy must know the importance of recording the finer details in the document and how to achieve this goal. In this chapter we shall consider what a good reproduction should contain and the various methods that might be used.

No reproduction, regardless of how skillfully it is made, is as satisfactory for a technical examination as the original. Each kind of reproduction imposes definite limitations on both the examination and the findings. Only the original document permits a study of the paper or chemical tests, and even the best photographs do not permit satisfactory ink or pencil examinations. If it appears that some portion of the document has been erased, further study of the suspected area and all attempts at restoration must normally await an examination of the original paper. With many commercial reproductions, especially those of poorer quality, there is a good chance that evidence of the erasure may not appear at all. Unless the original is carefully examined, an erasure may not be discovered. Finally, because most photography used in document work is black and white, colors may be reproduced only in tones of gray.[1] These disadvantages are present in the highest-quality reproductions, but unfortunately, many commercial photographs and photocopies are of inferior quality and contain other faults that further reduce their value.

Photographs

From the document examiner's point of view, a well-made photograph is the best copy of a document. Since a high-quality photograph is capable of recording the maximum amount of detail, except for the original document itself, a photograph permits the most extensive technical study.

Essentially, the black-and-white photographic processes consist of two distinct steps: first, the preparation of a negative copy from the original, and second, the production of a final (positive) print from the negative. This negative is made with a light sensitive photographic material consisting of an emulsion of silver salts mounted on a film base. When exposed and developed in a series of chemical solutions, transparent reproduction of the original is produced in which the various intensities and shades of color are shown as tones of grays, ranging from an almost clear transparency to a practically complete opaqueness. [This copy is called a negative because the white portions of the original here appear as black (opaque), and the black areas of the original are white (clear); the intermediate tones vary within these extremes but with opposite intensity to the original.] The positive print is made by passing light through the negative when in tight contact with the printing paper (thus producing a "contact print") or with a lens system by projecting an enlarged image onto the paper (thus producing a "projection print"). With document photographs the positive print is usually made on a glossy surface photographic paper,[2] which reproduces the greatest detail and is a facsimile copy in tones of gray. These tones should range from a white or slightly grayish-white reproduction of white paper to a pure black rendition of black print.

In this discussion photographs are arbitrarily divided into two groups based on the size of the negative film. The first, which may be termed "standard photographs," includes copies usually made with negatives ranging in size from 2¼ × 3¼ to 11 × 14 in. These films may record

---

[1]The use of color photography gives a full-color reproduction of the document, but these photographs are costly and difficult to make properly. When completed under the most accurate methods, the colors may not be perfectly reproduced, and the advantages gained are at best slight.

[2]Photographic papers are related to the negative materials in their basic composition. They consist of an emulsion of silver salts in a gelatin mounted on a paper base, rather than on film or glass. Unlike films, these papers are prepared with various kinds of surfaces, which range from rough (matte) to smooth (glossy).

a negative image the same size as the original document or slightly enlarged. Thus, natural size or slightly enlarged positive copies can be printed without resorting to further enlargement. When needed, positives can be enlarged by projection printing. Some workers copy documents at slightly reduced scale and prepare natural-size prints by projection.

The second class, which may be referred to as "microphotographs," includes all copies prepared from small size negatives, generally 35, 16, and 8 mm, with 16 mm the most common commercial film size. Thus microfilming obviously produces a greatly reduced negative image, and a corresponding degree of enlargement becomes necessary when printing a full-scale positive.

Standard Photographs

A full-tone photograph made with a film size that permits at least a natural-size negative image can lead to the very best document photographs. However, not all photographs prepared in this manner are necessarily good reproductions. Many commercial photographers, even when using good materials, fail to produce a top quality picture. While in part these faults are brought about by the manufacturers' recommendation of materials and processes that give too great contrast,[3] they can also be traced to the fact that progressive document examiners have not adequately publicized the results of their own investigations and experimentation on the correct way to photograph documents. Special equipment, good materials, and carefully controlled methods must be combined for superior results.

Good equipment is essential for the best document photographs. Highly corrected photographic lenses assure that the final print is sharp and free from distortion.

The camera should be of the view type, with the ground glass containing clear spots for accurate focusing. The document should be fastened to an adjustable object board, and in most instances it is better to place the paper under optically clear glass in order to hold it flat. The object board and film surface must be in parallel planes at right angles to the axis of the lens. A special camera base assures that these conditions are maintained. When the document is in place, the final accurate focusing is done with a magnifying focusing glass placed over the clear sections of the ground glass. The use of a small rule or scale

---

[3]Kodak, whose writings are generally among the most progressive, in *Photography in Law Enforcement* (Rochester: Eastman Kodak, 1959), p. 54, recommends the use of high-contrast films for document photography. Other companies make similar recommendations.

in the photograph is recommended to indicate exactly the degree of enlargement. These steps are basic and assure that the photograph is free from distortion.

Illumination of the document during film exposure is a critical consideration. Good photographs can be made with natural daylight from a north window, and this lighting method has been employed by many document examiners. If artificial illumination is used, for best results the lights should be arranged so that about 60% comes from one side and 40% from the other. Either technique gives the desired slightly uneven negative, which brings out details of the ink and pencil strokes or of the typewriting as well as the paper texture.

Incorrect selection of the negative material is a common cause of poor document photographs. Generally, a film with too high contrast is selected,[4] but occasionally the opposite course is taken. Manufacturers tend to recommend high-contrast emulsions, but these should only be used in making document photographs for special purposes, never for record copies nor for those to be submitted to a document examiner. Instead, films of a moderate contrast range (those which with normal development give between 0.9 and 1.1 gamma) should be used.[5] Among such films are Kodak Ektapan or Commercial Ortho. If the original document contains colors other than blue and black, then it is important to select a panchromatic film.

The exposure is calculated in accordance with the manufacturer's rated film speed. If a light meter is used, the exposure indicated by the meter reading is increased four times for a one-to-one scale negative, and then, if enlarging, by an additional enlargement factor.[6]

In making document photographs it is not absolutely necessary to record an entire document on a single film, although there are advantages in so doing if large-size films are available. If sectional negatives are made, these should overlap enough so that no detail of the document is omitted.

Development must also be carefully controlled if satisfactory results are to be achieved. Moderate contrast developers are recommended; a high-contrast solution should be avoided. By using the formulas sug-

---

[4]Contrast is the tonal difference between the light and dark portions of a photograph. A detailed discussion is to be found in *Basic Photography* (Technical Manual TM 1–219) prepared by the War Department (Washington, D.C.: U.S. Government Printing Office, 1935), pp. 162–163.

[5]Gamma may be considered as a measure of contrast and is defined as the slope of the straight-line portion of the density log of the exposure curve. Using gamma synonymously with contrast is only correct for the straight-line portions of this characteristic curve. See Keith Henney and Beverly Dudley, *Handbook of Photography*, (New York: McGraw-Hill, 1939), pp. 179–180 and 420.

[6]A table of enlarging factors for copying work can be found in Henney and Dudley, *Handbook of Photography*, p. 225, Table IV (Relative Exposure for Enlarging and Reducing Size of Photograph).

gested by the manufacturers for the recommended films and by following the instructions for obtaining the recommended contrast, the photographer can produce a negative that is snappy but also of good gradation of tone. A good practical guide is to select the film, exposure, and developer that give a negative that prints properly on a #2 contrast printing paper. Placing the final print beside the original document should give a comparable range of contrast. The result never should be black writing on a dead white background.

Occasionally, it may be desirable to include a correction or compensating filter[7] when exposing the negative to reproduce some detail accurately. Yellow stains tend to photograph too dark, but when a K-1 (light yellow) filter is used, the intensity of the stain is weakened enough to produce a final print with the visual appearance of the original. In the same way a yellow filter may improve the rendition of a lighter pencil stroke, which, because of the bluish-gray color, may otherwise appear too light. These corrections are necessary because the human eye and photographic film do not have identical color sensitivity. A contrast filter, however, should never be used in making a record copy of a document, although it is very useful in some special problems (Figure 17.1).

The final step is the preparation of the positive print. Prints made with the negative and paper in direct contact generally are slightly superior to those made by projection, although modern projection enlargers and printing papers can render fine detail. The appropriate contrast grade of glossy-surface printing paper should be used. Exposure and development must be controlled so that there is good detail in the writing stroke or typewriting and the paper background shows to a slight degree. The processed print is dried on a ferrotype plate to give a high-gloss finish and to retain every detail possible. With a document suspected of being a forgery, it is sometimes helpful to prepare additional prints slightly lighter and darker than normal. Thus, the faults of forgery contained in the original may be more clearly shown. After a negative has been completed any number of positive prints can easily be furnished, even at a subsequent date. These may be either enlarged, natural size, or reduced.

---

[7]There are two classes of photographic filters: correction or compensation filters and contrast filters. A correction filter transmits more light of specific wavelengths than the other wavelengths, such as yellow light with a K-1 filter. The color transmitted most readily then photographs slightly lighter than the other colors, thus correcting the film characteristics so that the final photograph appears more as the human eye sees the subject. Contrast filters, on the other hand, transmit light within only a narrow band of wavelengths. All colors outside this band photograph as black, while the color transmitted is recorded as almost white. Contrast filters are used to eliminate completely an undesirable color such as an interfering bank stamp.

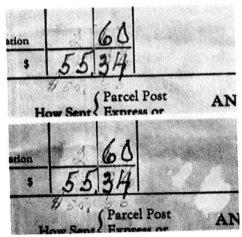

Figure 17.1. The proper selection of photographic films and filters permits either the elimination or the recording of spots and stains. The upper photograph was prepared on a panchromatic film without any filter; the lower one, on the same type of emulsion with a yellow (Wratten K-3) filter.

The original document contained stains and alterations. Fluid ink eradicator had partially removed the ball point pen notation and left a clear white spot on the blue paper in that area and to the right where chemicals apparently had been spilled. Because of the high blue sensitivity of all photographic emulsions (they tend to record lighter blues as white), these important telltale spots are lost in the upper photograph, but are recorded below.

The principal disadvantages of high-quality photographs are the restrictions inherent to all reproductions. Beyond these, however, there are not the many defects common to the other classes of reproductions. The cost of photographs and the time involved in their preparation might be classed by some as unfavorable. Compared to other reproductions, photographs are more expensive and their preparation requires more time. With important papers under investigation, however, these objections should be of minor importance compared to their superior technical qualities.

Microphotographs

The essential difference between microphotographs and standard photographs is the film size. With microphotographs the negative image must be greatly reduced rather than nearly actual size. Generally, the reduction is at least between one-tenth and one-twenty-fifth. Otherwise, the same steps are followed in microphotographs as in standard photographs (Figure 17.2).

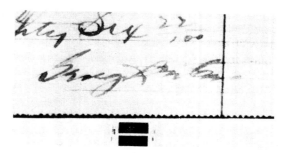

Figure 17.2. The signature was photographed on a commercial microfilm and enlarged by the manufacturer to demonstrate the quality of these photographs. When all steps are carefully controlled comparable results can be obtained, but Figure 17.3 more accurately portrays the typical better microphotographs from business and financial organizations. Below the signature is an actual-size reproduction of a portion of the film. The dark image on the film is the entire bank check.

The main advantage of microfilming lies in reduced unit cost and very substantial savings in storage space.[8] Consequently, microfilming is being widely employed by business firms, especially banks and insurance companies, and by libraries;[9] during World War II it was commonly used by the armed services V-mail.

The chief disadvantage insofar as the document examiner is concerned lies in the loss of detail and clarity in the final print. This loss is the result of the extreme image reduction coupled with the compensating enlargement necessary to make natural-size positives, as well as the high contrast and the grain size of the more popular microfilms, which in extreme cases produce coarse copies consisting of only two tones, black and white. These objections do not apply fully to the Kodak Micro-File film,[10] employed by libraries for copying an-

---

[8]Statistics on V-mail weight and volume give an accurate picture of the reduction brought about by microfilming. To quote from "Fleet Post Office," *Our Navy* (U.S. Navy Bureau of Personnel) (1944): 50: "When V-mail is used two transport planes can do the work of 100 similar planes carrying the same number of standard air mail letters. A V-mail letter weighs $\frac{1}{140}$ as much as the standard letter, and its use effects a saving of 98% in cargo space."

[9]Various types of microfilm cameras have been developed. They include high-speed automatic cameras designed to copy business documents; cameras suitable for the more exacting uses in libraries; and portable microcameras. The Recordak Corp., Remington-Rand Corp., and 3M are among the principal suppliers.

[10]In the specification sheet published in the *Kodak Reference Handbook* (Rochester: Eastman Kodak Company, 1956), p. 951, the general properties of Kodak Micro-File Safety Film are given as follows: "An extremely fine-grained, slow, panchromatic emulsion especially designed for making greatly reduced copies of newspapers, manuscripts, drawings, photographs, letters, etc." The resolving power is given as 130 lines/mm with development in Kodak D-11, and the contrast as 3.0 gamma, a high contrast.

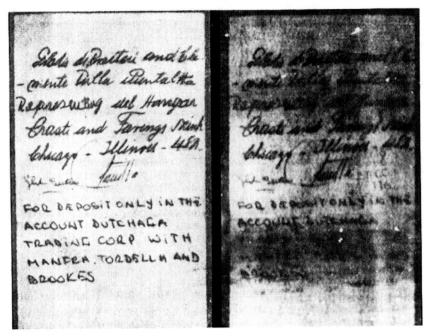

Figure 17.3. The two sections of the illustration contain microphotographs of the endorsement portion of a check. The left is a very good reproduction by microfilming, the right an average copy made at a New York City bank where a very great volume of checks are processed daily. The endorsement had been altered by carefully made over writings and added letters. This condition was even difficult to recognize from the left-hand microphotograph, but the examiner also had the opportunity to study the negative film from which it was made. The film actually contained greater detail, and most of the changes could be recognized. Neither the right-hand copy nor its negative was of sufficiently good quality to permit similar determinations.

cient and rare documents. This film has a very fine grain emulsion[11] with a high resolving power.[12] Its characteristics tend to retain the details of the original in the final actual-size print. On the other hand, the commercial microfilms, which are more commonly encountered in document problems, have a coarser grained emulsion with lower resolving power. In actual-size positives from these negatives fine strokes lack sharpness and details are obscured. Commercial micro-

---

[11] All photographic emulsions consist of a series of microscopic particles or grains of silver halides, which, when developed, are transformed into correspondingly small silver particles. The size of the silver salt particles, designated as "grain size," varies with different emulsions.

[12] The resolving power of a photographic material is its ability to reproduce sharply fine details or lines. The usual method of measuring this factor is in terms of the number of lines per unit length the material is capable of clearly separating.

filming is a high-volume automatic process in which equipment must be well maintained. Solutions must be fresh, lenses clean, and lighting properly balanced. Such standards often are not maintained, resulting in even poorer copies, far below the equipment's best work (Figure 17.3). Because of the importance of writing details in a technical examination, any loss is a serious handicap. Certainly, in view of these defects microphotographs are far from satisfactory reproductions for document examination.

Today's Dry-Photocopying Systems

Contemporary photocopying equipment has provided businesses and individuals with a fast, inexpensive means of copying documents. Today's copiers produce a readable, dry positive copy in a matter of seconds. This combination has led to widespread use of photocopies, in some cases to the extent that they have replaced multiple carbon copies. When an investigator needs to copy a document the original of which cannot be submitted to the document examiner, he may well have a positive photocopy prepared.

Three methods of photocopying are in common use today. They are the transfer electrostatic process, which is also referred to as the plain-paper process, the direct electrostatic or coated-paper process, and the dual spectrum process. Most copies are made by one of the first two methods, since the dual spectrum process is covered by 3M patents and has not been widely licensed. How good are these reproductions for expert study and to what extent may each method limit his work?

Transfer Electrostatic Copies

The transfer or plain-paper method of direct photocopies was developed by Xerox and introduced in March 1960.[13] Today, there are a number of other companies manufacturing copying machines using this process.[14] However, Xerox copiers are so widely used that despite Xerox's advertising that Xerox is a registered trade name, many people continue to refer incorrectly to all present-day photocopies as "xeroxes."

All of these copying machines consist of a built-in light system and a lens system that focuses an image of the document on an electrostatically charged drum or sheet. Xerox uses selenium as the metallic

---

[13]"The Revolution in Office Copying, Part II," *Chemical and Engineering News* (July 24, 1964): 84. This excellent survey of office copying machines has been a helpful source of information in preparing this section of the chapter.
[14]Around 1970 IBM was the first to challenge Xerox, but more recently a number of companies that had manufactured coated-paper machines have introduced plain-paper models.

surface for the drum. The material holds a positive charge until exposed to light. Thus, the reflection of white paper on the drum discharges that area while the darker ink or writing on the paper absorbs the light leaving this portion of the drum charged. A negatively charged toner is directed across the drum and adheres to the positively charged areas. This toner is in turn transferred to a plain sheet of paper by means of a positive charge, which also holds the toner to the paper until it is fused by heat to create the positive copies.

With machines in good mechanical operation, clear dry copies are quickly made and can be used immediately.

Direct Electrostatic Process

The direct electrostatic copier, called Electrofax, has a comparable light and lens system and works in a manner similar to that just described, except that zinc oxide–coated paper replaces the selenium drum and accepts the positive electrostatic charge directly. Again, the light dissipates the charge on the clear area of the document, leaving only the portions with the dark writing and printing charged. With machines manufactured for this process the toner may be either dry or in liquid form. Both are attracted to the charged area of the paper. The dry toner is finally bound to the paper by heat; the liquid simply air dried. The copies produced are not identical to those made by the indirect or transfer process and can be easily recognized by the coated paper surfaces. (When there is doubt about the paper, rubbing a coin across a clear area of coated paper will leave a dark scratch but across uncoated paper will not mark.) Copies are quickly made, legible, and virtually dry, even when liquid toners are used.[15]

Dual Spectrum Process

The dual spectrum copiers were developed by 3M Corporation.[16] They combine a photographic and thermographic technique to produce copies. The initial copy of the document is made by means of reflex photography on a very thin intermediate sheet. The intermediate sheet is coated with a material that is decomposed by visible light during the exposure process. The remaining portions of the intermediate sheet corresponding to the image on the document are then brought into

---

[15]Apeco (American Photocopy Equipment Co.) placed the Electrofax machines on the market in December 1961, followed by SCM in June 1962, and Bruning in November 1962. "The Revolution in Office Copying, Part II," p. 89.

[16]The Revolution in Office Copying Part I, Chemical and Engineering News (July 13, 1964): 128, discusses the development of this process and sets the date of introduction as October 1963.

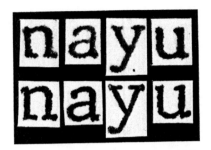

Figure 17.4. Typewriting reproduced by the dual spectrum process above is compared with the actual typewriting below. The slight damage to upper serif of the n, the lower right stroke of the a, the upper left serif of the y and u are sufficiently well reproduced in the dual spectrum copy to establish that the letter is defective even though the outline is not as sharp as it appeared in the original typing.

contact with a chemically treated copy sheet. The two are heated to about 100°C and the compound on the copy paper reacts with the undecomposed parts of the intermediate sheet to produce a final stable copy.[17] The final copy is permanent, records all colors, and is not affected by heat.

The special copy paper is manufactured by 3M and bears their pink or blue tulip mark on the reverse (noncoated) side. Thus the copies made by this process can be readily recognized. The copies record details rather well, so preliminary examinations can be made from them, provided the equipment is maintained in first-class condition.

Evaluation of Copies

All three modern methods produce within a few seconds positive dry copies that are fully satisfactory for reading purposes. If the copies are properly made directly from the original document, the examiner can generally carry out preliminary comparisons from them (Figure 17.4). The two electrostatic processes reproduce writing and drawings well, except for the weakness in the blue end of the spectrum. Many commercial copies tend to lose the lighter strokes. The present-day photocopying methods reproduce blue inks weaker, but dual spectrum copies record all colors more evenly. The transfer electrostatic process usually fails to record some ball point pen flaws and nib tracks in writing strokes. Copies on zinc oxide paper using liquid developers seem to record slightly finer details than those made by other methods.[18]

---

[17]"The Revolution in Office Copying, Part I," p. 128.
[18]Data derived from the author's testing of these copiers and reported on at the 1971 annual meeting of the American Society of Questioned Document Examiners.

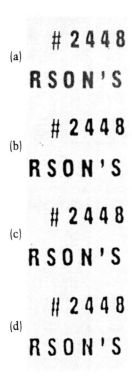

Figure 17.5. Repeated recopying of Xerox copies shows the gradual deterioration in the outline of printed characters from (a) the original to (d) the third copy. Note especially the # symbol, which shows slight breaks in the horizontal strokes in the third copy accompanied by the narrower outline of all characters.

From the document examiner's point of view good quality first-generation copies are usable for preliminary work. By "first generation" is meant copies made directly from the original. Recopying of any photocopy causes some loss of detail, often serious loss (Figure 17.5). In fact first-generation copies themselves can lose some detail, especially if prints are not carefully controlled. Many copying machines are designed to enlarge the copy slightly, about 1%. As a result, with certain types of examination in which accurate measurements need to be made (for example, in typewriting alignment problems), this imposes limitations on the document examiner's study.

Color Photocopying

Today Xerox and other companies are marketing photocopiers that reproduce color. These copiers reproduce a particular color by combining small toner particles of red, blue, and yellow. The black is a combination of these colors and all other nonprimary colors are a combination of two or three of the toners in varying intensity. Often when such a color is examined under magnification, halos of one primary color or another can be observed along the edge of a line. Under magnification, all colors appear as an accumulation of colored dots. The method is not ideal as yet, although the copy under direct viewing without magnification gives an approximation to the original color. As with color films, the reproduced color may not match the original exactly, but it does give a good idea of the colors involved in the original. However, at the present time, because of the shortcomings pointed out, there does not appear to be any particular advantage in copying a document for examination on a color-reproducing copier. In fact the dot problem is a serious disadvantage.

Earlier Reproduction Methods

Prior to the introduction of the current copying techniques several other methods had seen substantial use. Previously documents were copied by Photostat®, a photographic process that makes a negative copy on paper. It was not the type of equipment that any except large business organizations would purchase, and most copies were made by commercial firms specializing in copying documents. Until the late

Figure 17.6 The upper two signatures and typewriting were prepared by the diffusion transfer process and are typical of results that were often encountered with these copies. The lower signature was photographed from an original document. The loss of detail in the upper copy compared to the lower one occurred in even the better copies made by these methods. The reproductions are of three different documents encountered in a case problem. The very poor copy in the center shows the results of a poorly maintained copier and solutions.

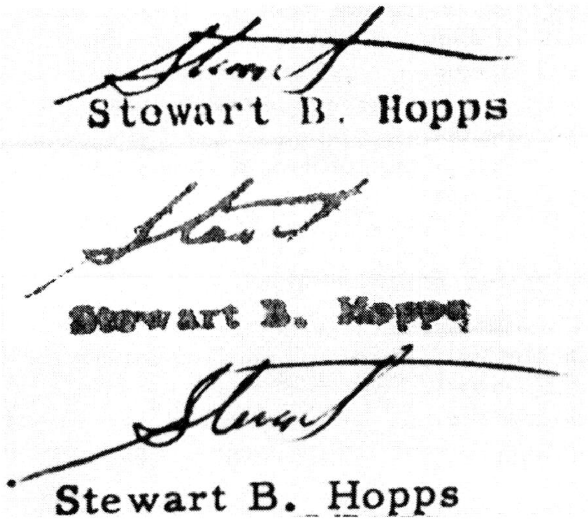

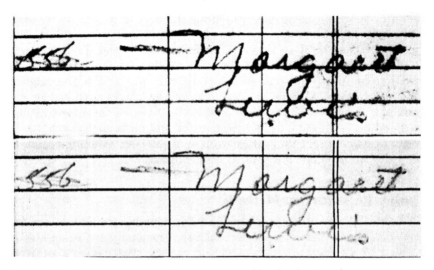

Figure 17.7. The upper reproduction was prepared by the dye transfer process and is compared with a positive Photostat, that is, the second Photostatic copy. The upper copy had been made from this Photostatic copy. The combination of the recopying and the inherent defects of the copying process produced the loss of detail in the e of "Margaret" and the final s of "Lewis" in the upper copy.

1940s only partially successful substitutes were available for smaller businesses. They were reflex devices using special photocopying paper and generally producing rather poor-quality copies.

During the 1950s three methods were developed for office copying: the diffusion transfer process, a gelatin transfer process (Verifax), and the thermographic process.[19] All were introduced at a time when Photostats were the most common and widely used photocopies, and all used a compact machine suitable for use in the small office or business. All three processes produced copies that in the eyes of the document examiner are inferior both to Photostats and to present-day methods (Figure 17.6).

Diffusion Transfer Process

Two different sheets are needed for a copy made by the diffusion transfer process. The first contains a light-sensitive silver halide emulsion and is exposed by means of reflex photography, that is, light passed through the sensitized paper and reflected back by the copy as it is held in tight contact with the negative paper. The reflected light exposes

---

[19]These methods are discussed in greater detail in "The Revolution in Office Copying, Part I."

the negative sheet, which is then separated from the original and placed face to face against the positive sheet. The two are immersed in a developing solution. In this solution, the unexposed silver halide is transferred to the second sheet and converted into metallic silver to create a positive copy. The positive copy is rolled virtually dry so that it comes out of the machine only slightly damp and must be air dried (Figure 17.7).

Gelatin Transfer Process

The Verifax method, developed by Eastman Kodak, is also a reflex copying technique. The light sensitive (silver halide) sheet or matrix contains an unhardened gelatin and a series of chemicals. After exposure, the matrix is immersed in a developing solution, which hardens the gelatin of the exposed areas while the remaining gelatin is unhardened. The unhardened gelatin combines with a dye, which can be transferred onto a second sheet to form the positive reproduction. With the gradual development of the remaining silver halides a permanent copy is obtained. Several positives can be made from a single matrix.

Again the copy is not absolutely sharp in the eyes of the document examiner and consequently is far from ideal. Nevertheless, good copies allow preliminary work and opinions. The process was designed to produce a quick readable copy, which, when handled properly, it did.

Thermographic Process

In 1950 the 3M Thermo-Fax copier produced the first dry copy. It is an infrared or heat process requiring specially treated paper. Again the method involves a reflex technique for exposing the document. Any material on the original document that absorbs infrared radiation, such as pencil, typewriting, and printer's ink, develops heat that is radiated causing the treated paper to form a colored compound in the area corresponding to the writing on the paper. A positive copy of the original is thus produced.

Thermo-Fax has certain serious limitations. Many colored inks cannot be copied simply because they do not absorb infrared (Figure 17.8). One cannot tell by inspection which fluid and ball pen inks will copy and which will not. Furthermore, the copies deteriorate with age, rapidly if they are exposed to excessive heat, darkening and becoming brittle. These problems ultimately lead to the development of the 3M dual spectrum process, which can copy all inks and whose copies do not deteriorate rapidly.[20]

---

[20]See "The Revolution in Office Copying, Part I."

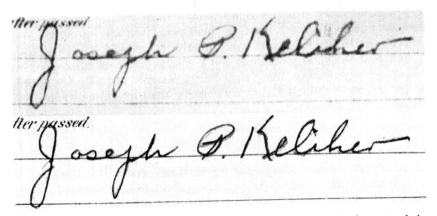

Figure 17.8. The poor quality of the signature in the upper copy, which was made by the thermographic process, strongly suggested that the signature was a forgery. The lower copy is a photograph of the original signature, which shows a genuine signature with a pencil outline along the strokes. The pencil stroke can be seen especially in the left-hand side of the P. The ink of the signature did not absorb infrared radiation and would not copy with the thermographic process. The salesman had suggested to the secretary that she trace the outline with pencil to make the copy which she admitted she had. This defect of the method lead to the development of the dual spectrum method and a superior copying process.

Photostats

Photostating was a common commercial method of reproducing documents prior to the introduction of Xerox and other electrostatic copiers. It involves a single step—the preparation of a negative (white on black) reproduction directly on a special light-sensitive paper. (A positive, black on white, Photostat, consisting of a photostatic copy of this negative, can be prepared, but this copy does not offer any advantage over the negative, and in fact intensifies the defects of the process.)

Photostatic copies are prepared with a specially designed camera, bearing the trade name Photostat. It is constructed for the rapid and automatic copying of documents directly on light-sensitive paper.[21] The image is developed in chemical solutions in the same manner as a photographic negative or print.

Among commercial copying methods Photostats gave superior results for technical examinations and for general usage. Many older

---

[21]The basic construction of a Photostat camera is the same as any other camera; i.e., it consists of a lens and shutter system which forms the opening to a light-tight box in which the photographic material is housed. However, the Photostat camera's lens system consists of both the usual lens and a reversing prism, the latter being necessary to invert the writing so that it runs from left to right in the negative (white on black) copy.

courthouse records were made by this process and when properly made recorded details well. Furthermore, they have remained in good condition for years. The method is not entirely free, however, from undesirable defects. Nevertheless, widespread preliminary studies can be and have been made from such copies, and with high-quality Photostats rather extensive work is possible. But the findings must be accepted as qualified, for they are always predicated on the assumption that the Photostats are good reproductions of the original, an assumption that may not be entirely valid.

Photostats are not entirely suitable for document examination because of certain inherent loss of detail that results from two factors, contrast and grain size. Photostatic papers have been developed for preparing clear, readable copies and for the most part tend toward high contrast. These papers were commonly used by many shops, so many document Photostats have too great contrast. Some papers have a rel-

Figure 17.9. The top section is an accurate photograph of a portion of a typewritten document in which parts of defective letters print very weakly. Note particularly the bottom of the A, a, and g.

The center section is a positive Photostat of the same document. This positive copy is actually the second Photostat, a copy of the first (negative) Photostat. Comparison of the two reproductions reveals a loss of details in the letters cited.

The bottom section is the fourth Photostatic copying of the document prepared by Photostating the copy above to create a negative and then re-Photostating this third copy. A very great loss of detail has occurred.

This kind of reduction in detail is found to some extent in all types of commercial recopying of a previous photocopy regardless of the method employed.

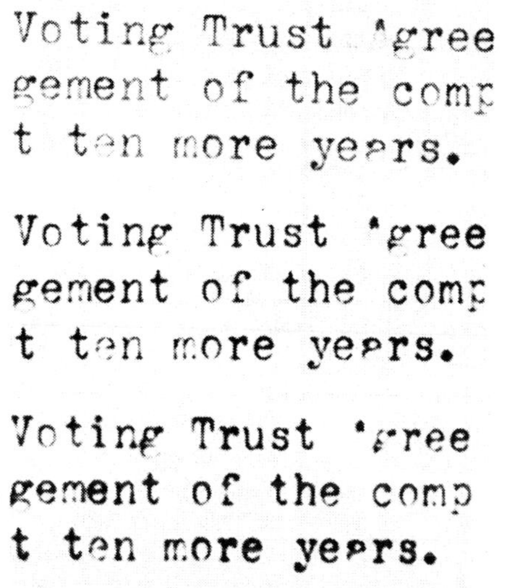

Voting Trust 'gree
gement of the comp
t ten more years.

Voting Trust 'gree
gement of the comp
t ten more years.

Voting Trust 'free
gement of the comp
t ten more years.

atively large grain size and low resolving power, which seriously restricts examination under magnification. When the image is examined under moderate magnification it lacks sharpness and clarity and discloses little more than can be seen with normal vision. Because of these conditions, a Photostat may not always permit an exhaustive examination. These restrictions of course are true today with contemporary copying systems.

Photostats have several additional minor disadvantages. While both enlarged and reduced copies can be prepared from the original or a Photostat of it, the best and actually only satisfactory ones are made directly from the original. With Photostats there is no negative transparency, as there is with photographs, from which a series of high-fidelity prints can be made. When additional copies are needed either the first photostat must be rephotostated, which always gives an inferior print (Figure 17.9) or the original document must be available to copy again. Many photostatic papers are not fully color sensitive and do not reproduce all colors in their proper tones of gray. If a document contains red or green ink or stamp impressions, papers that correctly record these colors must be used.[22]

Reflex Copies

The photostat camera was an elaborate and costly apparatus for a business establishment that had only a limited amount of copy work. Still there was a decided convenience in being able to copy the document in the office. The reflex method certainly filled this need with lower capital investment. It required a simple, inexpensive apparatus consisting essentially of a photographic printing box, i.e., a diffused light source beneath a glass surface.[23] To copy a document with this equipment the reflex paper[24] and document were laid one over the other and held in tight contact on the glass top during the exposure.

While reflex copies are readable, they are of a much lower quality

---

[22]Photostatic papers are supplied with different emulsion characteristics and surface texture. Some are only blue-sensitive while others are sensitized for the entire visible spectrum. Furthermore, papers of different contrast ranges can be obtained. Lower-contrast papers generally give better Photostats for technical study. Smoother surface papers likewise are more suitable.

[23]Several companies supplied reflex equipment that varied in complexity and basic design. Most of these were flat surface printing boxes, some of the more complex of which have automatic timing and exposure devices. At least one company built a printer in the form of a glass cylinder surrounding the light source.

For several years prior to World War II a phosphorescent plate device (Photoflor) was sold for making reflex copies. This booklike plate was charged by exposing to an ordinary light bulb for 15–20 sec before the reflex paper and documents were inserted in it for exposure.

[24]The most common type of photosensitive reflex material has characteristics very similar to Photostat paper. The emulsion consists of light-sensitive silver salts (silver halides), and development requires a series of solutions comparable to those used for photographic and Photostatic papers.

than Photostats. This results directly from their method of preparation.
In exposing the sensitized paper the light must pass through either the
reflex paper or the document, depending on the particular arrangement
used. The paper diffuses the light so that the image is less sharply
defined in the final copy than if a lens system had been used. When
the original contains writing on both sides, it is necessary to recopy
the first print to obtain a readable copy, and the defects are correspondingly intensified.[25] In either instance, with reflex copies the writing
strokes take on a slightly blurred appearance when viewed critically
with the naked eye and are certainly of little value for examination
under magnification.

It hardly seems necessary to point out that all of the defects of a
Photostat are encountered with reflex copies. Obviously, neither enlarged nor reduced copies can be prepared by this method. Fortunately,
today few such copies are apt to be found in old files or archives.

Other Methods

The methods of reproducing documents that have been described represent the ones commonly used to copy documents for technical examination as well as for general business purposes. Others, however,
have been developed for specific work but might be employed to copy
a disputed document. They include diazo prints, blueprints, photoengraving processes, tracings, and a now practically obsolete technique
of letterpress copy.

Diazo Prints

Within the last 40 or 50 years a simplified method for making direct
positive copies of line drawings has been introduced commercially in
this country. It is known as the diazo process. Two competing methods
have been available since the method was first introduced. Both employ
a special light-sensitive paper. With one method the exposed sheet is
developed by means of ammonia fumes; with the other development

---

[25]If the document contains writing on only one side, it is placed below the reflex paper with the
face of the document in contact with the glass top of the light box and the emulsion side of the
reflex paper against the back of the document. The light then passes through the document to expose
the paper. On the other hand, if the document contains writing on both sides, it is necessary to make
first a reversed negative copy and a readable positive from this. In this case, the reflex paper is laid
immediately on top of the light box, emulsion side up, in contact with the side of the document to
be copied. In exposing, the light passes through the reflex paper, and some is reflected from the face
of the document and brings about the exposure. In a copy made in this manner the writing is reversed,
running from right to left. Therefore, after the print is developed and dried, it must be recopied to
obtain a readable print with the writing running from left to right. Quality of the positive print is
inferior to the original negative copy.

is accomplished by moistening the sheet with a complex chemical solution.[26] Through a single exposure and development step, the final black on white positive print is produced without any intermediate negative.[27] More recently, a thermal diazo process was commercially introduced which eliminates the problems of solution maintenance and ammonia odors.[28] Because of the dry or semidry developing process and the direct positive printing, the time involved from the exposure to the finished print is measured in seconds, and the unit cost of the prints is low. Its primary field of application is the reproduction of drafting, architectural, and engineering drawings, but office record systems using thin, translucent paper stock lend themselves to copying with this equipment. Documents written on standard-weight writing and typewriting papers do not reproduce very well.

Printing machines are designed to make the exposure by a contact process, not unlike reflex printing.[29] The sensitized paper is automatically held tightly against the original document. The light must pass through the latter in order to expose the sensitized emulsion. After development those portions of the diazo paper that were shielded from the light by inked or penciled lines develop black while the remainder of the sheet is a clear white. The development is accomplished in a single step, and no fixing agent is required. With ammonia-developing machines the print is dry and immediately ready for use. When liquid developer is used the print is only slightly moistened as it passes between the developing rollers and is immediately fed through a drying chamber. With either method finished prints are ready in less than 2 minutes.

Although the diazo process has the advantages of speed and low cost, it was not intended to prepare copies for document examination. The high contrast of the paper is excellent for reproduction of line drawings, for which it was designed, but of course is objectionable in questioned document problems. Furthermore, the emulsion characteristics are similar to those of blue-sensitive films or Photostatic papers; i.e., all

---

[26]The Ozalid Products, Division of General Aniline and Film Corp., Johnson City, New York, is the principal manufacturer of the ammonia-developer equipment, but there are other suppliers. The dry-development process is especially advantageous, but the disposal of the ammonia fumes becomes a problem with these machines.

The Charles Bruning Co., Inc., Chicago, Illinois, introduced the liquid-developing machine. In order to overcome the loss of time due to print drying, each unit has a drying chamber built into it, through which the print passes in a few seconds and is ejected dry.

[27]Paper is also available for dry developing machines in which the lines are blue, maroon, and sepia on the white background. With the moist development method, modification of the developer achieves the same results. Further technical discussion of the paper and its coating appears in *Specialty Papers*, (R. H. Mosher, ed.) (Brooklyn: Remsen, 1950), pp. 231–236.

[28]General Aniline and Film Corp. introduced the first thermal diazo unit in 1964.

[29]Each manufacturer produces several models of his machine. They are specifically designed for different kinds and volumes of work. Readers interested in details of construction are referred to manufacturer's data sheets and publications.

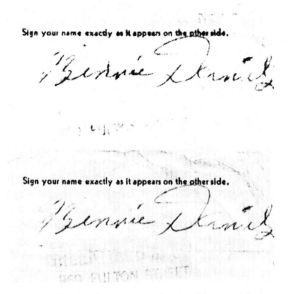

Figure 17.10. The same check is copied by the diazo process (top) and by careful photographing (below). The signature was lightly written ball point pen writing, and the stamp impression below was a weakly inked red imprint on green ribbed check paper.

Comparison of the two copies reveals that the fine lines of the signature are better retained in the photograph. The horizontal ending stroke below the top of the D is a good example. The paper background and the weak first line of the stamp impression are also lost in the diazo copy.

colors are not reproduced in their proper relationship as tones of gray. Instead, colors other than blue are recorded similar to black. Loss of detail is encountered with the reflex printing process. The sharpest line reproduction is obtained from drawings on translucent tracing paper, seldom the base for a disputed document, while the light diffusion caused by the texture of standard writing papers hides important details (Figure 17.10). As with reflex copies enlarged or reduced scale reproductions are not possible. In the case of the equipment of several manufacturers, the original document must not have writing on both sides. These restrictions do not recommend the method for copying disputed documents.

Blueprints

Blueprinting is an older, more established method than diazo prints of reproducing line drawings, but the same defects are present when the prints are used for document examination. They are of high contrast.

With this method the final copy consists of white lines against the blue background, and the strokes contain virtually no detail. Copies are made by contact exposure so that standard weight writing papers do not give satisfactory results. At best, therefore, blueprinting is a makeshift substitute for either photographing or other photocopying of an important document.

Tracings

Reproductions of handwriting in the form of handmade tracings may be an aid to criminal investigators, but are virtually valueless copies for identifying the writer. At best only the most qualified opinion can be rendered from them, while more often no identification is possible at all.

The usual and most satisfactory method of preparing a tracing is to cover the document with a thin paper and to follow as accurately as possible the writing outline. These copies differ in character little, if at all, from traced forgeries. They are only a slowly drawn outline of the writing, and their value varies with the skill of the individual tracer. Obviously, an opinion rendered must be based almost exclusively on the letter forms, and most likely they are not accurately reproduced.

Tracings have a second serious fault. In virtually every instance, a document that has been traced contains indentations corresponding to the traced copy. These indentations may seriously damage the document, especially in cases of suspected forgery, and consequently may be a handicap in subsequent studies. For this reason, tracings should never be made from important evidence.

In criminal investigations, however, tracings can be used to some advantage, particularly when mail or other written communications have been intercepted. Then in order not to arouse suspicion by retaining these documents for long, tracings can be quickly prepared and the document released. However, if identification of the intercepted writing is to be attempted, other types of reproductions, such as photographs or photocopies, should be made.[30]

---

[30]Various types of portable photographic cameras have been designed for field work. A useful, commercially made camera for photographing signatures is the Eastman Fingerprint Camera, a fixed-focus, 2½ × 3½ cut film camera, which contains a battery-powered built-in light source. (Details and specifications are to be found in Eastman Kodak Co. catalogs.) Highly mobile, it enables the investigator to prepare natural-size negatives of good quality. Some members of the American Society of Questioned Document Examiners have an improved design fixed-focus camera, developed by Elbridge W. Stein, which enlarges on a 5 × 7 film and employs a built-in 110-volt bank of lights. Photographs made with this kind of camera should be employed instead of tracings.

With photocopying machines readily available in many offices and public record rooms, it is relatively easy to photocopy rather than trace writing.

Photograving and Related Processes

Photomechanical engraving processes fall into three categories —photoengravings, photogravures or intaglios, and photolithographs or offset printing—depending on how the printing plate is prepared.[31]

Two classes of reproductions can be used with these processes: halftones, which give the optical illusion of a continuous tone picture, such as reproduction of a portrait or landscape; and linecuts, which consist entirely of solid, continuous lines, such as a line graph. Both halftones and linecuts have valuable applications, but not for the reproduction of material to be subjected to questioned document examinations.

These photomechanical engraving methods have been specifically developed to reproduce photographs and documents as illustrations in books, periodicals, and newspapers. No one would use them for making a record copy of a document since the cuts are costly and require a great deal of time to prepare. Nevertheless, occasionally handwriting or typewriting reproduced in this way may represent the only available known specimen. Photoengravings and photolithographs as a general rule are prepared from photographs, so that in these instances every effort should be made to locate either the original document or the photograph from which the cut was prepared. If neither can be procured, however, limited findings sometimes may be derived from the printed reproduction.

While line reproductions given an accurate outline of the letter forms with, of course, some indication of the width of the pen stroke and possibly the variation in pressure, they completely obscure such details as the finer tones of shading, nib tracks of the pen, retouchings, and ball point pen defects. There is also a tendency for these reproductions to completely lose all the lighter, hairline portions of the writing. Consequently, they have very limited value in a technical examination.

Halftones show more of the details of a document than linecuts, especially in the writing strokes. (All the specimens of writing in this book are halftones.) Variations in tone are achieved by employing a screen in the preparation of the plate to break the printing surface up

---

[31]Photoengravings, photolithographs or offset, and photogravures represent three distinct reproduction methods used in the printing trade. Photoengraving is a relief process in which the image is etched on the plate surface with the portions that are to print raised above the rest of the plate. In the case of photogravure or intaglio, the plate surface is etched in the reverse manner with the areas that are to print depressed. Lithographic or offset plates have no relief effect; instead the surfaces are treated so that the portions that are to print pick up the ink while the rest of the plate does not. The three processes are fully discussed by Charles W. Hackleman, *Commercial Engraving and Printing* (Indianapolis: Commercial Engraving Publishing Co., 1924), pp. 217–230, 242–275, 483–519, and 566–573.

into a number of small squares or dots of various sizes and shapes.[32] Instead of the writing stroke being a continuous line, it is actually discontinuous, made up of a series of small dots. The effect to the eye is a line of varying intensity and shading, but with the use of a low-power magnifier, the actual makeup becomes apparent even when a fine screen is used. This curtailment on the use of magnification is a serious limiting factor in document examination.

One of the more common problems in which published copies serve as standards involves the proof of writing of famous persons long since dead. Often this writing comes from an old book containing reproductions of letters or signatures. These older facsimiles are inferior to modern cuts since prior to about 1900 they were made by hand rather than by modern photographic methods. Thus, despite skillful workmanship, these reproductions were less accurate than modern photomechanically made illustrations.

Analysis of Photocopies

The document examiner can make certain examinations of good quality photocopies. In virtually all instances the somewhat defective methods common during the 1950s have been discarded. These methods, Verifax, diffusion transfer, and Thermo-Fax, limited the document examiners work significantly and more so than the better-quality present-day copies or good Photostats. Current photocopying techniques do not record the same degree of detail as properly made photographs, but the examiner can often reach a reasonably accurate conclusion from them.

Not all questions can be answered from a reproduction. However, general handwriting can often be tentatively and sometimes be positively identified. This condition also holds for signatures. These examinations many times lead to conclusions that are consistent with those reached after a review of the original documents, which should reveal greater detail. Photocopies of skillful forgeries can hide subtle defects, although in all probability some suspicious details will be inferred or recognized after careful study. A properly made photocopy of an average or poor-quality forged signature certainly contains typical flaws. Typewriting identifications can be undertaken, but as has been pointed out, if the reproduction is not exactly to scale, they may be significantly restricted when alignment factors are controlling. There

---

[32]The screen is a transparent plate cross-ruled with a series of fine opaque lines. Not all screens have the same number of lines per inch. A finer ruled screen, i.e., one with a greater number of lines per inch, has the advantage of increasing the detail in the finished printing. The type of paper used for printing, the intended use of the cut, and the cost are contributing factors in the selections of the screen size.

are problems in which initially only photocopies can be submitted. A document examiner consequently may need to express a tentative opinion from them despite the fact that he would prefer to make his study from the original documents.

The problems discussed are those most likely to be answered from photocopies. Others cannot. An actual erasure may not be recognized in some photocopies since certain types of flaws such as disturbed paper background are obscured. Differentiation between inks and writing instruments and determination of the sequence of strokes require examination of the original document. Of course proper paper examinations cannot be made, and there are other questions requiring the study of the original documents to reach any opinion.

Only the best photocopies, carefully made directly from the original document, allow accurate preliminary opinions. The second-generation photocopy, that is, a photocopy of a previous copy, can be very restrictive. Each subsequent recopying leads to a less valuable reproduction. One should inspect a copy to be submitted to a document examiner for study to assure that fine details are recorded. Those which cannot be seen in the photocopy cannot subsequently be made visible on the copy by any techniques available to the examiner. The only way to retrieve these lost details is to recopy the original document more carefully.

Should experts work from photocopies? It is debatable. Some workers refuse to examine all copies, but the practical examiner recognizes that it is necessary to rely on copies at times. There are problems in which the original can no longer be found. Certain questions still require some answers. He must reserve the right, of course, to inspect the copies and to reject those that in his judgment are inadequate. He may need to qualify his findings if after a study of the reproductions he should find key elements less clear that they originally appeared. The person who submits the problem must also recognize that not every questioned document examined from the original can necessarily be answered without qualification; qualified answers from somewhat restrictive photocopies must also be expected.

Fraudulent Photocopies

With the widespread use of photocopies, one can expect an occasional copy to have been manipulated in some way or other. Fraudulent photocopies are relatively rare, but they may be encountered in both criminal and civil problems. Their exposure combines thorough field investigation and careful study by the document examiner.

When there is any question concerning a photocopy, the obvious step is to compare it with the original material. However, circumstances may dictate that the document is not readily available or that it

386

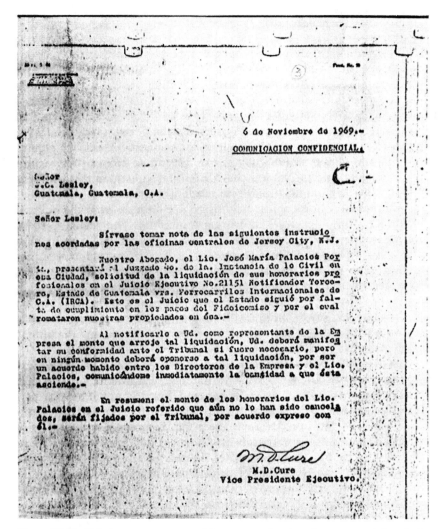

Figure 17.11. This letter was presented for an examination of a suspected forged signature. Comparison of the signature with known samples revealed that it was authentic, but study of the photocopy itself established the fraud. Note the double row of fingers along the top of the letter. They indicate that there had been a recopying of a previous photocopy, and the fact that the lower row has narrower spacing, together with the fingers, shows that an early model Xerox reducing copier had been employed to make one copy. Proof of the forgery appears in Figure 17.12.

has been reported lost. Under such circumstances it becomes necessary to subject the photocopy to technical study.

A number of photocopies are challenged because one of the parties involved denies any knowledge of it. Such denials, like signature denials, may or may not be accurate. Certain photocopies are questioned because no one except the party producing it had any knowledge of its existence. It may be claimed that a copy was made because of concern that the original might be lost. The original may have formerly seemed of no special value, whereas since the controversy has arisen, the copy is badly needed. Some photocopies are of documents that have little evidence to support them. Others, despite their obscure background, form sorely needed key evidence. A number of questioned photocopies, despite their suspect background, turn out to be authentic, but some definitely are not.

Modern photocopies may be more easily manipulated than were Photostats. Assembling an original by cutting and pasting was for years the normal way to manufacture the "original." It is still done, but parts of modern photocopies can be erased or covered up, others sections added by reexposing the copy, and careful recopying may eliminate shadow lines and other evidence of manipulation. These properties of photocopies may make proof of fraud difficult if all evidence of manipulation is virtually eliminated.

There are a number of factors in manipulated copies, nevertheless, that assist the examiner in establishing their lack of genuineness. A determination of whether a suspected photocopy is authentic or fraudulent, however, can require extensive study. It is unusual to find ob-

Figure 17.12. The typewriting below the signature has been placed adjacent to the typewriting of the body of the letter (a portion of the last three lines). The 26 typewriting spaces required to complete "Vice Presidente Ejecutivo." correspond to 28 spaces in the typewriting of the body of the letter. In other words, this establishes that the typewriting was not continuous, but that the signature and its typewriting had been superimposed on that of the letter.

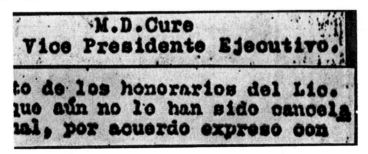

vious evidence, even evidence that is relatively obvious to the experienced examiner, in a suspected photocopy. Detailed study, careful measurements, and extensive comparison of various parts of the copy are usually needed to reveal flaws and to evaluate suspected elements.

Manipulation can be exposed by a number of small details. Background flaws around some parts of the writing, improper alignment of typewriting or printing, evidence of several recopyings (Figure 17.11), manipulation by a machine or model that had not been introduced when the copy was made, slight differences in the enlargement or printing quality of parts of the copy, or the presence of stray markings or fragments of letters must be considered (Figure 17.12). When they are detected and properly evaluated the proof of fraud can be strong. In some cases there is also other nontechnical evidence that raises serious questions about the photocopy and supplements the technical proof. While such combinations of evidence form ideal proof, there have been cases decided on the testimony and demonstration of the document examiner alone.[33]

When there is a question about a photocopy, one should seek competent expert assistance promptly. These examinations take time, may require additional field investigation or interrogation of witnesses under oath, and in a certain number of cases fail to reveal evidence to support a claim of fraud. In the latter cases it may be necessary to make significant changes in trial strategy. Furthermore, if the photocopy is fraudulent, early examination means that the document examiner has adequate time to prepare proper demonstration of his findings for trial.

---

[33]For additional technical details on this problem see O. Hilton, "Detecting Fraudulent Photocopies," *Forensic Science International* 13 (1979): 117–123.

THE DOCUMENT PROBLEM GOES TO COURT

When it is impossible to settle amicably a dispute arising from a questioned document, it becomes necessary to present the evidence to a court or jury for decision. This aspect of a document problem is obviously an important one. Now it is necessary to set forth the findings of the laboratory in a form that can be understood by the "man on the street"—the person in the jury box. Not only must the opinion be given, but the factors on which it is based must also be detailed. This task is not always simple. Careful pretrial preparation is necessary to assure an effective presentation. But when document testimony is given correctly, each juror gains the feeling of having reached the opinion independently. Then a verdict consistent with the facts is a reasonable expectation.

Effective presentation of this nature does not just happen. It depends on thorough and adequate work in arriving at the original opinion. It likewise depends on coordinated pretrial preparation by both the document examiner-witness and the attorney so that the document testimony is forceful and clear. The attorney must therefore understand the technical phase of the case; must know the special problems that can arise, how the testimony is to unfold, what points really control the opinion; and must give special attention to how he can best assist the witness during direct, cross-, and redirect examination.

18

Preparation for Trial

A very important step toward winning a case involving a favorable questioned document opinion is the preparation for trial. That this step is not only necessary but also involves extensive work may come as a surprise to attorneys who have never tried a case of this kind. For the most part, a document report states an opinion together with a short summary of the pertinent facts upon which it is based. It may not be illustrated, certainly not fully, nor are the supporting reasons necessarily discussed in detail. But when the matter is heard in court, the discussion must be complete so that those who decide the case will understand and appreciate the basis for the document examiner's opinion. To do this well means that both the document examiner and the attorney must be thoroughly prepared.

The Document Examiner's Preparation

The document examiner's preparation starts with a comprehensive review of the entire problem. Aided by his working notes and report he must organize the mass of details that his study has revealed into the coherent description that he, as a witness, will present in court. Virtually every document case should be illustrated to make the testimony clearer and more effective. Illustrations that are to accomplish this require planning and may involve long hours of highly specialized work. These are the essential steps in his preparation for trial and should precede the final pretrial conference with his attorney.

Organization of the Facts

Not all facts disclosed by the examination of a document pertain to the questions at hand. Even those that are pertinent will vary in their degree of importance. Questioned document testimony without organization has little value. Unorganized testimony wastes the court's time and fails to support the truth effectively. Therefore, the examiner must carefully review all the facts disclosed by his examination, eliminating those that have little or no bearing on the problem, evaluating and grouping the others so that his testimony can relate them in an orderly and convincing manner. This apparently simple task may actually require going over the problem several times and coming back to it on different days. Thus, the task of organization is a necessary step, often entailing a substantial amount of time.

Photographic Preparation

An important part of the preparation is the designing and making of photographic court exhibits. Photography is one of the examiner's most useful tools. It has already been shown how the camera helps to discover hidden facts; it also serves to organize and simplify the court presentation. Court exhibits, correctly made, increase the effectiveness of testimony by bringing related elements of the disputed and admitted documents together for easy comparison. In so doing they also reduce the time and effort expended by the court and jury. In simpler problems well-designed exhibits may virtually testify by themselves.

A good court exhibit does not just ornament the case; it tells a story. By means of photography it is possible to cut out pertinent parts of handwriting or typewriting, enlarge them, and place them beside material from other documents with which they are to be compared. For example, signatures from a series of documents can be put together and enlarged to show details (Figure 18.1); or typewriting from one

Figure 18.1. The signature at the top of this court exhibit had been denied by Morris. The document transferred stock in a family-owned company. The three lower signatures were admitted authentic signatures. While the second signature was not denied, Morris had refused to state that it was his, even though it appeared on his stock certificate. It was desirable to establish that it too was his. The exhibit used in the trial also contained a second section with five additional genuine signatures. All established that the denied signature was in fact the signature of Joseph J. Morris.

This arrangement of signatures allowed the witness to point out to the jury and court the strong similarity in its executions—a freely written, clear signature. He could with the enlargement of two diameters in the court exhibit call attention not only to the general design of the signatures, but to details as well. With illustrations of this type testimony becomes a demonstration, not just an opinion.

393

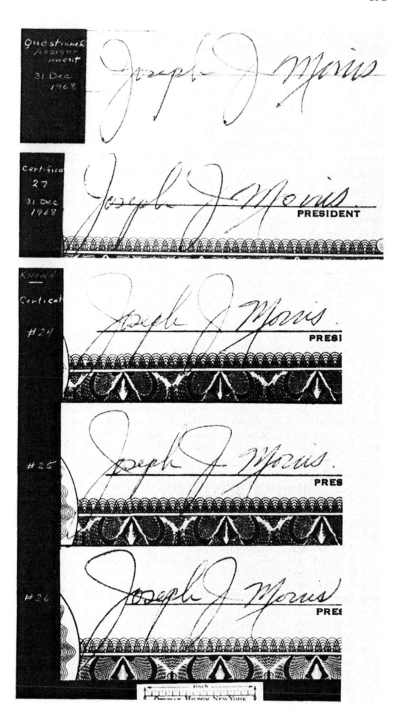

document can be put next to similar combinations of letters from a second to make differences or points of similarity more apparent (See Figures 11.20 and 11.21). This class of exhibit may be referred to as *comparison exhibits.*

A second class can be termed *fact-revealing exhibits.* They include many kinds of photographs. Skillfully made enlargements, or photomicrographs, show details of line crossings, patched strokes, suspicious disturbances of paper fibers, or other pertinent details of a document. Ultraviolet, reflected infrared, and infrared luminescence photographs disclose erased material. Color photographs are especially useful in illustrating differences in inks and other colored writing materials. With photographs the document examiner can disclose facts that his eye is trained to recognize or those that could otherwise be shown only with instruments whose use would be unfamiliar to many in the courtroom (Figure 18.2).

Figure 18.2. This fact-revealing exhibit shows the court exactly what the examiner saw as he studied the typewriting alignment under the test plate. The purpose was to demonstrate that the typewriting and underscores were all placed on the paper in one continuous typewriting. He was able to determine from other studies that both writers had signed after the underscore lines were on the document.

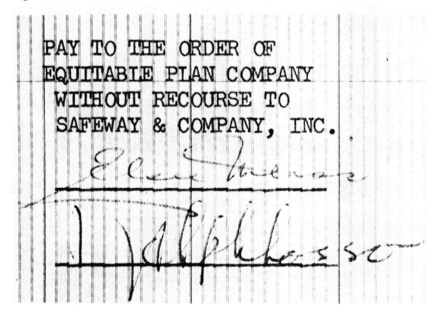

Comparison Exhibits

The factors that must be kept in mind for proper design of comparison exhibits are selection of material, arrangement, degree of enlargement, and simplification of the exhibit. What is made a part of the exhibit may influence its value and establish whether it is a true sample of material from which it was taken. Arrangement must be both functional and, in some measure, artistic. The degree of enlargement must be suitable for the problem at hand, and in order to simplify the exhibit, extraneous and unnecessary matter should be eliminated. Since these points are fundamental to correct comparison exhibits, it is well that they be dealt with more fully.

There must be a critical selection of the material that goes into a court exhibit. Actually, only with signature problems in which there are a small number of known signatures can all the material examined be included. In all other questions this plan is impractical.

Selection must achieve two ends: it must ensure, first, that the exhibit accurately presents those elements of the standards that control the identification, and second, that it forms part of an effective presentation. No scientific examiner would select only chance variations to establish nonidentity of two specimens when the fundamental points of identification stamp them as originating at a single source. But there is always the need to guard against slight bias. What is selected must represent fairly and truthfully the whole from which it was taken. On the other hand, the illustration can properly be restricted to the most significant points in the identification. Naturally, it cannot contain all points, so that as long as what has been omitted would not bring about a modification of the conclusions, the selection is justified. Court exhibits should tell a clear and concise story, and each element of them should be chosen with this end in view.

In arranging the parts of a comparison exhibit, its functional aspects should be the foremost consideration. It should be designed to bring close together the details to be compared so that the untrained observer can easily see the similarities or differences. Related elements are usually set in horizontal lines, for the human eye compares objects with greater ease when so arranged. Comparisons are also facilitated by bringing the elements near to one another. Thus, often with a signature exhibit, where its length must be considered, the horizontal array is discarded in favor of a vertical arrangement. This procedure puts the corresponding writing habits immediately adjacent. Even these may be improved by appending extra prints of the disputed signature at intervals alongside the standards. Repeated presentation of the disputed signature, clearly marked as such, is both correct and effective.

The exact physical arrangement is dictated by the particular problem. A traditional arrangement is the two-column exhibit with the known material on the left and the unknown on the right. Each line contains the units to be compared, and the paired items in the two columns are placed in proximity. It is far more important to set words and letters near together than it is to maintain a symmetrical pattern, and the order of the material should be consistent with the desired emphasis. An excellent variation on this two-column scheme is a three-column arrangement; the central section contains the disputed material, and the two outside ones, the known matter. This design is particularly useful when the known material contains a number of examples that can be compared favorably with the disputed, or when the questioned words are relatively long. In the latter case, writing habits occurring in the first part of the word can be compared with material in the left column, while those toward the end are related to the material in the right column. Occasionally, need dictates the use of a multiple-column display. With typewriting problems especially, these latter two arrangements permit the use of known typewriting from different dates and are especially useful in establishing the date of a typewritten document.

Whether comparison exhibits should be made up of words, sections of words, or single letters often depends on the problem at hand. Unique letter designs may suggest a comparison of a series of single letters. Handwriting identification normally involves consideration of movement, so that words and the larger segments of words illustrate movement as well as form, slant, interruptions, and connections among other identifying characteristics. Typewriting and handwriting are not necessarily illustrated in the same way. Damaged typefaces may be best handled with letter-by-letter comparison, but alignment defects often stand out best when several letters are combined or whole words are used. One cannot say that any particular choice is always the best or incorrect or improper.

Simplicity of arrangement is a goal that is not always easy to achieve, and often compromises must be made. A very simple exhibit consists of a single known and unknown example of each letter displayed individually. Examiners using color-slide projections may lean toward such a presentation. Yet this scheme may not be the best in many handwriting presentations, for important parts of the identification rest on continuity of the writing, how connections are made, and the proper consideration of natural writing variations. A more complex exhibit is required to illustrate these factors. A serious fault of many court exhibits, however, is a too complex arrangement resulting from the use of too much material. Thus, it is well to review every completed exhibit to see whether it could or should be simplified.

Artistic considerations in the design of court exhibits are most likely to be neglected. Balance and the pleasing appearance of any illustration attracts and helps to hold the observer's attention, certainly a worthy feature of every court exhibit.

The degree of enlargement is important and depends to some extent on the problem. Typewriting, for example, should be presented at a slightly greater degree of enlargement than that used for handwriting, but with either class of problem, each particular question leads to the selection of the proper degree of enlargement. The general rule to keep in mind is that too much enlargement may overemphasize unimportant details and minor variations, whereas too little makes it difficult for the layman to appreciate many identifying elements.

Court exhibits must emphasize important details, and all extraneous, distracting matter should be eliminated. With cutout exhibits, those made up of letters or words cut from the known and disputed matter, all other writing or typewriting than that to be compared can be cut away. It may mean that the cutouts are irregular in shape, but this is certainly better than having fragments of the words with which we are not concerned appearing in the exhibit.

Photographic illustrations must reproduce the writing or typewriting with clarity. The negatives and prints cannot have too much contrast or they will hide details; they cannot be too flat or they will obscure the finer identification points. The enlargement must be chosen to show clearly the small but significant elements, but not so large as to overemphasize many of the smaller details that do not have a definite bearing on the identification. Paper background and gradation of tones should appear in the photographs. In short, a court exhibit must be high-grade photography, accurately reproducing the original documents exactly as they are except for the enlargement factor and for being monochrome, in many instances, rather than color reproductions.

When color slides are used for court presentation the degree of enlargement can be varied by the position of the projector and screen. The slide area is limited, so too much information should not be included in a particular slide. Lighting and exposure should be controlled so that color is as accurate as possible. Some colors are not easily reproduced with the color balance of the films, especially the slight purplish-blues found in some writing inks, but reasonably accurate color reproduction can be achieved with proper care.

Marking and labeling of exhibits should be done in a neat and simple manner, and whatever labels are used should be virtually self-explanatory. However, the label terminology should not embody the examiner's opinion about the document. It should simply identify the exhibit for what it is conceded to be for litigation purposes. In other words, instead of labeling the disputed signature "forgery," it should be referred to as "disputed" or "questioned." Then, too, terms such as "known" and "unknown writing" are unobjectionable and clear to the layman, whereas "standards," "exemplars," and the like may have little meaning to him.

With cutout exhibits consisting of a number of words and letters, it is necessary to have some scheme for relating these to their source. Rather than marking along the margins of the document and possibly the lines and pages from which the words came, a typewritten schedule or chart listing each word and its exact source can be prepared and fastened to the back of the copy to be marked in evidence. Thus, the source information is certain to be made a part of the record, and at the same time the face of the photograph is not confused by numerous notations.

Fact-Revealing Exhibits

Because of the great diversity of problems, fact-revealing exhibits are composed of a variety of highly individual illustrations. The particular exhibit should reveal clearly the obscure physical facts. If it is to be effective, it must show them in such a way that very little explanatory testimony is required for its complete comprehension.

Three factors must be considered in order to accomplish the end: degree of enlargement, simplification of the exhibit, and the use of diagrammatic markings.

The degree of enlargement covers a much wider range with these exhibits than with comparison photographs. A photograph 10–15 times actual size or greater may be necessary to illustrate the sequence of line crossings, while an actual-size or just slightly enlarged photograph might form the best illustration with partially erased writing. Erased writing is one type of problem in which increasing the enlargement may actually reduce what can be determined from the illustration, but with every document problem some enlargement is generally needed. Experience and experimentation serve as the best guides in individual problems.

Fact-revealing photographs must be simple in their design. Many times a 4 × 5 or 5 × 7 print showing only the area of the document in which some physical fact is found is a much more effective exhibit than an 11 × 14 photograph of a large portion of the same document. The rule for deciding what should be used is to include only what is necessary to establish clearly the physical facts in question.

One of the most useful techniques in preparing fact-revealing court exhibits is to hinge together two prints of the same subject, one carefully marked to interpret the facts, the other entirely without markings.

A recent court presentation emphasized the importance of offering in evidence as a single exhibit this combination of marked and unmarked photographs. The problem involved a series of erasures, and all of the erased material that could be deciphered from examination of the photographs and original documents was sketched in with red ink on one print and hinged to a duplicate, unmarked print. Rather than undertaking extensive cross-examination regarding the witness's interpretation of the fragments of strokes, the opponents virtually admitted that the marked photographs were an accurate decipherment. Furthermore, the referee in the case did not find it necessary to review extensive portions of the record to refresh his recollection of just what the witness had said about these erasures.

It is inadvisable, if not actually improper, to offer a marked photograph without an unmarked one that the judge and jury can examine to decide whether they are to accept the witness's interpretation. Actually, the marked photograph leads the layman by the hand, for when he has been shown the interpretation he can see a great deal more in the unmarked print.

Special Reports and Conferences

Special Pretrial Reports

With highly technical presentations the examiner may find it desirable to prepare a special pretrial report based on his prepared court exhibits. This report should contain at least in brief all the elements of his testimony. By means of it, the attorney has a further opportunity to study the salient points his witness is to discuss, so that in the course of trial presentation he can be of greatest assistance. Compiling this sort of report, especially in problems of a more technical nature, is another important step in the pretrial preparation.

In some jurisdictions in which all parties have pretrial access to reports of experts who are listed as witnesses, or in those cases in which there is an agreement for complete exchange of experts' report, the trial attorney may not want detailed information about proposed testimony in written form. Under these circumstances he must, of course, be willing to spend longer conference time with his expert witness, so that he thoroughly understands the strengths and weaknesses of the document evidence. On the other hand, when a pretrial report is prepared, all these factors should be clearly set forth, but if there is any question about whether such a report fits into the trial attorney's preferences, definite approval of it should be obtained before submission.

Pretrial Conferences

A pretrial conference between the document examiner and the attorney is essential for a successful court presentation. Both will then have the opportunity to go over together all aspects of the case in which they both have interest. In this way they will understand what each must do during the presentation of the document evidence. If this conference is properly carried out, all testimony relating to the document question will be more effective and will be limited to the salient points in dispute.

The document examiner's contribution to this conference should include not only a survey of the technical problem and his findings, but also suggestions about when and how his testimony should be presented. He should be ready to discuss all phases of the contemplated testimony, including the proof of the standards upon which the examiner's preparation is based, his court exhibits, his opinion, and the controlling facts that lead him to his opinions. He should prepare for counsel either a suggested set of questions to introduce his qualifications and testimony or a summary of his qualifications and an outline of his ideas regarding the direct testimony. This step may sound presumptuous to an experienced trial attorney, but a document examiner of only moderate experience undoubtedly has participated in more trials of document matters than many of the most active trial attorneys. The examiner has a special and sometimes very extensive knowledge of this particular aspect of trial work, and as a consequence his contributions are derived from courtroom experience. It is unusual for any active trial attorney to have tried more than a handful of document problems, and most welcome the exchange of ideas with the document examiner. By the same token, the attorney who has knowledge of expert testimony in this field should be able to point out those parts of the technical testimony that may seem obscure to the layman and to work out means of clarification.

At this conference it is well to discuss such matters as the direct and cross-examination of all witnesses who are to testify regarding the documents. How the authenticity of the standards is to be established should be thoroughly covered, for failure to prove a standard may badly weaken or ruin the entire presentation. Preparation must now be made to cross-examine thoroughly any witnesses who testify against the facts established by the documents in dispute. An alleged eyewitness to a document's execution may make statements in his direct testimony that are absolutely false and by skillful cross-examination can be shown to be false. But the attorney must know the facts derived from the physical evidence and how convincing the testimony about them can be. Accurate knowledge of the truth and thorough preparation for its effective use during the heat of trial is a powerful tool in any legal battle.

If the identity of an examiner who has examined the papers for the opposition is known, his technical ability and ethical standing should be discussed. In a vast majority of cases testimony against the facts are given by poorly qualified or unscrupulous "experts." What might an uninformed or dishonest examiner say to attack the correct conclusions? How can he be most effectively cross-examined? Answers to these questions can lead to a detailed plan of cross-examination that is far more devastating than any last-minute courtroom consultation can devise.

Another phase of cross-examination that should be considered is a series of questions relating to important aspects of one's own examiner's presentation. They should explore those areas the opposing expert has omitted. To do this, the cross-examiner needs to know his witness's evaluation of the problem, the stronger elements in his reasoning, and what the details of his testimony will include. Especially when obvious important factors are skipped over, they should be emphasized with the understanding that his witness will cover these points in his direct testimony, emphasizing the full importance of the evidence.

The most important part of this conference, however, is for the attorney to understand the full significance of the technical evidence. During the trial he is not able to consult with his witness about the meaning or importance of statements made on the stand. What are the things that in combination lead to the opinion stated? What factors are controlling in arriving at the opinion stated? What meaning do apparent divergences have in this problem? If the cross-examination of the witness is along certain lines, what kind of questions should be asked on redirect examination to remove the sting or to clarify the situation? Cross-examiners try to restrict the scope of the witness's answers, and if successful, it remains for the informed trial counsel to be ready with redirect questions to allow his witness to discuss these details thoroughly. It must be remembered that questions concerning evidence contained in the physical aspects of a document cannot be answered simply yes or no, but may require detailed evaluation. What part do the various photographic exhibits play in the examiner's testimony? What are the governing principles supporting the opinion? This conference is the attorney's opportunity to inquire of his witness concerning every phase of the examination and the factors revealed so that in the end there remain no unanswered questions. The pretrial conference is the time when the trial attorney should come to understand the strengths and weaknesses of the technical aspects of his case.

The attorney must be familiar before trial with special legal decisions governing expert testimony on documents. He must know the appellate decisions on the admissibility of standards, or photographs, and of the expert opinions and extent of reasoning. Many document examiners keep files on key decisions involving their work and testimony and are glad to assist the attorney in this respect. One witness still recalls his first court appearance, in which the opposing attorney objected to the admission of a crucial enlarged photograph, and the delays and confusion this objection provoked when the court asked for appellate decisions on its admissibility. No preparation on the law had been made. Fortunately, in the end the exhibit was accepted, for otherwise the major portion of the testimony would have been seriously weakened. In many courts today expert testimony is common and is accepted without objection, but at the same time there are ample decisions in most jurisdictions to provide for testimony even over the opposing attorney's objection.[1]

By means of this conference the attorney and document examiner can organize their presentation and be prepared for most contingencies. Then, after each has looked into weaknesses revealed by this meeting and strengthened them, the matter is ready for trial.

---

[1]Modern reference texts that contain key legal citations on various phases of expert testimony and especially questioned document problems include Andre A. Moenssens, Ray E. Moses, and Fred E. Inbau, *Scientific Evidence in Criminal Cases* (Mineola, New York: 1973); Charles C. Scott, *Photographic Evidence*, 2nd ed. (St. Paul, Minnesota: West Publ. Co., 1969); and James R. Richardson, *Modern Scientific Evidence* (Cincinnati: Anderson, 1961).

19

In the Court Room

When it becomes necessary to try a matter involving questioned documents all that has been discussed to this point is of a preliminary, though very important, nature. The chief problem now is to present clearly the document examiner's findings to the court and jury. As was pointed out in Chapter 18, the correct presentation of this testimony is not the witness's responsibility alone. Before the witness can testify, known writings, typewriting, or other classes of standards must be in evidence. During testimony the document examiner's qualifications must be presented, the various documents shown to him and his opinions stated, his photographic exhibits admitted into evidence, and then the appropriate questions asked so that he can fully discuss the facts and reasoning upon which his opinions are based. This chapter will deal with these subjects and other aspects of testimony relating to a document problem.

Proof of Standards

The proof of standards, that is, the proof that certain writings on documents to be used for comparison purposes are what they purport to be, is an essential preliminary step. They are the cornerstones on which the document examiner's testimony rests.

How is handwriting proven so that it can be admitted into evidence as a standard? The best legal proof that a person wrote a particular document that is to be used as an example of handwriting is the testimony of someone who saw him write it, but there are many writing specimens that cannot be proven in this way. In some instances they form a part of permanent records, such as bank signature cards, and are used by the institution in the conduct of business.

To prove these standards, two steps are needed: first, to connect the writer in some way with the record or with the institution, and second, show the document is in fact this writer's record. For the second step, testimony must be given to the effect that a company employee supervised the preparation of the record, that these writings are regularly kept on file and referred to as specimen writings of this individual, and finally that the person who is presenting them in court has charge of their custody. With this background they may serve as competent standards. It may be that the known writing was received in the form of a letter or directive, and the recipient carried out the instructions or in some other way acted on its contents, all with the knowledge and tacit approval of the writer. Courts may accept this as adequate proof of a writing standard. Finally, while it is far from the best proof, it is possible in some courts to show that a specimen of writing was prepared by a particular individual through testimony of someone familiar with his writing. The governing legal rule is that the proof of standard writing must satisfy the trial court, and when this has been done, appellate courts rarely overrule the lower court.

In many instances the person who prepared the writing will freely admit the fact, especially when it in no way seems to incriminate him or to prejudice his case. Stipulations about the genuineness of certain standards can often be obtained if asked for, but an attorney should not depend on this means of proving standards if the question has not been raised prior to the trial.

In some jurisdictions, for example, Illinois, the attorney must give reasonable pretrial notice to his opponent that certain writings are to be used as standards. Failure to do so will prevent use of the standard at trial despite the most thorough proof. Attorneys should make sure that they have complied with all procedural rules of the court in which they are trying the case.

The usual manner for proving typewriting standards is to have the person who prepared the document testify about what machine was used. One who witnessed the preparation of the typewriting likewise would be competent to prove the standards. In some cases it is sufficient to show that a document, such as a letter, came out of a particular office and in such a case proof of identity of another document links it to the same source, but of course not to a definite machine in that office.

The Document Examiner's Testimony

Qualifications

The document examiner testifies in court under the usual expert-witness rules. Before he can testify, therefore, he must qualify as an expert by showing his special knowledge and skills in this field. The court must be informed about the extent of the special knowledge he has gained through study and experience. It is within the court's discretion to decide whether the background and work the witness has done is sufficient to classify him as an expert. Generally if an error is made in the determination, it is made in the direction of letting the poorly qualified testify rather than silencing a competent man.

The qualifying questions asked therefore depend on the witness's particular background. Their prime purpose, of course, is to show the witness's ability and competency. They should bring out his general and technical education, together with his special studies concerning the problem at hand. A court always wants to know how long the witness has done this work, whether or not it is his only occupation, and in which other courts he has testified. Many witnesses recite at length prominent cases in which they have appeared, a recital that undoubtedly impresses a jury but is actually of little value in determining their ability except to show that they have previously testified. Competency may be further established by calling attention to ways in which the witness has been recognized as an authority in his field, including membership in professional societies, schools, and seminars at which he has lectured, and special honors or degrees conferred upon him.

The most important qualification of a witness is his ability to do the work. There is no school at which a document examiner, unlike an engineer or a doctor, can study to prepare himself. Some universities have offered special courses on questioned document examination, but these have not as yet been of high enough caliber to develop a proficient worker.[1] Rather, they give only a survey of the principles of the work. Self-study is the chief means of gaining this special knowledge, and some men have been able to supplement this study by apprenticeship or association with a recognized document examiner or in a recognized laboratory. Self-education must include study by experimentation and systematic research. Publication of results in books and recognized journals is good evidence of this phase of compentency. The usual recital of the answers on the various qualifying points unfortunately tends to make even the most incompetent man sound qualified. But this method of determining the fitness of an expert witness is of long

---

[1]Recently, Antioch School of Law, Washington, D.C, has undertaken to develop a graduate program in questioned document examination at the Forensic Science Center. This program is designed primarily for examiners with some experience in the field. In the early 1970s Georgetown University offered a program in questioned document examination, which aimed toward the development and training of those interested in entering the field, but the program was discontinued after only a few years.

tradition, and at the present time there does not seem to be any better means for a court to determine who is and who is not qualified.[2]

Qualifications can generally be presented effectively by a series of short-answer questions, rather than with the general question, Will you state your qualifications. When the witness is asked questions that can for the most part be answered in one or two sentences, his qualifications are given with accuracy and proper emphasis. With this type of questioning jurors tend to listen more attentively. A good rule of trial procedure is to qualify the witness adequately but to avoid drawing it out with unnecessary detail.

Occasionally, the opposing attorney offers to concede that the witness is qualified. This act may seem generous, but actually it is a clever defensive trick. If accepted, it means that the court and jury know little of the special qualifications of the witness. His testimony may not be looked upon with the same confidence that it would have if his true qualifications had been known. In the event of appeal the appellate courts would be in the same position. By far the best procedure is to decline graciously to accept the concession by pointing out that the jury would undoubtedly like to know something of the witness's background and to continue qualifying the witness. If, on the other hand, the concession is accepted, counsel should nevertheless summarize the important parts of the witness's professional background and ask that it be made a part of the stipulation.

Direct Testimony

Direct testimony actually consists of two parts—the introductory questions leading up to and including the witness's opinions and that portion of the testimony in which he explains or gives the reasons for his opinion. It is this latter part that removes document testimony from the class of pure opinion and makes it a scientific demonstration.

The introductory questions are necessary to show what documents have been examined, the purpose of their examination, what photographs have been made and how they were prepared, whether the witness has arrived at an opinion, and finally, what the opinion is. In certain classes of problems it may be well to bring out how the ex-

---

[2]The American Board of Forensic Document Examiners, Inc., was organized in 1977 for the purpose of providing a nationwide program for certifying document examiners. The Board investigates the ethical and professional standing of any person it certifies and by 1980 had developed an examination program that applicants will be required to complete. In 1978 the Board started certifying examiners whose standing and reputation were of high order. It is the aim of this organization to develop a cadre of examiners whom the legal profession knows have and maintain proper qualifications.

amination was made. The order of the questions depends somewhat on the problem, but in all instances the witness should first be shown the various documents he has examined and on which his opinion is based. Before he can properly express an opinion, he must state that he has one. It seems preferable to introduce photographic illustrations or exhibits after a statement of the opinion, and in most instances to discuss the examinations that were made in conjunction with the reasons for the opinion. An early statement of an opinion is advantageous. This opinion is the chief reason for the witness's testimony. Consequently, it should be placed in evidence as soon as possible. If it precedes the introduction of photographs, then it can be properly restated in the answer to the general question, What are the reasons for the opinion which you have stated?, with a clear gain through the repetition.

Photographic illustrations are an essential part of the witness's testimony. Before these are admitted into evidence, it is necessary to describe clearly what they are and how they were made and to establish that they are true and accurate representations of what they purport to show.[3] If the witness has made the photographs himself, or if they were made under his supervision, their proof is simplified. However, it is possible to introduce them into evidence even though the witness did not make or supervise their production, provided he has compared them with the original documents and can state that they are true and accurate reproductions of the writing or typewriting contained in them.[4] It is also well to establish by the witness's testimony that he needs the photographs in order to explain his reasons fully. This step gives considerable protection to the side offering the photographic exhibits, because if the trial court errs in excluding them, the fact that the witness said they were necessary to his opinion and testimony may serve to show that the erroneous exclusion of the evidence should be considered serious enough to warrant a reversal of the case.[5] Because of the importance of photographs in completely understanding the witness's testimony, these steps should be faithfully followed to ensure their admissibility.

---

[3] In some jurisdictions court exhibits are premarked at a pretrial conference; these exhibits include photographic charts prepared by the document examiner. Under such procedure it is important that the exhibits are ready and marked at this conference so that they cannot be excluded on procedural grounds.

[4] Attorneys who are to try a questioned document problem in which photographic illustrations are to be used will do well to study Charles C. Scott, *Photographic Evidence*, 2nd ed. (St. Paul: West Publ. Co., 1969), Chapter 33, "Basic Rules for Photographic Evidence," Chapter 40, "Document Photographs," and Chapter 48, "Introducing Photographs in Evidence."

[5] The rule that a photograph must be shown to be relevant before being admitted into evidence is discussed and cases cited by Scott, *Photographic Evidence*, Vol. 2, Section 1022(6), pp. 329–333.

Court exhibits may be either of two kinds:

1. *hand exhibits,* i.e., enlarged photographs made up of one or more panels designed to be held and examined by the individual jurors or pairs of jurors; or
2. *display exhibits,* i.e., very large projection prints mounted on an easel before the bench or jury.

Which type will be used generally depends on the preference of the witness. The principal advantage of the hand exhibit is that the most effective degree of enlargement can be used; that is, since the exhibit can be held in the same position as the original, the full effect of its enlargement is gained by the viewer. The main disadvantage is that the witness using this kind of exhibit cannot always be sure that each juror is looking at the particular element he is discussing. This weakness can be overcome by the witness holding up his own copy to indicate the exact location and at the same time accurately designating the column and row in which the element under discussion is to be found. With the large display exhibits placed before the jury, the witness can point to the very detail that he is discussing. On the other hand, with this kind of exhibit every juror does not see the image enlarged in the same way—those close by see details more clearly than those in the far corners of the jury box, for whom a slightly enlarged hand exhibit might be more effective. With the present method of jury selection, no one may realize that not every juror has good far vision, and some people do not like to admit that they cannot see the exhibit clearly.[6] Furthermore, lighting conditions or courtroom design may make the large exhibit difficult to see and use.[7] As a consequence, the choice warrants thoughtful consideration, and there are certain cases in which both methods should be employed.[8]

The use of slide projections to illustrate document testimony has advantages and disadvantages similar to those of display exhibits. Furthermore, it is not always easy to darken the courtroom to show slides to best advantage, although of course top-quality color slides have significant advantages in illustrating some types of opinions. Some examiners find this kind of photographic procedure more convenient

---

[6]A. S. Osborn, whose long career in the questioned document field allowed him to observe many juries, states in *Problem of Proof* (Newark: Essex, 1926), p. 352, "There are a few partially blind men on many juries."

[7]A. S. Osborn discusses court room design in *Problem of Proof*, Chapter 15, "Designing and Lighting of Court Rooms," pp. 234–245.

[8]Over a period of years, George G. Swett studied jury reactions to various types of photographic illustrations by interviewing jurors at the conclusion of cases. This study disclosed that the individual or hand exhibit was the most effective type of photographic presentation. See George G. Swett, "The Use of Individual Photographic Charts in Presenting Questioned Document Testimony," *Journal of Criminal Law, Criminology and Police Science* 42 (1952): 826–832.

and consequently use it exclusively. The author, however, favors using more than one procedure, depending on the suitability to the problem at hand.

Only one exhibit should be before the jury at any one time. Upon completing all reference to it, all copies in the possession of the jury should be picked up and the next distributed. This procedure assists the witness to eliminate any confusion about the exhibit to which he is referring. It is a strong argument for the introduction of photographs individually rather than in bound albums, as practiced by some witnesses.

The preliminary aspects of expert testimony are time consuming. For this reason, both the attorney and the witness should have all details arranged and in order so that the procedure moves along smoothly. In far too many cases the attorney only starts looking for the exhibits that are to be shown the witness after he has been sworn. Frequently they are mixed among masses of other papers and notes, and the entire court must sit silently while the search goes on. Introducing and marking photographic exhibits takes time, but the witness himself can hasten their introduction by having them immediately at hand. If the witness must dig through a briefcase to find the next photograph, there is more delay. Smooth and rapid production of these items does much to prevent the court and jury from becoming exhausted, bored, and impatient.

With these preliminaries completed the witness is now ready to relate the reasons for his opinion. One general question will usually serve to introduce this phase of the testimony: Will you take the various exhibits that I have shown you, together with your photographic illustrations, and explain to the court and jury the reasons for the opinion that you have expressed? Now the entire matter rests in the hands of the witness.

After a responsive opening statement, the witness is free to continue with what he considers the most effective and emphatic discussion. The details depend on the individual problem, but good testimony is well organized. It is testimony that moves easily from point to point. It is succinct, simple, clear, and understandable. It points out the facts revealed by the examination and evaluates them in relation to the problem and the opinion given. It covers adequately all the points pertaining to the problem at hand, both those that lead to the conclusions stated and those that may point away from it. The latter should be carefully evaluated and explained. Testimony dealing with questioned document problems must to some extent be technical, but this is no excuse for the witness filling his testimony with many long technical terms that have little or no meaning to the layman. When it is necessary to use some such terms, each should be carefully defined.

If the witness fails to do this, his attorney should make a special point to clarify the term at the first opportunity. It is only the exceptional case in which the witness should refer to notes made during his laboratory study. He ought to be sufficiently well acquainted with the entire problem to be able to talk intelligently on it without recourse to any working notes or memoranda. His testimony should not go into details that have no bearing on the problem, nor should he labor over minor points. Finally, this phase of the testimony should be accurately summarized by relating each salient point to the opinion.

At the end of this phase of the testimony, it may be well for the attorney to ask a series of summarizing questions, or to ask further about those things that may need clarification or amplification. Here is where the trial attorney can profit from thorough pretrial preparation with his witness. Generally, though, if the witness has been effective, there will be little need for questions of this kind.

Some trial attorneys make a practice of interrupting their expert witness from time to time to inquire about a particular point just covered that is believed to be of particular importance. To a limited extent the procedure has advantages. It can break a long presentation and realert jurors who may be losing interest. It can emphasize the point by partial repetition without the witness appearing repetitive. It can clarify a hazy statement or one that might be misinterpreted. If it is overdone, however, it can weaken the presentation, especially if the questions break away from the direction of the witness's development and may make it awkward to resume the original approach. It is certainly a tactic that should be discussed before trial so that the best approach can be used by attorney and witness.

The witness and his attorney should realize that one important aspect of the testimony is to make an accurate record in the event of subsequent appeal. Vague references, such as "this letter" or "the upstroke here," are of no value to an appellate court in reviewing the case, even though the reference may be clear to those in the courtroom seeing as well as hearing the witness. Testimony should be precise, naming the exhibit and designating the portion of it to which each reference is made. A good record of the case can be just as important as effective testimony in the trial court.

Cross-examination of an Expert Witness

The cross-examination of an expert witness must have a definite end in view. It may be aimed toward showing that the witness is in error or has overstated the scope of his conclusion. A competent and honest witness would hardly be expected to appear in a case in which he is wrong. This is not to say that any expert witness is infallible, but his reputation has been built on his accuracy, his integrity, and the fact that he is very careful. If the witness is not too highly qualified, however, or is known to be superficial in his work, this cross-examination may be fruitful. To succeed, however, requires knowledge of the facts and principles of identification.

The incompetent witness should be attacked through his qualifications, and this ought to be done immediately upon completion of this portion of his testimony. In some jurisdictions this is the only time when it can be done; otherwise opposing counsel will be charged with having waived any qualification defects. A limited background of experience and study, or the fact that questioned document work is but a casual avocation, must be clearly brought out before the court. It is unfortunate that even the most extensive attack on an unqualified "expert" has very rarely prevented the witness from expressing an opinion. Nevertheless, it should weaken the effectiveness of the testimony.

A witness with a background of incompetence and a bad reputation has a higher likelihood of error in the case at hand. The attorney who has consulted with a competent examiner knows the facts. Before trial and cross-examination, he should have conferred at length with his examiner and have mastered the pertinent elements of the identification. He is now ready to cross-examine effectively, to show up error and weaknesses. It is regrettable how often an attorney, knowing very little, if anything, about the technical problem, attempts to attack an incompetent witness. Failure is almost certain. Good cross-examination cannot be composed under fire even with the best technical aide sitting at the counsel table. No cross-examination at all is frequently better than an inadequate attempt. The questions must be aimed at the weak points of the testimony and have a definite and continuous plan of attack. By clear, concise questions, the facts can be put before the court and the weaknesses of an erroneous conclusion revealed.

Incorrect document testimony sometimes grows out of opinions that go beyond what is justified by the facts. Questions about the age of ink are a common source of these errors. Likewise, an alleged identification of the forger based on only two or three points of similarity between his writing and an imitated signature is not scientific. Full understanding of the principles involved in such problems and their application to the particular one at hand is a powerful tool for cross-examination.

Another purpose of cross-examination is to seek information. It is proper to inquire about aspects of the testimony that, if more fully developed, may favor the cross-examiner's case. However, it may be that this course leaves the realm of cross-examination entirely. Some courts are more lenient about the scope of cross-examination of an expert than of an ordinary witness, taking the attitude, not always rightly, that the former can be asked anything in his special field.

Sometimes questions are based on documents that are not submitted to the witness prior to trial. This examination is fair only if the witness is given ample time to study the problem. Actually, this whole scheme can be very dangerous for the lawyer who is conducting the cross-examination unless he already knows the facts.

Another method of cross-examining an expert witness concerning his professional ability is to present a test problem. He is asked to examine a signature, for example, to determine if it is genuine. The facts concerning the signature can be established by independent, impartial testimony or by agreement of the adversaries and the court. It is essential that the test is comparable to the problem in dispute, that it is a fair one, and that the witness has ample time and proper facilities to examine the problem and to reach an opinion. In other words, he must be given more than a few minutes on the witness stand to answer the question. The problem of making the test comparable to the one in question is difficult since the known signatures should be as plentiful and representative as in the case at hand. Further not every forgery is detected with the same ease, but each depends on the skill of the imitator and on the type of signature being forged. If results are to be used to discredit the expert, then it is essential that the test material's true character be established to the satisfaction of the court.[9] Objections to the test include the introduction of collateral issues and delaying or extending the trial while the expert has time enough to make a proper study of the matter. Trial courts and review courts have ruled differently on the use of these tests.[10]

One important rule must be followed in cross-examining an expert witness. Each question should be framed to be answered yes or no. Never ask, Why, or What is the reason for that? These questions only allow the witness to discuss the problem in detail and to repeat parts of his direct testimony.

Redirect Examination

If the trial attorney fully understands the technical work of his witness, he is prepared to use the redirect examination to best advantage. In most instances one or two general questions are all that are needed,

---

[9]In a New Jersey case, State v. Bulna, a conviction was reversed because of the exclusion of a test of the document examiner testifying for the state. The Appellate Division, 46 N.J. Super. 313, 134 A.2d 738 (App. Div. 1957) recognized that the expert cannot be discredited without clear proof of the authorship of the test specimen used. The Supreme Court of New Jersey, in affirming the Appellate Division's decision, also recognized this requirement. For a more detailed discussion of the problem relating to this case, see O. Hilton, "Cross-Examination of a Handwriting Expert by Test Problem," *Rutgers Law Review* 13 (1958): 306–313.

[10]Courts that have prohibited this kind of testing of the expert's qualification usually hold that the test raises collateral issues and prolongs the trial or confuses the issues of the case. See, among others, State v. Griswold, 67 Conn. 290, 34 Atl. 1046 (1896); Nordyke v. State, 213 Ind. 243, 11 N.E. 2d 165 (1937); State v. Maxwell, 151 Kan. 951, 102 P.2d 109 (1940).

if any further examination is required at all. When cross-examination has consisted of pointing out a number of inconsequential divergences in the handwriting, the product of natural variation between two specimens by the same writer, the attorney might ask, On cross-examination you were shown a number of slight divergences between the known and disputed writing. Have these caused you to change your opinion in any degree? He might continue with, Why do they not change your opinion? This last question gives the witness the opportunity to rediscuss the problem of natural variation in handwriting and to analyze the suggested differences pointed out on cross-examination. Redirect examination should for the most part consist of this class of question and generally should be limited in extent.

Purpose of the Document Examiner in Court

Every document examiner who is called on to testify should remember that his fundamental purpose is to assist the court and jury in recognizing the facts and their meaning concerning those technical parts of the evidence about which he has special knowledge. He usually appears as a witness for one of the litigants, but he is still there to assist the court. He should not be an advocate for one party's cause, only an advocate for the truth as it relates to documentary evidence. He must be fair and unbiased at all times. His work in court must be just as scientific as his work in the laboratory. By following this code he will, to the greatest extent, promote justice, and those whom the facts favor will gain far more from his services than if he assumes a partisan stand.

Advocacy by the document examiner is a constant hazard. The American legal system is an adversary system. Some trial attorneys believe that their expert should favor their case and try to forget any adverse factors. Under these circumstances, it is always important that the expert witness remembers his true role. If the facts favors one's client, the role of advocacy may seem to be appropriate, but a strong though impartial presentation many times drives home the favorable facts much more effectively to those who decide the case than one that has clear overtones of partisanship.

Document Examiners as Opposing Witnesses

Conflicting testimony by document examiners of high professional standing tends to be a rare occurrence. One examiner has reported appearances in over 20 consecutive cases without an opposing expert witness to refute his testimony. Nevertheless, conflicts do occur. The usual situation involves at least one examiner of limited training and ability or experience. Unfortunately, there are a growing number of examiners trained by correspondence course practicing today who examine documents only on an occasional basis. Probably most should not be permitted to testify in the first place, but they are offering weak and often conflicting testimony.

There are a few examiners who expect to testify in the great majority of cases in which they are engaged because their work is to find some evidence supporting the client. They seem to believe that they should be an advocate for their client's case. The professional bias of these witnesses is generally well known around the courts in which they often appear, and they frequently present conflicting testimony.

Upon occasion, however, well-qualified examiners appear as opposing witnesses. Some of these conflicts represent differences in the shades of value put on the physical evidence, but others constitute sharper clashes of opinions. Some conflicts are brought about by the fact that the witnesses have not had an opportunity to examine the same known material and that one or both sets of standards may be defective and not truly satisfactory as a basis for an opinion. Still, these factors cannot account for every disagreement. It must be recognized that no expert is infallible. He must approach each problem with utmost care, aware that error may occur.

To summarize, the more common conflicts are brought about by a lack of scientific attitude or the poor qualifications of one or both witnesses, a witness's spirit of advocacy despite the preponderence of the evidence, or on rare occasions the basic dishonesty of one of the witnesses to the conflict.

Use of More than One Expert Witness

The concurring testimony of two expert witnesses greatly strengthens the case. First, there is intensified emphasis on the document question, an important consideration when the answer is controlling on the outcome of the case. Second, no two witnesses present their findings in the same way, and each slightly different presentation helps to clarify obscure, technical points. The skeptical juror is thus much more apt to be convinced. Certainly, there is value in a second and on occasion, even a third or fourth witness, and in important cases attorneys can resort with benefit to this procedure more frequently than is customary today.[11]

---

[11]In the late 1800s when expert testimony on handwriting was only beginning to be accepted the use of several experts was encountered in a number of important cases. Daniel T. Ames, *Ames on Forgery* (New York: Ames-Rollinson, 1900), and William E. Hagan, *A Treatise on Disputed Handwriting* (New York: Banks, 1894), both discuss cases in which they participated with a group of experts. In 1936 in State of New Jersey v. Bruno Hauptmann, eight highly qualified document examiners testified for the state. See Clark Sellers, "The Handwriting Evidence Against Hauptmann," *Journal of Criminal Law and Criminology* 27 (1937): 874–886. The practice is followed in some cases today. In the 1978 Nevada trial that resulted in a verdict that the alleged will of Howard Hughes was a forgery, the attorneys for the Hughes interests retained three experts who testified that the document was fraudulent.

Naturally certain disadvantages must be recognized. In the first place, of course, most cases are not of sufficient importance to warrant the additional expense. Sometimes, even if the case does warrant the expenditure, too many expert witnesses or a too exhaustive presentation may cause the jury to lose interest and become bored, to the detriment of the entire case. When to stop this phase of the presentation is a decision for the trial attorney. There have been attorneys who, in the course of a trial at which they had several expert witnesses available, realized it was time to turn to other evidence and did not call all the document examiners. If the question concerning the document is only part of the proof, too many witnesses or too great emphasis on this phase can turn attention from other important and favorable aspects of the case. It may not always be best to call a second expert witness, but failure to engage more than one witness is the more common mistake.

Occasionally, a trial attorney hesitates to use a second expert fearing that in their presentations there will be differences in the value placed on certain identifying factors by the two witnesses. In every document problem there are a great number of factors in the writing or typewriting that must be evaluated. Within a group of workers all are not necessarily going to agree on the importance of these points, but in reaching the final opinion each witness will have assembled a significant group of individual factors to support the findings. Undoubtedly with two or three independent workers the factors for the most part will be the same. Minor differences of emphasis do not weaken the opinion of either or both witnesses but merely add to the total picture. Under cross-examination, the writer normally would acknowledge that his colleague put greater emphasis on a point than he has, but would also point out that both factors are but part of the whole. It probably makes little difference which is more important; both help to identify along with a long series of other factors. It should be made clear that both experts concur in the total evaluation. In the final analysis several jurors may be more strongly impressed by one part of the technical presentation than others, while all jurors accept the ultimate opinion concerning the documents.

Affidavits and Depositions by Document Examiners

Some attorneys, often in the interest of economy, offer the document examiner's findings to the court by affidavit or deposition. Even if deemed acceptable in this form, it is not the most effective way of introducing the testimony. No affidavit can present the evidence as clearly and forcefully as the witness himself. If the facts are favorable, they warrant a strong presentation. Personal testimony can do this, and when for some extenuating reason it is necessary to resort to an affidavit presentation, it must be understood that an inferior course is being pursued.

Conclusions

The testimony on questioned document problems depends for its effectiveness on close cooperation between the witness and the attorney. If the facts are favorable, then proper preparation on the part of both, prior consultation on what is to be presented and how, and coordinated effort in the courtroom should bring about an effective presentation. Correct document testimony is a clear demonstration of the facts, and facts form the basis for a favorable decision.

Index